LATINO WRITERS and JOURNALISTS

JAMIE MARTINEZ WOOD

Facts On File
An imprint of Infobase Publishing

Latino Writers and Journalists

Facts On File, Inc.
An imprint of Infobase Publishing
132 West 31st Street
New York NY 10001

ISBN-10: 0-8160-6422-9
ISBN-13: 978-0-8160-6422-9

Library of Congress Cataloging-in-Publication Data
Martinez Wood, Jamie.
    Latino writers and journalists / Jamie Martinez Wood.
        p. cm. — (A to Z of Latino Americans)
    Includes bibliographical references.
    ISBN 0-8160-6422-9 (acid-free paper)
    1. Hispanic American authors—Biography—Dictionaries. 2. Hispanic American journalists—Biography—Dictionaries. 3. American literature—Hispanic American authors—Bio-bibliography—Dictionaries. 4. Journalism—United States—Bio-bibliography—Dictionaries. I. Title. II. Series.
    PS153.H56M36 2007
    810.9'868073—dc22
    [B]   2006017394

CONTENTS

LIST OF ENTRIES

ACKNOWLEDGMENTS

I thank my agent, Julie Castiglia, for bringing me this project; my editor, Nicole Bowen, for her assistance on all the fine details; and Liza Trinkle and Ania Antoniak for fielding my questions. My gratitude extends to Stephanie Gonzales of Arte Público Press and Bryce Milligan of Wings Press for putting me in touch with authors and helping arrange other matters. Thank you to the following authors, journalists, and editors who gave of their time so that the interviews found within this tome reflect the greatest spark of what makes an artist truly inspirational and encourage readers to find the gifts they were meant to share with the world: Leonard Adame, Marjorie Agosín, Kathleen Alcalá, Alfred Arteaga, Sandra Benítez, Juan Bruce-Novoa, Yvette Cabrera, Norma Elia Cantú, Denise Chávez, Betty Cortina, Frank Cruz, Yasmin Davidds, Junot Diaz, Ysabel Duron, Margarita Engle, María Amparo Escandón, Maria Espinosa, Carolina García-Aguilera, Sheila Sánchez Hatch, María Herrera-Sobek, María Hinojosa, Jorge Huerta, Nicolás Kanellos, Marcela Landres, Josefina Lopez, E. A. Mares, Rubén Martínez, Mary Milligan, Pat Mora, Alejandro Morales, Ed Morales, Julio Moran, Sylvia Moreno, Carlos Morton, Elías Miguel Muñoz, Yolanda Nava, Mireya Navarro, Ana Nogales, Deborah Paredez, O. Ricardo Pimentel, Mary Helen Ponce, Luis J. Rodríguez, Vicki L. Ruiz, Pam Muñoz Ryan, Maria Elena Salinas, Marcela Sanchez, Michele Serros, Frank Sotomayor, Virgil Suárez, Carmen Tafolla, Luis Alberto Urrea, Luis Alberto, Alisa Valdes Rodriguez, Ana Veciana-Suarez, Gloria Velásquez, Evangelina Vigil-Piñón, and Val Zavala. Big thanks to my homerun hitters, Julia Budd Bredek and Dana Wardrop, for their editing in the final moments of the game. Thank you to my friends and family for supporting me through this endeavor of deepening my love of my Latino inheritance.

INTRODUCTION

Colonial Latin America

Latino literature incorporates a multitude of ethnicities and sensibilities that spans at least two centuries. The definition and beginning of Latino literature is debated by scholars, writers, and literary critics. A Latino has either been born or has had ancestors born in any Latin country, a country in which Spanish or Portuguese is the dominant language. Some view the memoirs and written records of the early explorers of the mid-1500s to be the precursor to Latino letters. Others state Latino literature began with the establishment of the United States in the region where the author resided.

There is little biographical information known about the few who composed literature of the exploration and colonization era between 1542 and 1800. During this time Mexicans and Spaniards established colonial rule in New Spain, part of which is now the American Southwest and South. Many of these Mexican and Spanish soldiers who colonized this area for Spain requested and received large land grants upon retirement from duties, which they turned into ranchos. For much of this time, the Crown strictly prohibited printing and publishing among its colonial dependents. Only letters submitted to government officials in Spain or Mexico that reported on military or secular progress were permitted. For example, in 1785 Mexican governor Felipe de Neve wrote and delivered the Code of Conduct, a manifesto establishing proper treatment of California Indians due to the fact that an estimated 90 percent of the Native

population in Los Angeles, California, had been decimated by violence and disease since the Spanish arrived in 1769. These types of documents and an occasional journal on the flora and fauna of the new region or indigenous customs were written, but few survive. Therefore, oral storytelling began a rich tradition as the forerunner and foundation of Latino literature.

Political Foundation of Latino Literature

Political unrest in Mexico and the Caribbean as well as racist clashes between Latinos and Anglo Americans would prove to be the muse to much of Latino literature. In the early 19th century, insurgents began to rebel against the colonial dominance Spain held over the Caribbean islands of Puerto Rico and Cuba and in Mexico. Outspoken writers such as José Martí were exiled from their homelands and sought political refuge in the United States. Capitalizing on the freedom of speech policy in America, Cuban and Puerto Rican nationalists established newspapers to voice their opinions and call for cultural and political independence for their compatriots. Concurrently, Hispanics living in the northern regions of New Spain had established communities strong enough to support commerce among themselves. The first Spanish-language newspaper, *El Misisipi,* was published in 1808; *El Mexicano* followed in 1809. Both papers were founded in New Orleans, Louisiana. Similar papers appeared in Florida, Texas, Philadelphia, and New York. In 1821, Mexico freed itself from Spanish rule, New Spain was ceded to Mexico, and the dissemination of information began to blossom. The first Spanish-language printing press was established in 1834.

In time, the journalists and writers contributing to these papers demanded equal rights, implored their readers to preserve their Spanish language and Hispanic culture, and gave an alternate view of contemporary issues, often contesting the opinions held by English-language papers. Given the fact that local newspapers were sometimes the only Spanish-language printed material available to Latinos, the papers provided a forum for establishing solidarity.

During the course of the 19th century, Anglo Americans embarked upon an imperialistic expansion to claim the lands from the Atlantic Ocean to the Pacific Ocean. Under this policy, known as Manifest Destiny, Americans clashed with Mexicans and Spaniards living in northern Mexico. Texas and portions of New Mexico were annexed to the United States in 1845. The following year, Texas Rangers committed atrocious crimes against Latinos, all in the name of establishing peace for Anglo Americans. The conflicts culminated in the U.S.-Mexican War. When the United States won the war in 1848, Mexico was forced to cede one-third of its country to America. In this way, California, New Mexico, Arizona, Nevada, Utah, and Colorado became U.S. territory. Although the Rio Grande partially serves as the U.S.-Mexican border, the dividing line between the two countries often intersects major U.S. and Mexican cities, thereby ensuring international commerce and transnational customs, which have created an inevitable border culture. Writing about border culture became and still is quite popular.

Based on the Treaty of Guadalupe Hidalgo (1848), persons living and working on lands granted by either Spanish or Mexican governments had to prove the legitimacy of their land claims. While the rancheros attempted to make sense of the foreign laws, Americans from the East and Midwest flooded into the new American lands,

particularly California and Texas, to squat on the lands in litigation. Most rancheros lost their cases, resulting in dispossession and poverty. Little written information survived, with the exception of the novels of María Amparo Ruiz de Burton, which were not published until the later 1800s. The squatters were not as interested in New Mexico or Arizona. The Latinos of these regions maintained their land, wealth, and sense of self. Through newspapers and small presses they published folklore, character sketches, essays, memoirs, and biographies celebrating their Mexican heritage. Those who descended directly from Spanish predecessors claimed higher breeding than their Anglo-American counterparts. This high self-opinion served as a foundation for the majority of early Hispanic writers, such as Miguel A. Otero, Fray Angélico Chávez, Ruiz de Burton, and Fabiola Cabeza de Baca Gilbert. Writers of this era often idealized a romantic version of Hispanic life prior to the arrival of Anglo Americans.

By the late 1800s, some of the more successful newspapers grew into publishing houses. During this time, the frequent revolts besieging Mexico began to take their toll. Porfirio Díaz became the Mexican president in 1876, promising to reestablish the former greatness of Mexico. He instead began a dictatorship marred by extreme violence and oppression. Mexicans fled to the southern and southwestern United States in droves to avoid the wrath of Díaz and his military force, known as the Rurales. Insurgents such as Pancho Villa and Emiliano Zapata rose to fight Díaz, and thus began the Mexican Revolution in 1910, although the violence and waves of immigration to the United States continued until 1920.

Native, Exile, and Immigrant Experiences

At this point Latino literature began to truly establish itself and form three distinguishable types of expression as defined by Nicolás Kancellos in *Herencia* (2004): native, exile, and immigrant. Natives, Hispanics who lived in northern New Spain before it became the United States, such as Eusebio Chacón and Jovita Idar, wrote in a variety of genres calling for cultural and civil rights and the preservation of cultural traditions. The exiles were political dissidents such, as Félix Varela, who particularly originated from Cuba and Puerto Rico and wrote about their hopes for political and cultural independence. Lastly, the immigrants published works that spoke in large part to the establishment of identity, whether that meant the process of melding the Hispanic and American cultures or resisting Americanization. Jesús Colón was the major forerunner on this front, addressing the issues and ideologies of the working class. Another immigration factor came about during the depression, when scores of Mexican Americans were repatriated to Mexico regardless of whether they held U.S. citizenship. During this time, writers such as Américo Paredes and Jovita González wrote about their Hispanic experience but found little success while alive. It was not until after Paredes's death that his greatest works found publication.

The mid-1900s were rife with political upheaval in the United States and abroad. In 1953, the United States launched Operation Bootstrap in Puerto Rico, which industrialized a formerly agricultural economy. The result was unemployment for many and the largest migration of Puerto Ricans to the United States. A vast majority of Puerto Ricans immigrated to New York's Lower East Side, falling into a city suffused with racism based in large part on skin color. Piri Thomas and Nicholasa Mohr penned some of the first works to describe the racism and inequality they experienced. A few years later, Fidel Castro came to power in Cuba. His dictatorship resulted in violence for those opposed to him, a break with former congenial ties with the United States, and a wave of Cubans leaving their homeland for major U.S. cities such as Miami, Chicago, and New York. Dominican Republicans fled their dictators at about the same time. Women from these Caribbean islands, such as Julia Alvarez, Judith Ortiz Cofer, Esmeralda Santiago, and Cristina García,

in particular, wrote about their coming-of-age caught between Hispanic and Anglo-American cultures.

Civil Movement and Identification

Inspired by the Civil Rights movement of African Americans, Latinos began to demand their civil rights with more vehemence than ever before. As a forerunner to the Chicano movement, César Chávez unionized the Latino field-workers in 1965 in an event known as the Delano Grape Strike. Luis Valdez created plays to energize the people and the Chicano movement. *Chicano* refers to a political Mexican American. Poets read their works at political rallies, elevating their status to something akin to celebrity. Not only did poets demand equality, they also conveyed imagery of the mythic land of Aztlán, a place of belonging and beauty. The works of Lorna Dee Cervantes, Alurista, and Abelardo Delgado stand out. However, it was Rodolfo "Corky" Gonzales's poem "I Am Joaquin" that carried the furthest trajectory. These grassroots efforts trickled into the world of academia and with the leadership of Jorge Huerta and Tomás Rivera, among others, eventually established fields of study in literature and history on the contributions of Latinos in universities throughout the nation and the world.

At the height of the Chicano movement, lone Latino investigative journalist Rubén Salazar worked tirelessly to ensure Latino issues were covered in periodicals. On August 29, 1970, Chicanos held a peaceful march to protest the Vietnam War and demand equality. Salazar was killed in what was known as the Chicano Moratorium. Frank del Olmo rose to take his place at the *Los Angeles Times*. Salazar and del Olmo became role models for other Latino journalists, many of whom have won Pulitzer Prizes. The shooting of Salazar further incited Chicanos in their quest and fueled the fire for Chicano novelists such as Tomás Rivera, Rudolfo Anaya, Sandra Cisneros, and Rolando Hinojosa, who began to see publication by major houses and receive literary awards in the early 1970s.

Nowhere did Latino literature investigate the bilingual and bicultural existence more than in border cities. Authors and writers from these regions, such as Alicia de Alba Gaspar, Denise Chávez, Gloria Anzaldúa, Carmen Tafolla, and Jose Antonio Burciaga, validated the experience of living in two worlds simultaneously. They helped to authenticate the combination of both English and Spanish in their works and the amalgam of being Hispanic while living in the United States.

In 1972, Kanellos founded the *Revista Chicano-Riqueña,* a literary magazine dedicated to publishing the works of Latinos. The following year Miguel Algarín and Miguel Piñero created the Nuyorican Poet's Café, a cultural center for artists to share their work. Nuyoricans, New York Puerto Ricans, had finally established a forum to speak to their concerns in their unapologetic street style. Poetry slams, a precursor to rap, grew in popularity, as did the works of Tato Laveria, Pedro Pietri, and Victor Hernandez Cruz. During the 1980s and 1990s, Latinos such as Gary Soto and Helena Maria Viramontes built on the success of the Chicano and Nuyorican movements. The late 1990s witnessed an explosion of Latino literature. Contemporary writers such as Virgil Suárez, Alisa Valdes-Rodriguez, Isabel Allende, and Junot Diaz draw on their Latino heritage to inform their works while showing their talents in touching on universal themes. Latino literature will continue to evolve and contribute to world literature for years to come.

A

Acosta, Oscar Zeta
(Oscar Acosta)
(1935–) *novelist, autobiographer, activist*

Known for his charisma, intensity, and valor, Oscar Zeta Acosta is a provocative writer, lawyer, and activist who fought on the front lines of the Chicano movement when Mexican Americans worked for equality beginning in the mid-1960s.

Oscar Acosta was born in El Paso, Texas. Sources show varying dates; however, most references list Acosta's birth date as April 8, 1935. His family moved to the San Joaquin Valley near Modesto, California, while Oscar was still young. When his father was drafted during World War II, Oscar assumed much responsibility for his family. His later work suggests that he felt a keen sense of isolation and suspicion as a child. He was a bright student known for his brazen boldness and obsessive tendencies. He began to have problems with alcohol in high school, eventually developing ulcers that would bother him throughout his life.

Upon graduating high school, Acosta enlisted in the U.S. Air Force. During a tour of service in Latin America, he converted to Protestantism, eventually becoming a Baptist missionary in a leper colony in Panama. He eventually denounced Christianity. After four years in the military, Acosta was honorably discharged. He returned to northern California, where he enrolled in Modesto Junior College. In 1956, he married Betty Daves; they divorced in 1963. Acosta then took creative

writing courses at San Francisco State University. Upon graduation, he attended San Francisco Law School, passing the bar exam in 1966. Acosta's first position as a lawyer involved working for the Oakland Legal Aid Society, an antipoverty agency.

In the late 1960s, he moved to East Los Angeles and joined the Chicano movement. He was married to Socorro Aguiniga from 1969 to 1971. Acosta's charisma and pure strength became a dominant force in courthouses as well as on the streets where racist battles were fought. He represented RODOLFO GONZALES, Saint Basil 21, and other protest groups and prominent activists. His short story "Perla Is a Pig" serves as an example of how being excluded from society and prejudged does not allow one the right to condemn another. As a result of this awareness, Acosta adopted *Zeta* as part of his name as a resolute confirmation of his Chicano roots and identity. The story was published in 1974 in both *Con Safos,* a Chicano political magazine, and *Voices of Aztlán.* Unfortunately, according to many critics, his humanitarian approach did not include defending or honoring women.

Acosta gained a widespread notoriety, reaching the attention of America's mainstream population when Hunter S. Thompson immortalized him in his book *Fear and Loathing in Las Vegas* (1971). Thompson reveals in the book, which the *New York Times* called the "Best Book of the Dope Decade," his exploits with Acosta in Las Vegas,

1

Nevada, through his fictional dealings with Dr. Gonzo, a character based on Acosta.

Acosta released *The Autobiography of a Brown Buffalo* (1972), in which he used biotherapy to unravel the mysteries and obsessions that plagued him. His characters have been noted as closely resembling people who play major roles in his life, including Thompson. Again highly autobiographical in nature, *The Revolt of the Cockroach People* (1973) follows a main character who, like Acosta, is a lawyer defending the suppressed, marginalized members of society. The novel even includes an incident that strongly parallels the shooting of RUBÉN SALAZAR. This book ends on a hopeless note, in which Chicanos have not reached unity, and in fact many have assimilated into the dominant white culture.

Acosta traveled to Mexico in 1974. In May 1974, he called his son Marco from Mazatlán, Sinaloa, Mexico, and was never heard from again. Critics, family, and friends, including Thompson, presume he is dead. The cause of his death and/or disappearance is pure speculation but varies from drug overdose to murder and even includes the possibility of a nervous breakdown and decision to stay in Mexico.

Acosta's work bears importance in Chicano letters based on the level to which people use identification with ethnicity to define who they are as individuals. In the case of those who claim allegiance to people of a minority, the effect can result in a recurrence of victimhood and unworthiness. Acosta's roller coaster, insatiable hunt for acceptance in life from others and through his writings points to the need to bridge alliances rather than to focus on what separates ethnicities and people. An evaluation of Acosta's life and work, including his love and aptitude for the seemingly divergent modes of thinking of math and creative writing, supports the theory that struggling to seek the meaning of life and identity through mental delineation contains far less value and benefit to human beings than recognizing and honoring relationships can offer.

Further Reading

Acosta, Oscar Zeta. *The Autobiography of a Brown Buffalo.* San Francisco: Straight Arrow, 1972.

Heide, Rick, ed. *Under the Fifth Sun: Latino Literature from California.* Santa Clara and Berkeley, Calif.: Santa Clara University/Heyday Books, 2002.

Thompson, Hunter S. *Fear and Loathing in Las Vegas.* New York: Random House, 1971.

Adame, Leonard
(1947–) *poet, educator*

Leonard Adame creates poetry that speaks to the crux of human relationships. He uses Mexican-American themes to connect his readers to universal impulses held by all peoples, regardless of race, creed, or social status.

Leonard Adame was born on September 2, 1947, in Fresno, California. His father, Trinidad Concepción Adame, Jr., was born in Chihuahua, Mexico, and his mother, Jessie Contreras Adame, is Mexican American, born in Colton, California. Leopard's grandmother provided the consistency he needed when he entered the foreign world of English and Anglo-American customs at Jane Addams Elementary. In school, his Spanish language "sank into linguistic quick sand," Adame recalled in a 2006 interview, but at home, "every morning was the same: she [his grandmother] was up before anyone, the coffee boiling and the eggs popping in the lard-glazed frying pan, her hands patting and shaping tortillas, her hands moving as fast as hummingbird wings, or so it seemed." When he was not working in his father's restaurant, Adame spent hours devouring comic books and other periodicals at the local drugstore. His love of reading led him to John Steinbeck, William Faulkner, Ernest Hemingway, and others. Music also played a major influence in his life. His grandfather played the mandolin and guitar, and his uncles were professional musicians. Adame married Lupe Diaz in 1968, and the couple have two children.

Adame attended California State University–Fresno in the early 1970s. While at the university Adame met the future Pulitzer Prize winner Philip Levine. Levine inspired the group known as the Fresno School of Poetry, which included Adame, GARY SOTO, LUIS OMAR SALINAS, and Ernesto Trejo. Levine convinced Adame that his Mexican experience was important and that it should be an integral part of his poetry. Adame says of his mentor, "He is a true oracle, a man of great insight, compassion, expertise, and encouragement." Adame followed Levine's advice, and his poetry saw publication in various periodicals throughout the 1970s, including *Entrance: 4 Chicano Poets* (1975) and *Cantos pa' la memoria* (Songs for memory) (1979). During the 1970s, Adame worked in a variety of jobs, including teaching, social work, and playing in a band. Adame earned a B.A. in English in 1981, and an M.A. in English with an emphasis in creative writing in 1986.

Adame began his teaching career at California State University–Fresno in 1972. He has also held positions at Fresno City College and Kings River Community College. He is currently a full-time faculty member at Butte Community College. Adame has contributed his writings to various anthologies and periodicals. He creates images that combine tangible everyday items and chores with sublime lyricism. Additionally, his poetry establishes compassion for the plight and disillusionment of the immigrant experience.

Further Reading

Adame, Leonard. *Entrance: 4 Chicano Poets, Leonard Adame, Luis Omar Salinas, Gary Soto, Ernesto Trejo.* Greenfield Center, N.Y.: Greenfield Review Press, 1975.

Heide, Rick, ed. *Under the Fifth Sun: Latino Literature from California.* Santa Clara and Berkeley, Calif.: Santa Clara University/Heyday Books, 2002.

Lomelí, Francisco A., and Carl R. Shirley, eds. *Chicano Writers: First Series.* Vol. 82. Detroit: Gale Research, 1992, pp. 11–15

Agosín, Marjorie

(1955–) *poet, memoirist, short story writer, essayist, activist, educator*

Marjorie Agosín has established herself as a prominent figure in Latino letters, as well as a humanitarian with prestigious awards such as a Good Neighbor Award (1988) and the National Mujer Award (2004). Her poetry has earned her the Letras de Oro prize (1995) and the Latino Literature Prize (1995).

The daughter of Moisés and Frida (Halpern) Agosín, Agosín was born in Bethesda, Maryland, on June 15, 1955. When she was three months old, the family moved to Santiago, Chile, her parents' homeland. Even as a young child, Marjorie felt a strong kinship with fellow writers. The Latin-American literary culture was an extension of her family; established writers such as Gabriel García Márquez and María Luisa Bombal were her pen and ink grandparents. At the age of seven, Marjorie met the renowned poet Pablo Neruda. They shared a brief conversation that proved to be a pivotal moment for the budding writer and poet.

Agosín's writings are characterized by a humanitarian theme and a strong faith in life, family, and the wonders of nature. Agosín attributes much of this hope and conviction to her Jewish upbringing. She was regaled with stories of her Jewish ancestors who overcame obstacles through their inner strength and faith. The peace that arose from their courage wove its way into Agosín's nature, outlook on life, and writings. She found that writing restored and fortified her sense of faith. Agosín stated in a 2005 interview that "this kind of faith is not defined or restricted to religion, but wells up from the faith in possibilities, dreams, nature, and the planet." Through her connections to Latin-American culture, including its writers such as Neruda, and the grit of those who faced the Holocaust, she forged an identity. This identity served as a starting point, a window from which she could look out at the world and find her connection to the whole of humanity.

As the political tension in Chile mounted, Agosín's parents moved back to the United States in 1969, where her father accepted a professorship in biochemistry at the University of Georgia. Agosín remained in Chile with her maternal grandparents to complete her education. She joined her parents in 1971. During the 1970s, Agosín enjoyed a period of study and contemplation. Her identification with her Latin-American roots remained strong even during her self-imposed exile from Chile. She majored in philosophy at the University of Georgia, graduating in 1976. She married John Wiggins in 1977, with whom she would have two children, Joseph Daniel and Sonia Helene. She earned a Ph.D. in Latin-American literature from Indiana University–Bloomington in 1982. Her dissertation was on Chilean writer María Luisa Bombal.

The 1980s marked the beginning of a long and lustrous career as a writer for Agosín. Her first love in writing is poetry, in which she has a profound ability to elucidate the shared connection with all living beings. Agosín writes in Spanish, although her work is often translated into English or appears as a bilingual edition. She has been published in the United States, Spain, Chile, and Costa Rica. Agosín's collections of poetry include *Conchali* (1980), *Hogueras* (1986, published as *Hogueras/Bonfires,* 1990), *Zones of Pain* (1988), *Generous Journey: A Celebration of Foods from the World* (1991), *Toward the Splendid City* (1994), *Noche estrellada,* (1996, published as *Starry Night: Poems,* also in 1996), *An Absence of Shadows* (1998), *The Angel of Memory* (2001), *At the Threshold of Memory: New & Selected Poems* (2003), and *Poems for Josefina* (2004).

Bilingual editions of her poetry include *Brujas y algo más/Witches and Other Things* (1984), *Mujeres de humo/Women of Smoke* (1987), *La literatura y los derechos dumanos: Aproximaciones, lecturas y encuentros/Literature and Human Rights: Approaches, Lectures, and Meetings* (1989), *Círculos de locura: Madres de la Plaza de Mayo/Circles of Madness: Mothers of the Plaza de Mayo* (1992), *Sargazo/Sargasso: Poems* (1993), *Dear Anne Frank*

(1994 and 1998), and *Lluvia en el desierto/Rain in the Desert: Poems* (1999).

Agosín writes in Spanish to maintain connection to her Latin-American roots and the values and ways of life that most inspire her. In addition to this connection, Agosín delves deep into the heart of her Jewish ancestors and the trials they faced. In 1982, she accepted a position at Wellesley College, where she continues to instruct courses in Latin-American literature and Spanish. In this vein, she has been able to introduce the varied works of Latin-American writers to a widespread audience. She has edited or contributed to more than 40 books. Her tireless efforts to spotlight the works of Latin-American writers, particularly women writers, have earned her much acclaim and respect.

Agosín dives into the experiences of the oppressed and calls forth the light to chase away the shadows of tyranny and cruelty. She has expanded her writing skills beyond poetry and editing to memoirs, short stories, nonfiction, and essays. Writings from these varied genres include *La felicidad, cuarto propio* (1991, published as *Happiness: Stories* in 1993); *Sagrada memoria: Reminiscencias de una niña judia en Chile* (1994, published as *A Cross and a Star: Memoirs of a Jewish Girl in Chile* in 1995); *Tapestries of Hope, Threads of Love: The Arpillera Movement in Chile, 1974–1994,* photographs by Emma Sepulveda and Ted Polumbaum (1996); *Ashes of Revolt: Essays on Human Rights,* (1996); *Women in Disguise: Stories* (1996); *Las chicas desobedientes* (1997); *Council of the Fairies* (1997); *A Necklace of Words: Stories by Mexican Women* (1997); *Mujeres melodiosas,* translated as *Melodious Women* (1997); *Always from Somewhere Else: A Memoir of My Chilean Jewish Father* (1998); *An Absence of Shadows* (1998); *Las palabras de Miriam* (1999); *Uncertain Travelers: Conversations with Jewish Women Immigrants to America* (1999); and *The Alphabet in My Hands: A Writing Life* (2000).

Agosín has made significant contributions to the Latino communities both in the United States and in Latin America. Her ability to deal frankly with suffering and share the humanity she finds hidden within is a rare gift. She stated in a 2005 interview that "by allowing the silence to enter the spirit from that vortex, peace can be found within. With this peace, compassion and strength arise to fight injustice." Her weapons are not satirical or mean-spirited lyrics but an ever vigilant voice that illuminates the connection and universal needs that speak to the heart of all humanity.

Further Reading

Agosín, Marjorie. *A Cross and a Star: Memoirs of a Jewish Girl in Chile.* Albuquerque: University of New Mexico Press, 1995.

Kanellos, Nicolás, et al, eds. *Herencia: The Anthology of Hispanic Literature in the United States.* New York: Oxford University Press, 2003.

Scott, Nina. "Marjorie Agosín as Latina Writer." In *Breaking Boundaries: Latina Writings and Critical Readings.* Amherst: University of Massachusetts Press, 1989, pp. 232–235.

Alarcón, Francisco X.
(Francisco Xavier Alarcón)
(1954–) *poet, essayist, short story writer, children's book writer, educator*

Francisco X. Alarcón's short and powerful verses shatter rigid perceptions and prejudices about the disenfranchised members of society. His work is celebrated in the United States, as well as in Latin America.

Francisco Xavier Alarcón was born on February 21, 1954, in Wilmington, California, son of Jesús Pastor and Consuelo (Vargas) Alarcón. During his childhood, Francisco spent periods of time living with his parents just outside of Los Angeles; with his grandfather, a full-blooded Tarascan Indian in the mountains of Michoacán, Mexico; and with other relatives in Guadalajara, Mexico. While in Mexico, Alarcón had the pleasure of hearing generations-old stories, as well as his grandfather's tales of fighting alongside the Mexican revolutionary Pancho Villa. The Mexican Revolution, which occurred from 1910 to 1920, was a violent time when the common people sought to establish order. Living biculturally had a profound effect on Alarcón in both his patterns of thinking and the way he crafted words.

As a young adult Alarcón returned to Los Angeles with $5 in his pocket and a dream of becoming a writer and recording the stories he had been told. Alarcón earned his high school diploma at Cambria Adult School in Los Angeles. He studied one year at East Los Angeles College, then transferred to California State University–Long Beach, where he earned his B.A. in Spanish and history in 1977. Shortly thereafter, he obtained a graduate fellowship and enrolled at Stanford University, where he studied contemporary Latin-American literature. Alarcón wrote poetry while in college, joined literary circles in the San Francisco Bay area, and gave poetry readings. He found a forum to explore his mestizo roots and Latin-American solidarity when he joined the coordinating staff of *El Tecolote,* a Bay area monthly bilingual newspaper.

In 1981, Alarcón won the Rubén Darío Latin-American Poetry Prize from Casa Nicaragua in San Francisco. This award had a domino effect, with more recognition around the Bay area, more poetry readings, and eventually a Fulbright Fellowship in Mexico City. Alarcón was introduced to the best-known Mexican poets, members of the intellectual elite, and literary greats in Havana, Cuba. He became involved in theater and served as a visiting researcher at the Colegio de México. He gained notoriety from his readings, eventually appearing as a television guest on the daily literary program *Noche a Noche* (Night to night) in Mexico City. The turning point in his life, both socially and personally, came when Alarcón met Elías Nandino, one of "Los Contemporáneos" (The Contemporaries). The Contemporaries were a literary and intellectual avant-garde group of the late 1920s, which also included Octavio Paz, Carlos Pellicer, Celestino Gorostiza, and Salvador

Novo. Nandino greatly impressed Alarcón with his stand to be openly gay in his work and life.

Inspired and encouraged by Nandino, Alarcón wrote with a deeper honesty in his poems as well as his short stories and essays. He won second prize in the Palabra Nueva (New Word) University of Texas–El Paso literary contest in 1983 for his short story "Las repatriaciones de noviembre" (The repatriations of November), and he won a first prize in poetry from the Tenth Chicano Literary Contest of the Department of Spanish and Portuguese at the University of California–Irvine. These awards and his "showmanlike" poetry readings established Alarcón as one of the most exciting and influential young Chicano writers of the decade.

In 1984, as Alarcón was enjoying a peak in his career, a young boy was found sexually molested and murdered in San Francisco. Since Alarcón's car matched the description of a car abandoned at the scene of the crime, the police targeted him and mercilessly slandered him through print and broadcast media. His neighborhood rallied around him. Eventually the real killer was found, but not before the experience had had a deep impact upon Alarcón's life.

The following year, Alarcón released his first book, *Tattoos* (1985), in which the poet explores community, his roots, and his political convictions with clipped, piercing words. Later that same year, Alarcón collaborated with Rodrigo Reyes and Juan Pablo Gutiérrez to publish *Ya vas, Carnal (Right on, Brother)*. Alarcón then released *Quake Poems* (1989) in response to an earthquake that devastated Santa Cruz, California, where he was living and serving as a lecturer at California State University–Santa Cruz. *Body in Flames/ Cuerpo en llamas* is divided into five parts and deals directly with sexuality, sensuality, and the explosive joy of living as a self-expressed soul. Alarcón followed with *Loma prieta* (1990), *De amor oscuro/Of Dark Love* (1991), *Snake Poems: An Aztec Invocation* (1992), *No Golden Gate for Us* (1993), and *From the Other Side of Night/ Del otro lado de la noche: New and Selected Poems* (2002).

In the late 1990s, Alarcón wrote bilingual poetry for children. With widespread success he released *Laughing Tomatoes and Other Spring Poems* (1997), *From the Bellybutton of the Moon and Other Summer Poems* (1998), *Angels Ride Bikes and Other Fall Poems,* (1999), and *Iguanas in the Snow and Other Winter Poems* (2001). Inspired by children, Alarcón has translated many children's books into Spanish. He has edited several textbooks for teaching Spanish in college and high school, including *Mundo 21* (1995; World 21), *Pasaporte Mundo 21* (1997; World passport 21), *Tu Mundo* (1997; Your world), and *Nuestro Mundo* (2000; Our world).

Alarcón has won several awards including the Josephine Miles Literary Award, PEN Oakland, American Book Award, Before Columbus Foundation, and Pura Belpre Honor Award for Poetry. He has appeared in a number of anthologies, literary journals, and magazines. Alarcón currently teaches at the University of California–Davis, where he also serves as director for the Spanish for Native Speakers Program.

Further Reading

Heide, Rick, ed. *Under the Fifth Sun: Latino Literature from California.* Santa Clara and Berkeley, Calif.: Santa Clara University/Heyday Books, 2002.

Holder, Kathleen. "A Poet Who Writes Tattoos." *Dateline UC Davis* 13, no. 26 (April 14, 2000):3.

Lomelí, Francisco A., and Carl R. Shirley, eds. *Chicano Writers: First Series*, Vol. 122. Detroit: Gale Research, 1992, pp. 3–7.

Alcalá, Kathleen
(1954–) *novelist, folklorist, anthologist, playwright*

Best known for her trilogy on 19th-century Mexico, Kathleen Alcalá has received several awards and honors, including the Western States Book Award, Governor's Writers Award, Pacific Northwest Bookseller's Award, and Washington State Book Award.

Kathleen Alcalá was born on August 29, 1954, the youngest child of Lydia Narro, from Durango, Durango, Mexico, and David Alcalá, from San Julián, Jalisco, Mexico. She attended a two-room schoolhouse in rural Devore Heights, California, for kindergarten and first grade. The family then moved to San Bernardino, California, where she went to Eliot Elementary School. As a child, she wanted to play the flute and be an artist. She was a bright nonconformist, testing off the charts on IQ and aptitude tests. Mythology and science fiction literature drew Kathleen's attention as a child. Her favorite books were *Have Space Suit—Will Travel* by Robert Heinlein because one of the main characters is a girl and *A Wrinkle in Time* by Madeleine L'Engle. However, she did not fit any notion that educators had at that time of the good or promising student, so she spent a fair amount of time in the principal's office in elementary school.

Alcalá's aunt, Rosa Fe Narro Arrien, a world-traveled missionary and writer, greatly influenced Alcalá. Narro Arrien showered her love on Kathleen and her sisters and taught them that there was a bigger world than the one they knew. Later Kathleen attended Arrowview Junior High and wanted to be an anthropologist. She tutored other children, acting as a teacher's assistant to a class of "otherly abled" learners.

Alcalá's mother was from a large family, while her father was an only child. Kathleen grew up visiting her mother's many brothers' and sisters' families in Monterey Park and East Los Angeles. The stories told at family gatherings helped to shape the stories she would later write. Additionally, every summer Kathleen visited her aunt, uncle, and their five children in Chihuahua, Mexico. The experiences in Mexico provided a dual, almost binocular vision from both sides of the border. Alcalá felt that "we belonged to both sides, or rather, both sides belonged to us," as expressed in a 2005 interview with the author.

Alcalá attended San Bernardino High School, where tensions ran high. Robert Kennedy, Martin Luther King, and Rubén Salazar were all assassinated about this time. Race riots broke out consistently. As Mexicans who lived in a town that practiced real estate redlining, her family held a very precarious place in society. Alcalá's father, a junior high school teacher and one of the few Mexican Americans around with a white-collar job, was also a Methodist minister raising his children as pacifists. Alcalá's parents belonged to the Fellowship for Reconciliation, a group that advocated nonviolence, even during the Vietnam War. Former students came to the house to be counseled about their draft status by Alcalá's father. Juxtaposed to the freedom to choose a political stance, Alcalá's mother, a piano teacher, was very obsessed with proper behavior. Alcalá remembered in a 2005 interview, "[T]here was no sexual revolution in our house. I think I came of age right at the dividing line ending the 1960s."

Alcalá attended Stanford University from 1972 to 1976, where she wrote for the *Stanford Daily*. She came across *One Hundred Years of Solitude* by Gabriel García Márquez, which reminded Alcalá of her family stories. At the same time, a fellow student gave Alcalá an anthology called *The New Journalism,* with an essay by Joan Didion, which introduced Alcalá to the notion that others had similar family experiences and proved to be a source of inspiration for her own writing.

Alcalá obtained a B.A. in human language (linguistics) in 1976. Three years later, she married Wayne Roth. Alcalá worked in Democratic politics and public broadcasting and as a consultant to nonprofit groups. But in each case, her contributions always revolved around writing. She received her M.A. in English from the University of Washington in 1985. In 1989, Alcalá gave birth to a son she and Roth named Benjamin. Alcalá founded a magazine to represent voices of diversity called *The Raven Chronicles* with Phil Red Eagle and Phoebe Bosché in 1991. *The Raven Chronicles* sponsors readings and events and has an active Web site with different content from that of the magazine.

Alcalá released her first book, *Mrs. Vargas and the Dead Naturalist,* in 1992. This collection

Novelist Kathleen Alcalá cofounded *The Raven Chronicles,* a magazine dedicated to diversity. *(Jerry Bauer)*

Her second novel, *The Flower in the Skull,* is based on the story of Opata, Alcalá's great-grandmother, who was born in Rayón, Sonora. Released in 1999, this book reveals the intricacies of culture, self-identity, and assimilation through the lives of three generations of women. Alcalá entwines magic with everyday life by exploring the inexplicable connection to one's land and faith.

Treasures in Heaven, her third novel, released in 2002, is based on the feminist movement in Mexico of the late 19th and early 20th centuries, before the Mexican Revolution. The Mexican Revolution was a period from approximately 1910 to 1920 rife with terror, violence, and corruption as the people attempted to assert a stronger political voice and more control. Estela, a character in *Spirits of the Ordinary,* is the main protagonist in this book. Self-described as a writer of "counter-narratives to official history," Alcalá reveals throughout her trilogy how the larger movements and shifts of history change individual lives. She examines society on the level of the individual and unravels how each character fits into the whole. Research and writing have also proved a means of self-discovery. Alcalá discovered that her family was not an anomaly as she had once believed but that there are other Mexican Protestant Jews. Alcalá stated in a 2005 interview, "[W]riters have an innate need to 'relive' experience through narrative. That is how we understand the world around us, by showing the threads that connect seemingly disparate incidents."

In 2003, Alcalá cowrote a play based on her novel *Spirits of the Ordinary,* which was produced at the Miracle Theatre of Portland, Oregon. Her work has appeared in *Creative Nonfiction, The Raven Chronicles, Re-Markings,* and *The Pacific Northwest Writers Association Anthology.* Alcalá has served as a visiting professor at the University of New Mexico and taught at writing conferences throughout the nation. Her students and readers provide great inspiration. Alcalá reflected in a 2005 interview, "I have discovered that each person who reads one of my books is actually reading

of 14 short stories is based on those tales told by her aunts and uncles, their lives and attitudes, and the mode of storytelling. "People call it magic realism, but that is just how people told family history," commented Alcalá in a 2005 interview.

In 1997, Alcalá debuted her first novel, *Spirits of the Ordinary: A Tale of Casas Grandes,* which grew out of the last story in her previous book. Set in 1870s Mexico, the novel relates the story of Zacarias, who abandons his family and Jewish faith to pan for gold. He witnesses a massacre that brings him back to his ancestral religion. Skillfully Alcalá weaves mystery into ordinary events through Estela, Zacarias's bereft wife, and her journey to find strength and independence.

a different book, based on their own experiences. So it is very gratifying to provide narratives that alter the way people see the world, or that bring out their own experiences that they thought were isolated."

Further Reading

Alcalá, Kathleen. *Spirit of the Ordinary: A Tale of Casas Grandes.* San Francisco: Chronicle Books, 1997.

Flores, Lauro. *Floating Borderlands: Twenty-five Years of U.S. Hispanic Literature.* Seattle: University of Washington Press, 1998.

González, Ray, ed. *Mirrors Beneath the Earth: Short Fiction by Chicano Writers.* Willimantic, Conn.: Curbstone Press, 1992.

Johnson, Rob. *Fantasmas: Supernatural Stories by Mexican American Writers.* Tempe, Ariz.: Bilingual Review Press, 2001.

Alegría, Fernando

(1918–2005) *novelist, poet, essayist, educator*

Fernando Alegría was considered one of the preeminent Chilean writers living in the United States. Born in Santiago, Chile, on September 26 (some reports say September 18), 1918, Fernando Alegría was the son of Santiago Alegría Toro, a businessman, and Julia Alfaro. Fernando was a voracious reader as a child, who especially enjoyed the poetry of Pablo Neruda. Both his mother and grandmother encouraged his writing and his attendance at the country's best schools. By the time he was in high school, Santiago's daily newspaper had published several of Alegría's writings. He studied Spanish and philosophy at the University of Chile, later accepting a position as professor at the university.

In 1938, Alegría published *Recabarren,* a biography of a Chilean labor movement leader. Alegría became an activist for the peace movement and traveled to New York to attend an international conference for the Youth for Peace. Political unrest in his homeland forced him to stay in the United States. He enrolled in Bowling Green State University, earning a master's degree in literature in 1941.

In 1943, Alegría married Carmen Letona Meléndez, with whom he would have four children: Carmen, Daniel, Andrés, and Isabel. The couple moved to California so Alegría could pursue his doctorate at the University of California–Berkeley. He supported his family teaching Spanish and Portuguese at Berkeley from 1947 to 1967, later teaching the same subjects at Stanford University from 1967 to 1987.

During the course of his professorship at Berkeley, Alegría had a tremendous impact introducing Spanish literature to English readers and vice versa. He translated and promoted Spanish-language literature in the United States, publishing several books of short stories and poems, juvenile fiction, and novels. These include *Ideas estéticas de la poesía moderna* (1939; Esthetic ideas of modern poetry), *Leyenda de la ciudad perdida* (1942; Legend of the lost city), *Lautaro: Joven libertador de Arauco* (1943; Lautaro: Young liberator of Arauco), *Ensayo sobre cinco temas de Tomás Mann* (1949; Essay on five themes of Thomas Mann), *Camaleón* (1951; Chameleon), *La poesía chilena: Orígenes y desarollo del siglo XVI al XIX* (1954; Chilean poetry: Origins and development from the 16th to 19th century), *Walt Whitman en hispanoamerica* (1954; Walt Whitman in Latin America), *El poeta que se volvió gusano, cuadernos americanos* (1956; The poet who became a worm, American notebooks), *Caballo de copas* (1957; Queen of hearts), *Breve historia de la novela hispanoamericana* (1959, A brief history of the Latin American novel, with later revised editions), *El cataclismo* (1960; The catastrophe), *Las noches del cazador* (1961; The nights of the hunter), *Las fronteras del realismo: Literatura chilena del siglo XX* (1962, 1967; The borders of realism: 20th century Chilean literature), *Mañana los guerreros* (1964; translation by Carlos Lozano published as *The Maypole Warriors* in 1993), *Viva chile M!* (1965; Long live Chile!), *Genio y figura de Gabriela Mistral* (1966; Genius and form of Gabriela Mistral), and *La novela hispanoamericana, siglo XX* (1967; The Latin American novel, 20th century).

His greatest work of this era, *Caballo de copas*, was a lengthy essay that drew on the similarities in life for Hispanic laborers in the United States and the Chilean working class. The success of this work in Chile allowed Alegría to return to his homeland with a captive audience. Always of a political nature, Alegría became involved with the Popular Unity Movement in Chile. He returned to the United States but remained attached to his Chilean roots. He wrote *Los días contados* (1968; The days told), *Ten Pastoral Psalms* (1968), *Como un arbol rojo* (1968; Like a red tree), *La maratón del palomo* (1968, The dove's marathon), *Los mejores cuentos de Fernando Alegría* (1968; The best stories of Fernando Alegría), and *La literatura chilena contemporánea* (1969; Contemporary Chilean literature), *Instructions for Undressing the Human Race/Instrucciones para desnudar a la raza humana* (1969), and *Amerika (manifiestos de Vietnam)* (1970; Vietnam manifestos).

Beginning in 1967, Alegría taught at Stanford University and created opportunities for exiled Chileans to experience their homeland traditions. When in 1970 his old friend Salvador Allende was elected president of Chile, Alegría became his cultural attaché in Washington. He served in this post for three years, until Allende was assassinated in 1973. In 1977, he cofounded *Literatura Chilena en el Exilio* (Chilean literature in exile), a literary magazine. He continued to write, publishing *Retratos contemporáneos* (1979; Contemporary profiles), *Coral de Guerra* (1979; The warrior coral), *El paso de los gansos* (1980; The path of the geese), *The Chilean Spring* (1980), *Changing Centuries: Selected Poems of Fernando Alegría* (1984), *Los trapecios* (1985; The trapeze), and *The Funhouse* (1986). Alegría served as an editor for *Novelistas contemporáneos hispanoamericanos* (1964; Contemporary Latin American novelists), *Historia de la novela moderna* (1966; History of the modern novel), and *Chilean Writers in Exile: Eight Short Novels* (1982). With others he translated a book

of poetry by Nicanor Parra, *Poems and Antipoems* (1967). He contributed to *Literatura y praxis en América Latina* (1974), *Figuras y contrafiguras en la poesía de Fernando Alegría* (1981), and *Una especie de memoria* (1983).

Alegría became a professor emeritus of Stanford University in 1987. He then wrote *La rebelión de los placeres* (1990), *Creadores en el mundo hispánico* (1990), and *Encuentro por Martín Cerda* (1991). Deeply affected by his own exile, the author began collecting testimonies from other exiles. The result was *Paradise Lost or Gained?* (1992), a collection of essays, poems, and stories that explores the varied experiences of the exile process. With the personal touch that comes from deeply knowing the subject, he penned a quasi-fictional account of the overthrow of Salvador Allende in *Allende: A Novel* (1993). Alegría died October 29, 2005, at his home.

Further Reading

Flores, Angel, ed. *Spanish American Authors: The Twentieth Century.* New York: H. W. Wilson, 1992.

Heide, Rick, ed. *Under the Fifth Sun: Latino Literature from California.* Santa Clara and Berkeley, Calif.: Santa Clara University/Heyday Books, 2002.

Ryan, Bryan, ed. *Hispanic Writers.* Detroit: Gale Research, 1991, pp. 3–9.

Algarín, Miguel

(1941–) *poet, short story writer, educator, anthologist*

Miguel Algarín pioneered the Nuyorican poetry movement and cofounded the Nuyorican Poets Cafe in New York City.

Miguel Algarín was born to Miguel and María Algarín on September 11, 1941, in Puerto Rico. He immigrated to the United States when he was nine years old, arriving in New York City. His family gave him a strong sense of pride in culture that would later inform much of his work. Algarín says of his early years in *Shattering the*

Silences, "I came from a family where culture prevailed. My folks gave me a love of culture. So there is nothing surprising about Shakespeare being in my life. It would be surprising if he weren't. I work for him and he works for me. He wanted to have a place to tell the story of England; so I wanted to have a place in which to tell the story of the Lower East Side."

Algarín earned a B.A. from the University of Wisconsin–Madison in 1963 and an M.A. from Pennsylvania State University two years later. He lectured in English at Brooklyn College of the City University of New York from 1965 to 1967 and taught English at Middlesex County College in Edison, New Jersey. He released his first collection of poetry, *Realidades,* in 1970. In 1971, he accepted a position as associate professor of English at Rutgers University. He remained at Rutgers until the late 1990s, branching out to teach Shakespeare, creative writing, and U.S. ethnic literature.

In 1973, Algarín created a gathering place for fellow poets and artists, including MIGUEL PIÑERO, in the living room of his Manhattan apartment. Algarín and Piñero decided to edit and collect the works of their colleagues. While at the San Juan airport in Puerto Rico, the two poets overheard someone derogatorily refer to them as "newyoricans" (New York [Puerto] Ricans), as Algarín and Piñero spoke fluent English. Algarín transformed the insult into a positive affirmation by making it the title of their anthology. *Nuyorican Poetry: An Anthology of Puerto Rican Words and Feelings* was released in 1975. Concurrently, the collective energy and talent had outgrown Algarín's living room. They rented an Irish bar, the Sunshine Cafe, on East Sixth Street, which they renamed the Nuyorican Poets Cafe. Located in the eastern part of Manhattan's East Village, an area variously known as Alphabet City or Loisaida (a Hispanicization of Lower East Side), the Nuyorican Poets Cafe popularized slam poetry, a form of performance poetry.

Algarín published a collection of short stories, *Spread Your Cheeks,* in 1975. The following year, he translated and provided the introduction

Known as the "poet laureate" of Loisaida, the Lower East Side of New York City, Miguel Algarín cofounded the Nuyorican Poets Cafe with Miguel Piñero. *(Photo of Miguel Algarín is reprinted with permission from the publisher [APP Archive Files] [Houston: Arte Público Press—University of Houston, © 2006])*

to Pablo Neruda's verses, which was published as *Song of Protest by Pablo Neruda* (1976). Additional works of this time include *The Mongo Affair* (1978) and *On Call* (1980). In 1980, Algarín purchased a building on the same street to expand the café. The café now offers programs that include poetry and prose readings, theatrical and musical performances, and visual arts exhibits. The theater has won more than 30 AUBELCO Awards and was honored with an OBIE Grant for excellence in theater.

In addition to building an artistic community and venue, Algarín continued to work on his writing. He released *Body Bee Calling from the Twentieth Century* (1982), *Time's Now/Ya es tiempo* (1985), *Aloud: Voices from the Nuyorican Poets' Café* (1994), *Action,* with Lois Griffith (1997), and *Love Is Hard Work* (1997).

Algarín currently serves on the board of directors for the still popular Nuyorican Poets Cafe, which is now a nonprofit organization, multicultural venue, and one of the country's most highly respected arts organizations. He is working on a new book titled *Dirty Beauty.*

Further Reading

Algarín, Miguel. *Love Is Hard Work: Memorias de Loisaida/Poems.* New York: Scribner, 1997.

Algarín, Miguel, and Miguel Piñero. *Nuyorican Poetry: An Anthology of Puerto Rican Words and Feelings.* New York: William Morrow, 1975.

Kanellos, Nicolás, et al., ed. *Herencia: The Anthology of Hispanic Literature in the United States.* New York: Oxford University Press, 2003, pp. 220–222.

Allende, Isabel
(Isabel Allende Llona, Francisca Ramón)
(1942–   ) *novelist, short story writer, young adult writer, playwright*

Known the world over as one of most influential and acclaimed Latina authors, Isabel Allende has received more than 25 international awards and more than 35 international honors. Her books, translated into 27 languages, have been adapted into plays, operas, ballets, and major motion pictures. Allende's life is a surreal labyrinth filled with spirits, exile, international wanderings, tragedy, courage, love, rebellion, and outrageous family characters that have helped define her novels.

Born Isabel Allende Llona on August 2, 1942, in Lima, Peru, she was the first child of Tomás Allende Pesce de Bilbaire and Francisca Llona Barros. Trying to impress the Peruvian socialites, Tomás insisted his first child be born in a hospital.

The austere appearance of the hospital so frightened Francisca that she, along with her mother, conspired and succeeded in stealing little Isabel from the nursery. At three, Isabel found herself aboard a ship bound for her grandfather's charity and home in Santiago, Chile, with her mother; two brothers (Pancho and Juan); their maid, Magara; and dog, Pelvina Lopez Pun. Francisca obtained a miraculous annulment from her absentee husband, and although he could not obtain an annulment from his marriage, Ramón Huidoboro, her mother's new love, became the family's guardian and Isabel's stepfather.

Shy and quietly observant in public, Isabel often retreated to the underground world of her grandfather's cellar. There she created ritualistic games, told her brothers stories, and read many books by candlelight. She adored her grandfather, or Tata, Don Agustín Llona, a solid Basque, stubborn and strong as a mule, whose legacy to her was a love of language and stories. Before she had the opportunity to be fully trained as an *illuminata*, also known as a mystic or psychic, by her clairvoyant, ethereal grandmother, known as Memé, the grand dame gracefully died. Her maternal grandparents served as inspiration for her first novel, *The House of the Spirits.*

Isabel first attended school under the tutelage of German Ursuline nuns. She was expelled for "perversion" at six when she organized a contest to show off underpants. Her next school was Dunalastair, an English school with, as she put it, a "horrible uniform." Soon afterward Huidoboro was appointed secretary of the embassy in Bolivia, where Isabel went to a coeducational American school. In 1955, they moved to Lebanon, where they stayed for three years.

At age 15, Allende moved back to her grandfather's house. As a teen and young adult, Allende never thought she would become an author—that was considered beyond a woman's reach. Her first job was as a secretary for the United Nations in the Department of Information, later leading to the opportunity to host a television show. In 1962,

Allende married Miguel Frías. Within a few years, she gave birth to Paula and then Nicolás. Allende wrote a feminist humor column for a woman's magazine, *Paula* (under the pseudonym Francisca Ramón), a column for a children's magazine, *Mampato;* and three plays—*El embajador* (1971), *La balada del medio pelo* (1973), and *Los siete espejos* (1974).

On September 11, 1973, her world changed. Revolutionaries killed Allende's uncle Salvador Allende, the first Socialist president ever elected democratically in Chile. In the span of a few hours, a regime of terror replaced a century of democracy. Allende spoke out against the insurgents until it became too dangerous to stay. Eventually she fled her homeland with her husband and children.

They arrived in Caracas, Venezuela, in 1975. Paralyzed by nostalgia and desperately homesick, Allende found comfort in literature and for the next 11 years worked as a journalist for the newspaper *El Nacional.* Allende stated on her Web site, "Frankly, I think I would have not become a writer if I had not been forced to leave everything behind and start anew. In exile, literature gave me a voice, it rescued my memories from the curse of oblivion."

On January 8, 1981, she received a call that her grandfather was dying. Allende began a spiritual letter for her beloved grandfather. One year and 500 pages later, her debut novel, *La casa de los espíritus (The House of the Spirits),* was born. Steeped in magic realism, family secrets, and tragedy, the novel became an instant best seller when published in Barcelona in 1982. It was also very popular when it was published in English (1985) and made into a major motion picture (1994). Departing from magic, Allende's second novel, *De amor y sombras* (1984; *Of Love and Shadows,* 1987) recounts the true adventure of two journalists forced into exile.

In the mid-1980s, Allende divorced Frías. About that time, Celia Correas Zapata, a literature professor, began asking Allende to speak at San Jose State University in California. Finally, after two or three years, Zapata convinced Allende to do a book tour in California. When Zapata's friend William Gordon commented about *Of Love and Shadows,* "[T]he author understands love as I do," Zapata knew magic was afoot. She invited Gordon to a dinner party held after Allende's speech. Allende asked Gordon for his life story and was immediately enthralled. The next day, she returned home, packed her belongings, and within a week returned to California. Six months later Allende and Gordon exchanged wedding vows.

Always beginning on the auspicious January 8 and writing her fiction in Spanish, Allende shifted her setting to a tropical landscape in *Eva Luna* (in Spanish, 1987; in English, 1988). *Cuentos de Eva Luna* followed in 1989 (*Stories of Eva Luna,* 1991) as a collection of short stories featuring characters from the previous novel.

Eventually, Allende got around to writing Gordon's life in her 1991 novel *El plan infinito (The Infinite Plan,* 1993). In December, while on a book tour in Madrid, Allende discovered that her daughter, Paula, had porphyria, a rare genetic condition. Paula later fell into a coma and died one year later. Through the ordeal, Allende again found solace in writing. *Paula* (in Spanish, 1994; in English, 1995) is Allende's heart-wrenching memoir and truly a celebration of life. However, tragedy struck once more when a few months later Gordon's daughter, Jennifer, died. For three years, Allende faced an immense writer's block.

Inspired by Zapata in 1996, Allende began the Esperanza Grant, which rewards organizations working to make the world a safer, more compassionate place for women and children. The Paula Scholarships followed to help provide educational grants to selected male and female students.

In time, Allende gave herself permission to choose a subject as removed from grief as possible: lust and gluttony. Researched mostly in the porn shops of a gay neighborhood of San Francisco and with the love and support of her husband, the project pulled Allende out of depression. *Afrodita:*

cuentos, recetas y otros afrodisíacos (Aphrodite: A Memoir of the Senses, 1998), a collection of recipes with aphrodisiac powers and historical and literary musings, was warmly received by critics and readers alike.

Allende turned to a historical drama for her next book, *Hija de la fortuna (Daughter of Fortune),* published simultaneously in Spanish and English in 1999. It tells the story of Eliza Sommers who follows her lover to the California gold rush. In 2000, Oprah Winfrey announced the book as the featured title for Oprah's Book Club. That same year, Allende released *Retrato en sepia (Portrait in Sepia),* also a historical novel, which related the story of Aurora del Valle, the granddaughter of Eliza Sommers.

Ciudad de las bestias (The City of the Beasts, 2001), Allende's first young adult book, tells of the magical adventure of Alexander Cold, a 15-year-old American boy and his friend, Nadia Santos, among Stone Age Indians in the Amazon. That same year, Allende established the Espíritu Awards to celebrate, honor, and support positive and compassionate action in the areas of literacy, education, shelter, health care, and the pursuit of peace.

Reino del dragón de oro (Kingdom of the Golden Dragon) appeared simultaneously in Spanish and English in 2003. Also in 2003, Allende published *Mi país inventado: Un paseo nostálgico por Chile (My Invented Country: A Nostalgic Journey to Chile),* in which she connects the violent 1973 coup against the Chilean government and the 2001 attacks on the World Trade Center, which occurred on the same day. Allende released two books in 2005, *Zorro* and *Forest of the Pygmies,* the second and third volumes of her young adult trilogy. In 2006, Allende published *Inés of My Soul.* Allende has taught literature at the University of Virginia–Charlottesville, Montclair College in New Jersey, and the University of California–Berkeley.

Allende best summarizes her own work on her Web site: "There is something magic in the sto-rytelling. You tap into another world. The story becomes whole when you tap into the collective story, when other people's stories become part of the writing, and you know that it's not your story only. Fantasy, emotion, and memories make us who we are and create the stories of our lives. It's strange that my work has been classified as magic realism because I see my novels as just being realistic literature."

Further Reading

Allende, Isabel. *Paula.* New York: HarperCollins, 1995.

Heide, Rick, ed. *Under the Fifth Sun: Latino Literature from California.* Santa Clara and Berkeley, Calif.: Santa Clara University/Heyday Books, 2002.

Kanellos, Nicolás, et al., eds. *Herencia: The Anthology of Hispanic Literature in the United States.* New York: Oxford University Press, 2003, pp. 483–487.

Mendoza, Sylvia. *The Book of Latina Women: 150 Vidas of Passion, Strength, and Success.* Avon, Mass.: Adams Media, 2004.

Zapata, Celia. *Isabel Allende: Life and Spirits.* Houston, Tex.: Arte Público Press, 2002.

Alurista
(Alberto Baltazar Urista)
(1947–   ) poet, short story writer, children's writer, editor, educator, activist

Alurista has been called the poet laureate of Chicano letters, the creator of interlingual text, and the revolutionist who inspired Chicanos to reclaim the geographic and mythical land of Aztlán. An integral pioneer and champion of the Chicano movement, Alurista cofounded the Movimiento Estudiantil Chicano de Aztlán (MECA), the Brown Berets, the Chicano literary journal *Maize,* the Chicano Studies Center at San Diego State University, and the Festival Floricanto, a celebration and sharing of Chicano literature and art.

Alberto Baltazar Urista was born in Mexico City on August 8, 1947. He is the oldest of six children of Baltazar and Ruth (Heredia) Urista. As a child, he lived in the Mexican states of Morelos and Guerrero. An eloquent public speaker from an early age, Alberto became the official orator of his grade while in elementary school. He memorized poetry about country, nationalism, and culture, which he would deliver with passion and style. Later he wrote poetry, which turned an easy profit with the campaigning of a girl from a Catholic school across the street from his own school. Alurista recalled in a 1999 interview for *Metro,* "We were both on scholarship, and we were both in the same boat—no money. So we started talking one day about how we could get some of these rich students' money. She came up with this idea of my writing love poetry to girls at her school from boys at my school. We'd charge each of them 25¢. It worked. That's how I got going writing poetry. Cyrano de Bergerac, without knowing who the hell that guy was."

Intrigued by spirituality and humanity, Urista studied Catholicism, even spending three months in a preseminary school. While visiting his aunt in 1961, Urista became enamored with San Diego, California. He moved to the United States and began studying marxism. He quickly became inspired by the passion and valor of César Chávez and often organized students in support of the farmworkers' plight. At this point, Urista decided to use his writing skills to assist the Chicano movement.

Upon high school graduation, Urista enrolled in Chapman College in Orange, California. While he studied business administration, Urista worked as a counselor at the Friendly Center until 1967. He realized his chosen field of study was not congruent to his interests and talents and returned to San Diego, where he studied religion at San Diego State University. He explored Protestantism, Buddhism, Hinduism, Taoism, Zoroastrianism, Islam, and pre-Columbian religions of Mexico. Inspired by the Maya and Nahuatl cultures, Urista learned both languages, finding a depth and strength to his identity in these pre-Columbian societies. Fueled and inspired by his deep ancestral roots, Urista cofounded the Movimiento Estudiantil Chicano de Aztlán (Chicano Student Movement of Azlán; MECA). Due to the volatile nature of the times, Urista adopted the pen name *Alurista* to avoid any trouble for his family. The name change also provided a symbolic manifestation of his Marxist beliefs, which call for unity and bringing together, as in, *Alberto* and *Urista*.

At the Crusade for Justice–sponsored Denver Youth Conference in 1969, Alurista read his poem "El plan espiritual de Aztlán" (The spiritual plan of Aztlán). Aztlán is the mythic and geographic home of Chicanos, located in the American Southwest, which was lost to the United States as a result of the U.S.-Mexican War and Treaty of Guadalupe Hidalgo of 1848. Alurista called for a reclamation of culture, language, pride, and identity. The crowd at the conference rallied around Alurista's depiction of Aztlán and subsequently chose Alurista's poem as the preamble to "El Plan de Aztlán," which in turn became the community plan of action.

That same year, Alurista married Irene Mercado, with whom he would have two children, Tizoc, named after the 1486 Aztec emperor, and Maoxiim. They later divorced in 1976. Alurista changed his major to sociology and later psychology, graduating from San Diego State University in 1970. He helped establish the Chicano Studies Center and began lecturing in the Chicano Studies Department. A devotee of potentiality and power language as a means of identity, Alurista used a combination of Chicano and Mexican Spanish, English, and Mayan and Náhuatl dialects to represent the blending of languages and cultures within a people in his first collection of poems, entitled *Floricanto en Aztlán* (1971; Flower and song in Aztlán). Consisting of 100 provocative *cantos* (chants or songs), *Floricanto en Aztlán* was highly successful and remains his most widely read and influential work. Although today interlingual text is common, Alurista was the first to have his work published as such. Alurista persisted in his use of multilanguages because of his belief in a unique blending of the cultures. In an interview with JUAN BRUCE-NOVOA, in 1985 Alurista said, "The historical time-space in which we live is going to focus on this terrenal [earthly] belly button of consciousness between Hispanic America and Anglo-Saxon North America. Amerindia is going to bloom. That's inevitable."

In 1972, Alurista published *Nationchild Plumaroja, 1969–1972* (1972; Nationchild Redfeather). *Nationchild* is composed of 100 typically didactic poems divided into five Mayan *katunes* (units of 20). Each *katun* uses the symbol of an animal or flower—*nopal* (prickly pear), *xóchitl* (flower), *serpiente* (serpent), *conejo* (rabbit), or *venado* (deer)—to signify a particular mood. From 1973 to 1978, he served as the organizer of Festival Floricanto, an annual literary event.

Alurista has written nine volumes of children's stories, published as *Colección Tula y Tonán: Textos generativos* (Tula and Tonan collection: Generative texts) in 1973. *Timespace Huracán: Poems, 1972–1975* (1976) explores three levels of "time-space." In an interview with Bruce-Novoa, Alurista described three levels of "time-space" within which all individuals live and function: a historical or collective time-space "that describes reality as accorded by a consensus of people"; a personal, individual, psychological time-space; and a "mythological time-space that unifies the personal and historical time-spaces." Alurista draws on all three spaces, linking the Amerindian of history and mythology with the energy of the contemporary Chicano movement. *Timespace Huracán* is characterized by considerable experimentation with form, including shaped poetry, serial poems, prose poems, and haiku. Chants, songs, rhythmic patterning, and acoustic effects appear frequently.

Throughout his writing career, Alurista has lectured and given poetry readings at numerous colleges and universities and on radio and television programs. In 1976, he cofounded *Maize* (a literary magazine and publishing house) with Xelina Rojas, whom he married the following year. The couple had two children, Zamna and Zahi, and divorced in 1990. Alurista earned an M.A. in 1978 and a Ph.D. in 1983 from the University of California–San Diego.

Alurista's later writing, though not considered as revolutionary as his initial works, is nonetheless important. These works consist of *A'nque/Alurista: Acuarelas hechas por Delilah Merriman-Montoya* (1979; A'nque/Alurista: Watercolors made by Delilah Merriman-Montoya), *Spik in Glyph?* (1981), *Return: Poems Collected and New* (1982), *Tremble Purple: Seven Poems* (1986), *Z Eros* (1995), *Et Tu . . . Raza?* (1996; And You . . . Raza), and *As the Barrio Turns Who the Yoke B On* (2000).

"We [Chicanos] were never exclusivist," Alurista insists in the 1999 interview. "Our nationalism has always been inclusivist. The black-white conflict in America was a racial conflict. But with [Chicanos], the differences are more cultural and linguistic than racial. We have Asian blood. We have European blood. We have Indian blood. That's what makes us Mexicans. We are the Rainbow People. Aztlán is wherever we are. We don't recognize borders. It's more a matter of cultural/political identity. When I say this is our land, I don't mean that we own it. Who owns anything?"

Further Reading

Bruce-Novoa, Juan. *Chicano Poetry: A Response to Chaos.* Austin: University of Texas Press, 1982.

Candelaria, Cordelia. *Chicano Poetry: A Critical Introduction.* Westport, Conn.: Greenwood Press, 1986.

Kanellos, Nicolás, et al., eds. *Herencia: The Anthology of Hispanic Literature in The United States.* New York: Oxford University Press, 2003, pp. 205–206.

Lomelí, Francisco A., and Carl R. Shirley, eds. *Chicano Writers: First Series*, Vol. 82. Detroit: Gale Research, 1992, pp. 16–23.

Alvarez, Julia

(1950–) *novelist, poet, educator, essayist, young adult writer, children's writer*

Highly awarded and nationally acclaimed author and poet Julia Alvarez expertly captures the immigrant experience. As one of the most widely read and well-known Latina writers, she is sought after as a keynote speaker for universities, museums, associations, writers' conferences, and festivals.

The second of four sisters, Julia Alvarez was born in New York City on March 27, 1950. When she was three months old, her parents, both native Dominicans, returned the family to their homeland. Julia was raised among cousins, aunts, uncles, and maids on her maternal grandparents' compound. However, she was the only one born in America, a fact Julia would not let anyone forget. The extended family was completely captivated by the United States. She and her sisters wore American clothes, ate American food, attended American schools, read and wrote in English, and befriended American classmates.

Alvarez's father, a doctor who ran a local hospital, and his family had once been wealthy until they supported the wrong political party during the 1960 revolution. Julia's father would have drawn the wrath of the Dominican Republic dictator, Rafael Leonidas Trujillo Molina, had her mother's family not had such strong American ties and supported the political victors during the revolution. Julia's uncles had all attended Ivy League colleges, and her grandfather was a cultural attaché to the United Nations. The family was relatively safe until Julia's father secretly joined the insurrectionists attempting to overthrow Trujillo. In 1960, the police began surveillance of the compound where the Alvarezes lived in preparation to arrest the doctor. An American agent warned Julia's father, and they escaped the country. Most unfortunately, the Mirabal sisters, fellow activists against Trujillo, were brutally murdered by the dictatorship—a plight Julia would later write about.

The Alvarez family returned to New York City, where Julia's father had procured a fellowship at a hospital. On the plane, Alvarez fantasized about the homecoming of her dreams, but reality was much harsher. The English spoken in New York blurred together for Alvarez, forcing her to concentrate on each word—a fact she calls training for a writer. Her new classmates teased her, forcing the once gregarious Alvarez to the quieter world of books.

Julia left home at 13 to attend boarding school. When her English teacher assigned the composition of a personal essay, Alvarez delved into her feelings of alienation and displacement and found she loved writing. She continued to write throughout high school and later at Connecticut College, where she won the Benjamin T. Marshall Prize in poetry (1968 and 1969). She transferred to Middlebury College in Vermont after attending the Bread Loaf Writers' Conference. In 1971, she earned her B.A. with summa cum laude honors from Middlebury and was awarded the Creative Writing Prize. In 1974, Alvarez won the American Academy of Poetry Prize; the following year she was awarded her M.A. in creative writing from Syracuse University.

After graduation, Alvarez became a migrant poet and teacher. She served two years as a visiting writer at elementary schools and high schools and in communities with the Kentucky Arts Commission. She taught freshman English at California State College in Fresno, and College of the Sequoias in Visalia, California. Alvarez moved to Delaware, where she conducted daily bilingual creative writing workshops in English and Spanish. This work culminated in an anthology, *Yo Soy/ I Am* (1978).

Alvarez conducted 11 weeks of poetry workshops for senior citizens in rest homes and in civic and county centers. *Old Age Ain't for Sissies* (1979) is the anthology resulting from this work. Over the next several years Alvarez taught English at a private high school, the University of Vermont, George Washington University, and the University of Illinois. Alvarez continued her writing along with her teaching, receiving the La Reina Creative Writing Award for poetry, Third Woman Press Award for narrative, General Electric Foundation Award for Younger Writers, and PEN Oakland/Josephine Miles Award for excellence in multicultural literature.

The Housekeeping Book (1982) is Alvarez's first published work. This book of poetry celebrates basic household implements with simple yet elegant reverence to the stories inherent in them. *Homecoming* (1984) features 33 sonnets of self-exploration to match Alvarez's age at the time of publication. Alvarez added 13 new poems when the book was re-released in 1996.

In 1988, Alvarez accepted a position as professor of English at Middlebury College. She married Bill Eichner on June 3, 1989. In 1991, she was awarded tenure and released her first novel, *How the García Girls Lost Their Accents,* to considerable critical acclaim. Semiautobiographical in nature, the book weaves together 15 stories of the Dominican-born Garcia sisters—Carla, Sandra, Yolanda, and Sofia—and their immigration to the United States. The *New York Times Book Review* reported that Alvarez "beautifully captured the threshold experience of the new immigrant, where the past is not yet a memory and the future remains an anxious dream." Riding the crest of the literary boom of ethnic novels, *How the García Girls Lost Their Accents* became the exemplar of this new literary genre.

In 1994, Alvarez published her second novel, *In the Time of the Butterflies,* a fictional account based on the true story of the Mirabal sisters' assassination in the Dominican Republic. The sisters, whose code name during the resistance was Las Mariposas, "butterflies" in Spanish, continue to be honored throughout many Latin American countries on the anniversary of their death. Supported by Salma Hayek, Showtime produced a film version of *In the Time of the Butterflies* in 1999.

Alvarez's work continued to receive awards and honors such as Notable Book, Book of the Month Club, National Book Critics' Award, Best

Books for Young Adults, and the Jessica Nobel-Maxwell Poetry Prize. Alvarez released her second collection of poems, *The Other Side: El Otro Lado,* in 1995. Arranged in five sections, the poems lyrically depict the passage and experiences of sifting through class consciousness, establishing identity, childhood memories of the "old country," and the power of language.

Alvarez accepted a promotion to full professor at Middlebury College in 1996. The following year, her third novel, *¡Yo!,* was published. *¡Yo!* focuses on the struggles and triumphs of Yolanda from *How the García Girls Lost Their Accents.* Along the way, she discovers her voice and independence and how her unique expression fits into her identity as both an American and Dominican.

By 1998, Alvarez was torn between the joy of reaching her goal to earn a living while writing and the love of teaching. After much debate, she remitted her professorship at Middlebury College to become the school's writer-in-residence. The position created a better balance of teaching and advising students with time to devote to creative writing. She had also carved out time and energy to establish, with her husband, a sustainable coffee farm called Alta Gracia, named after the patron saint of the Dominican Republic. Funds gained from selling the coffee support programs to teach literacy to local children and adults. In that same year, *Something to Declare,* an autobiographical collection of essays on the author's life experiences, was released. She was also awarded the Literature Leadership Award by the Dominico-American Society of Queens.

In 2000, Alvarez published *In the Name of Salomé,* which covers 100 years and reveals the courage of Salomé Urena de Henriquez, the 19th-century poet laureate of the Dominican Republic, and her daughter, Camila Henriquez Urena, who left a quiet comfortable life to return to the old world and find her voice. Honored as Woman of the Year by *Latina* magazine, that same year Alvarez released a picture book, *The Secret Footprints,* based on a traditional Dominican fable about the *ciguapas,* a tribe of beautiful women who live underwater but come out at night to hunt for food. *How Tía Lola Came to Stay* was released the following year. This young reader tells the story of nine-year-old Miguel's struggles to adjust to his parents' divorce, a new town, and his flamboyant aunt, Tía Lola. Alvarez released *A Cafecito Story* in 2001, which chronicles events at Alta Gracia. Released in 2002, *Before We Were Free,* which won the Pura Belfre Award (2004), captures young Anita's coming-of-age in a dictatorship in the Dominican Republic. Anita records her feelings and the events that transpire in a diary while she and her mother go into hiding after her father is taken away by the secret police.

Alvarez returned to poetry with *The Woman I Kept to Myself,* released in 2004. This collection of 78 poems is self-exploratory in nature. The verses recall and reassemble what has passed to form a new meaning and direction for life. Alvarez published *Finding Miracles,* another young reader, in 2004. This book chronicles the search of Americanized Milly, originally named Milagros, for the truth and integrity of her roots. Alvarez released *Saving the World,* a novel, in 2006.

Alvarez's works have been translated into several languages and included in many anthologies. She writes from deep introspection and personal experience, yet her writings touch a universal chord for the need of self-discovery and a place to call home. With her words, readers across the land and from different cultures find a commonality that clarifies why Alvarez is so beloved and honored.

Further Reading

Alvarez, Julia. *How the García Girls Lost Their Accents.* Chapel Hill, N.C.: Algonquin Books, 1991.

———. *Something to Declare.* Chapel Hill, N.C.: Algonquin Books, 1998.

Barron, Jonathan N., and Bruce Meyer. *Dictionary of Literary Biography: New Formalist Poets.* Vol. 282. Detroit: Gale, 2003, pp. 16–23.

Heredia, Juanita, and Bridget A. Kevane., eds. *Latina Self Portraits: Interviews with Contemporary Women Writers.* Albuquerque: University of New Mexico Press, 2000.

Novas, Himilce. *The Hispanic 100: A Ranking of the Latino Men and Women Who Have Most Influenced American Thought and Culture.* New York: Citadel Press, 1995.

Tardiff, Joseph C., and L. Mpho Mabunda, eds. *Dictionary of Hispanic Biography.* Detroit: Gale Research, 1996, pp. 32–35.

Anaya, Rudolfo A.
(Rudolfo Alfonso Anaya)
(1937–   ) *novelist, short story writer, poet, essayist*

Rudolfo A. Anaya is hailed for helping the Latino way of life, traditions, and values become nationally recognized with his first novel, *Bless Me, Ultima* (1971). Throughout the 1970s and 1980s, Anaya was known as the premier voice of Chicano literature. Captured and inspired by the land and the mysteries of life, he has long sought to find the meaning in the mundane, the spiritual in the physical.

Born on October 30, 1937, in Las Pasturas, New Mexico, Rudolfo Alfonso Anaya, the fifth of seven children, would grow to be the bridge between his divergent parents. Martín Anaya, his father, was a vaquero, a horseman with a free spirit and wanderlust nature. His mother, Rafaelita Mares Anaya, came from a long line of poor, hard-working farmers who were devout Catholics.

Soon after his birth, the family moved to Santa Rosa, New Mexico. Rudolfo would spend the next 14 years in Santa Rosa roaming the *llano* (plains) and swimming and fishing in the Pecos River. The family spoke Spanish at home. It was not until Rudolfo entered school that he learned English. He excelled in school, encouraged by his mother, who valued a good education. Rudolfo was raised in the Catholic faith and earnestly asked difficult questions of spirituality that neither his older siblings, mother, nor his priest could answer to his satisfaction. Surrounded by the comforts and security of a supportive community, he learned to live with mystery as a natural part of his life. The mystique and superstitions of the Roman Catholic faith wove into the stories and legends of Mexico, forming a blended truth for Rudolfo Anaya that placed the wisdom of the land and his ancestors at its apex.

In 1952, the Anaya family moved to Albuquerque, New Mexico, taking Anaya out of the cocoon of pastoral life to the colder reality of urban life. Anaya was exposed to cultural and ethnic diversity, racism, and prejudice, which he was neither accustomed to nor prepared for. He steered clear of gangs, performed well academically, and otherwise adjusted until he had a life-altering experience. When he was 16 years old, while swimming with friends in an irrigation ditch, Anaya miscalculated a dive and broke two vertebrae in his neck. The near-death experience, long and painful recovery, and eventual return to his active lifestyle infused Anaya with an unquenchable passion and thirst for life.

Anaya graduated from Albuquerque High School in 1956. He attended Browning Business School from 1956 to 1958, intent on becoming an accountant. He found the business classes unrewarding and enrolled at the University of New Mexico at Albuquerque. None of his university classes offered anything that reflected his upbringing. Anaya felt engulfed by the dominant white culture and yearned for a mentor. Thankfully, a freshman English class sparked his interest in literature. He submersed himself in writing as a means of transcending his feelings of alienation and frustration. This writing process proved to be cathartic and became a lifelong practice. Anaya graduated with a bachelor's degree in English in 1963 and accepted a teaching job. Three years later, he married Patricia Lawless, who, while editing his work, encouraged Anaya to write. He earned his master's degree in English in 1968.

Throughout the 1960s, Anaya taught junior high and high school by day and wrote at night. He labored for many years trying to capture the essence of his memories and the people of his childhood. As he struggled to find his inner voice one night, he was blessed with a mystical experience. An elderly woman dressed in black entered his room. The vision became his muse for the *curandera,* or "healer," known as Ultima in his novel *Bless Me, Ultima.* Anaya wrote in a reprint of *Bless Me, Ultima,* "In the process of writing, the serious writer enters planes of visions and reality that cannot be induced by drugs or alcohol. That trance can only be explained as a sort of spiritual high." His writing flowed, and through many rewrites a classic was born.

Bless Me, Ultima (1972) revolves around Antonio Juan Marez y Luna, a bright six-year-old boy who comes of age with the assistance and wisdom of Ultima. Like Anaya, Antonio seeks a spirituality that can answer his questions and encompass his beloved land. He is also torn between his parents' desires for him to be either a vaquero or a farmer. *Bless Me, Ultima* was sent to several publishers before Quinto Sol Publications accepted the book. *Bless Me, Ultima* won the prestigious Premio Quinto Sol Award for the best Chicano novel of 1972. Selling hundreds of thousands of copies over the years, the book was well received and "inspired the largest body of criticism in contemporary Chicano literature," noted Antonio Márquez a well-respected Chicano studies scholar.

With his newfound acclaim and a recently acquired M.A. in guidance and counseling from the school, Anaya secured a faculty position at the University of New Mexico at Albuquerque, in 1971, where he taught and mentored in several capacities until his retirement in 1993. He published his second novel, *Heart of Aztlán,* in 1976. In it, he relates how members of the Chavez family become estranged when they move from their pastoral life to the barrios of Albuquerque. Although it won the Before Columbus Foundation American Book Award, *Heart of Aztlán* did not receive good reviews.

Tortuga, Anaya's third novel, published in 1979, completed his trilogy on the Chicano experience that spans several generations. *Tortuga* is set in a sanitarium for terminally ill teenagers. The main character is a teenage boy who lies in the hospital in a full body cast, partially paralyzed and unable to move. Because of confinement to his cast, he is nicknamed Tortuga, which means "turtle" in Spanish. In despair, he tries to kill himself but finds appreciation for life through the wisdom of a terminally ill boy. *Tortuga* won the Before Columbus Award. Critics reviewed Anaya's third book favorably, and many consider *Tortuga* to be Anaya's most complete and accomplished work.

Anaya next experimented with a variety of styles, composing a collection of short stories published as *The Silence of Llano* (1982) and *A Chicano in China* (1986), a nonfiction account of Anaya's travels to China. *The Legend of La Llorona* (1984) and *Lord of the Dawn: The Legend of Quetzalcoatl* (1987) are both retellings of traditional Mexican folk stories, and *The Farolitos of Christmas: A New Mexican Christmas Story* (1987) was Anaya's first children's story. In 1985, he published an epic poem, *The Adventures of Juan Chicaspatas.* Anaya also served as an editor for numerous publications as well as a translator of or contributor to other Chicano works.

In 1992, Anaya released *Alburquerque* (the original spelling of the city's name), the first in a new series of mystery novels. Abran Gonzalez, a former Golden Glove champ from the Barelas barrio, is the protagonist in *Alburquerque,* which won the PEN-West Fiction Award. The rest of the series, *Zia Summer* (1995), *Rio Grande Fall* (1996), and *Shaman Winter* (1999), features detective Sonny Baca. In *Jalamanta: A Message from the Desert* (1996), the spiritualist Jalamanta returns after a 30-year exile to teach his fellow villagers that higher consciousness is an individual path rather than a predescribed dogma. Critics dismissed *Jalamanta* as a preachy New Age book, missing the book's message as anything but didactic. In 2000, Anaya wrote another epic poem, this time aimed at middle and high school students. *Elegy on the Death of Cesar Chavez* celebrates the life and

struggles of the famed Chicano labor leader. The poem provides factual details while it takes readers on a journey through grief, hope, and call for action. Anaya released *Serafina's Stories* in 2004; *Jemez Spring* in 2005, and *The Man Who Could Fly, Albuquerque: A Novel,* and *Curse of the Chupa Cobra* in 2006.

The list of Anaya's awards is long and illustrious and includes the New Mexico Governor's Public Service Award, the Before Columbus Foundation American Book Award, and the New Mexico Governor's Award for Excellence and Achievement in Literature, among others. He is also the recipient of several fellowships, which include two National Endowment of the Arts Fellowships and a Kellogg Foundation Fellowship.

Anaya devotes his time to writing and traveling. He has visited Mexico, Costa Rica, Panama, Puerto Rico, the Caribbean, Europe, and China. However, like his mother, Anaya has strong roots to the land and has continued to call New Mexico his home throughout his travels. Anaya, who spends several hours a day writing, believes his role as a storyteller is to restore harmony and order with the assistance of legends, myths, mystery, and the ancestors. His feat is accomplished according to his millions of readers and fans who have felt the supernatural swell of inner spiritual strength in reading his works and listening to his lectures.

Further Reading

Anaya, Rudolfo. *Bless Me, Ultima.* Berkeley, Calif.: Quinto Sol, 1972.
———. *The Man Who Could Fly.* Norman: University of Oklahoma Press, 2006.
Bruce-Novoa, Juan. "Rudolfo A. Anaya." In *Chicano Authors: Inquiry by Interview.* Austin: University of Texas Press, 1980, pp. 183–202.
Kristovic, Jelena, ed. *Hispanic Literature Criticism.* Detroit: Gale Research, 1994.
Lomelí, Francisco A., and Carl R. Shirley, eds. *Chicano Writers: First Series.* Detroit: Gale Research, 1989, pp. 24–35.

Rogers, Jane. "The Function of La Llorona Myth in Rudolfo Anaya's *Bless Me, Ultima.*" *Latin American Literary Review* 5 (Spring 1977): 64–69.

Vassallo, Paul, ed. *The Magic of Words: Rudolfo A. Anaya and His Writings.* Albuquerque: University of New Mexico Press, 1982.

Anzaldúa, Gloria
(Gloria Evangelina Anzaldúa)
(1942-2004) *poet, essayist, short story writer, children's book writer, anthologist, activist, educator*

Gloria Anzaldúa was an internationally recognized writer, activist, and theorist whose passionate prose, poetry, and other writings defined and legitimized the experiences of disenfranchised minorities. One of the first Chicanas to openly declare her lesbianism, Anzaldúa is best known for her book of mixed genres, *Borderlands/La Frontera: The New Mestiza.*

Gloria Evangelina Anzaldúa grew up on a ranch settlement called Jesus Maria of the Valley, located near the town of Edinburg, Texas. Born on September 26, 1942, Anzaldúa was a seventh-generation Mexican American and the eldest child of Urbano and Amalia Anzaldúa. When she was 11, Gloria and her family left the ranch environment to be migrant workers. She worked in the fields of Arkansas alongside her family for one year until her father decided the migrant life was not conducive to obtaining a good education. The family settled in Hargill, Texas, part of the Rio Grande Valley, where Gloria developed a love of reading as a path to define personal freedom and pursue alternate perspectives. Her mother did not share her father's value of education for girls. Whenever Gloria was caught reading, her mother would call her lazy and state that only labor, such as washing dishes and scrubbing walls, could be called work or improve a person. Anzaldúa's father died when she was 15, which removed the buffer and contributed to an increasing tension between mother and daughter.

Despite a lack of support, Anzaldúa graduated from high school and continued her education at Pan American University, where she received her B.A. in English, art, and secondary education in 1969. She then earned an M.A. in education and English from the University of Texas at Austin in 1972. Upon graduating, she was hired by the state of Indiana to teach children of migrant families—a post she filled for a year and a half. Anzaldúa entered the comparative literature department at the University of Texas, intending to gain a Ph.D. in feminist studies, Chicano studies, or Spanish literature. She met with considerable resistance and could not gain Ph.D. candidacy during three years of unremitting effort. From 1976 to 1977, she taught Chicano culture and literature, with emphasis on the experiences of Chicanas, at the Mexican American Studies Center located at the University of Texas.

Frustrated yet undaunted, Anzaldúa enrolled in the Ph.D. dissertation program at the University of California–Santa Cruz in the late 1970s, where she studied feminist theory and cultural studies. She did not complete the doctorate program. She lectured on feminist journal writing and Third World women's literature in the Women's Study Program at San Francisco State University from 1979 to 1980. Anzaldúa teamed with CHERRÍE MORAGA to edit and collect writings from ethnic women. Their collaborative efforts produced *This Bridge Called My Back* (1981). This pioneering collection of essays and poems written by ethnically diverse women is widely considered the premiere multicultural feminist text. Anzaldúa's contributions are suffused with spirituality that transcends yet welcomes mundane experiences, a quality inspired by the fact that Anzaldúa's grandmother was a *curandera,* a traditional healer.

Anzaldúa taught creative writing at the University of California–Santa Cruz from 1982 to 1986. In the classroom, she was adamant about establishing a forum where women of color, whose voices were normally suppressed, could speak freely about personal experiences and feelings. She explained her teaching philosophy in a 1998 interview with Elizabeth Baldwin for *Matrix* magazine: "I wanted the context to be theirs and I wanted to hear from women of color first, men of color second . . and lastly, that I wanted to hear from white people. And that I was the teacher, I was the bridge." She occasionally taught creative writing, feminist studies, and literature in the adult degree program of Vermont College, Norwich University, from 1984 to 1986. While in Vermont, Anzaldúa was overcome with a feeling of alienation. *Borderlands/La Frontera: La Mestiza* (1987) was born from this estrangement and isolation. In her book, Anzaldúa mixes poetry, narration, and language offering a formidable exposition that forces readers to consider and reevaluate rigid assumptions on sex, gender, language, fiction, and identity. The author uses English as well as Spanglish, a combination and blending of Spanish and English, that may frustrate monolinguistic Anglos yet serves to parallel the frustration many border people experience. *Borderlands* succeeds in creating a space where people straddling two or more cultures can feel at home. *Library Journal* chose it as one of the Top 50 Best Books of 1987.

Anzaldúa's work appeared in several journals and magazines, including *Trivia, Third Woman, IKÔN,* and *Sinister Wisdom.* In addition to gender, cultural, and race differences, she explored spirituality in her writing. Anzaldúa was devoted to the Virgin of Guadalupe, Nahuatl/Toltec divinities, and the Yoruba *orishás* Yemayá and Oshún, to whom she had been introduced by author Luisah Teish. She released *Making Face, Making Soul/ Haciendo Caras: Creative and Critical Perspectives by Feminists-of-Color* (1990), a collection of writings dealing with issues of spirituality, sexism, racism, multilingualism, multiethnicity, and cultural identity. Anzaldúa brought her writing talents to children with three bilingual children's books: *Prietita Has a Friend/Prietita tiene un amigo* (1991), *Friends from the Other Side/Amigos del otro lado* (1993), and *Prietita and the Ghost Woman/Prietita y la llorona* (1995). She offered the foreword for the 1996 *Encyclopedia of Queer Myth, Symbol and Spirit.* Other writings include *Interviews/Entrevistas* (2000), a memoirlike collection of interviews, and *This Bridge We Call Home: Radical Visions for Transformation* (2002), a coedited collection (with AnaLouise Keating) of essays, poetry, and artwork that implores society to bring marginalized voices into the collective consciousness. Anzaldúa won numerous awards, including the Before Columbus Foundation American Book Award, the Lambda Lesbian Small Book Press Award, an NEA Fiction Award, the Lesbian Rights Award, the Sappho Award of Distinction, a National Endowment for the Arts Fiction Award, and the American Studies Association Lifetime Achievement Award.

Anzaldúa's life was cut short on May 15, 2004, when she died due to diabetic complications. She is affectionately remembered as *una vela de inspiración* (a candle of inspiration). Her writing and activism are exemplary of a person unwilling to be pigeonholed or forgotten, thereby giving permission and strength to the disenfranchised to be heard.

Further Reading

Heide, Rick, ed. *Under the Fifth Sun: Latino Literature from California.* Santa Clara and Berkeley, Calif.: Santa Clara University/Heyday Books, 2002.

Kanellos, Nicolas, et al., eds. *Herencia: The Anthology of Hispanic Literature in the United States.* New York: Oxford University Press, 2003, pp. 254–261.

Keating, AnaLouise. *Women Reading and Writing: Self-Invention in Paul Gunn Allen, Gloria Anzaldúa, and Audre Lorde.* Philadelphia: Temple University Press, 1996.

Lomelí, Francisco A., and Carl R. Shirley, eds. *Chicano Writers: Second Series.* Detroit: Gale Research, 1992, pp. 8–16.

Moraga, Cherrie, and Gloria Anzaldúa, eds. *This Bridge Called My Back.* Berkeley: Third Woman Press, 1984.

Premo Steele, Cassie. *We Heal from Memory: Sexton, Lorde, Anzaldúa, and the Poetry of Witness.* New York: Palgrave Macmillan, 2000.

Arias, Ron
(Ronald Francis Arias)
(1941–) *journalist, novelist, short story writer, biographer, educator*

Ron Arias writes well-crafted short stories and is commended for his journalistic work. However, he is best known for his masterful novel *The Road to Tamazunchale* (1975).

Ronald Francis Arias was born in Los Angeles, California, on November 30, 1941, the son of Emma Lou Estrada Arias. His mother remarried, after Arias's birth. Due to frequent moves required of his stepfather, Armando Estrada, who served as an army officer, young Arias spent much of his childhood with his maternal grandmother in Los Angeles. Arias spoke Spanish with his grandmother, who instilled in him a deep pride of his Mexican heritage. Arias discovered his love of writing at nine years old when he went to the hospital for a tonsillectomy. His mother gave him a journal to record the events and feelings about the surgery and his hospital stay. He went on to write for his high school and college papers.

After he graduated from high school, Arias attended Oceanside-Carlsbad College (now Mira Costa College) for a short time before deciding to travel. He hitchhiked through Spain, Argentina, and Peru. Throughout the 1960s, he attended the University of Barcelona, Spain, and National University in Buenos Aires, Argentina. He worked as a reporter and writer for the *Buenos Aires Herald* in Buenos Aires, Copley Newspapers, national and international wire services, and the *Caracas Daily Journal* in Caracas, Venezuela. From 1963 to 1964, Arias served as community development volunteer with the Peace Corps in Cuzco, Peru. In 1966, he married Joan Londerman. The next year, he earned a B.A. in Spanish from the University of California–Berkeley, followed by an M.A. in journalism from the University of California–Los Angeles in 1968. He was profoundly influenced by Gabriel García-Márquez's *One Hundred Years of Solitude.* Arias told Juan Bruce-Novoa in *Chicano Authors: Inquiry by Interview,* "For me, García-Márquez transformed, *deepened* reality in so many of its aspects—tragic, humorous, adventurous, wondrous. The work was alive, entertaining at every word."

Inspired by his introduction to magic realism, Arias wrote a slew of short stories that appeared in a variety of literary journals and magazines. He was awarded the Chicano Literary Contest first place award in fiction from the University of California–Irvine for his short story "The Wetback." From the early 1970s until 1985, he earned a living as an instructor at San Bernardino Valley College and then Crafton Hills College. He served as a member of the board of directors of the National Endowment for the Arts coordinating council of literary magazines from 1979 to 1980. After he enjoyed success composing short stories, Arias turned his attention to writing longer works. *The Road to Tamazunchale* (1975) is Arias's debut novel. Alejandro Morales, renowned Chicano scholar and critic, praised *The Road to Tamazunchale* (1975) for its "magical realistic imagination, its precise crisp prose, its relationship to the 'new reality' of Spanish American fiction and its compassionate treatment of death, its central theme." *The Road to Tamazunchale,* an exceptional blend of mysticism, death, transformation, and community, follows Fausto, an old, dying man, as he begins his journey in a Los Angeles barrio and travels to beautiful, mythical Tamazunchale in the mountains of Mexico. The book was nominated for a National Book Award in fiction and is recognized as a literary masterpiece.

In 1986, Arias joined the staff at *People* magazine as a senior writer, a position he still holds. He released *Five Against the Sea: A True Story of Courage and Survival* in 1989. Arias was awarded the Latino Literary Hall of Fame Award for biography in 2003 for *Moving Target,* a memoir that chronicles his youth and the development of his writing career.

Further Reading
Arias, Ron. *Moving Target: A Memoir of Pursuit.* Tempe, Ariz.: Bilingual Press, 2003.

Cárdenas de Dwyer, Carlota. "International Literary Metaphor and Ron Arias: An Analysis of *The Road to Tamazunchale*." *Bilingual Review/Revista Bilingüe* 4 (September–December 1977): 229–233.

Lomelí, Francisco A., and Carl R. Shirley, eds. *Chicano Writers: First Series*. Vol. 122. Detroit: Gale Research, 1992, pp. 37–44.

Tardiff, Joseph C., and L. Mpho Mabunda, eds. *Dictionary of Hispanic Biography*. Detroit: Gale Research, 1996, pp. 54–55.

Arteaga, Alfred
(1950–   ) *poet, editor, educator, essayist*

Recognized as a gifted poet and master of "heterotextual" prose, Alfred Arteaga is the recipient of the National Endowment for the Arts in Creative Writing Fellowship in Poetry (1995), a Rockefeller Fellowship, and the PEN Oakland Josephine Miles Award for Literary Excellence for *House with the Blue Bed*.

Alfred Arteaga was born in East Los Angeles on May 2, 1950, to Alfredo and Lilia Frias. He was raised in Whittier, California, where he dreamed of becoming a racecar driver or pilot. His mother often read him poetry and told her own stories, sparking Alfred's fascination for storytelling and poetry. During his youth, he was a quiet rebel, perfect for an upcoming poet. Being an introvert did not stop Alfred from opposing and organizing protests against the Vietnam War. His political activism and the injustice he saw profoundly affected his writing.

Another influence on his poetry was one of his first jobs, working at the Los Angeles coroner's

Alfred Arteaga is considered a master of heterotextual prose. *(photo by Alfred Arteaga)*

office. Being around so much death invoked much philosophizing about life and bereavement as well as human vulnerability and ultimate mortality. In the early 1970s, Arteaga married, and his budding family grew to include three daughters: Marisol, Xochitl, and Mireya. He was an editor for *La Raza,* a political journal, from 1974 to 1975. From age 28 to 30, Arteaga was an amateur racecar driver.

From 1977 to 1987, Arteaga was an instructor of Mexican-American studies and English at San Jose City College. During this time, he also worked as an editor for *Quarry West,* an annual literary journal published by the University of California–Santa Cruz. He earned an M.A. and Ph.D. in literature from the University of California–Santa Cruz in the mid- and late 1980s, as well as an M.F.A. in creative writing from the School of the Arts at Columbia University.

Arteaga next moved to Texas, where he served as an assistant professor of English at the University of Houston from 1987 to 1990. He then moved back to California with his family where he taught English at the University of California–Berkeley for the next eight years. His works from this time include *Cantos* (1991), *An Other Tongue: Nation and Ethnicity in the Linguistic Borderlands* (1994), *Chicano Poetics: Heterotexts and Hybridities* (1997), *House with the Blue Bed* (1997), and *Love in the Time of Aftershocks* (1998).

Arteaga has given several major readings, including on PBS and at the Library of Congress. His writings echo the travels of his life, reflecting on being Chicano and living biculturally with an intuitive, intelligent stroke. Fellow poets applaud Arteaga's work. FRANCISCO X. ALARCÓN describes *Cantos* "as a kaleidoscope in which reflections of the past mirror the changing patterns of the pres-

ent and the future, forming a time capsule that explodes in vivid images. The poet speaks in tongues and is moved by a telluric voice that keeps naming and reclaiming this continent, its people and its collective memory. The history of the Americas is invoked, conjured, and ultimately exorcised by the poet, who like Diego Rivera, paints through words a poetic mural of his world."

In 1999, Arteaga fell into a coma for six weeks. When he revived, his sense of self had changed dramatically. He became much more interested in the present moment than ever before. His writings began to reflect his need to experience life as a gift and to stay grounded. This newfound connection to the experience of the body informed the verses within *Red,* a book of poetry published in 2000.

Arteaga is currently a professor of ethnic studies at the University of California–Berkeley, where, as he commented in a 2005 interview, his works and teachings emphasize "as poets and writers, but especially poets, we have an important task, a tremendous capacity to shape humanity and define the soul."

Further Reading

Arteaga, Alfred. *Red.* Tempe, Ariz.: Bilingual Press/ Editorial Bilingüe, 2000.

D'Ooge, Craig. "Poets Alfred Arteaga and Lorna Dee Cervantes to Read at the Library of Congress." Available online. URL: www.loc.gov/today/ pr/1997/97-014.html. Downloaded on April 18, 2005.

Heide, Rick, ed. *Under the Fifth Sun: Latino Literature from California.* Santa Clara and Berkeley, Calif.: Santa Clara University/Heyday Books, 2002.

Hoffert, Barbara. "*Red:* Book Review." *Library Journal* 126, no. 10 (June 1, 2001): 559.

B

Baca, Jimmy Santiago

(1952–) *poet, essayist, novelist, playwright, screenwriter*

Much of Jimmy Santiago Baca's writing is based on personal experience and has earned him many awards, most important the National Endowment of Poetry Award, Vogelstein Foundation Award, National Hispanic Heritage Award, Berkeley Regents Award, Pushcart Prize, Southwest Book Award, and American Book Award. Baca turned a barren life void of comfort and security into a riot of color, verse, and family.

Born in Santa Fe, New Mexico, on January 5, 1952, Jimmy Santiago Baca was the youngest child of Cecilia Padilla, daughter of a Spanish Comanchero Indian, and Damacio Baca, of Apache and Yaqui descent. During Baca's early years, his father was often drunk, violent, or locked up in jail. His parents divorced when he was two. Eventually his father took a job in Santa Fe, visiting his family sporadically who had moved to Estancia, New Mexico. Tired of her husband's mistreatment, Baca's mother began an affair with and later married Richard Besgrove. In June 1959, when Baca was seven years old, his mother and her lover dressed her three children in their finest clothes and dropped them off unceremoniously at their paternal grandparents' home. All too quickly, Grandfather Baca died. Unable to care for the boys, his grandmother sent Baca and his brother Mieyo to St. Anthony's Orphanage.

Baca ran away at least a dozen times, until when he was 13, the only family member responsible, his mother's sister, signed papers relinquishing custody of Baca to the state of New Mexico. He was sent to live at a detention center where he was forced to toughen up. For a short time, Baca attended Harrison Junior High School, where he found encouragement from his football coach. However, an incident that accidentally caused the coach's child a minor affliction created a feeling of desolation and unworthiness to spring up in Baca. He quit school and the football team and returned to the detention center for a short time before leaving to stay with his brother Mieyo and father. Due to his untamable anger, he committed and was convicted of several crimes.

In the late 1960s, Baca lived briefly in San Diego, California, working as a plumber and selling drugs on the side. A few years later, he moved to Yuma, Arizona, with his girlfriend and another friend. All three became involved in the drug scene on a much deeper level. Baca tried to figure out how to stop the madness, but it was too late. The FBI raided a drug deal where Baca was present. A major shootout ensued, and one police officer was wounded. Baca escaped, but when the FBI put out an all-points bulletin for Baca's arrest, he turned himself in and was sentenced to five years in a maximum security prison in Arizona.

At 21, Baca entered the lawless, terrifying world of prison. He began to understand that education was vital to improving himself and his station in life. His desire to gain his G.E.D. was delayed twice by solitary confinement sentences doled out due to fights and refusal to work. Despite the dehumanization of incarceration and the bleak existence of struggling day by day with violence and fear, Baca discovered poetry while in prison. He eventually earned his G.E.D. and studied the works of poets such as Pablo Neruda and Walt Whitman and even read Mary Baker Eddy's spiritual pamphlets. Baca submitted his poetry to the national magazine *Mother Jones,* which published three of his poems. His chapbook, *Jimmy Santiago Baca,* was published in 1978. After six years of imprisonment, he was set free in June 1979. That same year, he published *Immigrants in Our Own Land,* with verses about his imprisonment.

Baca met Beatrice in 1981. She became pregnant the following year, and they moved in together. While Baca readjusted to his freedom, he directed his pent up energy into remodeling their home and writing. He released two additional poetry collections—*Swords of Darkness* (1981) and *What's Happening* (1982). In 1983, their son Antonio was born. Gabriel would follow several years later. At this point, Jimmy's mother reentered his life. He learned that she had told the two children she was raising with Besgrove about her former family. Aghast, Besgrove had shot her to death. Soon after, Mieyo died. In the face of this heartache, Baca gained a B.A. in English from the University of New Mexico. He released *Poems Taken from My Yard* (1986), a collection of poetry about his family and the building of his home.

Martin and Meditations on the South Valley and *Black Mesa Poems* were both released in 1989. *Martin and Meditations on the South Valley* received positive reviews from critics. Baca followed with *Immigrants in Our Own Land and Earlier Poems* (1990) and *Working in the Dark: Reflections of a Poet of the Barrio* (1992). In the same year he cowrote the script *Bound by Honor* (which appeared on

video as *Blood In, Blood Out*). He wrote the script *The Lone Wolf—The Story of Pancho Gonzalez,* for HBO Productions in 2000. The following year, he released *A Place to Stand: The Making of a Poet* (2001), which recounts the author's childhood, young adult years, and incarceration with chilling honesty and vulnerability.

Baca's collection of poems entitled *Healing Earthquakes* (2001) explores the depths of life's gritty experiences. Through the process of accepting one's humanity, Baca ends with zealous transcendence. *C-Train and Thirteen Mexicans: Dream Boy's Story* (2002) reveals the gruesome realities of the marginalized non-Anglo's existence and the impossibility of ever achieving the American dream. Baca later released selections of his poems on CD. Baca earned his Ph.D. in literature in 2003 from the University of New Mexico. He released two published works in 2004, *Winter Poems Along the Rio Grande* and *The Importance of a Piece of Paper.* Critics again hailed his writing. Garrett Hongo claimed Baca's words "heal, inspire, and elicit the earthly response of love . . . [Baca] writes with . . . an intense lyricism and that transformative vision which perceives the mythic and archetypal significance of life-events." Baca is at work on his third novel, currently titled *A Glass of Water.* In his work, he often takes the reader on a roller coaster ride that begins with images of anger and despair caused by oppression through the vibrancy of unabashed living and ends on a note that captures the strength of hope and endurance.

Further Reading

Baca, Jimmy Santiago. *A Place to Stand: The Making of a Poet.* New York: Grove Press Books, 2001.

Krier, Beth Ann. "Baca: A Poet Emerges from Prison of His Past." *Los Angeles Times,* February 15, 1989, pp. V5–V7.

Tardiff, Joseph C., and L. Mpho Mabunda, eds. *Dictionary of Hispanic Biography.* Detroit: Gale Research, 1996, pp. 79–81.

Benítez, Sandra
(Sandra Ables, Sandra Ables Benítez, Sandra Jeanette Ables)
(1941–) *novelist*

Unafraid to take the same journey she asks of her readers, Sandra Benítez pours her heart and soul into each page of the award-winning novels she writes. Frequently anthologized, Benítez is the recipient of several awards, grants, and honors, including the well-regarded National Hispanic Heritage Award for Literature in 2004.

The daughter of James Ables, an American diplomat, and Marta Benítez, a Puerto Rican, Sandra Jeanette Ables was the first of twin girls born on March 26, 1941, in Washington, D.C. Susana, her twin sister, died 37 days after they were born, leaving the family brokenhearted. Approximately two years later, the Ables moved to Mexico City, where her father worked at the American embassy, and younger sister Anita was born. When Sandra was four, the family moved to San Salvador, the capital of El Salvador.

Even though the family was not rich, because of Sandra's father's work at the embassy, they lived an affluent life. Servants and nannies fulfilled Sandra's every wish; there was nothing she lacked. From ages eight to 11 Sandra wrote letters for her nannies, who were illiterate, to send to their families. In these quiet moments Sandra's natural compassion allowed her to see the differences between her life and that of those who cared for her and empathize with them. The letter writing provided a mix of emotions. She was curious to see this other reality, and even though the impending sessions could sometimes give her a stomachache, Sandra complied out of a sense of duty as much as curiosity.

Sandra was pampered in some ways yet had to abide by a strict dress code, have a constant escort, and follow the rules of propriety so inherent in San Salvador in the 1950s. In 1955, when Sandra was 14, her father sent her to live with his parents in Unionville, Missouri. He wanted her to be "Ameri-canized" and understand that not everyone had the luxury of being waited upon. He wanted his daughters to learn how to do for themselves. In San Salvador, Sandra Ables had taken two showers a day, whereas, with no running water on the farm in Missouri, they had to carry in bucketfuls from a well. Alternatively, she was able to wear jeans or dungarees and go on a date, unchaperoned. Ables saw the move as an adventure. Her sister, Anita, objected, staying only one schoolyear. Ables went to high school in Unionville, returning to San Salvador for the summers. She missed her family, yet whenever she spoke about El Salvador as her homeland, her paternal grandmother would kindly rebuff such comments, saying America was her country. Ables's intuitive nature picked up on the unspoken belief that something was wrong with identifying with a Latino heritage. In El Salvador, Ables had been too white; in America, she was too brown. The dichotomy Ables found herself in not only included brown versus white; it also juxtaposed the life of the privileged with the hardworking.

After high school, Ables attended Northeast Missouri State University (now Truman State University), graduating with a B.S. in education in 1962. The same year, she married, and a year later, she gave birth to Christopher. Their second son, Jonathan, was born in 1965. Ables worked as a teacher before returning to school to earn an M.A. in comparative literature in 1974. For the next five years, Ables translated management training manuals at Wilson Learning Corporation. Her marriage was struggling when in 1976 Ables fell from a deck railing at a backyard party and broke her back. Ables divorced her first husband in 1977. Her boss, Jim Kondrick, came often to visit Ables in the hospital. They enjoyed intimate conversations, and by 1980, they were married.

With a renewed lease on life, Ables turned her creative energy to writing. Kondrick offered to support her until she could earn a living writing. She joined a writer's group, attended the Loft

Literary Center, and studied under children's book author Marion Dane Bauer. By admission, Ables's early writings were not very good, often bursting with long, complex sentences and florid language. She completed a mystery novel set in Missouri and took it to the prestigious Bread Loaf Writers conference in Vermont. An instructor spent two hours criticizing the manuscript, pointing out in lurid detail all the shortcomings of her writing. Her hopes dashed, Ables was ready to give up writing, but neither Kondrick nor her fellow writing buddies would hear of it.

Kondrick and Ables traveled through Mexico for three months. Immersed in Latin culture, Ables fondly recalled the stories her nannies had told her. She had been depressed until she decided it

Sandra Benítez received the 2004 National Hispanic Heritage Award. (© Ed Bock)

was high time to write about something she truly cared about. She wrote about the characters she was introduced to through her childhood letter writing and the dichotomy she experienced in El Salvador. Ables wanted to fully reclaim and embrace her Latina heritage. To do this and lend authenticity to her new book, she decided to adopt her mother's maiden name, Benítez. Out of respect, Ables asked for her father's blessing before becoming Sandra Benítez. Her manuscript was rejected by 10 New York publishers, but she continued to write short vignettes on life and won prizes through the Loft. She became a Hispanic Mentor and Writer in the Schools and won a fellowship and a grant for writing. However, writing for a living had not yet materialized.

After 10 years of submitting her book, Benítez was ready to quit when Coffee House Press called and offered her a contract for *A Place Where the Sea Remembers* (1993). Suffused with intimate details of life in Mexico, Benítez's first book is filled with memorable characters who linger well after the last page has been turned. At the center of the book lives Candelario, the salad maker, and Chayo, the flower seller, yet interwoven are the stories of several genuine characters and neighbors living in Santiago, Mexico. *A Place Where the Sea Remembers* received excellent reviews, the Barnes and Noble Discover Award, and the Minnesota Book Award and was selected as a finalist for the *Los Angeles Times's* First Fiction Award. The *Washington Post Book World* described it as "profound in its simplicity and rhythm . . a quietly stunning work that leaves soft tracks in the heart." In 1994, Benítez served as a tour member for the National Writers' Voice Project. She received the Jerome Foundation for Travel and Study Grant in Literature in 1995.

In her second book, *Bitter Grounds* (1997), Benítez recalled memories of living in El Salvador to tell a poignant tale from both the perspective of the oppressed and the fortunate. On the book jacket, author ISABEL ALLENDE called it "the kind of book that fills your dreams for weeks." Benítez was nominated for the renowned Orange Fiction

Prize and selected as a finalist for the Minnesota Book Award and won an American Book Award.

In 1998, Benítez received the Writers Community Residency for the YMCA National Writer's Voice program and in 2000 the Bush Foundation Fellowship. Benítez released *The Weight of All Things* in 2000. In her third novel, Benítez spins the story of Nicolás, a nine-year-old boy whose mother dies at the hands of terrorists during the El Salvador civil war. Unable to believe his mother is truly dead, Nicolás undertakes a quest to find her. Along the way, readers bear witness to life's fragile and beautiful state, the lunacy of war, and the people who live through it.

Benítez held the Knapp Chair in Humanities as associate professor of creative writing at the University of San Diego in 2001. She received many teaching residencies, including at the Bread Loaf Writers Conference, Flight of the Mind, University of Minnesota Split Rock Arts Program, and Hamline University in Minnesota.

Praised for her lyrical writing, Benítez once again hit the mark with readers and critics alike in *Night of the Radishes* (2004). In the book, Annie, a 34-year-old Minnesotan, travels to Oaxaca, Mexico, in search of her long-lost brother during the Christmastime celebration known as the Night of the Radishes festival. With Jane E. Brody, Benítez wrote *Bag Lady: A Memoir*, which was released in 2006.

Benítez's award-winning work is frequently anthologized. It has been translated into six languages and is often included on high school and university reading curricula. The most prestigious and rewarding of her many accolades is the 2004 National Hispanic Heritage Award, which was awarded at the John F. Kennedy Center for the Performing Arts and aired on television during Hispanic Heritage Month. Benítez is a gifted writer whose work touches the hearts of her readers and whose prose is as tangible and authentic as the artist who crafts it. Her role in literature is essential as it evocatively reveals in one person the symbiotic relationship between Middle and Latin America.

Further Reading

Abney, Lisa, and Suzanne Disheroon-Green, eds. *Dictionary of Literary Biography,* Volume 292. *Twenty-first-Century American Novelists.* Detroit: Gale Research, 2004, pp. 3–9.

Benítez, Sandra. *A Place Where the Sea Remembers.* Minneapolis, Minn.: Coffee House Press, 1993.

Flores, Lauro. *Floating Borderlands: Twenty-five Years of U.S. Hispanic Literature.* Seattle: University of Washington Press, 1998.

Bruce-Novoa, Juan
(Juan David Bruce-Novoa, Juan D. Bruce-Novoa, John D. Bruce-Novoa, John David Bruce-Novoa)
(1944–) *poet, essayist, short story writer, literary critic, editor, educator*

Juan Bruce-Novoa is a highly respected literary critic, educator, and writer who has interviewed and critiqued the works of the most prominent contemporary Hispanic writers.

Juan David Bruce-Novoa is the fourth and youngest child of Dolores Novoa and James H. Bruce. His father, an accountant, worked for 16 years with Price Waterhouse in Mexico City before accepting a temporary position in Costa Rica. During their brief stay Juan was born, on June 20, 1944, in San José, Costa Rica. Soon after, his father was drafted for World War II and positioned in Boston, where his accountant skills could best be put to use. During his absence, the family lived in San Antonio, Texas, where they could be close to Juan's uncle, a prominent doctor. In 1948, the reunited family moved to Denver, Colorado.

As a child, Juan did well in school, despite having dyslexia, which was not discovered until the fifth grade. His mother, born in Mexico City, came from a very well-connected and affluent family. As the director of the Bank of Mexico, his uncle played a major role in the Mexican ruling party. Juan often accompanied his uncle to Mexico

City during summer vacations. He believed that being Mexican made one superior, and, even though there were obstacles in his life, he never let them stop him. As a child he enjoyed acting, writing, and studying history.

Bruce-Novoa attended Holy Family High School. When he was a sophomore, his world history teacher became quite ill. Bruce-Novoa was the best qualified to substitute. He did such a fantastic job that he spent three years in high school teaching world history to fellow students. Upon graduation, Bruce-Novoa enrolled in Regis College. During college, he played base guitar and sang lead vocals for a rock band called Dr. Who and the Daeleks. In his senior year, he quit the band, which at the time was making good money, to take additional Spanish classes. In 1966, he graduated cum laude with a B.A. in European history and psychology. The summer after graduation he took intensive Spanish classes in Mexico City to qualify for the master's program at the University of Colorado at Boulder. He received an M.A. in 20th-century Spanish literature in 1968 and specialized in contemporary Latin-American literature for his doctorate, which he earned in 1974, also from the University of Colorado at Boulder.

After he became fluent in Spanish, Bruce-Novoa conversed with his mother on a deeper, broader level. He said in a 2005 interview that he "discovered my mother in the original language." From that point forward, his mother read everything he wrote, including his first collection of poems, entitled *Inocencia perversa/Perverse Innocence* (1976).

Bruce-Novoa is one of the first to confirm and create through imagery and concepts poetry that conveys Mexican Americans as neither Mexicans nor Americans but rather the space that exists between the two identities. From this concept of the space between two known realities, a new identity can be formed and allowed to constantly evolve and reinvent itself. With an aptitude for teaching, Bruce-Novoa instructed courses on Spanish and Mexican-American studies at the University

of Colorado at Boulder and Denver from 1967 to 1974. By the 1970s, he had become involved in the Chicano movement. Whereas most people within the movement fought to establish solidarity to fight oppression, Bruce-Novoa preferred to see what amalgam could be created between the Anglo and Hispanic populations, particularly related to language. He helped to establish legitimacy for the spatial relationships between people and cultures. He coined the term *interlingualism,* meaning the blending of two languages. This stance was first publicly witnessed in the mid-1970s when Bruce-Novoa presented "Revolutionizing the Popular Image: Chicano Theatre" at the International Theatre Conference, Pennsylvania State University, October 30, 1976. While reading the play *Esperanza,* he switched back and forth between English and Spanish. The paper was published as "Revolutionizing the Popular Image: Essay on Chicano Theatre," in *Latin American Literary Review.* Bruce-Novoa felt it was important, although not popular, to emphasize the dynamic, evolving state of being Chicano. He ran into criticism from the Chicano movement since unity was more prevalent and the idea of Spanglish, or the mixing of English and Spanish, was not quite as accepted as it is today.

In 1974, he joined the Yale University faculty. As director of undergraduate Latin-American studies, he assisted the Yale Latin American Studies Center in grant writing, represented the center in Washington, D.C., secured the establishment of Bildner Grants for research on Latin America, and organized three national and international conferences on Latin-American literature. He also was faculty adviser of the student literary magazine *Cambios Phideo.*

He accepted a position to teach at the University of California–Santa Barbara in 1983. Shortly after, he accepted a Fulbright Fellowship to teach American and Hispanic studies at Johannes Gutenberg University in Mainz, West Germany. While in West Germany, he organized and directed the first international conference on Chicano culture and literature. He served as an instructor and associate director of the Center for Chicano Studies at Santa Barbara from 1984 to 1985. In 1986, he organized and directed the second international conference on Hispanic culture in the United States, which was held at the University of Paris. In 1985, he accepted a tenured position in the foreign language department at Trinity University in San Antonio, Texas. In 1989, the University of California–Irvine (UCI) designed a position for him. He currently teaches at UCI.

Regardless of the fact that Bruce-Novoa never intended to be a critic, he has become one of the most well-respected critics of Chicano letters. A scholar at heart, Bruce-Novoa has compiled several anthologies and collections of Chicano literature. Among his works are *Chicano Authors: Inquiry by Interviews* (1980), *Chicano Poetry: A Response to Chaos* (1982), *RetroSpace: Collected Essays on Chicano Literature, Theory, and History* (1990), and *Only the Good Times* (1995). In a 2005 interview, Bruce-Novoa stated: "As a critic, one takes the written word and rearranges the form to understand what he likes and regenerates that information so that others can appreciate the writing. The creative writing process goes from idea to form, whereas the critic's creative process moves from form to idea."

Further Reading

Bruce-Novoa, Juan. "Pancho Villa: Post-Colonial Colonialism, or The Return of the Americano." *Kritikos,* March 2, 2005. Available online. URL: http://garnet.acns.fsu.du/%7Enr03/Pancho%20Villa.htm. Posted in March 2005.

Bryan, Ryan, ed. *Hispanic Writers.* Detroit: Gale Research, 1991, pp. 36–40.

Lomelí, Francisco A., and Carl R. Shirley, eds, *Dictionary of Literary Biography*, Volume 82. *Chicano Writers, First Series.* Detroit: The Gale Group, 1989, pp. 55–58.

Ortega, Felipe, and David Conde, eds. *The Chicano Literary World—1974.* Las Vegas: New Mexico Highlands University, 1975.

Burciaga, Jose Antonio
(1940–1997) *poet, journalist, educator, essayist, publisher*

Jose Antonio Burciaga was a humorist whose successful use of personal issues as a means to explore serious universal matters earned him widespread recognition and respect. Best known as a poet, Burciaga was also an accomplished journalist, muralist, and artist.

Jose Antonio Burciaga was born in the border town of El Chuco, Texas, on August 23, 1940. Some references report he was born in El Paso; however, all sources agree his family lived in the basement apartment of a synagogue where his father, Jose Cruz Burciaga, worked as a caretaker. Exposure to another culture and religion opened the young boy's eyes to a different perspective on life. He grew up enjoying the fluidity of border culture in El Paso, Texas. His mother, Maria Guadalupe Fernandez Burciaga, who worked as a teacher in Mexico, often read to her son and regaled him with oral stories. As a child, Jose loved to read. He enjoyed newspapers, popular magazines, and biographies.

After high school graduation, Burciaga served from 1960 to 1964 with the U.S. Air Force and wrote extensively as part of his duties. After one year in Iceland, he was transferred to Spain, where he discovered the writings of Spanish poet Federico García Lorca, who greatly influenced and inspired him. After being discharged, Burciaga enrolled in the University of Texas–El Paso to pursue his artistic talents. He graduated in 1968 with a B.A. in fine arts. Upon graduation, he worked as an illustrator in a civil service job in Mineral Wells, a cow town near Fort Worth, Texas. Away from a bicultural environment, Burciaga encountered prejudice and racism. He channeled his frustration into poetry and prose. He moved to Washington D.C., where he attended the Corcoran School of Art. While in the country's capital, Burciaga became involved in the Chicano movement. Through his political activism he met Cecilia Preciado, whom he married in 1972. The couple had five children: Lupita, Efrain, Conchita, Margarita, and Raul. Burciaga further developed his art at the Juarez-Lincoln Center of Antioch University and the San Francisco Art Institute. Burciaga wrote reviews and columns for local journals and newspapers in California. Eventually he published fiction, articles, and poetry in *Texas Monthly, Maize, Mango, Revista Chicano-Riqueña, Christian Science Monitor,* and the *Los Angeles Times,* among others.

Burciaga met fellow poets ALURISTA, RON ARIAS, and BERNICE ZAMORA in the mid-1970s. Zamora often hosted gatherings for her fellow writers to read their works and lend support and energy to one another. Burciaga and Zamora combined their work in *Restless Serpents* (1976), published by Diseños Literarios, a publishing company he founded. The majority of the 29 poems address social and political issues with a satirical tone. The other poems, most of which are written in Spanish, have romantic or philosophical themes. Burciaga released a collection of poems and drawings entitled *Drink cultura refrescante* in 1979.

In 1985, Burciaga accepted a teaching position at Stanford University. While at the institution he was a founding member of the comedy group Culture Clash and coordinated the painting of the murals in the student dorm Casa Zapata. The best known of the murals he painted himself is *Last Supper of Chicano Heroes. Weedee Peepo: A Collection of Essays* appeared in 1988. This bilingual collection, cowritten with Emy Lopez, gets its tongue-in-cheek title from the Spanglish pronunciation of the first words from the U.S. Constitution preamble "We the People." Burciaga reveals his insight as well as wit in satirical commentaries on American ethnocentricism and the Chicano plight. He explored his writing skills through the publication of *Undocumented Love: A Personal Anthology of Poetry* (1992), *Drink cultura: Chicanismo* (1993), *Spilling the Beans: Loteria Chicana* (1995), and *In Few Words (en pocas parabolas): A Compendium of Latin Folk Wit and Wisdom* (1997). Burciaga's work is collected in several anthologies.

He died of cancer on October 7, 1997. His imprint on Chicano letters is best summarized by Carlos G. Velez-Ibañez, who noted in *Aztlan,* "Those viewing [Burciaga's] art or reading his writings willingly suspend disbelief and become involved with their own beliefs about beliefs. He brings together interlinking cultural, spiritual and intellectual templates, and encourages people to learn how to learn. He offers a moral center that provides everyone with an insight into their potential selves and gives hope and optimism."

Further Reading

Heide, Rick, ed. *Under the Fifth Sun: Latino Literature from California.* Santa Clara and Berkeley, Calif.: Santa Clara University/Heyday Books, 2002.

Lomelí, Francisco A., and Carl R. Shirley. *Dictionary of Literary Biography*, Volume 82. *Chicano Writers, First Series.* Detroit: The Gale Group, 1989, pp. 59–64.

Rangel, Jesús. "Heirs of José Posada: Revolution Lives in Chicano Art." *San Diego Union,* February 24, 1980: no. D4.

Velez-Ibañez, Carlos G. "The Humanity and the Literature of José Antonio Burciaga." *Aztlán* 22, no. 2 (1997): 207–227.

C

Cabrera, Lydia
(1899–1991) *short story writer, folklorist, anthropologist*

Author of 23 books on Afro-Cuban themes, Lydia Cabrera is best known for her research on Cuba's indigenous religion and is considered a major figure of the island's letters.

Lydia Cabrera was born on May 20, 1899, in Havana, Cuba, to Raimundo Cabrera and Elisa Bilbao Marcaida y Casanova. Her father, a jurist, lawyer, historian, and writer, held many gatherings at which intellectual guests would discuss literary and artistic issues. Alternatively, Afro-Cuban nannies and household servants filled Lydia's imagination with tales and folk legends. Lydia absorbed it all. She pursued art and popular culture in Cuba without her father's consent. In her day, proper Cuban ladies were subordinate and bound to the house, not gallivanting about chasing higher education.

When Cabrera's father died, she was free to pursue her education unencumbered by secrecy. She attended the Lourve Museum art school in Paris in 1927, where the well-known theatrical Russian exile Alexandra Exter taught Cabrera drawing and painting. She graduated in 1930 and remained in Paris for a total of 11 years. During this time, Negro themes were of great interest in Paris's artistic and literary world. Cabrera recalled the Cuban tales told to her in her early years and recorded them. She frequently visited Cuba to gain additional insight by interviewing the people. She released her first book, *Contes nègres de Cuba,* in 1936.

Cabrera left Paris for Cuba in 1938. She became absorbed in recording everything she could of the ancient traditions, lore, and teachings of Cuban blacks. Crisscrossing the island, she was praised and known for speaking to virtually every Afro-Cuban in Havana. With great respect to the subject and those she interviewed, Cabrera made priceless contributions to literature, anthropology, and ethnology, helping Afro-Cubans integrate into the Cuban national culture. Her most famous book, *El monte* (The forest), released in 1954, is an invaluable tome for those interested in Santería, a combination of Catholic teachings and the traditions and religion of native African people. In *El monte,* Cabrera discusses the myths, rituals, and history of the religions derived from the Congo and Yoruba people who were brought as slaves to Cuba.

Due to the island's political situation, Cabrera left Cuba in 1960 as an exile. Living first in Madrid, she later settled in Miami, Florida. She received several honorary doctoral degrees, including one from the University of Miami in 1987. Her many works appear in Spanish and have yet to be translated into English. A selection of her writings include *Cuentos negros de Cuba* (1940; Black stories of Cuba), *Anagó: Vocabulario lucumí—El yoruba que se habla en Cuba* (1957, 1970; Anagó: Lucumí vocabulary: Yoruban spoken in Cuba), *La sociedad secreta Abakuá: Narrada por viejos adeptos* (1958, 1970; Abakuá secret society: Narration for the old initiates), *La laguna sagrada de San Joaquín* (1973; The sacred lagoon of San Joaquín), and *Yemayá y Ochún: Kariocha, Iyalochas y Olorichas* (1974).

Cabrera died in Miami on September 19, 1991. After her death, the Otto G. Richter Library received Cabrera's extensive collection of books, papers, photographs, and memorabilia, which is held in the Cuban Heritage Collection. At this time, the library is working on a digital imaging project in order to make this important collection available online to scholars.

Further Reading

Luis, William, and Ann Gonzales, eds. *Dictionary of Literary Biography,* Volume 145. *Modern Latin-American Fiction Writers, Second Series.* Detroit: Gale Group, 1994, pp. 82–90.

Meier, Matt S., Conchita Franco Serri, and Richard A. Garcia. *Notable Latino Americans: A Biographical Dictionary.* Westport, Conn.: Greenwood Press, 1997.

Simó, Ana María. *Lydia Cabrera: An Intimate Portrait.* New York: Intar Latin American Gallery, 1984.

Tardiff, Joseph C., and L. Mpho Mabunda, eds. *Dictionary of Hispanic Biography.* Detroit: Gale Research, 1996, p. 149.

Cabrera, Yvette
(Yvette Alma Cabrera)
(1972–) *journalist*

Yvette Cabrera is a member of the newest generation of committed journalists dedicated to ensuring the Latino experience is covered in prestigious and influential print media.

Cabrera's parents, Alma Xochil Cabrera, whose heritage is Salvadoran and Mexican, and Gabriel Cabrera Ruiz, born in Mexico, immigrated to California in the early 1970s. The middle child of three girls, Yvette Alma Cabrera was born on January 8, 1972, in Santa Barbara, California, shortly after her parents' arrival in the United States. Given their recent immigration, the Cabrera household was suffused with Mexican music, food, and language. When Yvette was eight years old, she spent a summer living in Mexico City with an aunt. This complete immersion helped her understand Mexico and its people, culture, mode of living, and values in a visceral way.

Gabriel loved to tell his daughters stories of his childhood in Mexico, infusing a love of storytelling in Yvette. She carried this enthusiasm for learning and participation into school. She was a songleader and one of the first Latinas to serve as student body president at Dos Pueblos High School in Goleta, California. With an affinity for leadership and a tenacity she gained from her mother, Cabrera worked as president to encourage the disenfranchised Mexican Americans, particularly the recent immigrants, to become involved in school activities.

Cabrera attended Occidental College in Los Angeles, California. She enrolled as a premed student majoring in biology but discovered she did not enjoy science classes. She joined the school newspaper and the Movimiento Estudiantil Chicano de Aztlán (MEChA), an organization that raises political, social, and cultural awareness of the Chicano experience. In a pivotal moment of her journalism career, Cabrera overheard fellow students discussing the impact of her article about the life journeys of her school's cafeteria workers. Cabrera changed her major to history with an emphasis on Latin-American studies and a minor in anthropology. She completed internships at the *Alumni Magazine* at Occidental College, the *Santa Barbara News-Press,* and United Press International.

After graduating in 1994, Cabrera was accepted into the competitive *Los Angeles Times* Minority Editorial Training Program (METPRO), which was a two-year program. Her apprenticeship included police reporting, general assignment reporting at the City Times zoned edition, and reporting for the Orange County daily edition of the *Los Angeles Times.* In the second year of the program, she served as a general assignment reporter at the *Morning Call* in Allentown, Pennsylvania. From 1996 to 1999, Cabrera worked at the *Los Angeles Daily News* as a staff writer covering Latino affairs, immigration, diversity issues, and the northeast San Fernando Valley. She joined the California Chicano News Media Association (CCNMA) and the National Association of Hispanic Journalists (NAHJ), serving the organizations in different capacities.

Early in her career, Cabrera was warned against pigeonholing herself by becoming a writer who primarily covered Latino issues. However, Cabrera felt she had a clear understanding of the community so vital to her heritage and integral to American society. Her instincts and integrity have proved to be an asset. She was awarded first place in the features category for the 1998 CCNMA La Pluma Award and was the 1998 outstanding journalist honoree for the Comisión Femenil of the San Fernando Valley. In 1999, Cabrera joined the *Orange County Register* as a Latino perspective columnist. In 2003, she was a finalist for the Livingston Awards for Young Journalists and a Women in the Media honoree for the Orange County Chapter of the Mexican American National Association (MANA), a national Latina organization. When veteran journalist FRANK DEL OLMO passed away in 2004, the CCNMA board elected Cabrera to his former position on the board as statewide professional vice president. The next year, Cabrera was honored with the Dart honorable mention for Excellence in Reporting on Victims of Violence for the series "The Women of Juárez." In 2005, she began writing a weekly column instead of a biweekly column so she could take on a new position as the *Orange County Register*'s Latino coverage coordinator. In her new position, Cabrera serves as a liaison for all of the *Register*'s departments and is responsible for improving the depth of the newspaper's coverage of the Latino community in Orange County, California. In 2006, Cabrera became one of the statewide board presidents of CCNMA.

Further Reading

"Daily News Staff Reporter Wins Media Award." *The Daily News of Los Angeles,* October 18, 1998.

"Freedom Orange County Information Appoints 2 to Focus on Latino Coverage." *Orange County Register,* March 10, 2005.

Levine, Ronn. "A Hire Purpose." *Newspaper Association of America, Inc. Presstime,* March 2000.

Candelaria, Cordelia Chávez
(Cordelia Chávez)
(1943–   ) *poet, literary critic, editor, educator, essayist, script consultant*

Cordelia Chávez Candelaria is nationally and internationally recognized for her brilliant analysis and insightful interpretations as a literary critic and editor as well as for her success as an accomplished and provocative poet.

The fifth of eight children of Eloida Trujillo and Ray J. Chávez, Cordelia Chávez was born on September 12, 1943, in Deming, New Mexico. Her father's road construction work required the family to move around frequently. As a youth, she enjoyed reading, language, and words. The southwestern terrain affected her deeply and later served as muse and inspiration for her writing. She graduated from Aztec High School in Aztec, New Mexico, in 1961.

Chávez married Jose Fidel Candelaria in 1961; the couple would later have one son, Clifford. Candelaria attended Fort Lewis College in Durango, Colorado, where her love for words and literature prompted her to study English and French. Candelaria graduated with honors in 1970. She later obtained her master's in English in 1972 and a doctorate in American literature and structural linguistics in 1976, both from the University of Notre Dame.

Candelaria's poems first appeared in periodicals in 1973. Her books, book chapters, articles, reviews, and poems have since appeared in several of the most prestigious journals and been included in anthologies. Drawn to higher education, Candelaria served as an assistant professor of English and Chicano literature at Idaho State University–Pocatello from 1975 to 1978. During her last year in Idaho, she also worked as the program officer for the Division of Research at the National Endowment for the Humanities. From 1978 through 1991, Candelaria held the position of associate professor of English and director of the Chicano Studies Program at the University of Colorado–Boulder.

While at Colorado, she was the founding director of the Center for the Studies of Ethnicity & Race in America (CSERA) and served as a writer and interviewer for Chicano Images in Film at the Bilingual Communication Center. Her excellent teaching abilities and contributions have earned her several awards, including the Thomas Jefferson Award (1983), Colorado University Equity and Excellence Faculty Award (1989), and a 15-year Higher Education Replication Study award from the National Sponsoring Committee in Denver, Colorado (1991).

Candelaria's first book, *Ojo de la cueva (Cave Springs)* was published by the renowned poet ALURISTA in 1984. The poems in this collection use images from nature to illuminate the struggles and triumphs of the human condition. She followed with *Chicano Poetry: A Critical Introduction* (1986), *Seeking the Perfect Game: Baseball in American Literature* (1989), and *Arroyos to the Heart* (1993).

In 1991, Candelaria joined the faculty at Arizona State University (ASU), where she teaches as a professor of English and Chicana and Chicano studies and is a research associate at the Hispanic Research Center. She chaired the Department of Chicana and Chicano Studies from 2001 to 2005 and currently serves as vice provost of academic affairs at ASU's downtown Phoenix campus. Candelaria is the recipient of several grants and awards that have funded her work as an editor for the following books integral to Chicano letters: *Women Poets of the Americas: Toward a Panamerican Gathering* (coedited with Jacqueline V. Brogan, 1999),

The Legacy of 1848 and 1898: Selected Proceedings from the 1998 Transhistoric Thresholds Conference (coedited with Gary Keller, 2000), and the two-volume *Encyclopedia of Latino Popular Culture,* for which she served as executive editor and senior literature and cultural studies editor (2004).

Candelaria's film and media projects include initiator and producer of the Major Topics in Latina/o Studies: Multimedia Learning Modules Project, in progress at ASU (1999–2004); project consultant and script coeditor for the SOMOS film production of *The Ballad of Gregorio Cortez* (1982); treatment and script consultant for the film *The Milagro Beanfield War* (produced and directed by Robert Redford and coproduced by Moctezuma Esparza in 1993); and writer of "Film Portrayals of La Mujer Hispana," in *Agenda: A Journal of Hispanic Issues* (May/June 1981). Candelaria's first husband, and lifelong friend continues ranching in northern New Mexico. She lives in Tempe, Arizona, with her second husband, Ronald Beveridge, a retired electrical power generation specialist and *futbolista* (football enthusiast).

Further Reading

Candelaria, Cordelia, et al., eds. *Encyclopedia of Latino Popular Culture.* 2 vols. Westport, Conn.: Greenwood Publishing Group, 2004.

Lomelí, Francisco, A. and Carl R. Shirley, eds. *Dictionary of Literary Biography,* Volume 82. *Chicano Writers, First Series.* Detroit: The Gale Group, 1989, pp. 65–67.

Telgen, Diane, and Jim Kamp. *Notable Hispanic American Women.* Book 1. Detroit: Gale Research, 1993.

Candelaria, Nash
(1928–   ) *novelist, short story writer, folklorist*

Nash Candelaria, a historical novelist, brings to life the struggles and personalities of New Mexicans, particularly during the U.S.-Mexican War and its aftermath as experienced by the participants' descendants through his acclaimed series. He offers dynamic characters whose trials and tribulations reveal the constant evolution of society and its people.

Nash Candelaria was born in Los Angeles, California, on May 7, 1928, to Flora Rivera and Ignacio N. Candelaria, a railway mail clerk. Although Candelaria spent most of his childhood in white Catholic neighborhoods of California, the summers spent in a rural area of Albuquerque, New Mexico, known as Los Candelarias, fed his soul with a deep love of and appreciation for New Mexico. He is often quoted as saying, "Although I was born in California, I consider myself a New Mexican by heritage and sympathy." Candelaria's ancestors were among the early Hispanic families who founded Albuquerque in 1706 and include Juan Candelaria, who wrote about the history of New Mexico in 1776.

During his youth, Nash experienced little prejudice. He was encouraged by teachers to further his education and thus entered the world without fear of rejection. He graduated from the University of California–Los Angeles with a B.S. in chemistry in 1948. While working for Baxter International as a chemist for four years, he felt himself drawn to writing. He entered the U.S. Air Force during the Korean War, where he became a second lieutenant. During his military service, Candelaria honed his writing skills and penned his first novel. He married Doranne Godwin, a fashion designer, in 1955. The couple later had two children, David and Alex. Candelaria enjoyed a long career in marketing and advertising. Candelaria wrote seven unpublished novels before *Memories of Alhambra* was published in 1977. Inspiration for the novel came while listening to *Recuerdos de la Alhambra,* a song recorded by Francisco Tarrega. Candelaria recalled, in an 1980 interview with JUAN BRUCE-NOVOA, ". . . the idea for the story came to me in a flash. It was a chilling, exhilarating experience—the book would be a culmination of much I would have gone through myself and much that I saw in my own family and others from New Mexico. It would be about 'Mexicanness' and the acceptance of it."

Memories of Alhambra set the stage for the Rafa family and the search for identity, pride, and acceptance of self and society. The book marks a turning point in Candelaria's life as he began to explore the constant movement of civilizations with a focus on Latinos in the Southwest. It is this realization that inspired Candelaria to tell Bruce-Novoa, "[W]e will evolve into a common culture, an American culture, in this country, or perhaps a world culture on this planet. We will all be more alike than we are now, but still different, whether Chicano, Black, Anglo, whatever. The current focus on minorities is but a transitory stage. While it impacts on our individual lives with all its pain and anguish, it in time will drop away so that we are only human—all of us, for better rather than worse."

Candelaria began work as a technical writer and editor and remained close to writing through work at advertising agencies and marketing communications companies throughout the 1970s and 1980s. *Not by the Sword* (1982) followed in the series and received the Before Columbus Foundation American Book Award in 1983 and was chosen as a finalist for the Western Writers of America Best Western Historical Novel Award. *Inheritance of Strangers,* released in 1984, deals specifically with an election that occurs after the 1848 Treaty of Guadalupe Hidalgo. The elected winner will determine who, within his jurisdiction, can maintain the most land. Candelaria departed from the Rafa saga to write a collection of 12 short stories about the Latino experience and published them under the title *The Day the Cisco Kid Shot John Wayne* in 1988.

Candelaria returned to the Rafa family in *Leonor Park* (1991), which revolves around sibling rivalry and land grabs of the 1920s. *Uncivil Rights and Other Stories* (1998) is a collection of seven short stories that explore border culture and its effects on people and relationships. An important voice in Latino literature, Candelaria uses his diverse literary talents to evoke the universal element within the individual's struggle against change to discover and maintain personal and cultural identity.

Further Reading

Bruce-Novoa, Juan. "An Interview." *De Colores* 5 (September 1980): 115–129.

Candelaria, Nash. *Not by the Sword.* Tempe, Ariz.: Bilingual Press, 1982.

Stavans, Ilan. *Wáchale! Poetry and Prose about Growing Up Latino in America.* Peru, Ill.: Cricket Books, 2001.

Tardiff, Joseph C., and L. Mpho Mabunda, eds. *Dictionary of Hispanic Biography.* Detroit: Gale Research, 1996, pp. 159–161.

Cantú, Norma Elia
(1947–) *short story writer, poet, essayist, editor, literary critic, educator*

Norma Elia Cantú is known for her ingenious method of combining literary creativity with cultural criticism in what the author calls "fictional autobioethnography." This technique is found in her most acclaimed book, *Canícula: Snapshots of a Girlhood en la Frontera.*

The eldest of 11 children of Virginia Ramón Becerra and Florentino Cantú Vargas, Norma Elia Cantú was born on January 3, 1947, in Nuevo Laredo, Mexico. Shortly after her birth, the family moved across the river that divides Mexico and the United States to Laredo, Texas. Cantú's mother had been born in Corpus Christi, Texas, in 1925 but was repatriated to Mexico in 1935, when her grandfather protested the unfair practices of the railroad company for which he worked. The return to the United States made a memorable reconnection to the land her mother was once thrust from.

Norma enjoyed writing from a young age. While at Saunders Elementary School, she wrote poetry beginning at age seven. Encouraged by her teacher Mrs. Treviño, Norma continued her writing practice, even winning an honorable mention

in a television contest. She has kept a journal since the age of 13 in which she records poems, short stories, and other writings.

Cantú attended Laredo Junior College with funds from a scholarship, where she earned her associate's degree in general education in 1970. She enrolled in Texas A&I University–Laredo, graduating cum laude with a double major in English and political science in 1973. During her studies, she served as a teaching assistant. Although she published some pieces in junior high and high school papers, Cantú has refrained from submitting her work throughout most of her adulthood. She has long viewed writing as an internal process. As she explained, in an unpublished 1999 interview, "To me, writing is like eating or breathing; it's not something for other people; I do it for myself, to nourish me."

But in about the mid- to late 1970s, Cantú began to read her writings in public venues, including scholarly gatherings and women's and ethnic conferences. Her work first appeared as articles and book chapters. She gained her master's in English with a minor in political science from Texas A&I University–Kingsville in 1975. While earning her doctorate at the University of Nebraska–Lincoln, which she received in 1982, she worked as a teaching assistant. Upon graduating, Cantú became an instructor, a post she filled at the University of Nebraska from 1976 to 1979. She wrote extensively during her stay in the Midwest, including the preliminary research for her first book, *Canícula* (1995). Concurrently, she applied her scholarly aptitude toward book reviews, eventually offering her expertise and critiques on 11 books. She deepened her literary and artistic interests by attending the Floricanto Festival where she was particularly inspired by Inés Hernández Tovar and LORNA DEE CERVANTES.

Cantú returned to Texas in 1980 to accept an assistant professorship at Laredo State University/ Texas A&M International University. Seven years later, she became an associate professor and began her involvement on the administrative level, coordinating events, activities, and education related to arts, science, folklore, and Chicano studies.

She taught at Georgetown University School for Continuing Education for one year then returned to Texas A&M International University as a full professor. She began a scholarly study of the popular tradition of the Matachines, the dancers in Indian dress who venerate the Holy Cross in Laredo during religious festivals on May 3, December 12, and Christmas Eve. However, she discovered personal stories captured her attention and decided to focus on these for her first book. *Canícula* features 85 vignettes and 23 family photographs and is well known and celebrated for creating and illustrating the symbiotic relationship between real and imagined events.

In 2000, Cantú accepted a professorship from the University of Texas–San Antonio, where she remains. The following year, she coedited with the Latina Feminist Group *Telling to Live: Latina Feminist Testimonios.* Her individual pieces included in it were "Getting there cuando no hay camino," "A Working Class Bruja's Fears," and the two poems Migraine" and "Reading the Body." In 2002, she coedited *Chicana Traditions: Continuity and Change* with Olga Najera Ramírez. She is currently working on *Soldiers of the Cross: Los Matachines de la Santa Cruz.*

Further Reading

Cantú, Norma Elia. *Canícula: Snapshots of a Girlhood en la Frontera.* Albuquerque: University of New Mexico Press, 1995.

———, and Olga Najera-Ramirez. *Chicana Traditions: Continuity and Change.* Champaign, Ill.: University of Illinois Press, 2002.

Lomelí, Francisco A., and Carl R. Shirley, eds. *Dictionary of Literary Biography,* Volume 209. *Chicano Writers, Third Series.* Detroit: Gale Group, 1999, pp. 34–39.

Rooney, Terrie M., and Jennifer Gariepy, eds. *Contemporary Authors.* Vol. 152. Detroit: Gale Research, 1997.

Carrillo, Adolfo
(1855–1926) *journalist, novelist, short story writer, publisher*

Adolfo Carrillo was a newspaperman of immense integrity and courage who used his words to attack the revolutionaries during the Mexican Revolution, a period from approximately 1910 to 1920 rife with terror, violence, and corruption as the people attempted to establish a stronger political voice and more control. In addition to his journalistic work, Carrillo recorded the stories of old California in his book *Cuentos californios.*

Adolfo Carrillo was born in July 1855 in the town of Sayula in Jalisco, Mexico. He spent most of his childhood in the nearby village of Tapalpa. He developed his writing and journalistic skills while studying at the Seminaro de Guadalajara, in the state's capital. Carrillo published two newspapers, *La Picota* (The gibbet), launched in 1877, and *La Unión Mercantil* (The mercantile union), starting in 1878. Carrillo was persecuted when his papers criticized the local government, forcing him to leave Guadalajara and find refuge in Mexico City. As the editor of *El Correo de los Lunes* (Monday's mail), he continued his assaults on the government, with particular attention on Mexico's president, General Porfirio Díaz. As a result of his work, Carrillo was tried and found guilty for crimes against the state. He served four months on an island prison, after which he was exiled to Cuba.

Carrillo chose instead to live in New York City, where he could visit his mentor, Sebastián Lerdo de Tejada. Lerdo had been Mexico's president when Díaz revolted and usurped the presidency. Through daily visits, Carrillo obtained enough information to write *Memorias inéditas del Lic. Don Sebastián Lerdo de Tejada* (Unpublished memoirs of Mr. Sebastián Lerdo de Tejada.) He found a publisher in Texas who released the book in 1889 without Carrillo's name due to the nature of the topic and the fact that the Díaz government continued to keep close tabs on Carrillo. The book enjoyed much success and served to unite the Mexican people who would later overthrow Díaz. Upon Lerdo's death, Carrillo moved to Europe. The Díaz government attempted to deport him and try him in court while he lived in Spain and France.

In 1897, Carrillo settled in San Francisco, married, and established a print shop. That same year the picaresque novel *Memorias del marqués de San Basilisco* was released anonymously. Many critics have attributed the work to Carrillo. As a result of the 1906 San Francisco earthquake, Carrillo suffered the loss of his daughter and demolition of his print shop. Four years later, the Mexican Revolution broke out. Carrillo joined the movement as a press agent. In 1914, he was appointed to head economic affairs of the Mexican consulate in Los Angeles and began publishing the newspaper *México Libre* (Free Mexico).

Carrillo spent time traveling throughout California, collecting stories and legends that he would later publish as *Cuentos californios* (ca. 1922). *Cuentos californios* consists of nine short stories that relate the stories of the pastoral life prior to U.S. invasion and the cultural loss from the Mexican and Californio (original Spanish colonists of California and their descendants) perspective, often using *pochos,* or caricatures, rather than fully fleshed-out characters. This use of sketches has been proven to be a precursor to current Chicano short stories and theater. Carrillo died on August 24, 1926, a man well respected throughout the Southwest.

Further Reading

Carrillo, Adolfo. *Cuentos californios.* San Antonio, Tex.: Lozano, ca. 1922.

Kanellos, Nicolas, et al., eds. *Herencia: The Anthology of Hispanic Literature in the United States.* New York: Oxford University Press, 2003, pp. 178–183.

Lomelí, Francisco A., and Carl R. Shirley, eds. *Dictionary of Literary Biography, Chicano Writers, Second Series.* Vol. 122. Detroit: Gale Group, 1992, pp. 53–55.

Castillo, Ana

(1953–) *novelist, poet, essayist, children's writer, young adult writer, editor, educator, activist*

Ana Castillo is an explosive writer who challenges the polarization of society based on race, gender, sexual orientation, and class in her award-winning novels, poems, essays, and short stories. She is well known for her feminism, activism, and articulate, powerful prose and lyrics, which make her a beacon of truth and understanding, piercing a path toward equality and fellowship.

Ana Castillo developed her particular style of writing from the rich oral storytelling of her youth. She was born to Mexican-American working-class parents, Raymond and Raquel Castillo, on June 15, 1953, in Chicago, Illinois. As a child, Ana dreamed of becoming an artist. However, the schools she attended did not shape or encourage young women for anything above menial work. A typist position was all she could hope to achieve. Undaunted, Ana practiced art and honed her literary skills at home, penning her first poem at age nine following the death of her grandmother. She became active in the Chicano movement while in high school and college, using her poetry to express her political opinions.

Castillo attended Chicago City College for two years before entering Northwestern Illinois University, where she received a B.A. in liberal arts in 1975. After receiving her degree, Castillo moved to northern California to teach ethnic studies at Santa Rosa Junior College. She contributed to the literary magazine *Revista Chicano Riqueña* (now *The American Review*). In 1977, she released her first collection of poems, *Otro Canto* (Another song), which was published as a chapbook. That same year, Castillo served as a writer in residence for the Illinois Arts Council. In 1979, she returned to Chicago and earned an M.A. in Latin-American and Caribbean studies at the University of Chicago and released her second chapbook, *The Invitation.*

Throughout the early 1980s, Castillo served as a poet in residence at Urban Gateways of Chicago, and lectured on the history of Mexican Americans and taught English as a second language at Northwestern Illinois University. Flamenco music and dancing caught her attention, inspiring Castillo to create and manage the Al-Andalus flamenco performance group and adapt *The Invitation* to music, which was performed at the 1982 Soho Art Festival in New York City. By this time, her poetry, which delved deep into the heart of women's issues and equality, had gained recognition and appeared in a number of esteemed anthologies, such as *Women Poets of the World* and *The Third Woman: Minority Women Writers of the U.S.,* as well as a high school text, *Zero Makes Me Hungry.* Castillo also released two books of her own poetry, *Women Are Not Roses* (1984) and *My Father Was a Toltec* (1988), and coedited and cotranslated *Este Puente, Mi Espalda* (This bridge, my back), a poetry anthology, in 1988. Castillo taught at various colleges throughout California, lecturing on creative writing, women's studies, humanities, and Chicano literature. From 1989 to 1992, she served as a writing instructor at the University of New Mexico–Albuquerque. She earned her Ph.D. in American studies from the University of Bremen in Germany in 1991.

Castillo's first novel, *The Mixquiahuala Letters* (1986), established Castillo as a leading Chicana feminist writer. The book, written in epistolary form, uses letters between two women who travel to Mexico to bare the realities, disappointments, and awakenings of the search for identity. *The Mixquiahuala Letters* garnered the Before Columbus Foundation American Book Award, as well as an award from the Women's Foundation of San Francisco. Castillo's second novel, *Sapogonia: An Anti-Romance in 3/8 Meter* (1990), which received a *New York Times* Notable Book Award, tells the story of Maximo Madrigal's obsession with Pastora Ake, the only woman he has not been able to conquer.

In 1993, Castillo reached mainstream recognition with her novel *So Far from God,* which received a *New York Times* Notable Book Award, the Carl Sandburg Literary Award in Fiction, and the Mountains and Plains Booksellers Award. Bordering on magic realism, this book follows the life of Sofi and her four daughters. Castillo continued to explore race and gender issues through her essays and poetry. She coedited *Chicano Poetry* (1994), released a revised *My Father Was a Toltec and Selected Poems* (1995), and published her first collection of critical essays, titled *Massacre of the Dreamers: Essays on Xicanisma* (1994). Through her writing and activism, Castillo examines *Xicanisma,* a term she coined in order to give name and authenticity to the struggles of politically active Chicanas. Critics praised Castillo's writings as bristly, provocative, and insistent for justice.

Castillo cofounded *Third Woman,* a literary magazine, for which she is a contributing editor. She delved deeper into the divine aspect of feminism with the anthology *La Diosa de las Americas/ Goddess of the Americas* (1996). In this collection of prose about the Virgin of Guadalupe, contributors such as Denise Chávez, Rubén Martínez, Pat Mora, and others write about the relationship with the Mother Goddess of Mexican, mestizo, and Indian societies. Throughout this feministic collection, Castillo strongly objects to the notion that sex is primarily for reproduction and insists that relegating sensuality and sexuality to an act of servitude denies a major component of the self.

Loverboys (1996) consists of 22 stories that explore the many kinds of relationships, including familial love, straight and gay sexual relationships, and friendship. The stories include racial and cultural issues and take place mostly in urban settings featuring strong hot-blooded Latina characters. This collection of short stories carries the typical power, earthy eroticism, and fresh humor for which Castillo is known. In 1998, Castillo was awarded the Sor Juana Achievement Award by the Mexican Fine Arts Center Museum in Chicago. Her next novel, *Peel My Love Like an Onion* (1999), tells the story of a worn-out flamenco dancer who yearns for her former life and the return of her gypsy lovers. It was well received by readers and critics alike.

With *My Daughter, My Son, the Eagle, the Dove* (2000), Castillo delves into her ancestral teachings to present two poems of Aztec and Nahuatl instructions for coming-of-age and traditional rites of passage. This, her first book for children, won the 2000 Américas Award for Children's and Young Adult Literature Commended Title. *Booklist* critic Linda Perkins found *My Daughter, My Son, the Eagle, the Dove* to be an "attractive addition to Aztec culture" with a "handsome blend of art and poetry [that] makes this a fitting offering for contemporary rites of passage." In 2001, Castillo published *I Ask the Impossible,* a collection of her poetry of the previous 11 years.

Castillo's work has appeared in a plethora of literary anthologies, periodicals, and literary journals. She is frequently asked to be a guest speaker and lecturer on an international level. Through her writing and activism, she strives to reunite women with themselves, helping them to uncover the dormant strength and power within. Her voice and writings stem from her experiences as a Chicana; however, they reach deeper into the human psyche to draw out the connection and spark the understanding and intelligence of equal power and strength for people of all races, gender, and class.

Further Reading

González, Ray, ed. *Mirrors Beneath the Earth: Short Fiction by Chicano Writers.* Willimantic, Conn.: Curbstone Press, 1992.

Hampton, Janet Jones. "Ana Castillo: Painter of Palabras." *Americas* 52, no. 1 (January 2000): 48.

Milligan, Bryce, Mary Guerrero Milligan, and Angela de Hoyos, eds. *Daughters of the Fifth Sun.* New York: Riverhead Trade, 1996.

Mills, Fiona. "Creating a Resistant Chicana Aesthetic: The Queer Performativity of Ana Castillo's *So Far from God.*" *CLA Journal* 46, no. 3 (March 2003): 312–336.

Navarro, Marta. "An Interview with Ana Castillo." In *Chicana Lesbians: The Girls Our Mothers Warned Us About.* Edited by Carla Trujillo. Berkeley. Calif.: Third Woman Press, 1991, pp. 113–132.

Platt, Kamala. "Ecocritical Chicana Literature: Ana Castillo's 'Virtual Realism.'" *Interdisciplinary Studies in Literature and Environment* 3 (Summer 1996): 67–96.

Tardiff, Joseph C., and L. Mpho Mabunda, eds. *Dictionary of Hispanic Biography.* Detroit: Gale Research, 1996, pp. 195–196.

Cervantes, Lorna Dee
(1954–) *poet, editor, publisher, activist*

Lorna Dee Cervantes is among the first Latina poets to be recognized outside the Chicano community. Her work inspired many people during the Chicano movement.

Lorna Dee Cervantes was born on August 6, 1954, in the Mission District of San Francisco, California. Cervantes is of mixed Mexican and Native American ancestry. Her mother's Mexican ancestors intermarried with the Chumash Native Americans of the Santa Barbara area. Her father's heritage derives from the Tarascan Indians of Michoacán, Mexico. When she was five years old, her parents divorced, and Lorna, her mother, and her brother, Steve, moved in with her grandmother in San Jose, California. Lorna often accompanied her mother to the houses she cleaned. In these homes, she discovered the works of Shakespeare, Byron, Keats, and Shelley. Lorna began writing poetry when she was eight years old. She became fascinated with the lyrical potential of language, which was fed by her brother's musical talent. She contributed her writings to her school paper at Lincoln High School in San Jose.

In 1974, she accompanied her brother, who played with the Teatro de la Gente (Theater of the People) of San Jose, to Mexico City for the Quinto Festival de los Teatros Chicanos. Wanting to add to their repertoire, the group asked Cervantes to read her work as part of their performance. She chose to read "Barco de refugiados/Refugee Ship." Impressed by the poet's ability to exquisitely capture the Chicano dilemma of belonging completely to neither Mexican nor American culture, *El Heraldo,* a Mexico City newspaper, printed the poem. Soon after, her poetry appeared in *Revista Chicano Riqueña* and subsequently in many journals and reviews.

After her poetry reading, Cervantes devoted herself to writing, editing for *Mango,* a literary review, and helping other writers. She learned the printing trade and bought an offset printing press. She soon published chapbooks for Chicano writers with the assistance of Centro Cultural de la Gente (People's Cultural Center) of San Jose and Mango Publications. By 1978, she was beginning to gain national recognition. She received a grant from the National Endowment for the Arts and spent much of the following year at the Fine Arts Workshop in Provincetown, Massachusetts, where she completed the manuscript for *Emplumada* (1981).

Emplumada is an amalgamation of the participle *emplumada* (feathered plumage, after or during molting) and the noun *plumada* (a pen flourish). The title and much of the verses throughout refer to Quetzalcoatl, the Mexican god of love, art, and creativity in his semblance as the plumed serpent, who symbolizes the full potential of human experience. *Emplumada* received national recognition. NICOLÁS KANELLOS wrote that the collection "presents a young woman coming of age, discovering the gap that exists in life between one's hopes and desires and what life eventually offers in reality. The predominant themes include culture, conflict, the oppression of women and minorities, and alienation from one's roots."

In 1982, Cervantes's mother was brutally murdered in San Jose. The devastating loss took its toll on the poet. She allowed herself a period of grief and introspection before delving back into her creative life. She received her B.A. at San Jose State University in 1984 and studied at the University of California–Santa Cruz. Her education continued

Lorna Dee Cervantes is one of the most well-known poets to emerge from the Chicano movement. *(Bryce Milligan)*

through the Ph.D. program in the history of consciousness at the University of California–Santa Cruz. She did not graduate from the program. She released *From the Cables of Genocide: Poems on Love and Hunger* in 1991. This collection includes stream of consciousness texts, surreal yet candid imagery, and a conviction that cannot be ignored.

Cervantes edited *Red Dirt* magazine and founded and directed Floricanto Colorado, which showcases Chicano and Chicana literature in Denver and surrounding schools. She joined the faculty at the University of Colorado–Boulder, where as a professor of English she teaches creative writing (poetry), poetics, cultural criticism, and aesthetics.

Her writings continue to be discussed as excellent interpretations of a life and perspective that synthesizes the divergent parts of being human. Her work has appeared in nearly 200 anthologies, including the second volume of the *The Norton Anthology of American Literature, Touching the Fire: Fifteen Poets of Today's Latino Renaissance, After Aztlán: Latino Poets of the Nineties,* and *Daughters of the Fifth Sun: A Collection of Latina Fiction and Poetry.*

She is the recipient of two fellowship grants for poetry from the National Endowment for the Arts and a Colorado Council on the Arts and Humanities fellowship. She has been awarded the American Book Award, Paterson Prize for Poetry, Latino Literature Award, and Lila Wallace–Readers Digest Award for her work. She continues to speak and inspire fellow writers and has been invited to speak at the Library of Congress, National Museum of Women in the Arts, and numerous universities and institutions across the United States, Mexico, Spain, and Colombia. Her latest book, *Drive: The First Quartet,* was released in 2005.

Further Reading

Gonzalez, Ray. "I Trust Only What I Have Built with My Own Hands: An Interview with Lorna Dee Cervantes." *Bloomsbury Review* 17, no. 5 (September–October 1997): 3, 8.

Ikas, Karin. *Chicana Ways: Conversations with Ten Chicana Writers.* Reno: University of Nevada Press, 2002.

Madsen, Deborah L. *Understanding Contemporary Chicana Literature.* Columbia: University of South Carolina Press, 2000.

Chacón, Eusebio
(Romeo)
(1869–1948) *journalist, novelist, poet, essayist*

A gifted orator and often credited as the first New Mexican to publish a novel, Eusebio Chacón contributed to the preservation of Hispanic culture in the Southwest with his essays and novels, as well as the distribution of rare Spanish-language writings.

Eusebio Chacón was born on December 16, 1869, in Penasco, New Mexico. He was the son of the well-known Mexican pioneer and colonist Rafael Chacón and Juanita Paez Chacón, a noblewoman. When Eusebio was young, New Mexico was still considered wild, untamed land. Even though the boundaries of present-day New Mexico were drawn by Congress in 1863, New Mexico did not become a state until 1912. Eusebio's father, who had once fought against the Americans in the U.S.-Mexican War of the 1840s, eventually became part of the U.S. Army, helping to settle the Southwest. Just before Eusebio's first birthday, the family settled in Trinidad, Colorado.

Chacón attended Las Vegas College in Las Vegas, New Mexico, obtaining his undergraduate degree at age 17. He gained his law degree from Notre Dame University in 1889, when only 19 years of age. He was such an eloquent speaker that he was asked to deliver the welcome address in Spanish to the Pan American Congress at St. Paul, Minnesota. After graduation, Chacón taught English and served as the assistant director at Colegio Guadalupano in Durango, Mexico. In 1891, he returned to Trinidad, Colorado, where he was admitted to the Colorado bar, and he married Sofia Barela, daughter of the affluent and influential Colorado senator and Mexican consul Casimiro Barela. The couple had two children, Rafael and Juanita. Chacón began his law practice and was named deputy district attorney of Las Animas County, Colorado. That same year he was appointed to the U.S. Court of Private Land Claims to serve as official translator and mediator for land grant disputes.

As a journalist, Chacón wrote and spoke out against anti-Hispanic prejudices in the Southwest. In 1898, he joined Jose Escobar to edit and write for the Spanish-language newspaper *El Progreso* in Trinidad, Colorado. He also contributed to the newspaper *Las Dos Repúblicas* (The two republics); both papers were under the control of his father-in-law. Chacón often used the pseudonym Romeo for his more evocative essays. He attempted to start a newspaper called *La Época* (The epoch), but it failed due to a lack of subscribers. In 1892, Chacón published *El hijo de la tempestad; Tras la tormenta la calma: Dos novelitas originales* (Son of the storm; calmness after the storm: Two original novelettes). These two novellas are the predecessors of Latino literature in the United States. In these works, the author offers the general public a Hispanic perspective on historical and cultural issues. He hoped to create a genre of Hispanic-American literature.

In response to slanders against Hispanics, Chacón penned what would become known as "La Junta Indignación 1901" (The Indignation Meeting of 1901) in Las Vegas, New Mexico. Chacón possessed rare early Mexican-American writings, such as the first American epic poem, *Historia de la Nueva México* (History of New Mexico), by Gaspar Pérez de Villagrá; *Noticias históricas y estadísticas sobre la antigua provincial de Nuevo Mexico* (Historic news—Statistics of the old province of New Mexico), by Pedro Baptiste Pinos; and the unpublished manuscripts of Manuel Alvarez, known as "New Mexico History of the First Half of the XIX Century." He ensured these writings were printed and circulated in *El Progreso* and *Las Dos Repúblicas*. Chacón is also known to have written poetry, though none of it has survived. Chacón died on April 3, 1948. Although he did not attain his goal of creating a new genre in his time, clearly Chacón is an essential brick in the foundation of Latino literature.

Further Reading

Kanellos, Nicolás, et al, eds. *Herencia: The Anthology of Hispanic Literature in the United States.* New York: Oxford University Press, 2003, pp. 130–135.

Lomelí, Francisco A., and Julio Martínez. "Eusebio Chacón: A Literary Portrait of 19th Century New Mexico." In *Chicano Literature: A Reference Guide.* Albuquerque: Southwest Hispanic Research Institute, University of New Mexico, 1987, pp. 1–60.

Lomelí, Francisco A., and Carl R. Shirley, eds. *Dictionary of Literary Biography.* Vol. 82. *Chicano Writers, First Series.* Detroit: Gale Group, 1989, pp. 78–82.

Chávez, Denise
(Denise Elia Chávez)
(1948–   ) *novelist, short story writer, children's book writer, essayist, playwright, activist, educator*

Deeply affected by the Southwest, family, community, and culture, Denise Chávez is one of the most prominent Latina writers to explore the themes of Chicano life, particularly in relation to women's issues. Her dramas and writings have won many awards, including the 1995 Governor's Award in Literature, and much critical acclaim as she paves the way for future generations of Chicana writers.

Born on August 15, 1948, in Las Cruces, New Mexico, Denise Elia Chávez is the daughter of Ernesto and Delfina Rede Chávez. She claims a long lineage to the town of Polvo (which means "dust" in Spanish), Texas. In a deliberate, mesmerizing way, Chávez captures the dust and the earthiness of her beloved Southwest in her writings. She was deeply influenced by her mother, a schoolteacher fluent in English and Spanish, who placed great emphasis on education. Delfina Chávez insisted Denise and her two sisters, Faride Conway and Margo, master both English and Spanish. Living 40 miles from the U.S.-Mexican border sparked in Denise a love affair with the richness inherent within a bilingual environment.

When Denise was 10 years old, her parents divorced. She then lived with her maternal grandmother, mother, sister, and half sister in Texas. Her grandmother loved literature, language, and reading. Chávez credits this matriarchal environment for the strong female characters in her writing. As a young girl, Denise kept a diary in which she recorded the oral stories that swirled around her. Her family's vibrant tradition of storytelling sparked an interest in theater. She attended Madonna High School, an all-girls Catholic school, in Mesilla, New Mexico, where she was encouraged to become whatever she could dream. Chávez pursued and nurtured her growing interest in live art by performing in drama productions. She found drama to be the perfect outlet for self-expression. As a teenager, she worked in a local hospital and aspired to be an actress.

In 1970, Chávez received a drama scholarship to New Mexico State University, where she studied with playwright Mark Medoff. That same year, she wrote her first play, *The Wait,* which won the New Mexico State University Best Play award. Chávez

Denise Chávez is one of the most widely recognized Latina authors among both mainstream and Latino readers. *(Photo of Denise Chávez is reprinted with permission from the publisher [APP Archive Files] [Houston: Arte Público Press—University of Houston, © 2006])*

followed with *Elevators* (one act) in 1972 and *The Flying Tortilla Man* (one act) in 1975. Blessed with strong literary friendships, she was encouraged by RUDOLFO A. ANAYA to continue her education. Chávez earned an M.F.A. in drama from Trinity University in 1974.

Chávez moved to Santa Fe, New Mexico, in 1975 after accepting a teaching position at Northern New Mexico Community College. Motivated by a strong sense to serve her community, Chávez became an artist in the schools for the New Mexico Arts Division from 1977 to 1983. She also worked in the Dallas Theatre Center.

She penned several more plays in these years, mostly one-acts, including *The Mask of November* (1977), *The Adobe Rabbit* (1979), *Santa Fe Charm* (1980), *How Junior Got Throwed in the Joint* (1981), *Hecho en México* (1982; Made in Mexico), *The Green Madonna* (1982), and *La morenita* (1983; The dark virgin). In 1982 she earned an M.A. in creative writing from the University of New Mexico.

Chávez returned to Las Cruces in 1983 when her mother died. She has lived there ever since in the house her grandmother once owned on La Colonia Street. Writing in the room in which she was born, she composed several poems, short stories, and a wealth of plays, including *Plaza* (1984), *Plague-Time* (1985), *Novena narrativas* (1986; The novena narratives), *The Step* (1987), and *Women in the State of Grace* (1989). Chávez, who considers herself a performance writer, has performed her one-woman play *Women in the State of Grace* throughout the United States. *Plaza,* one of her best-known dramas, has been produced at the Edinburgh Festival in Scotland and at Joseph Papp's Festival Latino de Nueva York. Chávez married Daniel Zolinsky, a photographer and sculptor, on December 29, 1984.

In 1986, Chávez released *The Last of the Menu Girls,* a collection of her short stories published as a novel. These short stories chronicle the coming of age of Rocio, a fiercely independent young waitress, who steps outside the repressive gender roles for Chicanas to create a path of her own making.

Chávez served as professor of theater at the University of Houston from 1988 to 1991. In her writing classes, she stresses the immeasurable value of keeping a journal. Chávez finds that a writer must be honest, respectful, and on the lookout for the deep meanings hidden in the crevices of all life.

Chávez also travels extensively, lecturing and teaching a variety of workshops, including International Body Language, Multi-ethnic Drama, The Art of the Monologue, Work as Metaphor, The Essence of Latina/Latino Writers, Performance Writing, and The Cuentista: The Storyteller. She traveled throughout the Soviet Union as a delegate in 1989 on an international arts commission sponsored by the Forum for U.S.-Soviet Dialogue. Chávez released *The Woman Who Knew the Language of Animals* in 1992. This magical fable teaches children how to get along in an ethnically, culturally, and linguistically diverse world.

In 1994, Chávez began the Border Book Festival, which features readings, storytelling, films, and more on issues that cover border life and concerns at the heart of borderland communities. The festival has included the works of award-winning producer Lourdes Portillo and acclaimed authors such as Anaya, Ana Castillo, Rubén Martínez, and Demetria Martínez. That same year, Chávez released the highly successful *Face of an Angel*. In this book, she continues in her usual approach to taboo subjects such as incest, alcohol abuse, sexuality, religion, and macho traditions with a frank intensity that shatters old world views. She commented in an interview with *Los Angeles Times* writer Julio Moran, "But that in itself is liberation for a woman to be able to speak the unspeakable. Latinas never talk about their sexuality . . . women writers want to confront the issues of sexuality in the family, especially in their complexity, as opposed to presenting an image of what the family is. That runs the gamut from abuse to personal relationships." She added, "[I]t's not airing dirty laundry. Latinos are human beings. We no longer need to create an image of what we're supposed to be to make ourselves acceptable to other people." *Face of an Angel* won an American Book Award and was selected for the Book of the Month Club.

Inspired by everyday dreams, integrity, hopes, and mercy, Chávez writes with a keen sense of life's vibrancy mixed with a compassion for human frailties. Her sensitive and perceptive tales transport and mesmerize readers to experience the intense beauty and heat of her beloved Southwest. *Loving Pedro Infante* (2001) captures the essence of the desert with a raw vulnerability and spicy desires. It tells the story of Tere who, along with her best friend Irma, carry on a cultish love affair with Pedro Infante, a Mexican movie star from the 1940s who died in a plane crash. Comparing the idealist view of love to reality is an awakening experience for Tere. In, 2006, Chávez released *A Taco Testimony: Meditations on Family, Food and Culture*.

Chávez's writings have been included in several anthologies, such as *Cuentos Chicanos: A Short Story Anthology, Shattering the Myth: Plays by Hispanic Women,* and *Chicana Creativity and Criticism: Charting New Frontiers in American Literature.* A deeply devoted community-based author, Chávez has been honored for her philanthropic and literary work, receiving the New Mexico Community Luminaria Award, the Soroptimist International of the America's Club's Woman of Distinction Award in Education, the New Mexico Governor's Award in Literature, and the El Paso Herald Post's Writers of the Pass award. Chávez currently serves as the executive director to the Border Book Foundation, which hosts the annual Border Book Festival, held in Las Cruces, New Mexico.

Further Reading

Anderson, Douglas. *American Women Short Story Writers.* New York: Garland, 1995.

Cortés, Eladio, and Mirta Barrea-Maryls, eds. *Encyclopedia of Latin American Theatre.* Westport, Conn.: Greenwood Press, 2003.

Flores, Lauro. *Floating Borderlands: Twenty-five years of U.S. Hispanic Literature.* Seattle: University of Washington Press, 1998.

González, Ray, ed. *Mirrors Beneath the Earth: Short Fiction by Chicano Writers*. Willimantic, Conn.: Curbstone Press, 1992.

Lomelí, Francisco A., and Carl R. Shirley, eds. *Chicano Writers: Second Series*. Vol. 122. Detroit: Gale Research, 1992, pp. 70–76.

Chávez, Fray Angélico
(Manuel Ezequiel Chávez, Angélico Chávez)
(1910–1996) *poet, biographer, novelist, essayist, short story writer, folklorist*

With 23 published works, Fray Angélico Chávez deftly produced a wide range of prose and poetry about the New Mexican landscape and Hispanic history, often laced with lyrical, ecclesiastical mysticism. His best-known and most widely discussed work is the highly personal *My Penitente Land: Reflections on Spanish New Mexico* (1974). Chávez held a great love for the hard and beautiful environment of New Mexico. Through his work, readers sense generations of dedication and symbiotic relationship with the land.

Born on April 10, 1910, in Wagon Mound, New Mexico, Manuel Ezequiel was the eldest of 10 children of Nicolasa Roybal, a teacher, and Fabián Chávez, a carpenter. Although his family was poor, Chávez was able to attend Mora Public School, run by the Sisters of Loretto. His love for New Mexico and its colorful history brought the Franciscan friars to his attention. The Franciscans' prominence in the region's history intrigued and inspired him to such a degree that at 14 years old Manuel entered the St. Francis Seminary in Cincinnati, Ohio. He loved to write and paint as a youth, publishing poetry in the school paper. In fact, in 1929, when he returned to Santa Fe, New Mexico, and entered the novitiate, he was given the name Fray Angélico in honor and recognition of the Italian Renaissance painter Fra Angelico.

Chávez attended Duns Scotus College in Detroit, Michigan, from 1930 to 1933. He continued his studies at the Franciscan House of Stud-

In his writings and actions, Fray Angélico Chávez exemplified the unbreakable connection between land, faith, and history typical of many New Mexicans. *(Photo of Fray Angélico Chávez is reprinted with permission from the publisher [APP Archive Files] [Houston: Arte Público Press—University of Houston, © 2006])*

ies in Oldenburg, Indiana, for the next four years. On May 6, 1937, he became the first native New Mexican to be ordained into the Orders of Friars Minor (Franciscan) as a Roman Catholic priest. Chávez immediately began to serve the towns and pueblos of New Mexico. He divided his time between working as a postmaster for Penablanca, New Mexico, missionary, and writer. In 1939, he released his first collection of poetry, *Clothed with the Sun*. The early written works of Chávez are primarily poetry, focused on the emotional spiritual life. Metaphors are often drawn with a deep connection to and reverence for nature. In 1943, he volunteered to serve in the South Pacific during World War II as a Spanish-speaking chaplain. He released *Eleven Lady-Lyrics and Other Poems* (1945) and *The Single Rose; The Rose Unica and Commentary of Fray Manuel de Santa Clara* (1948). In 1951, he spent one year in Germany as a chaplain during the Korean War.

By the end of the 1940s, Chávez began to fuse his love of history into short stories, articles, and essays. Chávez obtained and studied primary accounts and original documents of New Mexican history dating back to 1584 to stand as the backbone for these writings. With the help of original manuscripts, the perspective of the people who lived through events is clearly heard in his historical fiction. Selected works from this time include *Our Lady of the Conquest* (1948); *Origins of New Mexican Families in the Spanish Colonial Period* (1954); *The Virgin of Port Lligat* (1959), inspired by a Salvador Dalí painting and favorably commented on by T. S. Eliot; *The Lady from Toledo* (1960); and *Coronado's Friars: The Franciscans in the Coronado Expedition* (1968).

Chávez was named pastor of the church at Cerillos, outside Santa Fe, in 1959. He painted several murals and employed his artistic talents for restoration in towns and pueblos under his care. He retired from his parish duties in 1972 to devote himself to writing full time. *My Penitente Land: Reflections on Spanish New Mexico* (1974) marked perhaps his most seamless fusion of art, history, theology, and storytelling. In *My Penitente Land*, Chávez offers his personal reflections and intuitions to reveal how the land and its inherent mysticism formed Spanish New Mexicans. Additional works from this period include *The Dominguez-Escalante Journals* (as translator; 1976), *When the Santos Talked* (1977), *But Time and Chance; The Story of Padre Martinez of Taos, 1793–1867* (1981), and *Très Macho—He Said* (1985).

Chávez received the Catholic Poetry Society of America Award (1948), Cardinal Newman Key Award (1949), National Conference of Christians and Jews lyric poetry award (1963), and New Mexico Governor's literary award (1976). Chávez died on March 18, 1996. Through his voluminous collection, Chávez articulated the powerful connection between ancestry, faith, and terrain.

Further Reading

Kanellos, Nicolás, et al., eds. *Herencia: The Anthology of Hispanic Literature of the United States.* New York: Oxford University Press, 2003, pp. 191–194.

Lomelí, Francisco A., and Carl R. Shirley, eds. *Chicano Writers: First Series.* Vol. 82. Detroit: Gale Research, 1989, pp. 86–90.

Meier, Matt S. *Mexican-American Biographies: A Historical Dictionary, 1836–1987.* Westport, Conn.: Greenwood Press, 1988.

Riggs, Thomas. *Reference Guide to American Literature.* 4th ed. Detroit: St. James Press, 2000.

Tardiff, Joseph C., and L. Mpho Mabunda, eds. *Dictionary of Hispanic Biography.* Detroit: Gale Research, 1996, pp. 219–221.

Cisneros, Sandra

(1951–) *novelist, poet, essayist, short story writer, children's writer*

A resounding voice for the Chicana experience, award-winning novelist and poet Sandra Cisneros is one of the first Chicana writers to break the glass ceiling of mainstream literature. She is best known for *The House on Mango Street*, a coming-of-age story that is required reading in many high school and college curricula.

Born on December 20, 1951, in Chicago, Illinois, Sandra Cisneros is the only daughter and third child in a family of seven children. Her Mexican-born father came from a family of means but decided to travel to the United States in pursuit of higher education. He met Cisneros's mother, a Mexican American, in Chicago, and the two married and settled down. Cisneros's family had little money and constantly moved from house to house, from one barrio to the next. Finally, her parents borrowed a down payment and bought a house in a Puerto Rican ghetto on Chicago's north side. The move gave Sandra a sense of stability and a slew of eccentric neighbors and friends whom she would later write about in the highly successful *House on Mango Street.*

Due to the constant movement in her earlier years, Sandra became shy and had difficulty forming lasting friendships. She quietly observed others and wrote about her findings when at home. Her mother gave her a love of reading by insisting that Sandra and her brothers all had library cards. Years later, Cisneros would learn that some people actually bought books instead of always borrowing them. Sandra's introverted tendencies kept her from contributing in class or sharing her work until she was encouraged to do so by one of her 10th-grade teachers. Her teacher also encouraged Sandra to write for the school's literary magazine, ultimately becoming its editor.

After graduating from high school, Cisneros studied English at Loyola University. In her junior year, Cisneros discovered the works of Donald Justice, Mark Strand, and James Wright, whose poetry awoke a connection with and appreciation for her cultural roots. She graduated in 1976. A teacher encouraged Cisneros to attend the Iowa Writers' Workshop. Cisneros matured as a writer in the two years she spent in the prestigious writers' environment, studying poetry and earning her master's degree in creative writing in 1978. Cisneros was initially reluctant to share her work among fellow students who wrote about privileged childhoods. She eventually gained confidence and shared her poetry at public readings. Her poetry was published in literary magazines and selected to appear on public buses in Chicago. Cisneros published her first collection of poetry, entitled *Bad Boys,* in 1980.

Eventually, she learned to take pride in her iconoclastic writing and distinctive voice that portrayed a culture not readily seen, namely the experiences of a Mexican American. *The House on Mango Street* (1984) was the result. Esperanza is the protagonist in this novel, comprised of several vignettes that portray the hopes and dreams of a Mexican-American girl growing up in a Chicago barrio. With such a distinctive new voice and subject matter, *The House on Mango Street* was well received and became required reading for schools throughout the nation. In due course, the required reading would include elementary, middle and high school, and university-level programs. In 1995, *The House on Mango Street* was released in Spanish. Since then, Cisneros's books have been translated into several languages, including Galician, French, German, Dutch, Italian, Norwegian, Japanese, Chinese, Turkish, Greek, Thai, and Serbo-Croatian.

Throughout the 1980s, Cisneros received many grants and fellowships to fund her writing, including the Texas Institute of Letters Dobie-Paisano Fellowship, an Illinois Artists Grant, and two National Endowment of the Arts fellowships, one each for fiction and poetry. In 1986, Cisneros moved to San Antonio, Texas, and taught part-time as a guest professor throughout the United States. She received a fellowship that financially enabled her to write another book of poetry, *My Wicked, Wicked Ways,* which was published in 1987. Despite the success of her first book, she was unable to make a living from writing. Cisneros preferred Texan life and attempted to begin a writing program there. When the program did not succeed, Cisneros moved to California, where she accepted a teaching position at California State University–Chico.

She was awarded a National Endowment for the Arts grant to help her write *Woman Hollering Creek and Other Stories* (1991), a collection of vibrant vignettes of women's tales from life on the Mexico-Texas border. Random House published the book, making Cisneros the first Mexican-American woman to receive a major publishing contract for work about Latinas. Cisneros took on the responsibility to represent the formerly unheard voices with passion and respect. "I'm trying to write the stories that haven't been written. I feel like a cartographer; I'm determined to fill a literary void," Cisneros said. *Woman Hollering Creek* was awarded the PEN Center West Award for Best Fiction, the Quality Paperback Book Club New Voices Award, the Anisfield-Wolf Book Award, and the Lannan Foundation Literary Award. It was selected as a noteworthy book of the year by the *New York Times* and the *American Library Journal* and nominated Best Book of Fiction by the *Los Angeles Times.*

Cisneros wrote her first children's book, *Hairs/ Pelitos,* in 1994; it was released in 1997. *Hairs/ Pelitos* is a bilingual picture book based on one of the vignettes from *The House on Mango Street.* It won *Parenting Magazine*'s Best Children's Book of the Year Award and was acclaimed as an "exuberant bilingual picture book, with eye-catching artwork, . . . an affectionate picture of familial love and a cozy bedtime book" by *The Horn Book.* Cisneros returned to poetry with *Loose Women* (1994), which won the Mountains and Plains Booksellers Association's 1995 Regional Book Award in the poetry category.

In 1997, the writer returned to San Antonio. She bought a house in the historic district and painted it purple. The city objected, and Cisneros found herself in a two-year battle that made news in Texas. Eventually, Cisneros painted the house a mellow shade of lavender, which was deemed acceptable. Throughout her writing career, Cisneros has worked as a counselor to high school dropouts, as an artist in residence in the schools where she taught creative writing, a college recruiter, an arts administrator, and a visiting writer at several universities, including the University of California–Berkeley and the University of Michigan–Ann Arbor.

Cisneros released her second novel, *Caramelo,* in 2000. She is credited with spending a great deal of time and energy immersing herself in each character and studying community. The dedication has paid off. *Caramelo* was selected as a notable book of the year by several papers including the *New York Times, Los Angeles Times, San Francisco Chronicle,*

Chicago Tribune, and *Seattle Times.* The *Los Angeles Times* review glowed: "Cisneros writes along the borders where the novel and social history intersect. In this lovingly told and poetic novel, she uses the storytelling art to give the voiceless ones a voice, and to find the border to the past, imbuing the struggles of her family and her countries with the richness of myth." Cisneros released *Vintage Cisneros* in 2004; this collection features excerpts from her previously published works.

Cisneros is the recipient of several honors, including a MacArthur Foundation fellowship; a Texas Medal of the Arts Award; an honorary doctor of humane letters from Loyola University, Chicago; and an honorary doctor of letters from the State University of New York at Purchase. She secured her place in the Chicano literary canon with works that masterfully challenge stereotypes, explore racism, and unapologetically seek selfhood within communities and the larger society with divergent perspectives that reflect the growing and dynamic evolution of humankind.

Further Reading

Curiel, Barbara Brinson. "The General's Pants: A Chicana Feminist (re)Vision of the Mexican Revolution in Sandra Cisneros's 'Eyes of Zapata.'" *Western American Literature* 35, no. 4 (Winter 2001): 403–427.

Ganz, Robin. "Sandra Cisneros: Border Crossings and Beyond." *MELUS* 19, no. 1 (Spring 1994): 19–29.

González, Ray, ed. *Mirrors Beneath the Earth: Short Fiction by Chicano Writers.* Willimantic, Conn.: Curbstone Press, 1992.

Magill, Frank N. *Masterpieces of Latino Literature.* New York: HarperCollins, 1994.

Meier, Matt S., Conchita Franco Serri, and Richard A. Garcia. *Notable Latino Americans: A Biographical Dictionary.* Westport, Conn.: Greenwood Press, 1997, pp. 87–90.

Novas, Himilce. *The Hispanic 100: A Ranking of the Latino Men and Women Who Have Most Influenced American Thought and Culture.* New York: Citadel Press, 1995.

Cofer, Judith Ortiz
(Judith Ortiz)

(1952–) *poet, playwright, essayist, novelist, children's book writer, educator*

Judith Ortiz Cofer writes with a strong autobiographical slant about the Puerto Rican experience in the United States. She has an extensive collection of work that has received many prestigious awards.

The daughter of J. M. and Fanny Morot Ortiz, Judith Ortiz was born in Hormingueros, Puerto Rico, on February 24, 1952. When her younger brother was born, her father joined the

Judith Ortiz Cofer was one of the first Puerto Rican women to write an autobiographical work of her immigration experience. *(Photo of Judith Ortiz Cofer is reprinted with permission from the publisher [APP Archive Files] [Houston: Arte Público Press—University of Houston, © 2006])*

U.S. Navy, believing he could provide better for his growing family in the United States. At two years old, Judith moved with her family to Paterson, New Jersey. Ortiz learned English quickly and often translated for her Spanish-speaking mother. Whenever her father was shipped out to sea, Judith, her mother, and her brother stayed at her maternal grandmother's home in Puerto Rico. Judith enjoyed the many stories her mother's family told that taught her lessons of strength, friendship, and endurance. She attributes her storytelling talent to the oral teachings and *cuentos,* or "stories," of her childhood.

Fanny's strong ties to her native island conflicted with J. M.'s desire to assimilate into American culture. Their conflict and bicultural living inform Ortiz's writings. Judith attended public schools until the sixth grade, when she entered a private Catholic school. When riots broke out near their home in Paterson, she moved with her family to Georgia, a place far away from the unrest in the northeastern part of the United States. She completed her last two years of high school in Georgia. Ortiz met and subsequently married Charles John Cofer in 1971. She explored her love of language at Augusta College, where she received a B.A in English in 1974. In 1977, she earned an M.A. in English at Florida Atlantic University. During this time, she attended a graduate summer program at Oxford University, where she was an English Speaking Union of America fellow.

Cofer found herself incessantly writing poetry. A colleague convinced her to submit her work, and to her great excitement her poetry was published. She released her poetry in the chapbooks *Latin Women Pray* (1980), *The Native Dancer* (1981), and *Among the Ancestors* (1981). *Latin Women Pray* was produced as a three-act play in 1984. Cofer joined the staff of the University of Georgia as an English instructor that same year. First and foremost a poet, Cofer released *Peregrina* (1986, Pilgrim), *Reaching for the Mainland* (1987), and *Terms of Survival* (1987) while she was teaching. She contributed her work to *Triple Crown: Chicano, Puerto Rican and Cuban American Poetry* (1987). Her work garnered attention, national fellowships, and grants from the Fine Arts Council (1980), National Endowment for the Arts (1989), Witter Bynner Foundation (1988), and Bread Loaf Writers' Conference (1987).

In *The Line of the Sun* (1989), Cofer continues to write about her bicultural experiences as a means of unraveling and understanding her past. She explains, "[T]he reason I use so much autobiographical material in the novel is not so much that I think my life is important. I feel it is sort of an obligation. As a Puerto Rican immigrant my key experience was growing up bilingual and bicultural. Therefore I felt a need to share that with others, before I could go on. Perhaps you can call it a rite of passage or something similar . . . It was a kind of training for myself both as a thinking person and a writer to get my life straight." *The Line of the Sun* was nominated for a Pulitzer Prize. Other honors for her work include the Pushcart Prize (1990), O. Henry Prize (1994), and Anisfield Wolf Award (1994).

Silent Dancing: A Partial Remembrance of a Puerto Rican Childhood (1990), a collection of personal poetry and essays, explores her dual culturalism. *The Latin Deli: Prose and Poetry* was released in 1993. Cofer then focused on young adult writing in *An Island Like You: Stories of the Barrio* (1995).

In 1997, Cofer became a professor of English and creative writing at the University of Georgia, a position she filled until she was promoted to Franklin Professor of English. She taught poetry workshops and served as a visiting professor at numerous colleges and universities, including the University of Michigan, University of Arizona, and University of Minnesota–Duluth. Her work has appeared in periodicals such as *Georgia Review, Kenyon Review, Southern Review,* and *Glamour,* as well as anthologies and textbooks, including *Best American Essays 1991, The Norton Book of Women's Lives, The Norton Introduction to Literature, The Norton Introduction to Poetry,* and *The Heath Anthology of American Literature.*

In 1998, she received the Christ-Janner Award in Creative Research from the University of Georgia and released *The Year of Our Revolution: New and Selected Stories and Poems.* The following year, the Rockefeller Foundation awarded her a residency at the Bellagio, Italy, conference center. *Woman in Front of the Sun: On Becoming a Writer* (2000), a collection of essays, explains how the author's use of personal information is an attempt to create a sense of community and connectedness. During spring 2001, she was Vanderbilt University's Gertrude and Harold S. Vanderbilt Visiting Writer in Residence.

The Meaning of Consuelo (2003) was selected as one of two winners of the 2003 Americas Award, sponsored by the National Consortium of Latin American Studies Programs for U.S.-published titles that authentically and engagingly portray Latin America, the Caribbean, or Latinos in the United States. The New York Public Library included it on the "Books for the Teen Age 2004 List." Cofer released *Love Story Beginning in Spanish: Poems* in 2005 and *Call Me Maria,* a young adult novel, in 2006. A natural storyteller, Cofer engages and inspires her readers with her willingness to bare her life's experiences, thereby creating parables from which others might learn.

Further Reading

Cofer, Judith Ortiz. *Silent Dancing: A Partial Remembrance of a Puerto Rican Childhood.* Houston, Tex.: Arte Público Press, 1990.

Milligan, Bryce, Mary Guerrero Milligan, and Angela de Hoyos. *Daughters of the Fifth Sun.* New York: Riverhead Trade, 1996.

Tardiff, Joseph C., and L. Mpho Mabunda, eds. *Dictionary of Hispanic Biography.* Detroit: Gale Research, 1996, pp. 235–236.

West-Durán, Alan. *Latino and Latina Writers, Volume II.* Detroit: Gale-Thomas, 2004, pp. 917–934.

Colón, Jesús

(1901–1974) *poet, essayist, editor, journalist, activist*

Jesús Colón was among the first writers to chronicle the Puerto Rican immigrant experience in the United States. His pioneering efforts provided much of the foundation for those who would become Nuyoricans, or New York Puerto Ricans.

Of African descent and the son of a baker, Jesús Colón was born in Cayey, Puerto Rico, on January 20, 1901. Colón appreciated literature from an early age. He often visited the cigar factories and listened to the newspapers or classic books being read aloud. His family moved to San Juan, where he attended Central Grammar School. There, Colón served as director of the school journal *¡¡¡Adelante . . . !!!* and was the president of the Manuel Fernández Juncos Literary Society. He became active in political movements and joined the newly established Socialist Party. Upon the passage of the Jones Act of 1917, which declared Puerto Ricans U.S. citizens, many Puerto Ricans left their homeland to seek their fortunes in America. Colón stowed away on a ship (the SS *Carolina*) bound for New York. Just 17 years old, Colón began his search for work. When he could get work, he endured inhumane conditions and expectations and found that prejudice ran rampant everywhere. Colón documented his

Jesús Colón wrote one of the first books on the Puerto Rican immigrant experience. *(Photo of Jesús Colón is reprinted with permission from the publisher [APP Archive Files] [Houston: Arte Público Press—University of Houston, © 2006])*

experiences in essays, articles, and poetry while he supported himself through menial jobs such as dishwasher, waiter, post officer clerk, and longshoreman. He submitted his writings and was published in the Puerto Rican papers *Jusíticia, Unión Obrera,* and *Liberación.* He often wrote to his school sweetheart, Rufa Concepción (Concha) Fernández, about the discrimination he and fellow Puerto Ricans faced living in the Bronx.

Colón worked diligently to create social justice within his community. In 1918, he collaborated with others to form the first Puerto Rican committee of the Socialist Party in New York. He was a founding member and the first secretary of the Alianza Obrera Puertorriqueña and the Ateneo Obrero, where he taught courses for workers; a founding member of one of the most important civic organizations, La Liga Puertorriqueña Hispana, serving for a time as director of its *Boletín;* and a founding member and director of Sol Naciente, one of the earliest Hispanic fraternal societies. In 1925, he married Concha, who at that time joined him in New York. He served as the national head of the 30 Spanish- and Portuguese-speaking lodges of the International Workers Order (IWO), a multinational fraternal organization founded in 1930. He ran for public office as a Communist in both 1952 and 1969. Although he was not elected, he remained active throughout his life in various political, civic, and cultural organizations. He held offices in the American Labor Party and participated in strikes and other forms of orchestrated protest.

Colón wrote about his observations on racial discrimination primarily in English, which enabled him to reach a wider audience. He served as a newsman at the *Daily Worker,* the *Worker,* and *Mainstream,* often recording his firsthand experiences of injustice, hostility, and prejudice. Colón also wrote literary pieces in *Gráfico,* where he worked as a contributor. The newspapers *El Machete Criollo* and *El Nuevo Mundo* published his anecdotal writings and poems.

Colón's first book, *A Puerto Rican in New York: and Other Sketches,* was published in 1961.

The vignettes vary from humorous to poignant to didactic and offer a portrait of Puerto Ricans that vastly differs from assumed stereotypes. It was one of the first books written in English by a Puerto Rican about the Puerto Rican experience. The book was rereleased in 1981 and won the American Book Award in 1984.

Colón's most ambitious effort is considered to be the founding of his own company, Hispanic Publishers, also known as Editorial Hispánica. This small press published books of history, politics, and literary material. Colón is also recognized for translating works from English into Spanish, including poetry. He was listed as coauthor of a book by Kenneth B. Hoyt on vocational education, which was published by the U.S. Department of Health, Education, and Welfare after Colón's death in 1974.

Further Reading

Bryan, Ryan, ed. *Hispanic Writers.* Detroit: Gale Research, 1991.

Kanellos, Nicolás. *Hispanic-American Almanac.* Detroit: Gale Research, 1993.

———, et al., eds. *Herencia: The Anthology of Hispanic Literature in the United States.* New York: Oxford University Press, 2003, pp. 470–72.

Corpi, Lucha
(1945–) *poet, novelist, children's book writer, educator*

Lucha Corpi has created an understanding of diversity with her poems, novels, and children's books. She is best known for "The Marina Poems," a series of four poems that offers a different perspective on Malintzín Tenepal, the indigenous woman who served as translator and lover to Hernán Cortés.

Lucha Corpi was born to Angel and Victoria C. Corpi in Jaltipán, Veracruz, Mexico, on April 13, 1945. She lived her early years in a verdant landscape on the eastern coast of Mexico. When Corpi was nine, her family moved to San

Lucha Corpi is best known for "The Marina Poems," which depict a difference version of La Malinche, the lover of Hernán Cortés. *(Photo of Lucha Corpi is reprinted with permission from the publisher [APP Archive Files] [Houston: Arte Público Press—University of Houston, © 2006])*

Luis Potosí, Mexico, a place she felt was gray and distant, like its inhabitants. In 1964, she married Guillermo Hernández. At age 19, Corpi immigrated to the United States as a newlywed. She became part of the literary world in the San Francisco Bay Area during the height of the Chicano movement. In 1970, Corpi divorced and begin teaching English as a second language in the Oakland public school system, a position she held for many years. In 1971 she cofounded Aztlán Cultural, an arts service organization that years later would merge with Centro Chicano de Escritores (Chicano Writers Center). In 1975, Corpi earned a B.A. in comparative and world literature from the University of California–Berkeley. She received an M.A., also in comparative

and world literature, from San Francisco State University in 1979.

In 1980, Corpi released *Palabras de mediodía* (*Noon Words*); the book was rereleased in 2001. Corpi writes poetry in Spanish, enlisting Catherine Rodriguez-Nieto to translate the poetry into English. Her first volume of poetry explores death, love, and women's role in society and reinvents Malintzín Tenepal, better known by the derogatory name of La Malinche. Born in the early 16th century, Malintzín was of Aztec nobility when she was sold into slavery at the age of eight. Hernán Cortés made use of her translation skills and from him she had a child. Corpi gives a human face to the woman who had come to be known as an evil sorceress condemning the people of Aztlán to the cruel dictatorship of the Spaniards. Corpi suggests that Doña Marina (as Malintzín was renamed by the Spaniards after her Christian baptism) was not a willing accomplice but rather misunderstood and condemned for a fate she neither asked for nor relished. Corpi restores dignity to Malintzín, whom some refer to as the Mexican Eve.

Corpi's first novel, *Delia's Song* (1989), follows a woman as she escapes the male dominance of her native Mexico, only to find a more hostile form of oppression in Berkeley, California, during the Chicano movement. Her second book of poetry, *Variaciones sobre una Tempestad/Variations on a Storm* (1990), delves deep into the passion and pain of Mexico yet possesses a subtlety that creates a universal appeal. *Eulogy for a Brown Angel* (1992) marked Corpi's entrance into mystery novels. The protagonist, feminist detective Gloria Damasco, uses her intuition and dreams to solve crimes during the Chicano Moratorium, the march in Los Angeles for Latino equality during the Vietnam War. In *Cactus Blood* (1995), Damasco continues to use her clairvoyant talents to untangle mysteries surrounding the grape vineyards of Delano, California—the notorious town where activist César Chávez began the first Latino farmworkers strike.

Corpi combines imagination with childhood memories in her first children's book, *Where the Fire-*

flies Dance/Ahí, donde bailán los luciérnagas, (1997). *Kirkus Review* commented that Corpi's bilingual book is "a wonderful evocation of the early experiences and family love that give a child both roots and wings." In the same year Corpi edited *Máscaras* (Masks), a collection of essays written by 15 contemporary women writers. *Máscaras* represent the concealment of one's true feelings; however, in this collection, the writers courageously take off those masks to reveal journeys of personal identities as Latinas, Chicanas, and Americans. *Black Widow's Wardrobe* (1999) is the third mystery novel featuring Gloria Damasco. Critics have praised Corpi's protagonist as original, vulnerable, intelligent, and insightful with rare talents, not the least of which is her clairvoyant abilities. In 2004, Corpi released *Crimson Moon: A Brown Angel Mystery.*

Corpi has received several awards for her writing, including a National Endowment for the Arts creative writing fellowship, the PEN Oakland Josephine Miles Literary Prize in fiction, and the Multicultural Publishers Exchange Book Award of Excellence in Adult Fiction. Her novels use spirituality and mystery to explore the triumphs and trials of Chicanos, while her poetry reveals with intelligence, sensitivity, and valor the lives of disenfranchised people forgotten by the dominant culture. Corpi's writings give voice and texture to a nearly forgotten history that still breathes in many Mexican Americans.

Further Reading

Armstrong, Jeanne. *Demythologizing the Romance of Conquest.* Westport, Conn.: Greenwood Press, 2001.

Corpi, Lucha. *Palabras de Mediodía/Noon Words.* Houston, Tex.: Arte Público Press, 2001.

Gonzalez, Maria C. *Contemporary Mexican-American Women Novelists.* New York: Peter Lang, 1998.

Heide, Rick, ed. *Under the Fifth Sun: Latino Literature from California.* Santa Clara and Berkeley, Calif.: Santa Clara University/ Heyday Books, 2002.

Tardiff, Joseph C., and L. Mpho Mabunda, eds. *Dictionary of Hispanic Biography.* Detroit: Gale Research, 1996, pp. 243–244.

Cortina, Betty
(Beatriz Cortina)
(1970–) *journalist, editor*

Full of integrity and possessed of a strong work ethic, Betty Cortina rose through the journalism ranks by taking a humanitarian approach to "getting the story." Today, Cortina stands as one of the most visible Latina editors at a national magazine.

Beatriz Cortina was the first of her extended family to be born in the United States. The only child of Belén and Walfredo Cortina, who emigrated from Cuba to the United States in the 1960s, Cortina was born on July 17, 1970. She lived her early years in a culturally diverse neighborhood of Chicago, Illinois. Though her family ate different food, spoke a different language, and had different traditions, Cortina believed different was natural. Her parents ingrained in her that she was American just like everyone else. Cortina was unaware of racial or nationality differences between her and her best friends, who were black, Filipino, and Mexican. She just saw them all as American.

When she was 10 years old, Cortina moved to Hialeah, a town outside Miami, Florida. In a defining moment of her life, Cortina was asked to fill out a card by her teacher. This card required students to check a box to match their nationality. Cortina checked American. The teacher returned with a curt declaration that by proof of her surname, Cortina, she was Hispanic, not American. Cortina recalled in a 2005 interview, "It took years to unravel this ethnic slur and finally determine that one need never be branded nor whittle identity into a box; it is best to blend and weave together the many facets of self."

In elementary school, Cortina dreamed of becoming a teacher. She loved her teachers and school. When she reached junior high school, Cortina found she admired the intelligence and kindness of her English teacher, Gail Kelly. Kelly saw a budding writer in the student and invited Cortina to take her journalism class. Cortina accepted the offer and contributed to the junior high school paper. Ever since the eighth grade, including working at her high school paper, Cortina has worked in journalism.

After graduating from high school, Cortina obtained a Knight Ridder scholarship to study journalism at the University of Florida. As part of the scholarship, Cortina was required to intern every summer at a paper owned by Knight Ridder. During college, Cortina worked for the *Miami Herald,* spent one summer in California writing for the *San Jose Mercury News,* and wrote for the university's news and public affairs office. Since each summer was spent interning, Cortina's education took her one semester beyond the scholarship funds. Ever resourceful, Cortina entered writing contests that paid cash to finance the last semester. She won both the *Rolling Stone* magazine contest for a story covering a University of Florida alumni doctor who provided medical care to the homeless and a Hearst competition for feature writing. Cortina graduated from the University of Florida with a B.A. in journalism in December 1992. She then worked for the *Miami Herald* for two years as a local government reporter and crime reporter.

In 1995, Cortina moved to Los Angeles to work for *People* magazine. In March of that same year, Latina music sensation Selena was tragically killed. *People* covered the story of the young Tejana singer who had risen from the barrio to great heights without ever forgetting her roots. Latinos whose hopes were wrapped in Selena mourned for what she could have been with a poignant, visceral reaction. The critical mass the mourning reached caught the attention of mainstream Americans, who then realized, according to Cortina, "they had lost the biggest star they never knew they had."

Some 10 days after the burial, Cortina was assigned to speak to Selena's family. With great compassion and respect, Cortina wrote the story for *People*'s tribute issue dedicated to Selena. The issue sold out, which caused Time, Inc. to realize the power and presence of the "Sleeping Giant," a phrase used to refer to the growing Latino/Hispanic population. They decided to launch *People en Espa-

ñol.* As Cortina was the most Hispanic person at the magazine working on the prototype, the rest of the crew assumed she would want the editorship. When the magazine executives approached her, Cortina had only recently been named a correspondent and was merely 25 years old. She wisely declined and asked instead that she be involved with the launch of the magazine and perhaps work under a mentor. She got what she wanted and more—a move to New York and the second spot as an associate editor under the tutelage of a fantastic editor. Cortina worked for *People en Español* for three years. In 1999, she accepted a senior writing position at *Entertainment Weekly.* She wrote one year for the magazine, covering film festivals, lives of movie stars, and awards ceremonies.

Cortina turned 29 and began to seek work that reflected something deeper and more meaningful. Destiny's door opened when Oprah Winfrey called. Winfrey was launching *O, The Oprah Magazine* and needed Cortina's expertise. Cortina became the news editor in charge of finding the human element within the story. While at *O,* Cortina learned how to analyze her decisions, investigate her life's purpose, and seek thought-provoking issues and discussions from Winfrey. Cortina began to ponder what she would want to do with her life if she were not trying to build the perfect résumé. What would her life look like if she sought what inspired her and followed her own bliss?

Right on cue, *Latina* magazine called with an offer for their editorship. As editor in chief, Cortina brought fresh enthusiasm and a deep, honest desire to celebrate and honor the achievements of Latinas. A firm believer that the Latina community truly has many role models, Cortina strives to highlight Latina contributions, aspirations, and experiences. Readers' letters and the amazing women covered in each issue continue to inspire Cortina. She strives to give Latinas the applause they deserve and encourage others to be the best they can be—perhaps the first in the family to graduate from college or the first to carve out a career instead of just a job.

Cortina epitomizes the truism that if one keeps to her integrity and hard work, golden opportunities will present themselves. She writes and crafts stories first and foremost with a humanitarian style that not only brings the best out of the story but also sheds light on the best of the people she covers.

Further Reading

Albright, Mark. "Fashion Mag Speaks to Hispanic Women in English." *Chicago Sun Times,* June 20, 2003.
"Betty Cortina Founding News Editor of 'Oprah' magazine" *Communigator* (Fall 2000): 1.
Holt, Karen. "Say Hola to Your Next Consumer." *Folio: The Magazine for Magazine Management* (March 1, 2004): pp. 22–24.

Cruz, Frank
(Frank Henry Cruz, Frank H. Cruz)
(1939–) *journalist, educator, television executive*

Veteran broadcast journalist, cofounder of Telemundo, entrepreneur, and current vice chair of the Corporation for Public Broadcasting, Frank Cruz is a dedicated community leader whose business skills, compassion for his fellow citizens, and willingness to stand up for equality have influenced millions of people on a local and international level.

Frank Henry Cruz was raised by the strong love and discipline of his mother, Ruth Cruz. The Mexican Revolution was a period from approximately 1910 to 1920 filled with terror, violence, and corruption as the people attempted to establish a stronger political voice and more control. Cruz's grandfather, Rosendo Osuna, left Ruth and her four siblings, ranging in age from five to 14, in Nogales, Sonora, Mexico, on the U.S.-Mexican border in 1926, hoping they would find a better life to the north than in war-torn Mexico. Ruth found work as a laundress in Tucson, Ari-

zona, and eventually married Moses Cruz, a truck driver from Chihuahua, Mexico. When she was six months pregnant with Frank, and caring for their four-year-old son, Richard, her husband, Moses, died. Frank was born on October 4, 1939, in Tucson. Raising two boys in the Hollywood barrio, one of the poorest Mexican-American neighborhoods in the nation, as a single mother took untold strength and courage. Cruz never saw his mother smoke, drink, or carouse. She encouraged him to be a good student and work hard. By example, she taught him leadership. When Cruz was in junior high school, his mother opened a restaurant, forcing him to clean it and make *menudo*, a traditional Mexican soup.

Cruz excelled in school, graduating in 1957. He then entered the U.S. Air Force, where he served as a police officer stationed throughout the Far East. Other cultures, foods, and languages greatly intrigued Cruz. He immersed himself in the culture of each country he was stationed in, learning its language and customs. While in the air force, Cruz noticed his superiors gained higher rank through higher education. Focused on upward mobility, Cruz moved to Los Angeles after his military service to attend East L.A. City College, an institution, he affectionately called in a 2005 interview, "The Chicano Harvard of the West," due to its influential and prominent alumni, particularly those who graduated in the 1960s and 1970s. He married Bonnie Baldwin in 1964, who would give birth to their daughter Heather in three years' time. Cruz took history classes at East L.A. College from Dr. Helen Miller Bailey, who became his longtime mentor as a premier historian, an excellent teacher, and a true humanitarian.

Inspired by social and historical issues, Cruz transferred to the University of Southern California (USC) in 1964 to further his studies. He earned a B.A. in history in 1966, his teaching credentials in 1967, and an M.A. in Latin-American studies in 1969. While at the USC campus, a recruiter for the Los Angeles school district approached Cruz regarding teaching in affluent schools in West Los

Angeles. Cruz insisted he teach in East Los Angeles; he wanted to teach where he could make an impact on the community that helped form him. During the height of the Chicano movement, he gained a teaching position at Lincoln High School in East Los Angeles. The school was a central location for the 1968 East L.A. Blowouts, when high school students from five East Los Angeles high schools boycotted for nearly two weeks because of the inferiority of education and the inadequate and incomplete information relevant to Mexican-American history and culture. Cruz approached Dr. Bailey asking for any resources that could cover issues such as Mexican immigration to the United States. In light of the fact that no books

In 2006, former broadcast journalist Frank Cruz became the vice chair of CPB, the Corporation for Public Broadcasting. *(Courtesy of the author)*

had been published on the subject, Cruz and Bailey coauthored *Latin Americans: Past and Present* (1971) to address and record the different motivations and social context behind Mexican immigration waves.

While working on his Ph.D., Cruz taught ethnic studies at Sonoma State College (now University), later accepting a position teaching Chicano studies at California State University–Long Beach and eventually becoming chair of the department. The Chicano movement forced not only universities to change but also compelled the media to report the growing pains of a once exclusive American society. In 1969, Cruz hosted a series for NBC's *Sunrise Semesters* that consisted of 20 half-hour segments featuring the varied expertise of California Chicano studies professors. Cruz covered the U.S.-Mexican War and Mexican immigration for his two segments. Bill Fyffe, news director for KABC in Los Angeles, caught a rerun of the show in 1970 and asked Cruz if he would join their journalism team. Cruz viewed the new opportunity as exciting and challenging, with the benefit of reaching a wider audience for the uncovered issues in society and the probability of "making a greater impact and touching more lives," recalled Cruz in a 2005 interview. In 1971, twins Vanessa and Frank Richard joined the Cruz family.

Cruz worked for four years for ABC, covering the many aspects of being Latino in Los Angeles. He became so popular for his coverage of Mexican Americans that he often received calls from the community just prior to or while injustices were occurring. With his news team, he caught immigration services committing illegal acts of brutality, invasion of privacy, and other scenes that most Los Angelenos had never witnessed. He was promoted and became the first Hispanic anchor in Los Angeles. After four years with ABC, Cruz was told he had become known as a "bleeding heart" reporter and was beginning to turn off viewers. Cruz moved on to NBC, determined to be the best reporter, not just the best Hispanic reporter. He broadened the type of stories he reported while continuing to cover issues of importance to Hispanics. He won a Golden Mike and an Emmy for the *Latinization of Los Angeles* series.

In 1985, Cruz, with a group of investors, bought KVEA-TV in Los Angeles and established a Spanish-language television station. In 1986, he and other investors launched Telemundo, the nation's second-largest Spanish-language television network. Cruz served as the station's vice president and later as general manager. In 1990, he cofounded Gulf Atlantic Life Insurance, the first Hispanic-owned life insurance company in the United States. He served as the company's chair from 1991 to 1995. From 1990 to 1991, Cruz served as the president and executive director of the Latino Museum of History, Art, and Culture. In 1992, Cruz stood as one of 100 business owners nationwide who supported Bill Clinton's election. In August 1994, President Clinton nominated Cruz to his first term on the Corporation for Public Broadcasting (CPB) board. The Senate confirmed his nomination the following month. Cruz served as CPB board chair from 1999 to 2001, making him the first minority to head public broadcasting in the United States. He chaired the board's audit and finance committee from 1996 to 1999, and in 2002, he was elected as CPB vice chair. Cruz is particularly proud of being an integral figure in the airing of two Public Broadcasting Service (PBS) series—*American Family,* the first Mexican-American drama for television, and the children's program *Maya and Miguel.* Cruz is on the board of the James Irvine Foundation, a trustee of USC, and president of Cruz & Associates, a financial consulting firm.

Cruz strives to infuse media programming with balance, perspective, and responsibility to the community. Keen objectivity, innate empathy, and intolerance of inequality have made Cruz an invaluable leader and advocate of social and humanitarian concerns in broadcasting, business, and education.

Further Reading

Gershick, Zsa Zsa. "USC Honors CPBs Frank Cruz." *USC Trojan Family Magazine* (November 11, 1999): 3.

Villar, Arturo. "Diversity." *Hispanic Market Weekly* (October 4, 1999), 3–4.

———. "Frank Cruz Is the New Vice Chairman of the Corporation for Public Broadcasting." *Hispanic Market Weekly,* September 29, 1997, 9.

D

Davidds, Yasmin
(Yasmin Davidds-Garrido)
(1971–) *nonfiction writer*

Yasmin Davidds is one of few Latina authors who writes inspirational books. Her works have reached an international market through her radio show and favorable media attention.

Born on March 10, 1971, in Los Angeles, California, Yasmin Davidds was the second of three daughters of Irma Davila and Kleber Davidds. Her father and mother immigrated to the United States from Ecuador and Mexico, respectively, in 1968. The year Yasmin was born, her father began his entrepreneurial adventures. He quickly achieved financial success. However, the leisure her father's business success afforded the family was accompanied by his oppressive machismo behavior, which allowed him to rationalize extramarital affairs and emotional and physical abuse of his daughters and wife. While Yasmin was in high school, her parents separated. Although her father no longer lived with them, he promised to "command and direct their every move."

Upon graduation from Ramona Convent in 1989, Davidds enrolled in San Diego State University. In 1991, a minor dispute caused Davidds's father to cut all financial funding to his family, despite court decisions. In an emotional act of great courage, Davidds, her sisters, and their mother took Kleber Davidds to court. Defending their rights in the face of mortal fear gave Davidds the strength to build the foundation of her life's work, but within six months she spiraled into the world of drugs. She attended classes at the University of Southern California (USC) in a haze before voluntarily admitting herself into a rehabilitation program in 1994. She graduated from USC in 1995 with a business administration degree specializing in entrepreneurism. Davidds married Norberto Garrido, a professional football player, in 1996. The couple have one daughter, Divina. They divorced in 2002.

After a short time working at Phillip Morris, Davidds returned to San Diego State University to earn a master's degree in women's studies with an emphasis on Latina issues. During her studies, Davidds discovered a cultural misunderstanding and lack of information about how to help Latinas overcome cultural barriers. She dove into her research and gathered enough information for her first book, *Empowering Latinas: Breaking Boundaries, Freeing Lives* (2001), written with the assistance of Patricia Hernandez. This practical book outlines seven principles that promote and strengthen self-love and individual power. Based on the book, Davidds released seven CDs and a workbook entitled *The Latina Principles* in 2002. She launched a radio show, *¡Adelante Mujer!,* on KTNQ with Adriana Yañez in June 2005. *Taking Back Your Power* and *Never the Girl Next Door: 7 Steps to Raising Powerful Women* were released by Simon and Schuster in both English and Spanish in 2006.

Davidds has counseled thousands of young Latino boys and girls, in addition to working as an adviser for Latinas in several junior high schools. She applies her vast resources of energy into serving on various boards and activist committees. Davidds's books speak directly to the needs of Latinas, helping them maintain the beauty of their culture while discovering how to break the shackles that bind them. She specializes in restoring others' self-esteem.

Further Reading

Davidds-Garrido, Yasmin. *Empowering Latinas: Breaking Boundaries, Freeing Lives*. Roseville, Calif.: Penmarin Books, 2001.

Diaz, Katharine A. "Empowering Latinas, Yasmin Davidds' Life Story Inspires Others to Succeed." Available online. URL: http://www.hispaniconline.com/magazine/2003/june/Features/leading-yasmin.html. Downloaded on October 13, 2005.

Mendoza, Sylvia. *The Book of Latina Women: 150 Vidas of Passion, Strength, and Success*. Avon, Mass.: Adams Media, 2004.

de Acosta, Mercedes

(1893–1968) *poet, novelist, playwright, screenwriter*

Mercedes de Acosta's writings were among the first to feature strong female protagonists. She was ahead of her time in presenting characters who held equanimity regardless of the social confines of the day, while her poetry explored realities beyond strict heterosexuality.

Mercedes de Acosta was born on March 1, 1893, the youngest of eight children of Micaela Hernández de Alba y de Alba and Ricardo de Acosta. Her mother had come to America as a teenager to regain her family's fortune, which her uncle had stolen, through the New York supreme court. Her father emigrated from Cuba and met her mother in New York City. The family lived on the avant-garde 47th Street, between Fifth and Sixth Avenues. As a youth, de Acosta enjoyed many celebrations in her family home, where the likes of Theodore Roosevelt, William Vanderbilt, and producer Augustin Daly were entertained. Her sister, Rita Lydig, became a well-known, fashionable socialite. Lydig's personal wardrobe became the nucleus of the Costume Institute at the Metropolitan Museum of Art.

As a young child, Mercedes firmly believed she was a boy. She was raised Roman Catholic and tended toward the extremes. Mercedes played with boys, believing she was just like them, until age seven, when she realized her anatomy differed from her friends'. According to Hugo Victors, author of *Loving Garbo*, de Acosta recalled of that moment, "[E]verything in my young soul turned monstrous and terrible and dark." She was sent to a convent to adopt more feminine ways. She often ran away, claiming she could not be defined as either boy or girl but perhaps as both. This flexibility extended to her spirituality, whereby she proclaimed to have no belief or faith in dogma, but rather is reported as saying, "I believe in taking the essence from all religions and arriving at your own creed." Unfortunately, her confusion often led to bouts of depression.

De Acosta was an intellect who could not or would not be pigeonholed. A forerunner of the feminist movement, de Acosta was notoriously seen in New York City wearing pants, silver-buckled shoes, tricorn hat, and cape. She wore her black hair slicked back with brilliantine (an oily preparation used to make hair glossy), which, combined with her light complexion and thin red lips, inspired Tallulah Bankhead to call her Countess Dracula. In 1920, she married painter Abram Poole, whom she stayed with for 15 years. She wrote scripts for Hollywood, although none of her work made it to the screen. She possessed a deep integrity and would, if necessary, stand up to the biggest powers in Hollywood when their suggestions contradicted her view of a story.

De Acosta expanded her writing to include poetry, plays, and other genres. Collected works of de Acosta include *Moods: Prose Poems* (1919),

Wind Chaff (1920), *Archways of Life* (1921), *Sandro Botticelli* (1923), and *Until the Day Break* (1928). In 1931, de Acosta met Greta Garbo and became immediately infatuated with the intensity for which de Acosta was well known. The two carried on a love affair that reached its end for Garbo long before de Acosta felt complete. De Acosta had become obsessed with Garbo. She placed middle-of-the-night phone calls, clamoring for companionship and the need to discuss the meaning of life and other matters of deep thinking. Garbo ended the relationship with de Acosta, much to the latter's distress.

De Acosta was openly bisexual years before the sexual revolution came to pass. She lived a vivacious life and was a lover of many Hollywood goddesses such as Marlene Dietrich, Alla Nazimova, Isabella Duncan, and Eva Le Gallienne. She was often showered with gifts and letters from her lovers. Many of these letters between de Acosta and her lovers can be viewed at the Rosenbach Museum in Philadelphia. Her autobiography, *Here Lies the Heart* (1960), revealed the intimate relationships she held with the starlets without including vulgar details. However, many of her ex-lovers felt scandalized and refused to speak with her even late in her life.

In the 1960s, she and Andy Warhol became friends. She introduced the young artist's work to many of her well-connected friends. She extensively studied Eastern religions and became a strict vegetarian and follower of Krishnamurti. In the mid-1960s, she became quite ill. She soon became bereft and poor, having sold the last of her jewels to pay for medical expenses. De Acosta died in 1968. Her writings, which have been recently rediscovered, include acknowledgment in *Herencia: The Anthology of Hispanic Literature of the United States*. In this anthology, de Acosta was recognized for the "simple elegance of her literary style and for her perspective on the gay and lesbian arts world of the 20s and 30s." De Acosta pioneered writings for the marginalized that explored taboo subjects with grace and style.

Further Reading

de Acosta, Mercedes. *Women in Turmoil: Six Plays by Mercedes de Acosta.* Edited by Robert A. Schanke. Carbondale: Southern Illinois University Press, 2003.

McLellan, Diana. *The Girls: Sappho Goes to Hollywood.* New York: St. Martin's Griffin, 2001.

Schanke, Robert A. *"That Furious Lesbian": The Story of Mercedes de Acosta.* Carbondale: Southern Illinois University Press, 2003.

de Burgos, Julia
(Julia Constanza Burgos García)
(1914–1953) *poet, educator, journalist, activist*

Julia de Burgos was a forerunner of feminist poetry in Latina literature. She is known for poetry that expresses an elevated consciousness and creates space for the actualization of all human spirits outside of boxes and bars that delineate approved modes of behavior.

Julia Constanza Burgos García was the eldest child of Francisco Burgos Hans and Paula García de Burgos. She was born on February 14 (some reports say February 17), 1914, in Santa Cruz, a small barrio in Carolina, Puerto Rico. Julia gained her adventurous spirit from her father and her love of nature from her mother. She began school at age three, attending a grammar school in Carolina. Later while attending Muñoz Rivera School, she spent her weekdays with a family close to school and the weekends with her own family, often taking walks with her mother along the Río Grande de Loíza. The family moved from the small rural village to the city of Río Piedras when Julia was 14. She attended the University of Puerto Rico High School. The move proved to be a financial burden on the family, and they could not afford her tuition. Even though de Burgos was barred from school, her desire to learn was so great that she often climbed in through classroom windows. In 1931, she completed her high school education.

De Burgos earned her teaching certificate from the University of Puerto Rico in 1933. While at school, de Burgos became acutely aware of Puerto Ricans' struggle for independence. She worked at the Puerto Rico Economic Rehabilitation Agency, an organization that met basic needs of children. In 1934, she married Rubén Rodríguez Beauchamp. She spent the summer of 1935 studying for her bachelor's degree at the university. While there, she joined the leftist group Partido Nacionalista, which advocated independence. She divorced her husband in 1937 and released *Poemas exactos a mí misma* (Exact poems to myself) in a private edition. Her poetry vaulted her into the San Juan literary elite.

The following year de Burgos released *Poema en veinte surcos* (Poem in twenty furrows). That same year, she met Juan Isidro Jiménez-Grullón, who would become the great love of her life. Under the influence of love, she penned *Canción de la verdad sencilla (Song of the Simple Truth)*, which received an award from the Institute of Puerto Rican Literature when it was released in 1939.

In a stand for liberation and self-exile, de Burgos moved to New York City in 1940. She traveled with Jiménez-Grullón to Cuba, where de Burgos met the Chilean poet Pablo Neruda. Her most famous and widely anthologized poem, "Río Grande de Loíza," is a dedication to the untamable love she held for her lover, the spirit of life, and her beloved river. The metaphor of a river plays a major role in much of her work. In 1942, she and her lover parted ways. Deeply wounded by her unrequited love, she fled to New York. She married Armando Marín and worked on and off as a journalist for *Pueblos Hispanos*. De Burgos began a slow descent into alcoholism, during which she wrote very little. Diagnosed with cirrhosis of the liver, she spent time in and out of hospitals. On July 6, 1953, de Burgos collapsed and died on the streets of Harlem. She was taken back to her native land to be buried by the river she had made famous.

Since her death, de Burgos's work has become more widely recognized. *El mar y tú, y otros poe-mas* (1954; The sea and you, and other poems), a posthumous volume published with the assistance of her sister Consuelo de Burgos, deals with her disappointment with love. A compilation of her works, *Obra poética* (Poetic work), was released in 1961. *Roses in the Mirror,* a translation of selected works of de Burgos's poetry, was released in 1992. The English translation of *Song of the Simple Truth* followed in 1995. *Publishers Weekly* found de Burgos "ahead of her time in grasping connections between history, the body, politics, love, self-negation and feminism." Her feminism was a cry for gender equality and releasing restrictive roles and mores put upon both men and women by society.

Further Reading

Benbow-Pfalzgraf, Taryn. *American Women Writers: A Critical Reference Guide from Colonial Times to the Present.* Vol. 1: A–D. 2d ed. Detroit: St. James Press, 2000.

Chassen-López, Francie R. "Motherhood: Marianistas y Supermadres." *Journal of Women's History* 9, no. 1 (Spring 1997): 175–176.

De Burgos, Julia, and Jack Agueros. *Song of the Simple Truth: The Complete Poems of Julia De Burgos.* Willimantic, Conn.: Curbstone Press, 1996.

Kanellos, Nicolás, et al., eds. *Herencia: The Anthology of Hispanic Literature in The United States.* New York: Oxford University Press, 2003, pp. 488–490.

Meier, Matt S., Conchita Franco Serri, and Richard A. Garcia *Notable Latino Americans: A Biographical Dictionary.* Westport, Conn.: Greenwood Press, 1997, pp. 40–42.

de Hoyos, Angela
(1945–   ) *poet, activist*

Encouraged and supported by the Chicano movement, Angela de Hoyos's poetry, which passionately describes the cruelty and injustice of prejudice, has reached international acclaim.

Angela de Hoyos's poetry grew from a need to establish equality for Chicanos and inspired many activists during the Chicano movement. *(Moises Sandoval)*

Born in Coahuila, Mexico, on January 23, 1945 (some sources say 1940), Angela de Hoyos was badly burned by a gas heater at the age of three. During her lengthy convalescence, Angela comforted herself with rhymes and lyrics of her own creation. Her mother encouraged her word play and often read poetry to her daughter. After her recovery, Angela moved with her family to San Antonio, Texas, where she encountered oppression due to her Mexican heritage.

De Hoyos's high school newspaper first published her poetry. Upon graduation, de Hoyos created her own curriculum, attending creative writing courses at the University of Texas–San Antonio, San Antonio College, the Witte Museum, and the San Antonio Art Institute. Her poetry was published in literary journals, garnering international acclaim. She joined the Chicano movement, participating in literary festivals such as the Festival Flo-

ricanto III, Canto al Pueblo, and Sol y Sangre. In 1973, the National Association of Chicano Studies recognized de Hoyos for her contribution to Chicano letters. The following year, she received the Lifetime Achievement Award at the San Antonio Poetry Festival. As a result of the encouragement of Mireya Robles, de Hoyos's mentor, translator, and friend, the poet released *Arise Chicano! and Other Poems* (1975), a poetry collection that inspires and insists that Chicanos reclaim dignity and strength and make their voices heard.

Chicano Poems: For the Barrio (1976) contains 14 poems that concentrate on themes of poverty, racial discrimination, alienation, and loss of cultural traditions. It features the poem "Hermano" (Brother), which uses the fight at the Alamo to spark an awakening in readers that glorifying conquerors and denying or ignoring the original people of the land is terribly biased and inhumane.

De Hoyos's other poetry collections include *Selecciones* (1976), translated by Robles as *Selected Poems* (1979); *Woman, Woman* (1986), which explores the tension within relationships between males and females; and *Linking Roots: Writings by Six Women with Distinct Ethnic Heritages* (1993). Her two works in progress are *Dedicatorias,* a collection of poems dedicated to Chicano writers who have inspired de Hoyos, such as RUDOLFO A. ANAYA and ROLANDO HINOJOSA-SMITH, and *Gata Poems.* With Bryce Milligan and MARY GUERRERO MILLIGAN, de Hoyos coedited *Daughters of the Fifth Sun: A Collection of Latina Fiction and Poetry* (1995) and *Floricanto Sí: A Collection of Latina Poetry* (1998). Both collections include work from such prominent Latina authors as JULIA ALVAREZ and SANDRA CISNEROS and offer powerful insights and perspectives.

De Hoyos is perhaps the best known of Latina poets in Europe. Her poetry has been translated into 15 languages and received awards in Argentina, Germany, Italy, India, and the United States. De Hoyos's writings have appeared in international as well as national journals and publications, textbooks, and anthologies, including *Chicano Perspectives in Literature: A Critical and Annotated Bibliography* and *Latin American Women Writers: Yesterday and Today.* De Hoyos is the publisher and editor of *M & A Editions* and *Huehuetitlan,* a journal of Chicano culture and poetry. A preeminent poet, de Hoyos successfully captures imagery that invokes the unification of varied human experiences.

Further Reading

Aguilar-Henson, Marcela. *Multi-Faceted Poetic World of Angela De Hoyos.* Austin, Tex.: Relampago Press, 1985.

Amorim, Leanna, et al. "Angela de Hoyos." Available online. URL: http://voices.cla.umn.edu/vg/Bios/entries/de_hoyos_angela.html. Downloaded on November 11, 2005.

Milligan, Bryce, Mary Guerrero Milligan, and Angela de Hoyos, eds. *Floricanto Sí: A Collection of Latina Poetry.* New York: Penguin Books, 1998.

Tardiff, Joseph C., and L. Mpho Mabunda, eds. *Dictionary of Hispanic Biography.* Detroit: Gale Research, 1996, pp. 272–274.

Delgado, Abelardo
(Abelardo Barrientos Delgado, Abelardo B. Delgado, Lalo Delgado)
(1931–2004) *autobiographer, novelist, essayist, poet, short story writer, activist, educator*

Abelardo "Lalo" Delgado delivered passionate poetry at the height of the Chicano movement. Due to his prolific literary productivity, thematic versatility, and social commitment, he inspired and serves as a role model for contemporary Chicano poets, becoming known in some literary circles as "el abuelito" (the grandfather).

Son of Vicente Delgado (a rancher and cattleman) and Guadalupe Barrientos, Abelardo Barrientos Delgado was born on November 27, 1931, in La Boquilla de Conchos, Chihuahua, Mexico.

His early childhood years were spent in the cities of Parral and Juárez in northern Chihuahua. He moved to El Paso, Texas, with his family when he was 12. He had difficulty at Aoy Grammar School due to the language barrier. Eventually, he caught up and was promoted through two grades. While at Bowie Junior-Senior High School, he enrolled in college preparation coursework, coedited the school newspaper, and served as vice president of the National Honor Society.

Despite his academic success, Delgado heeded his teachers, who encouraged him to be a laborer, not a writer. After graduating from high school in 1950 at the top of his class, he spent several years working in restaurants and construction. In 1953, he married Dolores Estrada. The couple had eight children. From 1955 to 1964, Delgado worked as a special activities and employment director for Our Lady's Youth Center in El Paso. During the course of inspiring others to seek work and educational opportunities, Delgado decided to pursue a college degree. He enrolled at the University of Texas–El Paso, where he earned a bachelor's degree in secondary education in 1962. He joined the farmworker's movement led by César Chávez in the mid-1960s.

In the late 1960s, Delgado began to chronicle the Chicano experience through poetry. He began his own press, Barrio Publications, in 1969 and that same year released his first book of poetry, *Chicano: Twenty-five Pieces of a Chicano Mind.* This work appeared during the height of the Chicano movement, demanded social reform and equality for Latinos, and defined concepts of Mexican-American culture, such as *chicanismo* (identification with or belonging to Chicano Mexican-American activists), *carnalismo* (brotherhood), and machismo (Latino version of manliness). His poems such as "Stupid America," "La Causa," and "The Organizer" became known through his dramatic oral presentations rather than a vast circulation. He published through his own small press or other local presses, preferring to stay true to his adamant message instead of channeling his work through a larger publishing house that might soften his tone or ideas. Delgado released a collection of essays, *The Chicano Movement: Some Not Too Objective Observations* (1971); coedited and contributed to a collection of poetry with RICARDO SÁNCHEZ called *Los cuatro: Abelardo Delgado, Reymundo "Tigre" Perez, Ricardo Sanchez, Juan Valdez (Magdaleno Avila)—Poemas y reflecciones de cuatro chicanos* (1971; The four—poems and reflections of four Chicanos); and published the chapbook *Mortal Sin Kit* (1973) and the collection of poems *Bajo el sol de Aztlán: Veinticinco soles de Abelardo* (1973; *Under the Sun of Aztlán: Twenty-five Suns of Abelardo*). Delgado attended graduate courses at the University of Texas–El Paso in the early 1970s and at the University of Utah from 1974 to 1977. Throughout the 1970s, Delgado held a number of teaching and human services jobs, with particular focus on the migrant community.

Throughout his social service work, Delgado remained a productive writer. Among his many works are *It's Cold: Fifty-two Cold-Thought Poems of Abelardo* (1974), *A Thermos Bottle Full of Self-Pity: Twenty-five Bottles of Abelardo* (poetry, 1975), *A Quilt of Words: Twenty-five Quilts of Abelardo* (1976), *Seven Abelardos Reflexiones: Sixteen Reflections of Abelardo* (poetry and short stories, 1976), *Here Lies Lalo: Twenty-five Deaths of Abelardo* (poetry, 1977), *Under the Skirt of Lady Justice: Forty-three Skirts of Abelardo* (poetry, 1978), *Siete de Abelardo* (1979, Seven of Abelardo), *Totoncaxihuitl, a Laxative: Twenty-five Laxatives of Abelardo* (poetry and short fiction, 1981), *Letters to Louise* (novel, 1982), *Unos perros con metralla (Some Dogs with a Machine Gun): Twenty-five Dogs of Abelardo* (poetry, 1982), and *La Llorona: Forty-three Lloronas of Abelardo* (1987).

Delgado moved to Colorado in the late 1980s, where he taught at Aims Community College, St. Thomas Seminary, and the University of Colorado. Although his writing extended to a variety of genres, Delgado is best remembered for his poetry, for which he received many honors and awards.

His papers are part of the Nettie Lee Benson Collection in the Latin American Collection of the University of Texas at Austin. Delgado died of liver cancer on July 23, 2004, in Denver, Colorado.

Further Reading

Bruce-Novoa, Juan David. *Chicano Authors: Inquiry by Interview.* Austin: University of Texas Press, 1980.

Delgado, Abelardo. *Living Life on His Own Terms: Poetic Wisdom of Abelardo.* Denver, Colo.: Barrio Publications, 2001.

Johnson, Richard. "Abelardo Delgado: The Don of Chicano Poetry." *Empire: The Denver Post Magazine* (March 3, 1985), 6–9, 15, 19.

del Olmo, Frank
(Frank Phillip del Olmo)
(1948–2004) *journalist, editor*

Undeniably one of the strongest forces to ensure fair and complete representation of Latinos in print journalism in the United States and abroad, Frank del Olmo was an accomplished award-winning journalist and editor who instigated change through his persistence, professionalism, and leadership.

Frank Phillip del Olmo, born on May 18, 1948, was raised on the northeast side of the San Fernando Valley of southern California. His father, Francisco del Olmo, left when he was very young. His mother, Margaret, enlisted the love and support of her family to help raise the small boy. Her brothers-in-law, Joe and Frank, provided the paternal influence, and her sisters, Hope, Juanita, and Ramona, provided additional maternal support. They all worked together to shield Frank from "hoodlums" and other bad influences, including pooling resources to send him to a private Catholic school. His mother, the greatest influence on his life, advocated the need and benefit of a good education. She often read to Frank, but her influence did not stop there. She was a proud Mexican American who taught her son to always have self-respect, not accept insult, reach for his dreams, seek inner courage, and work hard to achieve his goals.

Another source of inspiration and encouragement came from Sister Agnes, Frank's teacher and principal at the Guardian Angel Catholic school in Pacoima. When he was 13 years old, Frank played hooky with his friends. They were caught and received severe punishments. Sister Agnes singled Frank out because he was a leader and "smartest boy in the school." She wistfully added, "If only you knew what you can achieve if you just set your mind to it." She gave Frank the *Boy Scout Manual* to help guide him with practical and philosophical advice. It was a turning point in his life.

When del Olmo graduated from high school, he tried to enlist in the U.S. Air Force. It was the height of the Vietnam War, and he wanted to be an officer and fighter pilot. However, del Olmo wore glasses and, therefore, did not meet the eyesight requirements. The recruiting officer recognized the young del Olmo's brilliance and drive and tried to enlist him in another branch of service, to no avail. Del Olmo wanted to be a pilot, an officer, and a leader, not a follower, and nothing less would do. He left the office and instead accepted a full scholarship to study journalism at the University of California–Los Angeles (UCLA). Two years into the program, UCLA closed its journalism department. Del Olmo was already committed to journalism and sought other programs nearby. He transferred to California State University–Northridge. In 1970, del Olmo, one of six Latinos out of 20,000 students, graduated and was chosen as the outstanding graduate of the entire university.

That summer, he began an internship at the *Los Angeles Times*. Rubén Salazar, well known in the industry as a prolific and unwavering journalist determined to reach Latino readers, mentored del Olmo. Del Olmo received a full scholarship in the master's journalism program at Columbia University as the Chicano movement was gaining momentum. He was preparing to leave for New York when

on August 29, 1970, 20,000 people marched down the streets of Whittier Boulevard in Los Angeles to protest the Vietnam War and the fact that Latinos, who were consistently put on the front lines, were dying in disproportionate numbers. Known as the Chicano Moratorium, the protest began peacefully. When a few demonstrators threw rocks and bottles at police who were responding to a looting at a liquor store, the police retaliated by attacking the entire crowd. A bloody battle ensued, resulting in three deaths. Perhaps the most well-known person killed was Rubén Salazar. The Latino community outcry was enormous. Salazar, a columnist for the *Times* and news director of KMEX, the first broadcast outlet for Latino concerns in the United States, had been covering police brutality,

Los Angeles Times journalist Frank del Olmo was an indomitable driving force who made certain that the concerns of Latino people were addressed in southern California print media. *(© 2005, Los Angeles Times, reprinted with permission)*

and now he was killed under what some labeled as suspicious circumstances. The *Times* found they had no one to cover the pertinent issues at stake— not one out of the thousands of employees spoke Spanish—except del Olmo.

Del Olmo rescinded his scholarship and began work at the *Los Angeles Times* in 1971, determined to carry on Salazar's work and cover the many nuances of the dynamic and vital Chicano civil rights movement. The following year, del Olmo co-led the founding of the California Chicano News Media Association (CCMNA). Del Olmo married Karen King, and in 1975, Valentina was born. Eventually the couple divorced, but del Olmo remained close to his daughter. That same year, he won an Emmy award for writing "The Unwanted," a documentary on illegal immigration. In the late 1970s, del Olmo teamed up with FRANK SOTO-MAYOR to begin a "hire list" of intelligent and motivated Latino journalists for the executives to consider to help increase the number of Latinos in the *Times* newsroom. In 1980, del Olmo became a columnist, dedicated to covering a wide range of Latino concerns and interests, such as bilingual education, immigration, farmworkers, and even pop culture. Often del Olmo wove in the impact of history on contemporary matters, providing a bird's eye view to sensitive issues.

Del Olmo chaired the first national meeting of Latino journalists in 1982. The result was the National Association of Hispanic Journalist, (NAHJ), an organization committed to helping Latinos get jobs as journalists. In 1983, del Olmo, along with Sotomayor, JORGE RAMOS, and a team of Latino journalists envisioned, wrote, edited, and photographed *Latinos in Southern California*. The series, which ran for three weeks and covered 27 stories, won the Pulitzer Prize for meritorious public service.

In 1987, del Olmo accepted the Nieman Fellowship to study journalism at Harvard. In 1991, del Olmo married Magdalena Beltrán. A year later, Frank, or "Frankie," as he is better known, was born. Specialists diagnosed infantile autism when Frankie was two years old. Del Olmo and Magdalena began research to unravel the mystery of autism and its effect on their beloved son. Del Olmo was ready to share Frankie's story in December 1995. He wrote 10 columns that followed the progress of young Frankie and offered a glimpse into the life of a young boy and the man who was proud to call himself his father. Del Olmo was the only journalist of national stature to write regularly about autism for nearly a decade. Del Olmo was named associate editor of the newspaper in 1998, having already been on the masthead as its first Latino since 1989—a major milestone for Latinos. In 2002, del Olmo was inducted into the NAHJ Hall of Fame.

In February 2004, at the age of 55, del Olmo died of a heart attack in his office at the *Times*. It was a heavy blow to journalism, the Latino community, and America as a whole. When he announced del Olmo's death to his newspaper staff, managing editor Dean Baquet said del Olmo was "one of the most beloved and valued members of the *Los Angeles Times* family." Editor John Carroll equally praised del Olmo as someone "known nationally as an accomplished journalist who always had time to help a colleague get a foot on the ladder. The number of Latino journalists who hold good jobs today because of Frank is beyond calculation."

Seven months after his death, Magdalena and Sotomayor selected 90 of the nearly 450 columns written by del Olmo for the *Los Angeles Times*–published book *Frank del Olmo: Commentaries on His Times*. It includes tributes by Gabriel García Márquez, Carlos Fuentes, and Félix Gutiérrez, among others.

During del Olmo's nearly 34-year career at the *Times,* he was an intern, a staff writer, an editorial writer, deputy editor of the editorial page, a Times-Mirror Foundation director, and an assistant to the editor of the *Times*. Del Olmo forever changed the face of the *Los Angeles Times*. His dedication and fortitude made him a giant in journalism; the way he lived his life made him a man of honor and integrity and a bit of a legend.

Further Reading

Beltrán–del Olmo, Magdalena. "A Bittersweet Remembrance of Frank del Olmo." Available online. URL: http://www.cureautismnow.org/home/article/news/4216.jsp. Downloaded on August 3, 2005.

Luther, Claudia. "Times Editor Was a Voice for Latinos." *Los Angeles Times.* February 20, 2004.

Sotomayor, Frank, and Magdalena Beltrán–del Olmo. *Frank del Olmo: Commentaries on His Times.* Los Angeles: Los Angeles Times, 2005.

de Uriarte, Mercedes Lynn
(Mercedes Carolyn de Uriarte)
(1939–) *journalist, educator*

Well respected and honored, Mercedes Lynn de Uriarte is the recipient of many firsts for women and Hispanics in journalism. She is the first Latina journalist to receive an Alicia Patterson Fellowship or a Kellogg Fellowship and has received many honors, including being the highest-ranking Latina in mainstream journalism and journalism education.

Mercedes Carolyn de Uriarte was born in Philadelphia on December 28, 1939, to Frances and Guillermo de Uriarte. Her father, whose family had lived in Mexico since 1838, wanted his daughter to have the opportunity for a bilingual environment and education, so the family moved to Mexico City in the mid-1940s, where de Uriarte attended an American school. Her school days were divided between a curriculum in Spanish from a Mexican perspective and a curriculum in English from an American perspective. This early education conveyed the fact that history is subjective—excellent training for a journalist.

Living simultaneously in two cultures taught Mercedes an appreciation for diversity, yet it also invoked a feeling of division within—she never fully fit into either culture. Books became the bridge, an opportunity to find wholeness. De Uriarte's Hungarian-American mother, read often to the girl from an early age. Reading gave Mercedes her love of writing. She wrote for her school paper and yearned to be a professional writer.

Higher education became a point of dissent in the family. De Uriarte's mother felt college was unnecessary and preached the importance of marrying well to ensure financial security. On the other hand, her father and paternal grandfather stressed how important it was for a woman to be autonomous. She often heard the phrase "Any woman can have a baby—you should do something more with your life."

De Uriarte received a scholarship to the University of Missouri, but the college was deemed too far away by her parents. Frustrated and temporarily thwarted from higher education, de Uriarte married and subsequently had two children, Cristina and John. They lived in 18 different places in 10 years, finally settling in Orange County, California, in 1966. De Uriarte enrolled in Fullerton Community College. She soon divorced and became the sole support for her family. When her grandparents became ill and moved in as well, the real juggling act began. De Uriarte coped daily with discrepancies in financial aid, conflicting demands on her time between wanting to learn and improve her future and the desire to be with her children, and sometimes a lack of support from advisers.

Ever determined, de Uriarte graduated with a B.A. in comparative literature and American studies in 1972 from California State University–Fullerton. Cristina had just graduated from high school and John from junior high school, so the three of them packed a U-Haul truck and headed east to Yale University. De Uriarte had been granted a Ford Foundation Fellowship that paid tuition, a book allowance, and a small stipend. When she arrived in New Haven, Connecticut, de Uriarte found herself the lone Latina pursuing higher education. She earned an M.A. in 1974 from Yale. One of the most trying moments of de Uriarte's life occurred on the second day of her second semester. A drunk driver hit de Uriarte's car, seriously injuring her and John, then 13. The greatest price of her education came when de Uriarte had to leave

John in Mexico with his grandparents for a year so that she could keep her only source of income (her stipend) and attend school (Yale did not provide medical leave), while he rested enough to heal properly. Six years later, de Uriarte graduated with an M.Phil. in American studies, and Cristina, with a B.A.—making them the first mother-daughter team to share a Yale graduation.

De Uriarte then gained a Ph.D. in American studies at Yale University in 1996. She received a Russell Sage fellowship to research her dissertation *Crossed Wires: Newspaper Constructions of Outside "Others"—The Case of Latinos.* She went to observe how the *Los Angeles Times* functioned and how the press constructs foreign and domestic news in ways that perpetuate myths and stereotypes, particularly about Latinos. Because of emerging conflicts in Central America and the fact that she is bilingual and bicultural, the editors offered her a job at the *Los Angeles Times* in 1977. She worked at the paper for almost 10 years as an assistant editor of the opinion section and a staff writer on urban affairs. She was responsible for expanding coverage of Mexico and Central America as well as of U.S. minority communities. She wrote about foreign land investments, immigration, assimilation, and patterns of social and neighborhood change.

From 1979 to 1985, de Uriarte served as a visiting lecturer in Latin-American studies at the University of California–Los Angeles, teaching courses in such subjects as media analysis and the sociology of literature. She taught communications courses at other University of California campuses: San Diego, Riverside, and Santa Barbara.

In 1982, she became the first *Los Angeles Times* journalist awarded an Alicia Patterson Fellowship, which supports travel and writing for a year. She spent most of it in Central America covering revolutionary conflict. She subsequently led a team of journalists for the New York–based Committee to Protect Journalists to document conditions faced by the press as Uruguay moved from a dictatorship to a democracy.

De Uriarte received a 1986 Fulbright appointment to teach feature writing and journalism to both college students and professionals in Lima, Peru. De Uriarte joined the University of Texas faculty in September 1986 as an assistant professor in journalism and Latin-American studies. There, she designed and pioneered two undergraduate skills courses later used as models on campuses across the nation. The first gave nonminority journalism students the opportunity to learn how to cover underrepresented communities. *Journalism Educator* and other publications covered this revolutionary course and called it a remarkable contribution to education.

Students inspired the second breakthrough course in 1989. A group of representatives from 15 University of Texas Latino organizations sought de Uriarte's assistance to have their voices included in campus media coverage. It had come to de Uriarte's attention that minority journalism students had few if any published clips. They often worked to cover college expenses and had little or no time to devote long volunteer hours at the campus press. This disadvantaged them in competitions for scholarships, internships, and jobs. To meet both the need for fair media representation and competitive clips, de Uriarte designed a course on community journalism that produced the news magazine *Tejas,* a publication for diverse experiences and voices. The course was listed in additional fields to encourage other students to consider a press future. The first such publication in the nation produced in a classroom laboratory, *Tejas* received national awards, including the prestigious Robert F. Kennedy Memorial Award for Outstanding Journalism in 1996.

Recipient of 13 grants and fellowships, de Uriarte was a resident research fellow at the Freedom Forum Media Center in New York in 1992 and received the Hogg Foundation grant toward production of a Latino USA radio series on Latino children in 1997. In 2000, she received a Ford Foundation grant to produce the first assessment of the 25-year attempt to integrate U.S. newsrooms. The result, *Diversity Disconnects: From Classroom to Newsroom,* includes an unprecedented profile of intellectual diversity drawn from a representative national survey of 615 journalists.

She has served on 20 consultancies to major foundations, newsrooms, and educational programs on matters related to diversity, including the Ford Foundation advisory committee, Parity Project for PBS, and the fellows selection committee for the Rockefeller Foundation Humanities Fellowship/Guadalupe Cultural Arts Center.

De Uriarte has been selected by several organizations for high honors and awards, including the Communicator of the Year award in 1998 from the Hispanic Link Journalism Foundation for her exceptional role as a mentor. She received an Award for Academic Excellence in Journalism from the National Association of Hispanic Journalists in 2000. In 2004, she was honored with the Trailblazer Award for Career Excellence by Dialog on Diversity.

De Uriarte writes frequently for mass media and academic publications. Her articles and chapters have appeared in numerous anthologies, including *Women Transforming Communications* and *Learning and Knowledge for the Network Society.* She currently teaches interdisciplinary journalism courses cross-listed in Latin-American studies and in American studies, with Latin American and U.S. Latino focus at the University of Texas. De Uriarte's work and tenacity to overcome a variety of obstacles has created a path for generations of minorities to find a voice in journalism, as well as a guiding light to follow.

Further Reading

de Uriarte, Mercedes Lynn. "Strangers among Us: How Latino Immigration Is Transforming America." *The Progressive* (September 1998): 32–38.

———. "Today I Couldn't Get Here from There: A Latina Mother's Journey." In *The Family Track, Keeping Your Faculties While You Mentor, Nurture, Teach, and Serve.* Edited by Diana Hume George and Constance Coiner. Urbana: University of Illinois Press, 1998, pp. 32–39.

Martindale, Carolyn. *Pluralizing Journalism Education: A Multicultural Handbook.* Westport, Conn.: Greenwood Press, 1993.

Rodriguez, Roberto. "Journalism Schools Change Their Standard on Diversity." *Black Issues in Higher Education* (July 24, 1997): 6–10.

De Zavala, Adina
(Adina Emilia De Zavala)
(1861–1955) *folklorist, short story writer, essayist, nonfiction writer, historian*

Adina De Zavala is known for her preservation of the historical documents, legends, and folk narratives of the Alamo in the *History and Legends of the Alamo and Other Missions in and Around San Antonio.*

Born on November 28, 1861, in Harris County, Texas, Adina Emilia De Zavala was the eldest of six children of Augustine, a Mexican-American captain in the Confederate navy, and Julia Tyrrell De Zavala, a patrician, Dublin-born woman. (She and her parents purposely capitalized and used *De* as the beginning of their surname.) As the granddaughter of Lorenzo de Zavala, the first vice president of the provisional government of Texas, De Zavala grew up absorbing Texas history and developing a love for reading and learning. She often created plays with historical themes with her sister.

Home-schooled for the first 10 years of her life, Adina attended Ursuline Academy from 1871 to 1873. She enrolled in Sam Houston Normal Institute at Huntsville, Texas (now Sam Houston State University) in 1879, graduating in 1881. She later attended a school for music in Chillicothe, Missouri. De Zavala taught high school from 1884 to 1886 in Terrell, Texas. She moved to San Antonio in 1887 to be closer to her family and secured a teaching position at an elementary school—a job she maintained until 1907.

Around 1889, De Zavala organized a group of women who discussed and studied Texas heroes.

In 1893, these women became affiliated with the Daughters of the Republic of Texas and were known as the De Zavala Chapter, after Adina's grandfather. De Zavala and her group first turned their attention to the preservation of four missions south of San Antonio and to the Alamo. At this time, grocery firm Hugo and Schmeltzer Company owned the two-story former quarters and offices of the Alamo missionaries, a building known as the Convento. In 1892, De Zavala persuaded Gustav Schmeltzer to grant her historical society first option to buy the Convento.

In 1903, Schmeltzer was prepared to sell the Convento. De Zavala went to ask the owners of the Menger Hotel for financial assistance and instead gained the support of hotel guest Clara Driscoll, daughter of a wealthy oilman, banker, cattle rancher, and commercial developer, also well known for her interest in the Alamo. Driscoll joined the De Zavala Chapter and agreed to help purchase the Alamo structure. After raising sufficient funds, in 1905 the governor of Texas formally conveyed the Alamo property, including the Convento and the mission church, to the Daughters of the Republic of Texas.

Driscoll believed that the mission had the most historical value and was prepared to remove the remaining Convento wall, allowing visitors to enjoy a parklike atmosphere. De Zavala adamantly opposed this plan, believing the long barracks building to be where most of the action in the famous 1836 Battle of the Alamo took place. In February 1908, she barricaded herself for three days in the long barracks in protest of its destruction. Time would prove most of her historical contentions correct. In 1912, the De Zavala Chapter formed the Texas Historical and Landmarks Association. Members of the historical society worked to preserve the Spanish Governors' Palace in San Antonio and marked 28 other historical sites in San Antonio and 10 other sites throughout Texas.

Experts describe De Zavala's work as inestimably valuable to Texas historians. She was a pro-

lific writer on Texan history and author of *History and Legends of the Alamo and Other Missions in and Around San Antonio* (1917), the pamphlets *The Story of the Siege and Fall of the Alamo* (1911) and *The Margil Vine: Legend of the First Christmas at the Alamo,* (1916), and *The Alamo, Where the Last Man Died* (1956). She also contributed to the *Handbook of Texas* (1952).

De Zavala died on March 1, the eve of her revered Texas Independence Day, in 1955. Her dedication to preserving Mexican-American history is honored by a bronze marker placed at the Alamo and the honor of "First Lady of Texas Historic Preservation."

Further Reading

De Zavala, Adina. *History and Legends of the Alamo and Other Missions in and Around San Antonio.* Houston, Tex.: Arte Público Press, 1996.

Hutchingson, Kay Bailey. *American Heroines: The Spirited Women Who Shaped Our Country.* New York: William Morrow, 2004.

Kanellos, Nicolás, et al., eds. *Herencia: The Anthology of Hispanic Literature in the United States.* New York: Oxford University Press, 2003, pp. 176–177.

Williams, Docia Shultz. *The History and Mystery of the Menger Hotel.* Austin: Republic of Texas Press, 2000.

Diaz, Junot
(1968–   ) *short story writer, essayist, anthologist, educator*

Junot Diaz is an electric writer whose short stories in his first book, *Drown,* won remarkable critical acclaim for a debut work.

Junot Diaz was born to Virtudes and Rafael Diaz on December 31, 1968, in Santo Domingo, Dominican Republic. With an older brother and sister and a younger brother and sister, Diaz is the middle of five children. His father left for the United States to support his family while Junot was quite young. Junot spent his early childhood in the barrio known as Villa Juana, and was raised by his mother, grandparents, and aunts. When Junot was six years old, his father returned to the Dominican Republic to gather his family and return to the United States. Despite his family's presence, Junot felt alone and scared during the immigration process. The family moved to central New Jersey, where they had to learn English quickly. No one around them, even immigrants from Puerto Rico, spoke Spanish. Junot's adjustment to his new life was further compounded by the severe disappointment of living with the brutality of his father, with whom he had long dreamed about reuniting but whom he soon learned to fear.

In what he called "a case study in social Darwinism" in a 2005 interview, Diaz was bused to a privileged public high school, which he attended with African-American and Latino kids from his neighborhood. During high school, he washed dishes and delivered pool tables. Upon graduating, Diaz attended Rutgers University, from which he graduated with a B.A. in English in 1992. History also held sway for Diaz; he remains three units shy of being a history major as well. Diaz then enrolled in Cornell University, where he earned an M.F.A. in creative writing in 1995. At Cornell, Diaz became involved in Latino activism.

After college, Diaz spent much of his time writing a novel that he never completed. He soon turned his attention to short stories and found a wellspring of talent and capability. *Drown* (1996) features 10 gritty yet tender stories that are based in both New Jersey and Santo Domingo. Critics lauded Diaz's work as well-crafted, unflinching, and insightful. He received several prestigious awards, including the Pushcart Prize XXII in 1997, the Eugene McDermott Award in 1998, a Guggenheim fellowship in 1999, and the PEN/Malamud Award in 2002. *Newsweek* magazine named him one of the "New Faces of 1996" and praised him as having "the dispassionate eye of a journalist and the tongue of a poet."

Without intending it, much of Diaz's work contains an autobiographical vein. The first-person narration parallels some of the events and situations of Diaz's life, while the complex characters of his work are reminiscent of the people in his life. Diaz's first-person narration of a Dominican's experience in the United States found in *Drown* is frequently associated with PIRI THOMAS's first-person narration of a Puerto Rican's experience in *Down These Mean Streets*. Diaz's writing style makes sparse use of words, an ability he gained from his mother, who was from a region of the southern Dominican Republic where people are known for their few words, or *pocas palabras*.

The success of his first book eventually garnered Diaz the attention of the scholarly world. He was offered a position at Syracuse University, where he taught writing from 1997 to 2002. During this time, he published numerous short stories and essays in periodicals and journals, including four separate volumes of the Best American Short Stories series. He edited the *Beacon Best of 2001: Creative Writing by Women and Men of All Colors and Cultures.* In 2002, he joined the faculty of the Massachusetts Institute of Technology, where he continues to teach writing.

Further Reading

Diaz, Junot. *Drown.* New York: Riverhead Trade, 1997.

Doctorow, E. L., and Katrina Kenison. *The Best American Short Stories, 2000.* New York: Houghton Mifflin, 2000.

West-Durán, Alan. *Latino and Latina Writers, Volume II.* Detroit: Gale-Thomas, 2004, pp. 803–816.

Duron, Ysabel
(1947–   ) *journalist*

Deeply committed to community, award-winning journalist Ysabel Duron has brought a sense of power, pride, and purpose to her 30-plus years in television broadcasting. She has been bestowed with many honors, including America's Top 100

Hispanic Women in Communications by *Hispanic USA Magazine* and an image award from Chicago's Latino Institute.

Born in Salinas, California, on April 14, 1947, Ysabel Duron is one of six children. Her Mexican-American parents, Jesusa "Jessie" Salgado and Eligio Duron, raised their children in an environment committed to education. Ysabel attended private Catholic schools from elementary through high school. Her mother worked nights at the local cannery to pay tuition so that all six of the children would have the education she felt was so vitally important. With education, one had choices. To Duron, education equaled liberation, empowering each person with an opportunity to make better choices in his or her life.

Duron credits her mother for being her role model. Sometimes Ysabel and her siblings would get rowdy, provoking their father to threaten to withdraw them from Catholic school if they did not stop. Nothing could get her mother's attention faster than a threat to her children's education. In these moments, she would remind her husband it was her salary that paid for the children's Catholic education and that he could do nothing about it. Watching her parents' confrontation, Ysabel realized that economic freedom gave people control of their own lives. She also learned that education would assure her a decent job and economic independence.

Duron's mother became involved with the local Mexican church about the time Ysabel was in junior high school. Jessie became the church club president and labored to build a new church. Her mother's hard work and efforts taught Ysabel the value of becoming engaged in community and the pride that comes with taking the lead. Jessie also encouraged her children to read. Every other Saturday she took them to the library to get an armful of books. Through reading Ysabel engaged her imagination. She loved literature. Her other love was travel. When she was 14 years old, she decided she wanted to be a foreign correspondent—that

way she could travel, write, and meet interesting new people.

Duron grew up protected from outright prejudice, though she always felt outside the norm. She was sometimes called a black sheep by a schoolmate for being dark skinned, or *prietita*. At San Jose State University, the difference was even more perceptible. Late in 1968, Duron became pregnant. Believing she was in no position to maintain her dream of becoming a journalist while raising a young child on her own, Duron decided to give her son up for adoption. She told very few people, not even the child's father or many members of her family. She graduated with a B.A. in journalism in the late 1960s, when less than 5 percent of Latinos were going to college. She received a fellowship intended to increase the number of minorities studying journalism at Columbia University in 1970. She was one of only five Latinos in that program, another signal that she was still a rarity.

Duron wanted financial independence; rich and famous sounded good to her. She chose broadcast journalism over print and found the medium suited her temperament. In 1971, she worked as a part-time writer at KRON4 in San Francisco, California. The following year, she served as an intern-reporter at San Francisco's CBS affiliate, KPIX-TV. From 1972 to 1979, Duron worked as an anchor and reporter for KTVU in Oakland, California. In 1974, she won an Emmy Award for her spot news coverage of the Patricia Hearst kidnap story. Duron moved to Boston for a brief time, where she worked at NBC affiliate WBZ-TV as a reporter and weekend anchor. Duron left because of a disagreement over journalism values.

Duron moved back to California to work as a reporter for KCST-TV in San Diego. Her career then moved the ambitious Duron back to California's Bay Area to work at KICU as an anchor and reporter in 1981, helping the independent station to launch its first newscast. Duron produced and reported a four-part news series, *Trouble with Teachers*. This series was honored with a Radio and

Television News Director Association Award and the John Swett Award, the highest award given by the California Teachers Association.

In 1986, Duron joined WMAQ in Chicago, Illinois, where she anchored the *Channel 5 News at Sunrise.* At this station, Duron's dreams of being a foreign correspondent were realized. Several times she reported from Mexico, capturing the stories of Guatemalan refugees pouring into Mexico a year after the 1985 earthquake that shook Guatemala to its roots. She also won an Emmy for her coverage of a horrific shooting spree in a Chicago suburb.

Duron returned to work in San Francisco at KRON4 in 1990 as a general assignment reporter, becoming the *Daybreak* weekend anchor a year later. At KRON, Duron tackled two of her toughest and most personal assignments. *The Child I Never Held,* a series focused on Duron's reunion with the son she had given up for adoption, was honored by the Radio and Television News Director Association. In 1997, Duron was inducted into the National Academy of Television Arts and Sciences "Silver Circle" for 27 years of meritorious work as a journalist. She also received the Living Legacy Award from the Chicana Latina Foundation and the Pioneer Award from the Bay Area's La Raza Media Association. In 1998, Duron's doctor detected a suspicious dark spot that turned out to be a cancer called Hodgkins lymphoma. The disease was caught early. Duron agreed to an aggressive treatment of 12 weeks of chemotherapy, followed by one month of radiation. She suffered from intestinal paralysis that forced her to be hospitalized twice. However, the battle with cancer only made her stronger. In 1999, Duron received an Excellence in Journalism Award from the Northern California Society of Professional Journalists and an honorable mention from the American Women in Radio and Television's Gracie Awards for *Life with Cancer,* a series about her winning battle with cancer.

In 1978 and 1987, Duron was mentioned in *Who's Who of American Women.* Duron is also a

Emmy Award–winning broadcast journalist Ysabel Duron was nominated as one of America's Top 100 Hispanic Women in Communication by *Hispanic USA Magazine. (Courtesy of the author)*

board member of the International Women's Media Foundation, a 1990 fellow of the National Hispana Leadership Institute, and a member of the National Association of Hispanic Journalists. Throughout her impressive journalism career, Duron continues to grow as a leader to serve the community. She helped create the nonprofit agency Las Isabelas in San Jose, California, to provide support services to Latinas with breast cancer. In 2003, owing to her experiences with cancer, Duron started Latinas Contra Cancer, a nonprofit organization, also in San Jose, organized to fill the void around issues of cancer care and education with culturally and linguistically appropriate services for the Latino community. Her work includes service on the Susan G. Komen Breast Cancer Foundation National Latina/Hispana Advisory Council, the grants committee of the Komen San Francisco affiliate, and Roche Pharmaceutical's Latino Cancer Advisory Board.

Further Reading

Díaz-Méndez, Marynieves. *Awareness: Las Isabelas.* Redes Report 4, no. 2 (Summer 2003): 3.

National Television Academy. "NATAS/Norcal Chapter—Silver Circle Member—Ysabel Duron." Available online. URL: http://www.emmysf.tv/duron/duron.html. Downloaded on February 18/26, 2005,

Rico, Yrma. *A Vida Rica, the Latina Guide to Success.* New York: McGraw-Hill, 2004.

E

Engle, Margarita
(Margarita Mondrus)
(1951–) *poet, novelist, short story writer, journalist*

Margarita Engle is best known for her novels *Singing to Cuba* and *Skywriting,* both of which deal frankly with stark realities of the Cuban Revolution.

Born on September 2, 1951, in Pasadena, California, Margarita Mondrus is the youngest daughter of Eloisa Ferrer y Uria and Martin Mondrus. Her mother was a native from the town of Trinidad de Cuba, located on the south-central coast of the island. Pictures featured in *National Geographic* depicting the town's beautiful colonial architecture inspired Martin Mondrus, a painter and native Los Angeleno, to visit Cuba in 1947. During his visit to paint the picturesque architecture, he fell in love with Eloisa, an art student.

Writing grew naturally from Margarita's love of reading. As a young child, she wrote poetry and fables. Her mother encouraged reading and told her that she could be anything she wanted to be. Engle recalled in a 2005 interview, "At the time I was skeptical, due to lack of confidence, but now I believe she is right. We need to stick to the one thing we really love. There is no life more satisfying than one that allows us to work at a job we are passionate about."

Eloisa engaged her children's imaginations by playing Cuban music, retelling family stories, and describing the homeland she missed dearly. The family visited Cuba when Margarita was two and again when she was nine. Margarita adored her relatives and her great-uncle's wild and tropical *finca* (farm) at the foot of the Escambray Mountain. At the end of the last visit, Eloisa, who was still a Cuban citizen, had a difficult time getting an exit visa. They were barely able to get on one of the last commercial flights before the United States and Cuba ended diplomatic relations. Shortly after their visit, her great-uncle was arrested on suspicion of sympathizing with counterrevolutionaries. Mondrus would later write about this experience in her novel *Singing to Cuba.* She recalls, "I have always wondered what my life would be like if we had ended up staying in Cuba. For that reason, I almost feel like I have a secret double, an invisible twin who represents my other self, the one that would have existed if we had stayed in Cuba."

Mondrus attended Washington Irving Junior High School and John Marshall High School in Los Angeles. Her family traveled extensively through Mexico and visited Europe. Despite the fact that the schools forced children to fill out forms declaring one nationality, Mondrus remained loyal to her mixture of Cuban, Ukrainian, and American heritage. As a teenager, she hoped to become a cultural anthropologist like Margaret Mead and visit remote rain forest villages.

Mondrus began studying at the University of California–Berkeley in 1968, a time rife with antiwar protests and civil rights marches. She dropped out of college for a couple of years, during which she lived in San Francisco's Haight-Ashbury district then hitchhiked to New York. She attended Los Angeles City College, where Professor Barbara Joe Hoshizaki helped her discover a love of botany and agriculture. She gained a B.S. from California State Polytechnic University–Pomona in 1974. She served as a teacher's assistant and received an M.S. at Iowa State University–Ames in 1978. In 1979, she married Curtis Engle, with whom she would have two children, Victor and Nicole. From 1982 to 1987, Engle taught agronomy at California State Polytechnic University–Pomona. In the final stages of the Ph.D. program in botany and plant science at the University of California–Riverside, she took a creative writing seminar offered by

Margarita Engle represents a new voice in the burgeoning Cuban-American literature. *(Courtesy of the author)*

Tomás Rivera. Inspired by the possibilities of writing, she resigned her tenured position as an associate professor of agronomy and engaged fully in writing.

Engle's interest in flora and fauna are evident in her writing. She released a book of haiku entitled *Smoketree* in 1983. During the late 1980s and early 1990s, she served as director of an irrigation water conservation program for a resource conservation district near San Diego, California, and published journalistic and scientific pieces. Her short stories appeared in anthologies in the 1990s. Engle's first book, *Singing to Cuba* (1993), was written in response to her great-uncle's arrest in Cuba and the secret war against counterrevolutionary peasants in the mountainous eastern provinces of Cuba during the 1960s. *Skywriting: A Novel of Cuba* (1995) details the journey of a woman who endeavors to save her brother from the horrors of prison life in Cuba. Engle published the poetry chapbooks *Tzintzuntzan* (1984), *In the Garden of Dreams* (2001), *Dreaming Sunlight* (2002), and *Salt: Poems of Peace* (2004). She also cowrote with Sean Qualls a young adult book entitled *The Poet Slave: A Biography of Juan Francisco Manzano* (2006), a biographical novel in verse based on the Cuban poet-slave who lived in the mid-1800s.

Engle's writings challenge repressive political environments and, instead of calling for unity under a single national, political, or ideological banner, seek ways to bond together. She said in a 2006 interview, "We all descend from common ancestors, so dividing ourselves into fractions is destructive. We need to find common ground, not ways to separate ourselves." Her contribution as a second-generation Cuban-American writer and the experience of acculturation and biculturalism is just beginning to be recognized and to receive significant critical attention. Her demand for humanitarian evolution will continue to spark interest and establish her as a prominent figure in Latino literature.

Further Reading

Hospital, Carolina, ed. *Cuban American Writers: Los atrevidos.* Princeton, N.J.: Ediciones Ellas/Linden Lane Press in association with Co/Works, 1988.

Perez-Firmat, Gustavo. *Next Year in Cuba: A Cubano's Coming-of-Age in America.* New York: Anchor Books, 1995.

West-Durán, Alan. *Latino and Latina Writers, Volume II.* Detroit: Gale-Thomas, 2004, pp. 581–590.

Escandón, María Amparo

(1957–   ) *novelist, short story writer, educator, screenwriter*

María Amparo Escandón is best known for *Esperanza's Box of Saints,* her debut book that topped the charts on the *Los Angeles Times's* best-seller list the same day the film based on the book won the Latin American Cinema Award at the Sundance Film Festival. *Esperanza's Box of Saints* is required reading in many Chicano and Latin-American studies departments across the country.

María Amparo Escandón is the eldest child of Julio Escandón and María Amparo Palomino, with all the typical traits, such as independence and responsibility, that come with the position of first born. The impulsive Escandón, born on June 19, 1957, in Mexico City, was taught to "set the example" for her two younger brothers and sister, not necessarily a role fit for such a maverick. She was an active child, always thinking, always in an exquisite world of her own imagination. Escandón's mother was a constant source of support, dealing with her daughter's hyperactivity and wild ideas and guiding her with spunk, determination, amazing strength, and intelligence.

Her parents transferred María among 10 different schools to see which one would fit best with her personality; however, María was expelled from two of them. Nine of the schools were in Mexico City. When she in the seventh grade, her parents sent her to live at a pig farm in Minnesota for the school year to learn English. None of the seven kids or their parents spoke a word of Spanish, so she had to learn fast.

María became a writer at age seven, as she commented in a 2005 interview, "[W]hen I realized that telling stories was a legit way of telling lies." She spent most of her weekends and summers at the family's hacienda, Tecajete, in the state of Hidalgo, Mexico. The hacienda, some 200 acres, was founded in 1834 by Mexican president Manuel González. Escandón's family has owned it since the 1930s. María was most fond of Tecajete's wonderful Catholic chapel and spectacular baroque altar. Most of her family's baptisms, first holy communions, weddings, and funerals have taken place before it. Every weekend, María rode horses, particularly an Arabian horse named Granadina, with her grandfather, José Escandón, who was a quarter horse breeder and president of the Jockey Club in Mexico City for more than 25 years. As a small child, María was afraid of saints, virgins, and Jesus Christ, the latter of whom was often gruesomely depicted in Mexico. However, in time her relationship with saints changed, and they became more like uncles and aunts.

Escandón married in 1979, but the marriage ended in 1981. She attended the Universidad Anáhuac, a Catholic university in Mexico City, and earned a B.A. in communications with a minor in linguistics in 1981. The next year, Escandón met and fell in love with Benito Martínez-Creel. They decided to elope in the United States. They sold their cars and with the money traveled to Los Angeles, California. Together, they opened a Hispanic advertising agency in a borrowed room on the second floor of a run-down theater in downtown Los Angeles: the Teatro Fiesta. Since they had no money and no credit, they also lived there in a tiny room by the projection room. Today, Acento Advertising is one of the largest independent, minority-owned ad agencies on the West Coast. Escandón's immigrant experience is covered in Jorge Ramos's book *The Other Face of America*

In this 2001 photograph, María Amparo Escandón stands before saint and Virgin Mary paraphernalia, a major theme in her best-selling book *Esperanza's Box of Saints*. (© Max Gerber)

in a chapter titled "The American Dream Mexican Style (or María Amparo's Santitos)."

In 1988, Escandón gave birth to a son, Marinés. Her daughter, Iñaki, came the following year. Her love for her daughter sparked her to write *Esperanza's Box of Saints* (1999). *Esperanza* means "hope" in Spanish. As she writes in the back of the book, "What if I was told that my daughter had died and I wasn't able to confirm her death? My immediate answer would be to deny it." The plot of the book is based on Esperanza's desperate search for her daughter, who mysteriously died and disappeared after a routine tonsillectomy. On her journey through Mexico, eventually landing in Los Angeles, Esperanza brings her box of saints and discovers herself along the way. Invoking laughter and a sense of wonderment in the middle of tragedy, Escandón succeeds in making magic palpable and attainable.

When Escandón first began writing *Esperanza's Box of Saints,* she realized her dialogue was too literary, so as an exercise she wrote the screenplay while writing the book. She used her advertising skills and included with the manuscript she sent to New York editors prayer cards, scapularies, and religious paraphernalia that she had picked up during a visit to the shrine of the Virgin of Guadalupe in Mexico City. It worked. She also sent the script to the Sundance Screenwriters Lab and was invited to attend the writer's program. There she met Alejandro Springall. He took the script to John Sayles, who ended up financing the film. The book and the film, which was called *Santitos,* came out simultaneously in January 1999, both enjoying much acclaim.

Escandón attributes the appeal of saints to the need people have to believe and hope. She commented in a 2005 interview, "Changing the world is too large a task to do on one's own. So, we resort to third parties, usually those who are larger than us, and place that responsibility on them. It is the best way to deal with issues beyond our control (illness, war, famine, personal matters involving other people). This is the essence of hope: Placing the future in someone else's hands . . . and praying that the outcome will be the one we wish for." At first, Escandón thought that trusting one's destiny to saints was a Latin American thing because life in the region is so accidental, volatile, ephemeral, and vulnerable. But as her book gained worldwide recognition, being translated into 18 languages, Escandón took the opportunity to visit all the countries where her book was published. In her travels, she discovered that the phenomenon of faith in saints or similar guides is almost universal.

Escandón has worked as an advertising copywriter, a creative director, and a creative writing teacher in a high school in Mexico. She currently teaches creative writing at the University of California–Los Angeles, where she has taught since 1993. Escandón commented in a 2005 interview about her teaching approach, "I always tell my students that we all have a story to tell. Just by living and observing how circumstances affect us and others we have enough material to write not one, but many, stories. But in order to take full advantage of this experience as writers, we must use it in conjunction with the art of expression. We must translate this experience into words that will convey unique meanings to others."

Escandón advocates the fact that language is ever-changing. She enjoys listening to people's stories and experiences in the form of gossip, confessions, and chit-chat. Her newest novel, *González & Daughter Trucking Co.: A Road Novel with Literary License* (2005), is the result of this habit of hers.

Further Reading

Escandón, María. *Esperanza's Box of Saints.* New York: Simon and Schuster, 1999.

Heide, Rick, ed. *Under the Fifth Sun: Latino Literature from California.* Santa Clara and Berkeley, Calif.: Santa Clara University/Heyday Books, 2002.

La Salle Caram, Eve. *Palm Readings: Stories from Southern California.* Austin, Tex.: Plain View Press, 1998.

Ramos, Jorge. *The Other Face of America: Chronicles of the Immigrants Shaping Our Future.* New York: Rayo, 2003.

Santiago, Esmeralda, and Joie Davidow. *Las Mamis: Favorite Latino Authors Remember Their Mothers.* New York: Knopf, 2000.

Espinosa, Maria
(Paula Cronbach, Maria Cronbach)
(1939–   ) *novelist, poet*

Maria Espinosa's writing is valued in Chicano canons for its authentic depiction of issues of identity as a process of unfolding.

She was born Paula Cronbach on a cold snowy night on January 6, 1939, in Boston, Massachusetts. The eldest of three children of Robert Cronbach, a sculptor, and Maxine Silver, a poet, she learned the value of art as a spiritual path and a deep respect for following one's personal muse from her parents. Her mother's ancestors had migrated in the 18th century from Spain to the United States via Brussels, where they were finally able to proclaim their Jewish inheritance. Paula grew up on Long Island with her two younger brothers, Michael and Lee. Her parents set unspoken but strict limitations around what feelings, emotions, or ideas were allowed to be expressed. Although she felt an intuitive, sometimes telepathic connection with her mother, neither close personal relationships nor social skills were bequeathed to her as a child or young adult. Paula felt, as she described it in a 2006 interview, like a "wild child without a mirror or counterpart to share her innermost feelings and insights." She attended Westbury Public School in her early years and at 11 years old transferred to a private school, which she hated. She begged her parents to allow her to attend a different school, but her cries for help fell upon deaf ears. Espinosa attributes this experience to the beginning of a spiral of emotional disturbance that would last for many years.

Cronbach began writing at age 13 and at that time had a vision that this would be her calling, although it clashed with her desires to be an actress, dancer, or singer. She began to write down her emotions and unravel the ideas she had but could not express. In her 20s, Cronbach followed a longtime desire to change her name to Maria, a choice she has stuck by ever since. After high school graduation, she enrolled at Radcliffe (at that time the women's division of Harvard University), where she studied from 1956 to 1958. During this period she experienced a helpless feeling that she was being programmed to lead a life that was not of her choosing and became involved in a series of reckless and self-destructive experiences resulting in her expulsion from college. Cronbach was admitted into a

Maria Espinosa's works have been included in a number of anthologies and periodicals, including *Anthologies of Underground Poetry*. *(Courtesy of the author)*

mental hospital, where she bonded with bright, talented, and sensitive girls who like herself did not fit into the system. She regained a sense of self through friendships and the discipline of dance.

Cronbach returned to school at Columbia University, earning a bachelor's degree in English and French in 1962. She then traveled to Europe, where she met Chilean journalist Mario Espinosa Wellmann. The couple were married the following year, and soon afterward their daughter, Carmen, was born. The marriage was turbulent and lasted only a few years. Espinosa returned to the United States, settling in San Francisco, California, with her daughter. She taught English as a second language for San Francisco Adult Schools from 1968 to 1970.

By her 20s, Espinosa sensed her writing must move beyond therapeutic outpouring and that she must write about her unique sensibility in a different way. Her resolution was to release two books of poetry, *Love Feelings* (1967) and *Night Music* (1969). Throughout the 1970s and 1980s, Espinosa taught a series of workshops on creative writing, visualization, development creative skills, and dream interpretation with Jungian psychologist Josephine Michael. In 1978, she married Walter Selig, a German-born Israeli scientist and refugee from Nazi Germany. That same year, her translation of George Sand's novel *Lélia* was published.

She produced two works of fiction in 1995, *Dark Plums* and *Longing*. *Dark Plums* is an authentic, moving portrayal of a woman's redemption and rediscovery of self after being lost in shallow sexual encounters that stripped her of sanity. *Longing,* a psychological novel that relates the evolutionary development and relationship between two people from different cultures, won an American Book Award from the Before Columbus Foundation. It has been translated into Greek.

Incognito: Journey of a Secret Jew (2002) explores the effects of religious intolerance on people forced to conceal their identity to survive. Her work uncovers the greater truth hidden underneath layers of hypocrisy and pretense. She lends her experiences as a guiding light and gives voice to the unspeakable. She currently teaches English as a second language for City College of San Francisco and is at work on a sixth book, *Dying Unfinished,* in dedication to her mother.

Further Reading

Espinosa, Maria. *Dark Plums*. Houston, Tex.: Arte Publico Press, 1995.

———. "Dying Unfinished." *Tertulia Magazine* 1, no. 3 (January 2004): pp. 6–8.

Peacock, Scot, ed. *Contemporary Authors Autobiography Series.* Vol. 30. Detroit: Thomson Gale, 1999.

Estés, Clarissa Pinkola
(Clarissa Pinkola, Clarissa Reyes)
(1943–   ) *nonfiction writer, essayist, poet, activist*

Clarissa Pinkola Estés created a phenomenon and initiated a spiritual awakening for thousands of readers with the release of her first book, *Women Who Run with the Wolves.* As a Jungian analyst, she was the first writer to explore the lacerations affecting the female psyche through storytelling, myths, fairy tales, and folklore.

On January 27, 1943, Clarissa Reyes was born in northern Indiana to Cepción Ixtiz and Emilio Maria Reyes, both mestizos of Spanish and American Indian descent. (Some reports give a later birth year; however, primarily and most often it is listed as 1943.) Her parents gave her up for adoption when she was very young. When Clarissa was four years old, she was adopted by Maruska Hornyak and Joszef Pinkola, first-generation Hungarians. Clarissa Pinkola grew up surrounded by the rich woodland nature of Michigan. She was often beguiled with many stories from her aunts, four widowed women who left Europe after World War I. She was expected to remember and repeat the stories that she was told. Clarissa came to understand storytelling as medicine and laughter as fortification for life.

Upon high school graduation, Pinkola moved to Colorado, at which time the wolf was quickly disappearing, a fact that inspired her to seek this wild animal. What she found instead was a multitude of stories about the wolf. These stories would later inform and serve as the major foundation for her first book. She married in 1967 and gave birth to three daughters before divorcing her husband in 1974. At the age of 25, Pinkola developed the habit of writing every day, often recording the stories told to her as a child. She deepened her knowledge and wealth of stories when she traveled to Mexico to reunite with her birth family. Her family embraced her lovingly and noticing the spirit of the storyteller—the *cantadora,* or keeper of old stories—in Pinkola, discovered their ancestral stories as well.

In 1971, Pinkola began writing the 100 fairy tales, myths, and psychological commentaries that Pinkola describes as "compris[ing] my work," as she explained to Contemporary Authors Online. "In essence, it is a work that de-pathologizes the innate and instinctual nature, and that asserts that all women are born gifted. Upon beginning a scholarly inquiry, I had found that the central issue was an ages-old reviling of various innate and powerful aspects of the feminine that not only constitute the feminine inheritance, but which are absolutely essential to women's psychic life, and to the strong living of that life in the outer world. Without these aspects, women psychically die."

She earned a B.A. in psychotherapeutics from Loretto Heights College in Denver, Colorado, in 1976. She was awarded her doctorate in philosophy in ethnocultural psychology from the Union Institute in Cincinnati, Ohio, in 1981 and a postdoctoral diploma from the Inter-Regional Society of Jungian Analysts in Zurich, Switzerland, in 1984.

In 1989, Pinkola married a master sergeant in the air force. A few months later, she spoke on the radio about Carl Jung to a receptive audience. Her expertise and warmth caught the attention of Sounds True Recordings, who wanted to record her wisdom. Her audio recordings include *Warming the Stone Child* (1990), *Creative Fire* (1991), *In the House of the Riddle Mother* (1991), and *The Radiant Coat: Myths & Stories about the Crossing Between Life and Death* (1991). She eventually combined her separate recordings into a series entitled the *Jungian Storyteller.* With a proven audience, soon publishers were vying for the right to publish Estés's first book. She trimmed more than 2,500 pages of research and writings to create *Women Who Run with the Wolves: Myths and Stories of the Wild Woman Archetype* (1991).

Within a few weeks, *Women Who Run with the Wolves* captured the imagination and hope of thousands of readers. The book reached the *New York Times* best-seller list and remained there for more than 70 weeks. In her book, considered a must-read for those on a spiritual path, Estés retells stories and myths of Inuit, Asian, European, Mexican, and Greek traditions using pictorial language to underlie and reinforce the healing power and potential of women. However, the wisdom is not held singularly by women. This sagacious understanding can also be felt and shared by men in touch with their feminine nature. Estés uses the archetype of the wolf to help women get in touch with their wild nature and natural instincts. She writes that women must embrace "wolf rules for life: eat, rest, rove in between; render loyalty; love the children; cavil in moonlight; tune your ears; attend to the bones; make love; howl often."

Estés followed her highly successful first book with *The Gift of Story: A Wise Tale about What Is Enough* (1993); *The Faithful Gardener: A Wise Tale about That Which Can Never Die* (1995); an excerpt called "Guadalupe: The Path of the Broken Heart," published in *Goddess of the Americas/ La diosa de las Américas: Writings on the Virgin of Guadalupe* and edited by Ana Castillo (1996); and the essay "Healing from Terrorism Sickness," originally posted at The Shalom Center Web site (www.shalomctr.org). Building on the strength and success of her audio recordings, Estés also recorded *The Gift of the Story* (1993); *How to Love a Woman* (1993); *Theatre of Imagination, Volumes 1 and 2* (1995); *Voices of Wisdom* (2000); *Bedtime Stories* (2003), *The Beginner's Guide to Dream Interpretation* (2003); and *Intuition and the Mystical Life* (2003).

Estés is the recipient of a Rocky Mountain Woman's Institute fellowship and grant (1990), for *Las Brujas* (a work in progress); a Las Primeras award (1993), MANA, National Latina Foundation (Washington, D.C.), for lifetime social activism and literature; a Book of the Year Honor Award, American Booksellers Association and the Colorado Authors League Award both in 1993 for *Women Who Run with the Wolves: Myths and Stories of the Wild Woman Archetype;* and the Joseph Campbell Keepers of the Lore Award, Joseph Campbell Festival of Myth, Folklore, and Story (1994).

Estés is a social activist, speaker, author, and performance poet, profoundly and steadfastly dedicated to uplifting the female archetype. Despite the sorrow that she empathically feels, she is driven to replenish hope and light in the world. Estés summarizes her drive with the German word *Schmerzenreich,* which means "rich in sorrow" or "ability to bear sorrow," or the Hebrew *tikkun olam,* which represents the moral duty to help repair the world soul on a daily basis.

Further Reading

Castillo, Ana. *Goddess of the Americas: La diosa de las Américas: Writings on the Virgin of Guadalupe.* New York: Riverhead Books, 1996.

Estés, Clarissa Pinkola. *Women Who Run with the Wolves: Myths and Stories of the Wild Woman Archetype.* New York: Ballantine, 1992.

Mendoza, Sylvia. *The Book of Latina Women: 150 Vidas of Passion, Strength, and Success.* Avon, Mass.: Adams Media, 2004.

Telgen, Diane, and Jim Kamp. *Notable Hispanic American Women.* Detroit: Thompson Gale, 1993.

F

Fornes, Maria Irene
(1930–) *playwright, director, educator*

A prolific playwright, Maria Irene Fornes is a pioneering force and influence in American theater. With 45 years of experience as a playwright, Fornes has amassed awards and honors, including nine Obies for her sensitive, experimental plays.

Daughter of Carlos Luis and Carmen Hismenia Fornés, Maria Irene Fornes was born in Havana, Cuba, on May 14, 1930. Following her father's sudden death in 1945, she immigrated with her mother and her sister to the United States. Maria spoke only Spanish when she arrived in Manhattan. As a teenager, Maria attended a Catholic school in New York but left school before graduating to work at a variety of unskilled jobs. Fornes then trained with the painter Hans Hoffman in New York City's Greenwich Village. On the advice of a friend, in 1954 she moved to Paris, where she spent three years pursuing her painting studies. She became intrigued by performance art after she saw the original Roger Blin production of Samuel Beckett's *En attendant Godot (Waiting for Godot).*

Returning to Greenwich Village in 1957, Fornes worked as a self-employed textile designer creating scarves and selling them on commission. She saw Burgess Meredith's 1958 New York production of *Ulysses in Nighttown* (adapted by Marjorie Barkentin from James Joyce's *Ulysses* with Zero Mostel as Leopold Bloom), which, in combination with the Paris experience of seeing *Godot,* secured Fornes's imagination and dedication to write. Over the next 19 days, she became completely immersed in writing what would become the absurdist *Tango Palace* (1964). Written in English, like the majority of her work, initially it was staged by the Actors Workshop in San Francisco and directed by Herbert Blau. However, her first produced play was *La viuda/The Widow* in 1961.

During the 1960s, Fornes became an established member of the avant-garde Greenwich Village artistic community. Supported by fellow forward-thinking artists, Fornes wrote *The Successful Life of 3* (1965), *Promenade* (1965), *The Office* (1966), *A Vietnamese Wedding* (1967), *The Annunciation* (1967), *Dr. Kheal* (1968), *The Red Light Burning* (1968), and *Molly's Dream* (1968). Known for her stylistically innovative work, she received the 1962 John Hay Whitney Foundation Award, a 1962–63 Centro Mexicano de Escritores residency, a 1965 Obie for Distinguished Plays *(Promenade* and *The Successful Life of 3),* a 1967 Cintas Foundation fellowship, Yale University fellowships in 1967 and 1968, and a Boston University Tanglewood fellowship. At this time, Fornes also became well established as an important participant at the annual summertime Padua Hills Playwrights Festivals in Claremont, California.

In 1972, Fornes created the New York Theatre Strategy with Ed Bullins, Rosalyn Drexler, Adrienne Kennedy, Rochelle Owens, Sam Shepard, and Megan Terry. This space afforded playwrights opportunities to test out their ideas and have control over their work. Although Fornes spent considerable time and energy on the administration of this project, she was able to write *The Course of the Langston House* (1972), *Aurora* (1974), *Cap-a-pie* (1975), *Washing* (1976), *Fefu and Her Friends* (1977), *Lolita in the Garden* (1977), *In Service* (1978), and *Eyes on the Harem* (1979). During the 1970s, she received a Guggenheim fellowship, two Creative Artist Public Service grants, a National Endowment for the Arts grant, and two Obies, one for playwriting *(Fefu and Her Friends* and the other for directing *(Eyes on the Harem). Fefu and Her Friends* was published in 1980 and is recognized as an innovative and important American play. It is one of Fornes most frequently produced works. During the 1970s, Fornes began teaching at INTAR (International Arts Relations), Hispanic American Arts Center, in New York City.

Fornes continued to write and direct many of her own plays throughout the 1980s and 1990s. Her works from this time include *Evelyn Brown (A Diary)* (1980), *A Visit* (1981), *The Danube* (1981), *Mud* (1983), *Sarita* (1984), *No Time* (1984), *Drowning* (1985), *The Conduct of Life* (1986), *Lovers and Keepers* (1986), *A Matter of Faith* (1986), *The Mothers* (1986), *Art (Box Plays)* (1986), *Abingdon Square* (1987), *Hunger* (1988), *And What of the Night?* (1988), *Oscar and Bertha* (1991), *Terra Incognita* (1991), *Springtime, Enter the Night* (1993), *Ibsen and the Actress* (1995), *Manual for a Desperate Crossing* (1996), *Balseros/Rafters* (1996), *The Summer in Gossensass* (1997), and *The Audition* (1998). Even though the mainstream audience knew little of Fornes's work, theater critics, professionals, and scholars praised the playwright's allegorical style and her tender and imaginative use of relationships to connote the play's meaning and message. She received several awards and honors, including a 1982 Obie for sustained achievement; a 1984 Obie for direction for *The Danube, Sarita,*

and *Mud;* a 1985 Obie for best new American play for *The Conduct of Life;* an Academy Award from the American Academy and Institute of Arts and Letters; a 1988 Obie for best new American play for *Abingdon Square;* and a 1990 New York State Governor's Arts Award.

In 2000, Fornes was awarded an Obie Special Citation for her most recent play, *Letters from Cuba.* Three years later, she was the first recipient of the Mujeres (Women) Advancing, Culture, History and Art/MACHA Award for outstanding achievement in mentoring emerging Latina writers. Some of Fornes's papers are collected in the Lincoln Center Library of the Performing Arts in New York. Fornes has written more than 40 plays that provoke the audience to ascertain a personal lesson or insight. Fornes's characters often possess an innocence and satirical humor in an absurd world. Her close attention to aesthetics forged her popularity. The visual impact of her plays is characterized by simple elegance—an understated yet highly individualized style. Her art is neither moralistic nor static but constantly evolving, providing audiences with entertainment as well as the opportunity to reinvent themselves.

Further Reading

Betsko, Kathleen, and Rachel Koenig. *Interviews with Contemporary Women Playwrights.* New York: Beech Tree Books/Quill, 1987.

Cortés, Eladio, and Mirta Barrea-Maryls, eds. *Encyclopedia of Latin American Theatre.* Westport, Conn.: Greenwood Press, 2003.

Delgado, Maria M., and Caridad Svich, eds. *Conducting a Life: Reflections on the Theatre of Maria Irene Fornés.* Lyme, N.H.: Smith & Kraus, 1999.

Rabillard, Sheila. "Crossing Cultures and Kinds: Maria Irene Fornés and the Performance of a Post-Modern Sublime." *Journal of American Drama and Theatre* 9, no. 1 (Spring 1997): pp. 33–43.

G

Galarza, Ernesto
(Ernest Galarza)
(1905–1984) *poet, autobiographer, children's book writer, activist, educator*

Ernesto Galarza was a renowned union leader, poet, storyteller, educator, and activist whose indefatigable battles for farmworkers' rights and the preservation of Mexican culture stressed the value Americans need to place on humanity. Of his many works, his best known book is *Barrio Boy* (1971), a fictionalized autobiography.

The son of Ernesto and Henriqueta Galarza, Ernesto Galarza was born on August 7 (some reports say August 15), 1905. Just prior to his birth, Galarza's mother left his father to live with her family in the mountainous village of Jalcocotán, Mexico. Young Ernesto spent his early years in this small village, whose inhabitants claimed heritage from the Huichol Indians who had escaped enslavement by the Spaniards centuries before. The violence and corruption of the imminent Mexican Revolution caused people to either fight against the government or leave the country. Ernesto, his mother, and two maternal uncles fled north, traveling through northern Mexico and the American Southwest before finally settling in Sacramento, California.

With the aid of an Italian huckster, Ernesto learned English quickly. His mother and one uncle died during the influenza epidemic in 1917. Galarza completed his high school education while working in a number of occupations. His assiduous dedication to gaining an education earned him a scholarship to Occidental College in Los Angeles, California. The only Mexican-American student in his graduating class, Galarza earned a B.A. in Latin-American studies from the school in 1927 and qualified for Phi Beta Kappa. He went on to graduate school, and while studying, his first book, *The Roman Catholic Church as a Factor in the Political and Social History of Mexico,* was published in 1928. He earned an M.A. in science and history from Stanford University in 1929.

He met his future wife, Mae Taylor, while at Stanford. After graduation, the couple married in December 1928 and soon moved to New York, where Galarza entered the doctoral program at Columbia. Together they introduced a kinesthetic approach to teaching while serving as coprincipals in a Long Island school district from 1932 to 1936. During this time, he wrote his first collection of poetry, *Thirty Poems* (1935). Galarza became involved with labor issues when he accepted a research associate position and later served as the director of labor and social information at the Pan American Union (PAU), now known as the Organization of American States. He remained with the PAU for 11 years, traveling extensively and researching labor and social conditions—particularly related to the Bolivian tin miners' strike and the Mexican bracero program. He wrote numerous pamphlets, most of the Latin America for Young Readers series, and the book *Labor Trends and Social Welfare in Latin America*. Galarza earned a Ph.D. from Columbia University in 1944, delayed in large part due to his political activism on behalf of farmworkers. He left the PAU in 1947, asserting that the U.S. government and the PAU tolerated exploitative practices.

Galarza, his wife, and their two daughters then moved to San Jose, California, where he served as director of research and education with the Southern Tenant Farmer's Union (STFU), which had recently become the American Federation of Labor's (AFL) National Farm Labor Union (NFLU). Galarza was involved with approximately 20 unsuccessful strikes in the West and Southwest. He accepted a grant to document the effects of the bracero program and Public Law 78. His findings were published in *Strangers in Our Fields* (1956). The book was well received, but even more important to Galarza, it succeeded in bringing the atrocities faced by American and Mexican farmworkers to the attention of the U.S. government's top officials. Galarza continued to send a barrage of articles about labor issues to newspapers, using his pen as a most effective sword.

Galarza left the AFL in 1959 and took on a number of jobs in support of the labor union. He recorded the tragic 1963 accident that killed 32 braceros near Chualar, California, in *Tragedy at Chualar: El crucero a las treinta y dos cruces/ The Thirty-Two Cross Crossing* (1963) and the self-published *Merchants of Labor* (1964), a history of the bracero program. *Merchants of Labor* not only sold out; it also assisted in the demise of Public Law 78, thereby contributing to the success of the historic Delano Grape Strike headed by César Chávez.

During the 1960s Chicano movement, Galarza accepted several teaching appointments at various institutions, including the University of Notre Dame, University of California–San Diego, and Harvard University. He also served on several boards, including the Ford Foundation and the Mexican-American Legal Defense and Educational Fund. He released *Mexican-American in the Southwest* (1969), *Spiders in the House and Workers in the Field* (1970), *Barrio Boy* (1971), and *Farm Workers and Agri-Business in California, 1947–1960* (1977). *Barrio Boy* chronicles his life with colorful, albeit perhaps exaggerated, memories from his childhood. Galarza admitted in an epigraph that precedes the text that "the actual journey may have been quite different," yet it is his contention that "[t]he memory [is] all that matter[s]." Critics hailed *Barrio Boy* as an epic of a Chicano family.

Galarza then turned his efforts back to education and children. He penned 11 children's books, five of which were poetry, among them *Zoo-risa/ Zoo Laughter* (1968), *Poemas párvulos/Short Poems for Youngsters* (1971), *Más poemas párvulos/More Short Poems for Youngsters*. Much of his works loosely translated the Mother Goose tales in an effort to capture the imagination of childhood and the lyricism of Mexican culture but were typically not constrained to a direct translation. He became affectionately known as the Father Goose for Mexican children.

Galarza died on June 22, 1984. He left behind the legacy of a man with great integrity whose impact on literature, social reform, and farmworkers continues to enrich and inspire innumerable lives.

Further Reading

Heide, Rick, ed. *Under the Fifth Sun: Latino Literature from California*. Santa Clara and Berkeley, Calif.: Santa Clara University/Heyday Books, 2002.

Kanellos, Nicolás, et al., eds. *Herencia: The Anthology of Hispanic Literature in the United States*. New York: Oxford University Press, 2003, pp. 465–469.

Meier, Matt S., Conchita Franco Serri, and Richard A. Garcia, eds. *Notable Latino Americans: A Biographical Dictionary*. Westport, Conn.: Greenwood Press, 1997, pp. 159–161.

Tardiff, Joseph C., and L. Mpho Mabunda, eds. *Dictionary of Hispanic Biography*. Detroit: Gale Research, 1996, pp. 357–359.

García, Cristina
(1958–   ) *novelist, journalist, educator*

Cristina García has been hailed as one of the most important Cuban-American voices in U.S. literature. Critics highly acclaimed García's debut novel, *Dreaming in Cuban,* comparing her work to literary giants such as Gabriel García Márquez and thereby securing her position as an exemplary literary figure for years to come.

The daughter of Esperanza Lois and Francisco M. García, Cristina García was born in Havana, Cuba, on July 4, 1958. Her father, a cattle rancher, moved the family in 1960 when Fidel Castro's power grew so immense he was confiscating personal property. The García family joined relatives in the Brooklyn Heights neighborhood of New York City, entering the restaurant business. When Cristina was a child, the family would regale her with stories of the homeland, instilling a sense of love and pride for Cuba and its culture in her. Cristina attended Catholic schools in her early years, and through her preteen and teen years, she attended the Dominican Academy in Manhattan. She then began studying political science at Barnard College at Columbia University. While at Barnard, until her graduation in 1979, García worked in her parents' restaurant and tutored younger students. She discovered a love of literature in an undergraduate class. García intended to join the foreign services when she enrolled in the School of Advanced International Studies at Johns Hopkins University. She worked part time as a copy girl for the *New York Times,* spent a year in Italy, and in 1981 earned an M.A. in European and Latin-American studies.

Upon graduating, García lived in West Germany for three months, working at Proctor and Gamble in a marketing position. From 1980 to 1983, she honed her journalism skills as a reporter intern at the *Boston Globe,* a reporter for United Press International, a reporter and arts critic for the *Knoxville Journal* in Tennessee, and a news assistant for the *New York Times.* She covered a variety of topics, including medicine, environment, business law, and technology. She served as a national correspondent for *Time* magazine from 1983 to 1990. Her work at *Time* took her to San Francisco, Miami, Los Angeles, and New York City. The longing to write a novel tugged at García until in 1990 she left *Time* to write fiction full time. García married Scott Brown in 1990.

In 1992, García gave birth to her daughter, Pilar, and released her first novel, *Dreaming in Cuban,* a finalist for the National Book Award. *Dreaming in Cuban,* which received unprecedented critical acclaim for a debut work, seamlessly weaves together three generations of women of the Del Pino family to explore the many facets and diametrically opposed emotional range rampant within Cuban exiles and their descendants. Haunted by feelings of longing, unfulfillment, and abandonment, her characters seek to absolve themselves through national identity. Only in the end does Pilar, the youngest of the Del Pino women, realize that homeostasis and peace can only be found when she equally acknowledges and forges her Cuban ethnicity and American upbringing into one being. Pilar's awakening seems autobiographical in nature when compared to García's life.

As a result of the critical response to *Dreaming in Cuban,* García received the Whiting Writers Award as well as Hotter, Cantos, and Guggenheim Foundation fellowships. An excerpt of her book was included in *Iguana Dreams* (1992), an anthology. That same year, she was invited to become a creative writing teacher for the University of California–Los Angeles Extension Program. She taught similar courses and English at the College of Creative Studies at the University of California–Santa Barbara and at the University of Southern California.

García released her second novel, *The Agüero Sisters,* in 1997. This young adult novel brings to life the entangled intimacies between two sisters, Reyna and Constancia, who have not spoken in 30 years. The sisters became estranged when Constancia left Cuba to completely immerse herself in American culture. The sisters' reunion is forged by the need to uncover the truth about their childhood and is assisted by the voice of their father. Critics admired García's evocative depictions of exile and homeland but did not find her second book as praiseworthy as her debut work.

García edited an anthology of works by Cuban writers called *¡CUBANÍSIMO! The Vintage Book of Contemporary Cuban Literature* in 2003. Divided into five sections named for Cuban dance styles, the book includes stories, essays, poems, and novel excerpts. The same year, García released her third novel, *Monkey Hunting,* which explores five generations and journeys through three countries. In this book, García reveals the effects of family dynamics on the individual and the plight of Chinese Cubans. She offered a foreword for *Cuba: Mi amor* (2003), a photography book featuring the work of Xavier Zimbardo that captures the exquisite beauty of her native country. She released *A Handbook to Luck* in 2007. García has found a large audience because her writing addresses the need to explore, accept, and celebrate the multicultural texture of all Americans.

Further Reading

Gomez-Vega, Ibis. "The Journey Home: Defining Identity in Cristina García's *Dreaming in Cuban.*" *Voces: A Journal of Chicana/Latina Studies* 1, no. 2 (Summer 1997): 71–100.

Kanellos, Nicolás, et al., eds. *Herencia: The Anthology of Hispanic Literature in the United States.* New York: Oxford University Press, 2003, pp. 503–508.

Meier, Matt S., Conchita Franco Serri, and Richard A. Garcia, eds. *Notable Latino Americans: A Biographical Dictionary.* Westport, Conn.: Greenwood Press, 1997, pp. 165–167.

Poey, Delia. *Iguana Dreams: New Latino Fiction.* New York: Perennial, 1992.

García-Aguilera, Carolina
(1949–   ) *novelist*

Carolina García-Aguilera is best known for her six-book mystery series featuring the smart and sexy Lupe Solano, a private investigator from Miami, Florida. Born in Havana, Cuba, on July 13, 1949, Carolina García-Aguilera is the second child of Lourdes Aguilera and Carlos García. Her early years were rather idyllic, and she spent her days fishing, horseback riding, and playing in the neighborhood or on team sports. In the late 1950s, Fidel Castro came to power, and the whole of Cuba changed. In December 1959, while Carolina ate lunch with her fifth-grade class, she was abruptly taken from everything she knew and understood and put on a plane bound for the United States. She lived for nine months in a convent in Palm Beach, Florida, with her older sister until her parents and younger brother could join them. They settled in New York City, where Carolina grew up.

Carolina read a lot of Sherlock Holmes as a child. She was drawn to the fact that in detective stories there was always justice and a tidy ending— "the bad guy always got his," she concluded in a 2005 interview. She dreamed about being an archaeologist until math became an obstacle. Carolina then focused on history, English, and creative writing. She attended Miss Porter's School in Connecticut for four years. In the late 1960s, she moved to Florida and attended Rollins College, graduating with a dual degree in history and political science. García-Aguilera married and traveled throughout Asia from 1973 to 1981 with her husband, living in Hong Kong, Tokyo, and Beijing. During this period, she gave birth to two daughters, Sarah and Antonia.

Upon her return to the United States, García-Aguilera attended the University of South Florida, graduating in 1983 with an M.B.A. in finance. García-Aguilera then divorced her husband and moved to Miami to be close to her brother and sister. She worked in the special services department of Jackson Memorial Hospital for two years and began studying at the University of Miami for a Ph.D. in Latin-American affairs. She remarried and had another daughter, Gabriella.

García-Aguilera took a job at a private investigator agency to research her first novel in 1986. She discovered she was good at the work, enjoying the research and assembling of clues. She worked as a private detective for 10 years before she decided the time had come to write a book. García-Aguilera made her literary debut with *Bloody Waters* in 1996, featuring Lupe Solano, a sassy private investigator who is devoted to Cuba, family, and her Catholic convictions. Solano has the best wardrobe in town, carries her gun in a Chanel bag, and possesses a willingness to use sex to get what she wants. She is as honest as the day is long and a self-proclaimed CAP (Cuban-American princess). In *Bloody Waters,* Lupe is asked to track down the birth mother of the Morenos's adopted daughter for an immediate bone marrow transplant. Through the plot, García-Aguilera reveals the history of the Cuban mass exodus and the impact of Castro's dictatorship on Cuban-American exiles. *Bloody Shame* followed as García-Aguilera's second novel in the series in 1997. Lupe Solano investigates a suspicious car accident that killed her childhood friend while helping her sometimes lover in a case of his own. Politics returned with the release of *Bloody Secrets* in 1998. The heroine tackles a case involving a raft refugee from Cuba who claims a wealthy Cuban couple has hired someone to kill him. García-Aguilera takes a new approach with *Miracle in Paradise* (1999). In this volume, Lupe Solano investigates the miracle of the Virgin at Ermita de la Caridad who is prophesied to shed tears on Cuba's Independence Day, October 10. The suspense returns in *Havana Heat* (2000), in which Lupe Solano hunts down a highly sought-after tapestry believed to have been a present to Queen Isabella. In *Bitter Sugar* (2001), Lupe Solano unravels the mystery surrounding financial interests in her father's friend's sugar plantation, which had been confiscated by Castro.

García-Aguilera breaks from the Lupe Solano series in *One Hot Summer,* published in 2002, to follow Margarita Maria Santos Silva and her confused yet wildly comical deliberation over whether to return to work or remain at home with her son. *Luck of the Draw,* another mystery thriller, released

in 2004, introduces Esmeralda Navarro, who must find her missing sister who has disappeared in Las Vegas, Nevada.

The Lupe Solano series, which has won Flamingo and Shamus Awards, is under option to DePasse Entertainment, and a screenplay is underway. García-Aguilera entertains with a good story as she reveals the politics in Cuba and the loves and fears of Cuban-American exiles.

Further Reading
García-Aguilera, Carolina. *Bloody Waters: A Lupe Solano Mystery.* New York: Berkley Publishing Group, 1997.

———. *One Hot Summer.* New York: Rayo, 2003.

Sutton, Molly, Sara Mozayen, and Nubia Esparza. "Carolina García-Aguilera." Available online. URL: http://voices.cla.umn.edu/vg/Bios/entries/garcia-aguilera_carolina.html. Downloaded on May 2, 2006.

Wilkens, Mary Frances. "García-Aguilera, Carolina. *Luck of the Draw.* Book review." *Booklist,* (May 1, 2003), p. 1,544.

Gaspar de Alba, Alicia
(1958–) *poet, novelist, short story writer, essayist, educator*

Proficient in the world of academia as well as art criticism and prose in both long and short forms, Alicia Gaspar de Alba originally found critical acclaim with her poetry. Alicia Gaspar de Alba was born in El Paso, Texas, on July 29, 1958. El Paso is situated across the Rio Grande from the Mexican city of Juárez. The two cities, El Paso and Juárez, although polar opposites in many ways, began to coalesce and merge customs during Gaspar de Alba's childhood. This long and painful process of creating a border culture came at a heavy price. Her parents had unwillingly left Mexico for the United States and resisted their new country's traditions and language. She was forbidden to speak English at home and beaten for speaking Spanish at the Catholic school she attended. She found it difficult and lonely to live in the undefined space between the worlds. She was the first of her family born in the United States and the first among fellow Mexican Americans to live in the Anglo-American section of town. Eventually, she would find a voice for the confusion she felt as a Mexican-American hybrid in her writings.

In the late 1970s, Gaspar de Alba attended fiction classes taught by James Ragan at the University of Texas–El Paso. Professor Ragan validated Gaspar de Alba's Mexican-American inheritance and the need to write about it. Gaspar de Alba was awarded the Ford Foundation fellowship for minorities offered by the National Research Council in 1979. She began teaching English as a second language to Mexican executives and other staff members of the General Motors maquiladoras at the Instituto Interlingua in Juárez, Mexico. She

Alicia Gaspar de Alba is a poet, professor, and novelist whose works defy antiquated traditions and mores, particularly those related to homosexuality. *(Photo of Alicia Gaspar de Alba is reprinted with permission from the publisher [APP Archive Files] [Houston: Arte Público Press—University of Houston, © 2006])*

also worked as a teacher's assistant in the English department at the University of Texas–El Paso. She earned a B.A. in English in 1980, magna cum laude, and an M.A. in English with a creative writing concentration in 1983 from the University of Texas–El Paso. She wrote the poem "Beggar on the Córdoba Bridge" as her master's thesis. The poem brought her notoriety and critical acclaim when published later in *Three Times a Woman: Chicana Poetry,* an anthology she coedited with María Herrera-Sobek and Demetria Martínez in 1989.

Her poems were anthologized in a variety of publications, including *Revista Chicano Riqueña, Imagine: International Chicano Poetry Journal,* and *Iowa Journal of Literary Studies.* Her short stories in Spanish appeared in the 1984 and 1985 editions of *Palabra nueva: Cuentos chicanas* (New word: Chicano stories). Gaspar de Alba won a CIC Minorities Fellowship and began pursuing her doctorate in American studies at the University of Iowa in 1985 but left the program after one year due to culture shock. She won the Massachusetts Artist's Fellowship in poetry for "Beggar" and moved to Boston, where she worked for the National Braille Press, translating children's books into Braille from 1986 to 1990.

Gaspar de Alba returned to the Southwest in the early 1990s. She wrote *The Mystery of Survival and Other Stories* (1993), which explores the boundaries between sexes, lovers, cultures, generations, and beliefs. She enrolled in the University of New Mexico–Albuquerque, earning a Ph.D. with distinction in 1994. Her dissertation, entitled "Mi Casa [No] Es Su Casa: The Cultural Politics of the Chicano Art: Resistance and Affirmation Exhibit," received the Ralph Henry Gabriel Prize for the best dissertation in American studies in 1994 and served as the basis for *Chicano Art Inside/Outside the Master's House* (1998). Gaspar de Alba was a minority scholar in residence at Pomona College from 1994 to 1995. She was hired as an assistant professor in the Cesar Chavez Center for Interdisciplinary Instruction in Chicana/Chicano Studies at University of California–Los Angeles in 1994 and was tenured in 1999.

Gaspar de Alba turned her attention to the life and works of Sor Juana Inés de la Cruz, a 17th-century Mexican nun and controversial writer, for several years. Her research culminated in *Sor Juana's Second Dream* (1999), a novel that combines excerpts from Sor Juana's writings with explicit, fictionalized journal entries to create an exciting version of a complex life. The book won the award for best historical fiction in the Latino Literary Hall of Fame, 2000. In 2003, Gaspar de Alba released *Velvet Barrios: Popular Culture & Chicana/o Sexualities,* a collection of essays, and *La Llorona on the Longfellow Bridge,* which features verse poems and prose poems that recount her physical and metaphorical travels between 1981 and 2001. Her novel *Desert Blood: The Juárez Murders* (2005) investigates the unaccountable serial murders that have taken place in Juárez, Mexico, for several years.

Gaspar de Alba has received many grants, including a Rockefeller Fellowship for Latino/a Cultural Study at the Smithsonian and a University of California Mexus Grant. Her work has been widely anthologized and awarded. She stands as one of the most prominent Chicana authors in her portrayal of border life for those segregated by class, race, and sexual orientation. She is a self-proclaimed lesbian, and her writings bring to light the experiences of the marginalized.

Further Reading

Davidson, Cathy N., and Linda Wagner-Martin. *The Oxford Companion to Women's Writing in the United States.* New York: Oxford University Press, 1995.

Norris Cristine, Shelby Amundsen, Mike Gleason, et al. "Alicia Gaspar de Alba." Available online. URL: http://voices.cla.umn.edu/vg/Bios/entries/alba_alicia_gaspar_de.html. Downloaded on May 1, 2006.

West-Durán, Alan. *Latino and Latina Writers, Volume II.* Detroit: Gale-Thomas, 2004, pp. 269–279.

Gilbert, Fabiola Cabeza de Baca
(Fabiola Cabeza de Baca, Fabiola Cabeza de Baca y Delgado y Delgado de Gilbert)
(1894–1991) *novelist, folklorist*

Fabiola Cabeza de Baca Gilbert is fondly remembered as the "first lady" of New Mexican cuisine. Through her respect, compassion, and dedication, she maintained a symbiotic relationship with Hispanic and Indian communities throughout the Southwest. She taught them about nutrition and modern food preservation, and they shared their recipes, folklore, and history, which she recorded in her books and other writings.

Fabiola Cabeza de Baca was the daughter of Indalecia Delgado and Graciano Cabeza de Baca. Both parents claimed heritage from Spanish gentry who had owned land in New Mexico since the 1600s. In 1823, her ancestor Don Luis María Cabeza de Baca received a land grant of a half million acres in the *llano,* or plains, region near Las Vegas, New Mexico. Cabeza de Baca was born on May 16, 1894, at the family headquarters ranch in La Liendre, New Mexico. Her mother died when she was four, and she was thereafter raised by her father and her Spanish and very proper paternal grandmother, Estefanita Delgado Cabeza de Baca. Cabeza de Baca attended school at the Sisters of Loretto in Las Vegas, New Mexico, graduating in 1916. She furthered her education at New Mexico Normal School (now Highlands University), gaining a B.A. in pedagogy, also called a teaching degree, in 1921. She studied art, history, and language at the Centro de Estudios Históricas in Madrid, Spain, the following year.

Cabeza de Baca taught in rural public schools across New Mexico from 1922 to 1929. When she received an assignment to teach "domestic science," she was immediately intrigued and thus began her pursuit of higher education on the subject. She earned a B.A. in home economics from the College of Agriculture of the New Mexico State University–Las Cruces in 1929. For the next 30 years, Cabeza de Baca dedicated her energy and time serving as the home demonstration agent for the New Mexico State Extension Service in Las Cruces. She traveled throughout New Mexico visiting many Native American pueblos and Hispanic villages teaching the use of the pressure cooker (which many people used throughout the Great Depression), nutrition, and food preservation. She encouraged families to plant gardens to provide fresh fruits and vegetables throughout the food shortages.

Cabeza de Baca became intimate with the indigenous Pueblo people of northern New Mexico and even learned their Tiwa and Tewa dialects. She was the only agent able to work with the women and was therefore able to establish many community organizations for women and children. Cabeza de Baca taught the people, particularly the women, how to market their products, including native rugs, baskets, pottery, canned delicacies, and other handcrafted items. She succeeded in empowering and liberating the women by giving them the means of independent economic revenue.

Cabeza de Baca wrote two pamphlets about nutrition and food preparation and preservation: *Los alimentos y su preparación* (1934, reprinted in 1937 and 1942; Food and its preparation) and *Boletín de conserver* (1935, reprinted in 1937 and 1941; Conserver's bulletin). In 1939, she released *Historic Cookery,* a book of recipes compiled from copious notes taken throughout her travels. This definitive description of Indian and Hispanic cooking in the upper Rio Grande area sold more than 100,000 copies. Also in 1939, she married Carlos Gilbert. She continued to write about nutrition, offering recipes in columns for the *El Nuevo Mexicano,* a newspaper of Santa Fe, New Mexico, and hosting a weekly bilingual radio broadcast on nutrition.

Through her work with indigenous people, Gilbert became enthralled in their folklore and traditions. She wrote *The Good Life* (1949), which describes the annual cycles of food gathering, preparations, and festivals in a fictitious New Mexican village. The book presents country living realistically rather than as overly bucolic or romantic. In 1951, Gilbert served as a representative for the United Nations Educational, Scientific and Cultural Organization (UNESCO). She established a home economics program for the Tarascan Indians in the state of Michoacán, Mexico. She set up her home base on the edge of Lake Pátzcuaro and established 18 training centers throughout northern Mexican villages, where she instructed the Tarascan in cooking and preserving techniques.

Gilbert discussed the history and lives of the early Spanish settlers, focusing on the women, in *We Fed Them Cactus* (1954). The title of this part historical, part memoir, and part folkloric work refers to how cattle were kept alive during droughts. The book delineates the critical role of women and promotes historical regional awareness. Gilbert wrote of her students and their families, "[M]y education was from books; theirs came the hard way. It was superior to mine."

Gilbert retired in 1959. She was awarded the Superior Service Award from the U.S. Department of Agriculture. During the 1960s, she trained Peace Corps volunteers. Despite the loss of a leg due to an automobile accident and her divorce from Carlos, Gilbert remained active. She served on many boards, including the New Mexico Museum Board, Red Cross, Girl Scouts, Santa Fe Opera Guild, International Relations Women's Board, and La Sociedad Folklórica de Santa Fe. She received the National Home Demonstration Agents Association Distinguished Award for Meritorious Service. In 1976, the American Association of University Women honored Gilbert by including her works in the Museum of New Mexico bicentennial exhibit.

Gilbert died on October 14, 1991. She was an imaginative, insightful pioneer whose legacy will be remembered as the one who "first taught them that beans and tortillas are not just 'poor people's food' but the proud, ancient, and nutritional staples of the New World."

Further Reading

Bullock, Alice. "A Patrona of the Old Pattern." *Santa Fe New Mexican,* May 19, 1968.

Cabeza de Baca, Elba. "Fabiola Cabeza de Baca y Delgado y Delgado de Gilbert." Available online. URL: http://perso.wanadoo.fr/rancho.pancho/Fabiola. htm. Downloaded on December 3, 2005.

Lomelí, Francisco, and Carl R. Shirley, eds. *Chicano Writers: Second Series.* Vol. 122. Detroit: Gale Research, 1992, pp. 44–47.

Meier, Matt S., Conchita Franco Serri, and Richard A. Garcia, eds. *Notable Latino Americans: A Biographical Dictionary.* Westport, Conn.: Greenwood Press, 1997, pp. 171–173.

Goldemberg, Isaac
(1945–) *poet, playwright, novelist*

Isaac Goldemberg is best known for his brutally honest depiction of his Peruvian-Jewish experience in his writings. Isaac Goldemberg was born on November 15, 1945, in Chepen, La Libertad, Peru, the son of Isaac, a merchant, and Eva (Bay). Many Latinos face the great difficulty of bridging their familial nationality and culture with the contemporary American dream and way of life. This melding combines food, language, temperament, social mores, and sometimes religion. Distinguishing one's spirituality is made more difficult if identifying with one side versus the other is almost forbidden. Such was the case for Goldemberg and his desire to attune himself with the Jewish faith in a predominately Hispano-Christian society.

In his late teens, Goldemberg spent a year in Israel and a short sojourn in Spain. He began to write poetry and penned a collection titled *Tiempo de silencio* (1969; Time of silence) and, with José Kozer, *De Chepen a la Habana* (1973; From Chepen to Havana). He married Mona Stern in 1963, and the following year immigrated to New York City. He worked as a clerk in the Dorot Jewish Division of the New York Public Library from 1965 to 1966.

He then served as the Spanish editor for Grolier from 1968 to 1969 and worked the following year at American Book Company. In 1976, he wrote *The Fragmented Life of Don Jacobo Lerner.* The author described his first novel to Contemporary Authors Online as "an attempt at reconstructing my own past and that of the Peruvian Jewish community at large. Even though my work deals mainly with the Jewish experience in Peru, the burdens of exile and spiritual rootlessness, I am also concerned with Peruvian life as a whole, particularly that of provincial Peru, marked by narrowness and claustrophobia. This is the world depicted in my first novel, where I attempted to draw the life of the Jewish immigrant as a tragic and heroic parody of the legend of the Wandering Jew."

Peruvian Jews and non-Jews attacked Goldemberg's book. He therefore attempted to write a book that would appease his readers and critics. The author found he could not bring himself to compose dishonest work and instead wrote the novel *Tiempo al tiempo; o, La conversión* (1983), translated by Hardie St. Martin and published as *The Conversion* (1983) and then as *Play by Play* (1985). The book's narration offers an honest perspective of the problems of racial and spiritual integration in Peru. Goldemberg's poetry includes *Hombre de paso* (1981; Just passing through) and *La vida al contado* (1989; A rare life), among other works. He composed *El gran libro de América judía* (The great book of Jewish America) for the Editorial de la Universidad de Puerto Rico in 1998. After more than 20 years in New York, Goldemberg returned to Peru. While in his native land, the author wrote *El nombre del padre* (2000; The name of the father).

Goldemberg's relentless and frank look at the life of the exile is a building block that can help readers reconcile the separation they feel as a result of leaving their native lands and trying to establish an identity and home in America. Although this blending of cultures, mores, and traditions is of particular importance to immigrants and Latinos, his work establishes a framework for anyone needing to create a bridge between what has been and what is now and thereafter establish an amalgamation of what can be.

Further Reading

Goldemberg, Isaac. *The Fragmented Life of Don Jacobo Lerner.* Albuquerque: University of New Mexico Press, 1999.

Kanellos, Nicolás, et al., eds. *Herencia: The Anthology of Hispanic Literature in the United States.* New York: Oxford University Press, 2003, pp. 475–476.

Peacock, Scot, ed. *Contemporary Authors.* Detroit, Mich.: Gale Research Group, 2001, pp. 206–208.

Gonzales, Rodolfo
(Corky Gonzales)
(1928–2005) *poet, essayist, activist*

Rodolfo "Corky" Gonzales is best known for his epic poem *I Am Joaquín/Yo Soy Joaquín*. The poem rallied many Mexican Americans who identified with the poem's character and his struggle with the apparent need to forgo his culture to achieve economic stability in the United States.

The youngest of five boys and three girls of Federico and Indalesia Gonzales, Rodolfo Gonzales was born in Denver, Colorado, on June 18, 1928. His mother died when he was two years old, but his father managed to keep the family together with discipline, stories of Mexico's history, and love. Gonzales's father, who had emigrated from Mexico to Colorado early in life, often regaled his children with tales about the pride of the Mexican people and the Mexican Revolution, a period from approximately 1910 to 1920 filled with terror, violence, and corruption as the people attempted to establish a stronger political voice and more control. The stories of Mexican people and their trials and tribulations gave Rodolfo a sense of personal and social identity. Although Rodolfo went to work in the sugar beet fields during the spring and summer from the time he was 10 years old, he attended public school in the barrios of east Denver during the fall and winter. He was an intelligent youth and graduated from high school at the age of 16.

During his teen years, Gonzales acquired a love for boxing and became a Golden Gloves, winner. With a keen interest in education, Gonzales saved money to attend college. He enrolled in the University of Denver to study engineering. The costs proved to be insurmountable, and Gonzales left college after one semester and returned to boxing. In 1947, he began his professional boxing career and rose to become the third-rank contender in the World Feather Weight category of the National Boxing Association. Gonzales left boxing eight years later to enter the political arena. He was elected the first Chicano district captain of the Denver Democratic Party in 1957. He coordinated the "Viva Kennedy" presidential campaign in Colorado in 1960 and was appointed chairman of the Denver antipoverty program. Determined to create equality for Chicanos, Gonzales organized and worked with several organizations, conferences, and efforts, including the War on Poverty, Colorado Raza Unida Party, and Los Voluntarios (The Volunteers), a grassroots organization and predecessor of the Crusade for Justice. He wrote plays for LUIS VALDEZ and his El Teatro Campensino, gave eloquent and electrifying speeches, and led rallies throughout the 1960s and 1970s. During this tumultuous time, Gonzales and his wife, Geraldine Romero Gonzales, raised a family of six daughters and two sons.

In 1967, Gonzales wrote and self-published *I Am Joaquín/Yo Soy Joaquín*. This epic poem provided a standard for grassroots-level and academic poets. The name in the title is believed to be based on the spirit of Joaquín Murietta, who became one of early California's most feared outlaws when his wife was raped and he was dispossessed of his land. By acknowledging the symbiotic yet diametrically opposed cultural and national aspects of Mexican Americans, it shaped an ideological foundation for activism. In his poem, Gonzales explores the victim and victor in Mexican history by identifying with the Aztec leaders and deities as well as the Spanish conquistadores and their deities and enemies on either side of the Mexican Revolution (when Mexicans sought to diversify political power, which had formerly been centralized in a dictatorship). This recognition of the polar opposites within Mexicans helped them establish harmony within themselves and solidarity with fellow Chicanos to fight the prejudice rampant in the 1960s.

Gonzales never strayed far from the needs of his own family as he fought to overcome the discrimination against Chicanos. In 1970, Gonzales founded the Escuela Tlatelolco, an alternative elementary and secondary school for Chicano students in Denver, Colorado. His daughter Nita still runs the school. When Gonzales suffered a heart attack in 1968, he withdrew from the public eye. In 2001, Antonio Esquibel, professor emeritus of Metropolitan State College of Denver, edited *Message to Aztlán: Selected Writings.* This first collection of Gonzales's diverse writings includes *I Am Joaquín* along with a new Spanish translation; seven major speeches (1968–78); two plays, *The Revolutionist* and *A Cross for Malcovio* (1966–67); various poems written during the 1970s; and a selection of letters.

On April 12, 2005, Gonzales died due to heart failure. Gonzales is considered one of the most influential leaders in the Chicano movement. He inspired others to take political action and find personal strength and pride within their dual culturalism through a bigger-than-life persona in his public and personal relationships.

Further Readings

Bruce-Novoa, Juan D. "The Heroics of Sacrifice, 'I Am Joaquín.'" In *Chicano Poetry: A Response to Chaos.* Austin: University of Texas Press, 1982, pp. 48–68.

Gonzales, Rodolfo "Corky." *Message to Aztlán: Selected Writings.* Edited by Antonio Esquibel. Houston, Tex.: Arte Público Press, 2001.

Lomelí, Francisco A., and Shirley, Carl A, eds. *Dictionary of Literary Biography.* Vol. 122: *Chicano Writers, Second Series,* Detroit: Gale, 1992, pp. 111–114.

González, Jovita
(Jovita González de Mireles)
(1899–1983) *essayist, short story writer, folklorist, educator, novelist*

One of the earliest folklorists for Mexican-American border culture, Jovita González was the first Mexican-American woman to receive a master's degree in Texas and served as a prominent member of one of the earliest Chicano organizations, League of United Latin American Citizens (LULAC). Jovita González was born in Roma, Texas, in 1899. (Some sources indicate her birth year as 1904.) She was raised on the

Jovita González is one of the most significant female writers of the first half of the 20th century. *(Photo of Jovita González is reprinted with permission from the publisher [APP Archive Files] [Houston: Arte Público Press—University of Houston, © 2006])*

family ranch that had been granted to her great-great-grandfather by the king of Spain when the American Southwest was considered the northern frontier of New Spain. González enjoyed a privileged childhood and was able to receive higher education when many minorities were refused such opportunities. In the late 1920s, she earned a B.A. with a teaching certificate in Spanish and history from the Lady of the Lake College in San Antonio, Texas. While teaching at St. Mary's Hall in San Antonio, González enrolled at the University of Texas–Austin.

At this time, she came under the tutelage of J. Frank Dobie at the Texas Folk-Lore Society, who encouraged González to research and later write about Mexican folklore. González joined the Texas Folk-Lore Society and became involved in the League of United Latin American Citizens (LULAC). Her essays and folklore stories began to appear in various publications of the Texas Folk-Lore Society, the *Southwest Review,* and the *LULAC News* in 1927. She earned an M.A. from the University of Texas–Austin in 1930. Her master's thesis, "Social Life in Cameron, Starr, and Zapata Counties," continues to be respected as a well-documented work. González collected the oral lore and traditions of Native Americans. She created picturesque stories that brought to life characters of the Southwest and illuminated the socioeconomic conflicts among Mexican Americans produced by the Anglo-American colonization of the Southwest. González wanted to establish awareness and foster better understanding between Mexican- and Anglo-American populations. She also employed her upper-class perspective to discuss the caste system Spanish conquistadores established in the New World. Her work was included in the 1937 Prentice-Hall publication on the United States minority populations, *Our Racial and National Minorities,* edited by Francis J. Brown and Joseph Slabely Roucek.

González married educator Edmundo E. Mireles in the 1930s. Together they produced the three-volume series *Mi libro de español* (1941–43; My Spanish book) and the six-volume reader *El español elemental* (1949; Elemental Spanish). She taught Spanish and history at W. B. Ray High School in Corpus Christi, Texas, from 1959 to her retirement in 1966. She died in 1983. Author GLORIA VELÁSQUEZ, who wrote her dissertation on González, claims that Jovita González and JOSEPHINA NIGGLI created a "female space" that addressed concerns related to being women. In reference to González's folklore, Velásquez believes that "[A]lthough Jovita did not focus so much on women's concerns, she did reveal an awareness of patriarchy." She wrote in her 1985 dissertation, "In exploring the limited role of women in border society, Jovita Gonzalez offers a realistic evaluation of the contradictory social position of women in which they are excluded from authority and yet exercise informal power." Arte Público Press posthumorously published two novels written by González. The first was *Caballero* (1996), and the second was *Dew on the Thorn* (1997).

Further Reading

Kanellos, Nicolas, et al., eds. *Herencia: The Anthology of Hispanic Literature in the United States.* New York: Oxford University Press, 2003.

Lomelí, Francisco A., and Carl A. Shirley, eds. *Dictionary of Literary Biography.* Vol. 122: *Chicano Writers, Second Series.* Detroit: Gale, 1992, pp. 122–126.

Velázquez-Treviño, Gloria. "Jovita González: Una voz de resistencia cultural en la temprana narrativa chicana." In *Mujer y literatura mexicana y chicana: Culturas en contacto: Primer coloquio fronterizo 22, 23 y 24 de abril de 1987.* Tijuana, Mexico: El Colegio de la Frontera Norte, 1988, pp. 76–83.

Haslam, Gerald

(1937–) *novelist, essayist, short story writer, script writer, editor, educator*

A prolific writer of varied genres, Gerald Haslam is considered one of the best short story writers, in league with John Steinbeck, and is valued as a major influence in western American and Hispanic literature. Gerald Haslam was born on March 18, 1937, in a suburb of Bakersfield, California, known as Oildale. He is the son of Fred Martin, an oil worker, and Lorraine Hope Johnson Haslam. His mother was raised by her Latino grandparents and brought a strong Hispanic influence to Gerald's mixed cultural inheritance of Irish, Spanish, Portuguese, Danish, German, Welsh, Native American, and Sephardic roots. She encouraged her son's friendships with people of diverse races and backgrounds. Gerald attended Garces Memorial High, graduating in 1955, with his participation in athletics reinforcing this cultural openness.

He attended Bakersfield College for two years; however, he enjoyed the extracurricular activities more than the educational aspects of the college experience. He dropped out in 1958 and joined the U.S. Army, serving until 1960. In 1961, he married Janice E. Pettichord, with whom he would have five children: Frederick, Alexandra, Garth, Simone, and Carlos. Haslam then returned to college with renewed vigor. He earned an A.A. in 1960 from Bakersfield College, a B.A. from San Francisco State College (now San Francisco State Uni-

versity) in 1963, and an M.A. from San Francisco State in 1965. Haslam taught English at San Francisco State University from 1966 to 1967. He then accepted a position at Sonoma State University, serving as professor of English from 1967 to 1997, specializing in western American literature and in linguistics. He was awarded a Ph.D. in 1980 from the Union Graduate School (now the Union Institute in Cincinnati), by which time he had proved himself proficient at varied forms of writing.

Haslam found inspiration for his creative writing from the stories his maternal grandmother told him. Haslam explained to Contemporary Authors Online, "I was, in any case, raised in a richly varied area—California's San Joaquin Valley—where oral tale-telling was a fine art. I was a good listener and I still am. Since no one ever told me a novel, I have always considered the story, not its longer counterpart, to be fiction's most natural expression. It is a continuing source of both wonder and satisfaction to me that I have evolved into a storyteller." He has contributed to several hundred magazines and journals, including *The Nation, Los Angeles Times Magazine, This World, Sierra,* and *Poets & Writers.*

Haslam's nonfiction works include *The Language of the Oil Fields* (1972), *Voices of a Place: Social and Literary Essays from the Other California* (1987), *Coming of Age in California* (1990; revised edition, 1992; second, enlarged edition, 2000), *The Other California: The Great Central Valley in Life and Letters* (1990; second, enlarged edition, 1994),

The Great Central Valley: California's Heartland (1993), and *Workin' Man Blues: Country Music in California,* with Richard Chon and Alexandra Haslam (1999).

Haslam's fiction is heavily influenced by a life led by inclusion rather than exclusion. He was a multiculturalist before the term was well known. Sympathetic to prejudice heaped not only on Latinos, but "Okies," a term Californians use to identify unintelligent "white trash," Haslam's works are laced with humor and wise insights that offer a means of embracing all races with an encompassing humanity. His fiction includes *Okies: Selected Stories* (1973), *Masks: A Novel* (1976), *The Wages of Sin: Collected Stories* (1980), *Hawk Flights: Visions of the West* (1983), *Snapshots: Glimpses of the Other California* (1985), *The Man Who Cultivated Fire and Other Stories* (1987), *That Constant Coyote: California Stories* (1990), *Condor Dreams & Other Fictions* (1994), *The Great Tejon Club Jubilee* (1996), *Manuel and the Madman* (2000), *Straight White Male* (2000), *Haslam's Valley* (2005), and *Grace Period* (2006).

Haslam has edited several anthologies. Among them are *Forgotten Pages of American Literature* (1970), *Many Californias: Literature from the Golden State* (1992; second edition, 1999), and *Where Coyotes Howl and Wind Blows Free: Growing Up in the West* (1995). *Many Californias* is one of the most widely used and influential of multicultural anthologies for classrooms and the general reader.

Haslam's list of publications is impressive and plays a major role in bringing a universal element to regional and personal experiences. However, his inexhaustible output of writing has not created an overblown ego. As Haslam put it to Contemporary Authors Online: "Perhaps because I came to writing directly from the oral tradition, I've never yearned to be an author, although I'm certainly pleased to see my work published. No, for me the act of writing is the most important thing, experiencing the emergence of a new reality. Like love, it remains an enduring thrill. I can't wait to face the typewriter each morning. I'm always amazed at what's in there. It's a great privilege to be able to write."

Haslam has been the recipient of well more than 25 awards and honors, including a Distinguished Achievement Award from the Western Literature Association, Laureate of the San Francisco Public Library, Benjamin Franklin Award from Publisher's Marketing Association (for *Many Californias*), and Pushcart Prize (for "The Man Who Cultivated Fire").

Haslam retired from teaching full time in 1997. During his education career, he served as adjunct professor for the National Faculty, Union Graduate School, and Fromm Institute, University of San Francisco. He is currently a professor emeritus at Sonoma State University and a commentator for *The California Report,* on KQED-FM. Haslam continually reinvents himself as a writer, evolving and experimenting with varied forms of writing.

Further Reading

Breiger, Marek. "Haslam's Oildale, Our California." *California English* 28, no. 4 (September/October 1992): 22–23.

Heide, Rick, ed. *Under the Fifth Sun: Latino Literature from California.* Santa Clara and Berkeley, Calif.: Santa Clara University/Heyday Books, 2002.

Locklin, Gerald. *Gerald Haslam.* Boise, Idaho: Boise State University Press, 1987.

Hatch, Sheila Sánchez
(Sheila Francine Hatch, Sheila Hatch)
(1963–   ) *poet, short story writer, children's story writer*

Sheila Sánchez Hatch offers literary images in her poetry that reflect personal and global issues. Her work carries immense value for its ability to imbue the passion of the precursory Chicano writers into contemporary concerns.

Sheila Francine Hatch was born on September 17, 1963, in San Antonio, Texas. Her mother,

Diamantina Sánchez Hatch, is Mexican American, born in Crystal City, Texas. Her father, James Hatch, was of English, Scotch-Irish, Spanish, and Alsatian heritage. Sheila learned early on to appreciate the contributions of people from various cultures because of her mixed ethnic inheritance. Although she loved people of all races and backgrounds, as a child Shiela felt very different and alienated from most of the people in her Mexican-American community on the west side of San Antonio.

Her father carried the most influence in Hatch's life due to his illimitable dreams and granite faith. During her youth, Hatch dreamed of becoming practically everything for a while—she craved adventure. She began writing at an early age—as soon as she learned to put sentences together—and wrote poems for her grandmother and father. Virtually everyone she read, but particularly Langston Hughes, inspired Hatch to write. When she attended Woodlawn Elementary, the class studied poetry. Hatch noticed there were no Latino writers in the book. Hughes showed Hatch that people of color could overcome great obstacles and take pride in themselves, including where and what they come from. Hatch attended Horace Mann Middle School then graduated from Thomas Jefferson High School.

Hatch received a B.A. in English from the University of Texas–San Antonio in 1989. She then attended Vermont College, of Norwich University (now the Union Institute), graduating with an M.A. in creative writing and literature in 1993. At Vermont College, Hatch met ANGELA DE HOYOS, the poet who inspired many during the Chicano movement. De Hoyos was of great assistance to the young poet. Hatch also frequently volunteered at the Guadalupe Cultural Arts Center, which was a powerful learning experience that changed her forever because she met many Latinos who took great pride in their culture and people. About this time, Hatch assumed her mother's maiden name, in part to reassert her full identity. Her work began to be published, and she found work teaching at the college level. She has also worked with young children in various arts programs. Hatch currently teaches English for the Alamo Community College District in San Antonio, Texas.

Hatch married Benito Tremillo in 1995 and has one daughter. Ideas of alienation and reclamation are present frequently in Hatch's poetry, whether in terms of culture, sex, or politics. She submitted a children's story to *Express-News,* a San Antonio newspaper, believing it was a regular submission. In fact, at the time the publication was hosting a literary contest. Her story was published, and she received a $300 check. Her family from all

Sheila Sánchez Hatch is known for her inventive metaphors and unique vision and is an emerging Latina writer. *(Stella Hatch Cody)*

over the valley called her mom to say how excited they were about it.

Hatch released *Guadalupe and the Kaleidoscopic Screamer,* a collection of poetry and short fiction, in 1996. De Hoyos wrote about Hatch, "If Sheila Sánchez Hatch did not exist, we would have to invent her—so necessary is she as a bonafide role model for the young Latina writer of today. A serious writer of depth and integrity, she is 100% Tejana . . . and her mestiza guns are loaded." Hatch released a book of poetry, *Strong Box Heart,* in 2000. She is currently working on a book of poetry called *(Working) Mom.*

Further Reading

Hatch, Sheila Sánchez. *Strong Box Heart.* San Antonio: Wings Press, 2000.

Milligan, Bryce, Mary Guerrero Milligan, and Angela de Hoyos, eds. *Floricanto Sí!: A Collection of Latina Poetry.* New York: Penguin, 1998.

Silver, Kate. "Sheila Sánchez Hatch." Available online. URL: http://voices.cla.umn.edu/vg/Critique/review_poetry/strong_box_heart_by_sheila_sanchez_ha tch.html. Downloaded on December 5, 2005.

Hernández-Ávila, Inés
(Inés Hernández)
(1947–) *poet, essayist, editor, activist, educator*

Inés Hernández-Ávila's literary contributions as a writer and editor stand primarily on her ability and strength to bring indigenous culture and language, as well as a re-creation of the feminine archetype, to the forefront of Latino and Chicano literature. Born on December 27, 1947, in Galveston, Texas, Inés Hernández drew strength and kinship from both her parents' heritage. Her mother, Janice Tzilimamúh Andrews Hernández, is a proud member of the Nimiipu (Nez Perce), Chief Joseph's tribe from Nespelem, Washington.

Of Mexican descent, her father, Rodolfo Hernández, was born in Eagle Pass, Texas.

Hernández saw the connection between these cultures, and by the time she entered college at the University of Houston, she became an activist in the Chicano movement. Hernández found the term *Chicana* was a political choice and recognized that the word has roots in the Nahuatl language (*mexica, mexicano, Chicano*). With a drive to speak for the voiceless, disenfranchised members of society as well as the ancestors of the Americas, Hernández wrote essays and poems, performing much of her work through song at festivals and book fairs across the nation. Her work was characterized by a symbolic use of words and larger than life, or surreal, imagery. She often created new words, such as *pensavientos* (pensive winds), thereby illustrating the need for constant evolution of terms and ways to identify with culture, nature, identity, and history.

Hernández earned a B.A., M.A., and Ph.D., all in English, from the University of Houston in 1970, 1972, and 1984, respectively. She taught English at La Marque High School from 1970 to 1971. She was the recipient of the Ford Foundation Doctoral Fellowship for American Indians from 1971 to 1976. Hernández released her *Con razón, corazón (No Wonder, Heart)* in 1977. During the 1980s, she worked at several academic institutions, including San Fransisco State University, Fresno State University, D-Q University, and the University of California–Davis. In 1989, she accepted the post of assistant professor at the University of California–Davis and received tenure in 1995. She married Juan Ávila in 1992, and together they raised her two sons, Rodolfo Valentino Tovar and Tomás Carlos Tovar, from a previous marriage. Hernández-Ávila served as chair of the Native American department from 1996 to 1998, during which time the department established an M.A. and Ph.D. program in Native American studies. This was the first Native American studies graduate program in the country with a hemispheric perspective. In 2002, she was promoted to full professor of Native American studies.

In addition to her teaching responsibilities, Hernández-Ávila has edited several works, including *Reading Native American Women: Critical/Creative Representations, Telling to Live: Latina Feminist Testimonios, Frontiers: A Journal of Women's Studies, Entre Guadalupe y Malinche: Tejanas in Literature and Art* (coedited with Norma Elia Cantú), *Indigenous Intellectual Sovereignties: A Hemispheric Approach to Native American Studies* (coedited with Stefano Varese), *Indigenous Intersections in Literature: American Indians and Chicanas/Chicanos* (coedited with Domino Renee Perez), *From Where the Songs Are Born: De donde nacen los cantos: Indigenous Literature of the United States and Mexico,* and *Dancing Earth Songs: Poems and Stories.*

Hernández-Ávila's editing skills are not her only contribution to Chicano letters. Her poems and essays have appeared in several anthologies, including *This Bridge We Call Home: Radical Visions for Transformation, The Floating Borderlands: Twenty-five Years of U.S. Hispanic Literature,* and *Chicano Culture and Folklore.*

Hernández-Ávila's powerful verses employ a rhythmic chanting with a foundation in Native American storytelling. With a focus primarily on the indigenous aspects of Chicana/o culture and identity, her work redefines Native American symbology as tangible realism rather than an etherical secret language. Her spirituality and sense of ritual is so embedded in her being that she lights candles and chants as a prelude to public poetry readings. Her work calls for solidarity for humankind not only within culture, class, and race but within gender as well. She stands out as a writer, educator, and activist who embraces the constant evolution of thought and the ability to reinvent cultural and personal identity. Hernández-Ávila is currently at work on research projects focusing on writers in indigenous languages in Mexico.

Further Reading

Arkin, Marian, and Barbara Shollar. *Longman Anthology of World Literature by Women, 1875–1975.* New York: Longman, 1989, pp. 1,019–1,022.

Hernández-Ávila, Inés. "My eyes breathe fire and my fingers bleed tears that are the ink of my dreams." *Social Justice* (December 22, 2004): 13–14.

Lomelí, Francisco A., and Carl A. Shirley, eds. *Dictionary of Literary Biography* Vol. 122: *Chicano Writers, Second Series.* Detroit: Gale, 1992, pp. 132–136.

Ordóñez, Elizabeth J. "The Concept of Cultural Identity in Chicana Poetry." *Third Woman* 2 (1984): 75–82.

Hernandez Cruz, Victor

(1949–) *poet, editor, essayist, short story writer, educator*

Victor Hernandez Cruz has made an integral contribution to the canons of American literature with his highly inventive, distinctive, and elusive poems. Hernandez Cruz is known and admired as one of the principal writers who helped define the Nuyorican experience for a mainstream American audience.

Victor Hernandez Cruz was born with the assistance of a midwife in the agricultural village of Aguas Buenas, Puerto Rico, on February 6, 1949. In his early years, Victor listened attentively to the tales spun by his grandfather Julio "el Bohemio," a tobacco roller. Victor was six years old when the agricultural system of the island collapsed. With no means to earn a living, many Puerto Ricans, including the Cruz family, formed a mass migration to the United States.

Soon after reaching the Lower East Side of Manhattan, his parents divorced. His mother, Rosa, worked very hard to keep the family together, which instilled great pride and strength in her son. By his mid-teens Victor began to write poetry. He had long played around with images and words, comparing and contrasting the divergent cultures of New York urbanism with the island traditions of Puerto Rico. This constant marrying of his Puerto Rican memories and the current experiences of New York in his writing helped the Nuyorican (New York Puerto Rican) find his place in American society.

At the age of 17, Hernandez Cruz had written enough poems to form a collection, which he self-published under Calle Once (Eleventh Street) Publications, as *Papo Got His Gun!* (1966). He and his friends distributed 500 copies of the book, whose verses told of a Puerto Rican struggling for an identity and a place in America. Fred Jordan of *Evergreen Review,* an avant-garde New York magazine, came across one of these copies and ran a seven-page spread featuring the vulnerable and explicit poems from *Papo* and photographs of Hernandez Cruz's barrio. In 1967, Hernandez Cruz joined *Umbra* magazine as an editor and cofounded the East Harlem Gut Theatre in New York. The theater, which supported the works of actors, musicians, and writers, closed after one year of operation.

Hernandez Cruz combined Spanish, Indian, and African influences in his second book, *Snaps* (1969). Hernandez Cruz strengthened his inner voice in this second collection with tightly controlled syntax and snapshot imagery. Critics varied on their opinions of Hernandez Cruz's latest work, although most agreed he was emerging as an influential, revolutionary poet. By the late 1960s, Hernandez Cruz's poems had begun to appear in prestigious magazines and journals. He moved to Berkeley, California, and found himself in a maelstrom of ideas, books, performance art, music, language, and comrades to explore the boundaries of ideologies, dogma, and cultures. Hernandez Cruz captured his journey across the country in *Mainland* (1973), wherein he blends together the natural and supernatural as the narrative poems move through major cities across the United States.

Hernandez Cruz received a Creative Artists Program Service (CAPS) grant in 1974 in order to write *Tropicalization* (1976). In this work, Hernandez Cruz uses lyrical Spanglish, a combination of Spanish and English, to superimpose tropical warmth, culture, and rhythm onto New York City, thereby creating a textured world that marries the best and worst in both cultures. Along with Piri Thomas, Hernandez Cruz established a trend and legitimacy for Nuyoricans and other Spanish-speaking poets to incorporate Spanglish in their varied forms of writing. Hernandez Cruz returned to New York City and married Elisa Ivette in 1975. The couple would have two children, Vitin Ajant and Rosa Luz. They returned to San Francisco, California, in 1976.

Hernandez Cruz joined the San Francisco Neighborhood Arts Program and worked with schools, senior citizens' centers, prisons, and city festivals. He was awarded another CAPS grant to write fiction. His short pieces were published extensively in journals and magazines, including the avant-garde reviews *New World Journal* and *Invisible City.* He was invited to the One World Poetry Festival in Amsterdam, Holland, in 1979 and 1980 and received a National Endowment for the Arts fellowship. Throughout his writing career, Hernandez Cruz has served as an instructor at many universities, including the University of California–Berkeley, San Francisco State College, University of California–San Diego, and University of Michigan–Ann Arbor.

In 1982, Hernandez Cruz released *By Lingual Wholes,* a collection of poetry and prose noted for its wit, pathos, and sardonic view on political issues. Often self-reflective in his poems, Hernandez Cruz included two decades of his work in *Rhythm, Content and Flavor: New and Selected Poems* (1988). He was awarded the New York Poetry Foundation award in 1989. The title of his *Red Beans* (1991) represents the pun "red beings," referring to the indigenous Puerto Rican descended from Spanish and African ancestors. *Panoramas* (1997) evokes emotions with an evolving and impulsive look at the artist's life. *Maraca: New and Selected Poems, 1965–2000* was published in 2001.

Hernandez Cruz is a leader among Nuyorican writers. His ability to infuse *ritmo* (rhythm), *música* (music), and *espiritismo* (spiritualism) brings the heartbeat of his Latino heritage into the modern world. Images of nature are sprinkled throughout his work, enabling readers from anywhere in the world to identify with the passion that permeates his prose and poetry.

Further Reading

Harris, Trudier, and Thadious M. Davis, eds. *Dictionary of Literary Biography.* Vol. 41: *Afro-American Poets Since 1955.* Detroit: Gale Group, 1985, pp. 74–84.

Lee, Michelle, ed. *Poetry Criticism.* Vol. 37. Detroit: Gale, 2002. pp. 1–38.

Riggs, Thomas. *Contemporary Poets.* 7th ed. Detroit: St. James Press, 2000.

Sheppard, Walt. "An Interview with Clarence Major and Victor Hernandez Cruz." In *New Black Voices.* Edited by Abraham Chapman. New York: New American Library, 1972, pp. 545–552.

Wallenstein, Barry. "The Poet in New York: Victor Hernandez Cruz." *Bilingual Review* 1 (September–December 1974): 312–319.

Herrera, Juan Felipe
(1948–) *poet, children's book writer, young adult writer, educator*

Juan Felipe Herrera artistically combines literary work and performance art with passionate style, intelligence, and sensitivity. His dedication to community, renegade willingness to challenge traditions and typecasting, and visceral writing has made him an inspirational model for Latinos.

Juan Felipe Herrera is the only child of Felipe Emelio Herrera, originally from Chihuahua, Mexico, and María de la Luz (Lucha) Quintana de Herrera, a native of the Niño Perdido (Lost Child) district in Mexico City. Herrera was born in Fowler, California, on December 27, 1948. During his earliest years, Herrera moved around with his parents, who were field-workers. He enjoyed the freewheeling lifestyle, allowing his imagination to take him anywhere he chose. Herrera recalled in a 2006 interview, "I was a dreamer without specific dreams, Chagall-like, Miro-like, open skies and red fields, roads and beaches, trees and dirtbugs, rainy winds, there was no talk about careers, just life, big life, respect and kindness." When he was eight years old, he settled with his family in San Diego, California. Accustomed to the camaraderie of the farmworker's life, Juan had difficulty adjusting to what he called "the phantasmagoria of downtown San Diego in the early 60's." His mother influenced him with her love of language, family history, humor, deep philosophical thought, and campesino style. At 13 years old, Juan met ALURISTA, who helped the youngster develop critical thoughts on literature and art and "the Chicano thing," as Alurista referred to it.

Juan attended Roosevelt Junior High School and graduated from San Diego High School in 1967. As a youth, he enjoyed music, poetry, and art. However, when he entered the University of California–Los Angeles, he studied sociology and earned a B.A. in social anthropology in 1972. In the early 1970s, a performance of El Teatro Campesino troupe inspired Herrera to form his own theater group, known as Teatro Tolteca, and study indigenous theatrical expression in Mexico. Upon his return to San Diego, Herrera worked with the Centro Cultural Toltecas en Aztlán, now called the Centro Cultural de la Raza. This experience provided the foundational work for Herrera's first book, *Rebozos of love we have woven sudor de pueblos on our back* (1974). The poems of this book form a kaleidoscope of chants that speak to a unification of Chicano identity within an ideal environment complete with pre-Columbian myths, heroes, and deities.

Herrera entered Stanford University in 1977, obtaining an M.A. in social anthropology in 1980. For the next several years, the poet conducted creative writing workshops for children in grades 3 through 12; performed and read his poetry at

Juan Felipe Herrera is well known for his successful combination of the written word with performance art. *(Randy Vaughn-Dotta)*

creative writing, and theater. Once settled in his professorship, Herrera released several books in succession. His books of poetry include *Memorias of an Exile's Notebook of the Future* (1993), *The Roots of a Thousand Embraces: Dialogues* (1994), *Night Train to Tuxtla* (1994; "Camino del Sol" series), *187 Reasons Why Mexicanos Can't Cross the Border* (1995), *Love after the Riots* (1996), *Loteria Cards and Fortune Poems: A Book of Lives* (1999), *Border-Crosser with a Lamborghini Dream* (1999), *Thunderweavers* (2000), and *Giraffe on Fire* (2001). *Mayan Drifter: Chicano Poet in the Lowlands of America* (1997) is a book of prose, while *Notebook of a Chile Verde Smuggler* (2002) is written in loose diary form and includes a selection of family photographs. Herrera penned books for younger readers, too. Some of these are *Calling the Doves/Canto a las palomas* (1995), *Laughing Out Loud, I Fly* (poetry, 1998), *Crash Boom Love: A Novel in Verse* (1999), *The Upside Down Boy/El niño de cabeza* (2000), *Grandma & Me at the Flea/Los Meros Remateros* (2002), and *Cilantro Girl/La superniña del cilantro* (2003). Herrera released *Cinnamon Girl* and *Downtown Boy* in 2005.

The Upside Down Boy was adapted as a musical for young audiences and was well received in New York City in 2004. The following year, Herrera took the position of professor in the creative writing department at the University of California–Riverside. Herrera is a community arts leadership builder with youth at risk and migrant communities and an actor with appearances in film and on stage.

During the last three decades, Herrera has received numerous awards and fellowships, including various National Endowment for the Arts writers' fellowships, four California Arts Council grants, the University of California–Berkeley Regent's Fellowship, the Bread Loaf Fellowship in Poetry, and the Stanford Chicano Fellows Fellowship. Appearing in more than 60 anthologies, Herrera's literary endeavors have garnered the Ezra Jack Keats Award, the Hungry Mind Award of

schools; released three books, *Exiles of Desire* (1985), *Facegames* (1987), and *Akrílica* (1989); and taught intercultural studies at De Anza Community College. He married Margarita Nirvana Robles in 1985, with whom he would have five children: Almasol, Joaquín Ryan, Joshua Ryan, Marlene Segura, and Robert Segura. Herrera instructed students in creative writing at the New College of California, the University of Iowa Writers' Workshop, and the University of Southern Illinois.

In 1990, Herrera earned an M.F.A. at the prestigious University of Iowa Writers' Workshop in poetry and accepted a position at California State University–Fresno to teach cultural studies,

Distinction, the Americas Award, and the Focal Award.

Further Reading

Bell, Marvin. "A Poet's Sampler: Juan Felipe Herrera." *Boston Review* (October 14, 1989): 6.

Heide, Rick, ed. *Under the Fifth Sun: Latino Literature from California.* Santa Clara and Berkeley, Calif.: Santa Clara University/Heyday Books, 2002.

West-Durán, Alan. *Latino and Latina Writers, Volume I.* Detroit: Gale-Thomas, 2004, pp. 281–298.

Herrera-Sobek, María
(María Díaz Herrera)
(1942–   ) *poet, literary critic, historian, folklorist, nonfiction writer, educator*

María Herrera-Sobek has authored or edited 17 books on Chicano culture and helped create Chicano studies programs at two major universities. She has been awarded 23 grants and 16 honors.

The fourth child of María Díaz and Roberto Herrera, María Díaz Herrera was born on January 21, 1942, in San Pedro de las Colonias in the Mexican state of Coahuila. Her father was killed in a rodeo accident just three months prior to his daughter's birth. Díaz, who already had three children to take care of, promised the unborn María to her parents, Susana Escamilla and José Tarango. Escamilla and Tarango had recently adopted a child, but the child had died. María's birth supplanted her grandmother's deep grief. Upon her father's death, Herrera's mother had moved in with Escamilla and Tarango, so María was raised among her siblings yet fell under the direct care of her grandparents. María moved with her grandparents to the border town of Reynosa, Tamaulipas, Mexico, as a baby. At the age of three, she learned to read Spanish and began reading the newspaper to the local residents. Soon afterward American farmers recruited Tarango to work in the fields

of Rio Hondo, Texas. Herrera and her grandmother followed, as eventually did her mother and siblings.

The fertile soil of the Rio Grande Valley provided a surplus of crops and stable work for field-workers. While cleaning houses with her grandmother during the colder months, María read the many magazines to which the woman of the household subscribed. In this way she discovered the possibility of college scholarships through *Seventeen* magazine. María was determined to reach the highest education possible. While in the fourth grade at Northward Elementary School, María wrote a poem that garnered considerable praise from her teacher. Encouraged by this incident, María wrote poetry from this point on. She convinced her grandparents to move to California after her graduation from Northward Junior High School. En route to California, they stopped at Gilbert, Arizona, where they were offered work. It was late August, and the studious María did not want to miss school, so she consented to stay.

After graduating from Gilbert High School, Herrera attended Arizona State University. She graduated with a B.S. in chemistry in 1965. After graduation, she moved to California and worked in a biochemistry laboratory at the University of California–Los Angeles (UCLA). César Chavez had recently begun the Delano Grape Strike in support of farmworkers' rights. Herrera became involved in the Chicano movement, participating in demonstrations and protests and advocating Chicano and women's rights and the end of the Vietnam War. Inspired to assist farmworkers, she changed her major when she was accepted into UCLA's graduate program. Herrera earned an M.A. in 1971 in Latin-American studies. From 1972 to 1974 Herrera taught at California State University–Northridge. In 1974, she married Joseph George Sobek, with whom she would have one son, Erik Jason Sobek. Herrera-Sobek earned a Ph.D. in Hispanic languages and literature in

1975. She then accepted a post in the Spanish and Portuguese department at the University of California–Irvine.

Herrera-Sobek's poetry saw publication in *Revista Chicano Riqueña* in 1978. Since then Herrera-Sobek has published *The Bracero Experience: Elitelore versus Folklore* (1979), *The Mexican Corrido: A Feminist Analysis* (1990), and *Northward Bound: The Mexican Immigrant Experience in Ballad and Song* (1993). In addition, she is the editor or coeditor of numerous anthologies, including *Beyond Stereotypes: The Critical Analysis of Chicana Literature* (1985), *Chicana Creativity and Criticism: Charting New Frontiers in Chicana Literature* (with HELENA MARIA VIRAMONTES, 1988 and 1996), *Gender and Print Culture: New Perspectives on International Ballad Studies* (1991), *Saga de México* (1991), *Reconstructing a Chicano/a Literary Heritage: Hispanic Colonial Literature of the Southwest* (1993), *Chicana (W)rites: On Word and Film* (with Viramontes, 1995), *Culture Across Borders: Mexican Immigration and Popular Culture* (with David Maciel, 1998), *Recovering the U.S. Hispanic Literary Heritage: Volume IV* (2000), *Power in Academe: Race and Gender—Strangers in the Tower* (2000), *Chicana Literary and Artistic Expressions: Culture and Society in Dialogue* (2000), *Chicano Renaissance: Contemporary Trends in Chicano Culture* (with Maciel and Isidro Ortiz, 2000), *Santa Barraza: The Life and Work of a Mexica/Tejana Artist* (2001), *Dreaming on a Sunday in the Alameda and Other Plays: Chicana and Chicano Visions of America* (with CARLOS MORTON, 2004), and *Chicano Folklore: A Handbook* (2006).

During her 21 years at the University of California–Irvine, Herrera-Sobek cofounded the Chicano Studies Program and the Latin American Studies Program and helped develop the Women's Studies Program. She was the first Chicana to win tenure and to become a full professor at that university. She accepted a professorship at the University of California–Santa Barbara in 1997. As the chair of the strategic planning committee,

Herrera-Sobek spearheaded the establishment of the university's Ph.D. program in Chicano studies, which accepted its first doctoral students in 2005. Throughout her career, Herrera-Sobek has held four visiting professorships, including one at Stanford University and another at Harvard University; contributed more than 100 articles and chapters to various books, periodicals, and anthologies; and advised on two documentary films. She has also received numerous grants, scholarships, and distinctions, including a nomination into the prestigious American Fulbright Society and a Distinguished Teacher's Award from the Chicano/Chicana Modern Language Society. In addition to playing an integral role in securing the infrastructure for Latino/a literature in the world of academia within the United States, Herrera-Sobek is currently bringing Chicano literature to the world, participating in conferences in Russia, Turkey, and Spain.

Further Reading
Herrera-Sobek, María. *The Mexican Corrido: A Feminist Analysis.* Bloomington: Indiana University Press, 1990.

Olivas, Daniel. "Spotlight on Maria Herrera-Sobek." La Bloga. Available online. URL: http://labloga.blogspot.com/2005/10/Spotlight-on-maria-herrera-sobek.html. Downloaded on October 5, 2004.

Palmisano, Joseph M. *Notable Hispanic American Women, Book 2.* Detroit: Gale Research, 1998, pp. 137–141.

Hijuelos, Oscar
(1951–) *novelist, short story writer, educator*

As the first Latino novelist to receive the Pulitzer Prize for fiction, Oscar Hijuelos was among the first to introduce Hispanic culture and people to the mainstream American audience. With his Cuban ancestry as a starting point, Hijuelos is well known for his ability to write with a universal appeal that is not limited by a cultural or national identity.

Oscar Hijuelos was born on August 24, 1951, in New York City, the son of Pascual, a hotel worker, and Magdalena Torrens Hijuelos, a homemaker, both of whom had emigrated from Cuba. New York City provided Oscar with an environment rich in Hispanic culture. He particularly enjoyed mambo music and played in several Latin American bands throughout his youth and early adulthood. After graduating from high school in New York, he enrolled in City University of New York, where he received a B.A. in English in 1975 and an M.A. in English with an emphasis on creative writing in 1976.

After college graduation, Hijuelos worked at an advertising agency for seven years. During this time, he wrote several short stories. His literary prose began to win awards such as the Outstanding Writer citation from Pushcart Press in 1978 for his short story "Columbus Discovering America"; an Oscar Cintas fiction-writing grant in 1978–79; a Bread Loaf Writers' Conference scholarship in 1980; and fiction-writing grants from Creative Artists Programs Service in 1982 and the Ingram Merrill Foundation in 1983.

Hijuelos released his first novel, *Our House in the Last World,* in 1983. The book follows a Cuban family who immigrated to the United States in the 1940s and contains elements of magic realism. Shortly after the release of his first book, Hijuelos was able to devote his efforts to writing full time for several years as a result of its success.

In 1989, Hijuelos accepted the post of professor of English at Hofstra University in Hempstead, New York, and released his Pulitzer Prize winner, *The Mambo Kings Play Songs of Love.* His best-known work, the novel follows brothers Nestor and Cesar Castillo, both highly talented musicians, as they leave their native Cuba to seek fame and fortune in America. Critics raved at Hijuelos's ability to create vivid characters with many dimensions, magical imagery, and a realistic depiction of the American dream.

Hijuelos followed with *The Fourteen Sisters of Emilio Montez O'Brien* (1993), which covers the female perspective of assimilation and ties to cultural and national homeland. *Mr. Ives' Christmas* (1995) introduces characters with Cuban or ethnic background as a foundation to explore one's faith in the face of tragedy. *Empress of the Splendid Season* (1999) returns to the struggles and tribulations of a Cuban immigrant. *A Simple Habana Melody: From When the World Was Good* (2002) is loosely based on the life of Moises Simons, a Cuban composer who introduced the rumba rhythm to an American audience.

Hijuelos's work has appeared in several literary journals, periodicals, and anthologies. He has received many awards and fellowships throughout his career, including a Fellowship for Creative Writers award, grants from the National Endowment for the Arts, and an American Academy in Rome Fellowship in Literature. However, the most prestigious was the Pulitzer Prize for *The Mambo Kings Play Songs of Love* in 1990.

Hijuelos's writings have been adapted to various media. *The Mambo Kings Play Songs of Love* was adapted as the film *The Mambo Kings* in 1992 and as a stage musical that opened in 2005. *Empress of the Splendid Season* was adapted for audiobook in 1999. Also, *A Simple Habana Melody: From When the World Was Good* was adapted for audiobook in 2002.

Hijuelos's novels are lauded for their ability to take readers on journeys of self-discovery and the formulation of personal identity that can be adapted to any culture or background. They begin with a clearly defined, tangible environment and expand to a sentimental yet realistic overview that is readily accessible to all readers.

Further Reading

Fernández, Enrique. "Exiliados on Main Street." *Village Voice,* May 1, 1990, pp. 85–86.

Kanellos, Nicolás, et al., eds. *Herencia: The Anthology of Hispanic Literature in the United States.* New York: Oxford University Press, 2003, pp 271–279.

Pérez Firmat, Gustavo. "Rum, Rump, and Rumba: Cuban Contexts for *The Mambo Kings Play Songs of Love*." *Dispositio* 16, no. 41 (1991): 75–86.

Stavans, Ilán. "Oscar Hijuelos, novelista." *Revista Iberoamericana* 155–156 (April–September 1991): 673–677.

Hinojosa, María
(María de Lourdes Hinojosa)
(1961–   ) *journalist, autobiographer, activist*

A socially committed reporter proud of her Mexican heritage, María Hinojosa is a highly influential journalist who has helped Americans understand their country's diversity, as well as the effects of oppression and prejudice. Her warmth, sensitivity, and ingenuity in portraying unsung heroes as well as covering international events have garnered her many prestigious awards.

María de Lourdes Hinojosa was born in Mexico City, Mexico, on July 2, 1961, as the fourth child of Raúl and Berta (Ojeda) Hinojosa. The family moved to the East Coast of the United States when María was 18 months old. After a few years in New England, her father, a medical research doctor, moved the family to Chicago. Every summer, María enjoyed family trips by car to different parts of Mexico. These summer vacations instilled in her a deep pride in her cultural heritage. However, they also made her distinctly aware of socioeconomic injustice. When she witnessed young wealthy kids in her private school being apathetic about poverty in her hometown, Hinojosa organized fellow students at her school to join the activist group Students for a Better Environment.

María first dreamed of becoming an actress. She attended Barnard College and pursued her dream until she found that the limiting world of theater could place her in neither the white nor Mexican box. Undaunted, Hinojosa turned to radio. She created the show *Nueva Canción y Demás,* becoming the first bilingual radio show host on WCKR-FM

in New York City. She changed her major from theater to Latin-American studies and political economy, graduating magna cum laude in 1985.

After graduation, Hinojosa applied for an internship at National Public Radio (NPR) and received a position as a production assistant in the Washington, D.C., office. She produced news stories and minidocumentaries for one year. She then moved to Tijuana, Mexico, to work as the associate producer of *Enfoque Nacional,* a weekly Spanish national news program at NPR in San Diego, California. In 1987, Hinojosa returned to New York, accepting a position as producer at CBS radio. Among the many shows she produced were *Where We Stand with Walter Cronkite, The Osgood File,* and *Newsbreak.* In 1988, she became a freelance reporter and began building altars in celebration of the Day of the Dead, a tradition she still continues. She won the Silver Award from the Corporation for Public Broadcasting for the show *Day of the Dead* in 1989.

In 1990, Hinojosa began work at WNYC Radio. She also worked as a general reporter for NPR's New York bureau and began to host *New York Hotline,* becoming the first Latina to host a prime-time public affairs news television show in New York. She married Germán Pérez, a critically acclaimed painter from the Dominican Republic, in 1991. The amalgamation of Pan-American and Mexican-American culture in her city and in her home continues to excite and inspire Hinojosa.

Throughout the 1990s, Hinojosa amassed several awards and honors, including the International Radio Festival of New York Silver Award, the Unity Award, a Top Story and first place Radio Award from the National Association of Hispanic Journalists, a first place from the New York Newswomen's Club, and an Associated Press award for her coverage of Nelson Mandela. In 1995, *Hispanic Business Magazine* named her one of the 100 most influential Latinos in the United States. She provided the foreword to *Daughters of the Fifth Sun: A Collection of Latina Fiction and Poetry* and received the Robert F. Kennedy Award for an NPR documentary exploring how jail has become a right of passage for men of all races. That same year, Hinojosa released *Crews: Gang Members Talk with Maria Hinojosa,* a book based on her award-winning NPR report. She gave birth to Raul in 1996, followed by her daughter, Yurema, 1998. In 1997, Hinojosa joined CNN to cover urban affairs in New York.

In 1999, Hinojosa wrote a memoir entitled *Raising Raul: An Adventure Raising Myself and My Son,* in which her vivaciousness suffuses her journey through the early stages of motherhood with poignancy and sincerity. It is particularly this type of honest and down-to-earth writing that has earned Hinojosa a reputation as a trustworthy, perceptive journalist as well as several awards, including the 2002 Latino Heritage Award from Columbia University, the RUBÉN SALAZAR Award from the National Council of La Raza, selection as one of the 25 Most Influential Working Mothers in America by *Working Mother* magazine, an Associated Press Award, the Robert F. Kennedy Award, the National Association of Hispanic Journalists Radio Award, the New York Society of Professional Journalists Deadline Award, the Unity Award, and the NAMME Catalyst Award from the National Association of Minority Media Executives in 2005.

In 2001, Hinojosa reported a weeklong CNN/*Time* magazine series, *The New Frontier/La Nueva Frontera,* which chronicled issues along the U.S.-Mexico border in a post-NAFTA era. She followed with a column for *Time* magazine called "Living La Vida Latina," in which Hinojosa wrote about balancing Mexican heritage with American childhood. In October 2004, Hinojosa produced the documentary *Immigrant Nation: Divided Country,* becoming the first Latina to produce a documentary for CNN. Hinojosa, who became a correspondent for the PBS newsmagazine *NOW* in 2005, said in a 2005 interview: "I hope that my journalism inspires people to feel things deeply, to question the world around them. And I would hope it makes people see what draws them together as human beings as opposed to what sets us apart."

Further Reading

Hinojosa, María. *Crews: Gang Members Talk to Maria Hinojosa.* New York: Harcourt Paperbacks, 1995.
———. *Raising Raul: Adventures Raising Myself and My Son.* New York: Penguin Books. 2000.
Milligan, Bryce, Mary Guerrero Milligan, and Angela de Hoyos, eds. *Daughters of the Fifth Sun.* New York: Riverhead Trade, 1996.
Tardiff, Joseph C., and L. Mpho Mabunda, eds. *Dictionary of Hispanic Biography.* Detroit: Gale Research, 1996, pp. 428–430.

Hinojosa-Smith, Rolando
(Rolando Hinojosa)
(1929–   ) *novelist, biographer, educator*

Rolando Hinojosa-Smith was the first Chicano author to receive a major international literary award. He is best known for his series of novels based in the fictitious Klail City of Belken County, Texas.

Rolando Hinojosa-Smith was born in Mercedes, Texas, on January 21, 1929, the youngest son of Carrie Effie Smith, an Anglo homemaker, and Manuel Guzman Hinojosa, a Mexican-American farmer. Although his paternal family had lived in Texas for two generations, they maintained a strong loyalty to Mexico. His father had fought in the Mexican Revolution. The Mexican Revolution of 1910 was an uprising of common folk who overthrew the dictator Porfirio Díaz, and violence continued throughout Mexico until 1920. Originally from Illinois, his mother was raised among Mexican Americans and comfortable with both the English and Spanish languages and customs. Rolando's first language was Spanish. An avid reader, he attended schools that reinforced Mexican culture with the daily singing of the "Himno Nacional," the Mexican national anthem. Surrounded primarily by other Mexican-American students, Hinojosa-Smith did not encounter many Anglo children nor the English language in school until he attended junior high school.

During high school Hinojosa-Smith enjoyed football, theater, and membership in the science, theater, and Pan-American clubs. At the age of 15, he had his work published in *Creative Bits,* an annual literary magazine. After graduating from high school in 1946, Hinojosa-Smith moved out of the Rio Grande Valley but would return there many times in the following years. From 1946 to 1948, he served in the U.S. Army. He then attended the University of Texas until he was reactivated in 1950 when the Korean War erupted. His experiences in Korea informed some of his later work, particularly *Korean Love Songs from Klail City Death Trip* (1980). Hinojosa-Smith edited a camp publication while stationed at Fort Eustis, Virginia. He was later sent to the Caribbean, where he became a radio announcer and the editor of the Caribbean Army Defense Command newspaper. Hinojosa-Smith returned to school in the early 1950s. In 1954, he graduated from the University of Texas with a B.A. in Spanish.

After graduation Hinojosa-Smith began his teaching career at Brownsville High School, located at the southern tip of the Rio Grande Valley. After two years, he quit to earn more money as a common laborer in a chemical processing plant. From 1954 to 1958, he wrote little but read voraciously, particularly Spanish literature and Russian novelists. In 1959, he went to work for a clothing manufacturer in Brownsville, then spent two more years as a high school teacher. He decided to begin graduate studies at Highlands University in Las Vegas, New Mexico, at the urging and support of the dean of humanities in the summer of 1960. He married Patricia Louise Mandley in 1963. The couple has three children. He earned an M.A. in Spanish from Highlands and received a Ph.D. in Spanish in 1969 from the University of Illinois–Urbana.

Hinojosa-Smith began a close friendship with TOMÁS RIVERA in 1971. Rivera sent excerpts of Hinojosa-Smith's *Estampas del valle y otras obras* to *El Grito,* an important early Chicano journal of the humanities and the social sciences, which published the excerpts. Hinojosa-Smith published *Estampas del valle y otras obras* in 1972. The bilingual edition, with translation by Gustavo Valadez and Jose Reyna, was published as *Sketches of the Valley and Other Works* in 1980. A revised English-language edition was published as *The Valley* in 1983, and *Estampas del valle* was released in its original form in 1992. This first novel in the Klail City Death Trip series is difficult to pigeonhole into a specific genre, a fact that frustrated many critics. The *estampas,* "or sketches," offer insight into the lives and characters of the people living in a fictional town located in the lower Rio Grande Valley. A total of 25 characters are introduced in the book, leaving an impression of a community rather than an individual as the protagonist. Hinojosa-Smith was awarded the third annual Quinto Sol prize for *Estampas del valle y otras obras* in 1973.

Throughout the 1970s Hinojosa-Smith continued his work in education, moving into administration. He placed many short pieces with literary journals and magazines such as *Bilingual Review, Mester, Revista Chicano Riqueña, Caracol,* and *Hispamérica.* He published *Klail City y sus alrededores* in 1976 (rereleased as *Klail City* in 1987). Winner of the prestigious Premio Casa de las Américas, the second novel in the Klail City Death Trip series weaves together the divergent points of view of 100 characters living ordinary lives. The distinguished judges commented on the author's skillful use of dialogue and humor, descriptive vigor, innovative use of time and space, richness of imagery, and extraordinary control of dialect.

Korean Love Songs from Klail City Death Trip (1978) followed as a book of several long poems and the third in the Klail City Death Trip series. Hinojosa-Smith conjures his memories of time spent in Korea to inform this work. *Claros varones de Belken,* the fourth novel in the Klail City Death Trip series, was published 1986 and reprinted in a bilingual edition, with translation by Julia Cruz, as *Fair Gentlemen of Belken County* in 1987. This novel focuses on four principal characters, Rafa Buenrostro, Jehú Malacara, P. Galindo, and Esteban Echevarría, through the use of dialogues and monologues.

Mi querido Rafa (1981, translated by Hinojosa and published as *Dear Rafe* in 1985) received the Southwestern Conference on Latin American Studies prize for best writing in the humanities in 1982. The book is divided into two parts, with the first half written in epistolary form and the second comprised of commentaries from the Klail City inhabitants. In *Rites and Witnesses* (1982), Hinojosa-Smith uses dialogue, vignettes, and reportage to depict life in Klail City during the late 1950s and early 1960s. In 1983, Hinojosa was inducted into the Texas Institute of Letters. He released *Partners in Crime: A Rafe Buenrostro Mystery* (1985), which critics praised for its lyricism, dialogue, and perfection of classic detective style.

Hinojosa-Smith took a short break from his series to translate the late Tomás Rivera's critically acclaimed *. . . y no se lo tragó la tierra/ . . . and the Earth Did Not Devour Him*. Hinojosa-Smith's translation was released as *This Migrant Earth* in 1986, two years after Rivera died from a heart attack. In 1988, Hinojosa recorded the life and work of his friend in *Tomás Rivera, 1935–1984: The Man and His Work* (coedited with Gary D. Killer and Vernon E. Lattin). He returned to Klail City with *Los amigos de Becky* (1990, *Becky and Her Friends*), which employs the opinions of 26 characters from previous novels in the Klail City Death Trip series (including Becky) to discuss Becky's divorce from Ira Escobar and her subsequent marriage to Jehú Malacara. *The Useless Servants* (1993) contains only one narrative voice, Rafa Buenrostro, who in diary form relates his experiences as an infantryman in the U.S. Army during the Korean conflict. Hinojosa-Smith's other works include *El condado de Belken—Klail City* (1994; Belken County—Klail City) and *Ask a Policeman (Rafe Buenrostro Mysteries)* (1998).

Hinojosa-Smith has been widely translated and celebrated throughout Europe and Latin America. His work has been anthologized and included in high school and college curricula. His papers are in the Nettie Lee Benson Latin American Collection at the University of Texas–Austin. Hinojosa-Smith's skillful and sensitive portrayal of the Southwest, with more than 1,000 characters, creates a rich tapestry of the complexities as well as the simple joys of living. He breaks down the barriers between reader and character with a multiplication of points of view that helps readers readily relate to various events, situations, and relationships. In this style, Hinojosa-Smith transcends the Chicano microculture in the Rio Grande Valley to offer a collective look at the many facets of life anywhere in the world.

Further Reading

Kanellos, Nicolás, et al., eds. *Herencia: The Anthology of Hispanic Literature in the United States*. New York: Oxford University Press, 2003.

Lee, Joyce Glover. *Rolando Hinojosa and the American Dream*. Texas Writers Series. Denton: University of North Texas Press, 1997.

Saldívar, José David. *Rolando Hinojosa Reader: Essays Historical and Critical*. Houston, Tex.: Arte Público Press, 1985.

Tardiff, Joseph C., and L. Mpho Mabunda, eds. *Dictionary of Hispanic Biography*. Detroit: Gale Research, 1996, pp. 430–432.

Huerta, Jorge
(George Alfonso Huerta, Jorge A. Huerta)
(1942–   ) *literary critic, educator*

Jorge Huerta is considered the foremost authority on and guiding presence of contemporary Chicano and U.S. Latino theater. Often called "Daddy" by his students, former and present, he has more than 80 published works on Chicano theater, including a number of articles, reviews, and research

Jorge Huerta is responsible for establishing much of the prestige Chicano theater has reached in the world of academia. *(Courtesy of the author)*

papers; three anthologies of plays; and two landmark books, *Chicano Theatre: Themes and Forms* (1982) and *Chicano Drama: Performance, Society, and Myth* (2000).

George Alfonso Huerta was born in Boyle Heights, California, at Japanese White Memorial Hospital on November 20, 1942, to Jorge Rodriguez and Elizabeth Trevizo Huerta. His mother had arrived in Arizona with her family in 1908, when she was four years old, while his father had immigrated to the United States during the Mexican Revolution. The Mexican Revolution of 1910 was an uprising of peasants who overthrew the dictator Porfirio Díaz, and violence continued in

Mexico through 1920. Jorge and Elizabeth married when she was 14, first settling in the El Paso, Texas–Juárez, Mexico, area before moving to Los Angeles, California, in the early 1920s. Jorge was light, or *güero,* while Elizabeth was darker, *la prieta,* and George, the only boy out of six children, came out *café con leche.* He was the youngest and *el consentido,* "the pampered one."

Huerta's father was a musician and played everything from Bach to mariachi music on all the stringed instruments. In the 1950s, Huerta's eldest sisters took their siblings to musicals in Los Angeles. They were Protestant and a very cultured family growing up in Lincoln Heights in northeastern Los Angeles. Huerta's father may have been a socialist. He would read the Mexican newspapers when Fidel Castro was coming into power and taught George that capitalism was not good for the working class. He was a union man and a great influence on George, as were his older sisters.

George attended Loreto Street School in Cypress Park, Nightingale Junior High, and Benjamin Franklin High School in Highland Park, all in northeastern Los Angeles. He dreamed of becoming a Broadway musical comedy star or a movie star. Huerta acted in Hollywood on television in the 1950s, which gave him, as he put it in a 2005 interview, "a very good taste of the ups and downs of the profession at an early age."

Despite his refined upbringing, Huerta felt he constantly had to prove he was as good as or even better than the dominant culture. Huerta attributes the family's Protestant upbringing to why all his siblings got so far in life. His sisters were in college in the 1940s—when few Chicanos or Chicanas were graduating from high school, much less going to college. His parents and older sisters taught him to fight for the rights of all peoples, regardless of ethnicity, class, gender, or race.

Huerta received a B.A. and M.A. in theater from California State College at Los Angeles in 1965 and 1967, respectively. Huerta married Virginia "Ginger" DeMirjian, who would later bear two sons, Ronald DeMirjian Huerta and Gregory DeMirjian Huerta. The boys have their mother's maiden name so they would never forget their dual heritages: Mexican-Chicano and Armenian.

Huerta served as the director of theater at Rubidoux High School from 1966 to 1969. He then taught at Pasadena City College for a year. In 1971, Huerta, along with six undergraduates at the University of California–Santa Barbara, founded El Teatro de la Esperanza, a Chicano theater troupe. Huerta served as the artistic director for El Teatro de la Esperanza until 1974. Always a lover of reading plays and translating the dialogue to the stage, in 1972 Huerta wrote and published a one-act play, *El renacimiento de Huitzilopochtli* (The rebirth of Huitzilopochtli), which he directed with members of El Teatro de la Esperanza. In that same year, Huerta released *A Bibliography of Chicano and Mexican Dance, Drama, and Music.* In 1974, Huerta became the first Chicano to earn a Ph.D. in dramatic arts. He graduated from the University of California–Santa Barbara.

Huerta became an assistant professor of theater at the University of California–San Diego in 1975. He held the position until 1981, when he accepted a promotion to associate professor. Huerta released *Chicano Theatre: Themes and Forms* in 1982. This book was the first to examine Chicano theater and drama as a field of study and stands alone today as a tome of critical analysis and consideration of Chicano theater's roots.

Huerta has received 28 fellowships and/or awards. The most impressive in this long list are the Ford Foundation Dissertation Fellowship (1974) and the Ford Foundation Post-Doc Fellowship (1980). From 2000 to 2002, Huerta and two other professors, CARLOS MORTON of the University of California–Santa Barbara and Jose Luis Valenzuela of the University of California–Los Angeles (UCLA), raised $175,000 to host the Festival of Chicano Theatre Classics at UCLA in 2002.

Huerta was awarded full professorship in 1988 at the University of California–San Diego. In 1989,

he released *Necessary Theatre: Six Plays about the Chicano Experience.* This anthology provides introductions to six plays and offers an analysis of how they work together to represent the Chicano experience. He also coedited with NICOLÁS KANELLOS *Nuevos Pasos: Chicano and Puerto Rican Drama,* a collection of eight plays by the most renowned Chicano and Puerto Rican playwrights. In 1990, Huerta cofounded and served as artistic director for Teatro Máscara Mágical in San Diego. Four years later, Huerta was appointed chancellor's associate professor of theater at the University of California–San Diego, which is a permanent endowed chair.

Huerta published *Chicano Drama: Performance, Society, and Myth* in 2000. This book begins in 1979, when LUIS VALDEZ's play *Zoot Suit* appeared on Broadway. Through biographies of each playwright and enlightening analyses of their plays, Huerta examines the Chicano/a experience by exploring a variety of issues including identity, community, and spirituality.

In 2005, Huerta became the chief diversity officer at the University of California–San Diego. In his new position, Huerta is eager to make a difference in the color and gender of the campus. Huerta stated in a 2005 interview, "[M]y students have always been and continue to be my inspiration. Benicio del Toro is the most visible of the people I have directed and taught, but there are people all over the country who I have introduced to theatre and teatro and who are carrying the baton onward and upward. That's what teaching is all about and I am very, very proud of having made a difference in the lives of so many wonderful young (and old) people through my work. My writing and my directing have reached across oceans and continents, I am proud to say."

Huerta has presented lectures and workshops on Chicano theater in the United States, western Europe, and Latin America, including Venezuela, Panama, and Mexico, and represented the United States at international theater festivals in Colombia and Cádiz, Spain. Huerta has been a panelist and reviewer for the National Endowment for the Arts, the California Arts Council, the National Research Council, and the Corporation for Public Broadcasting.

Huerta's books, reviews, training, directing, and teachings have brought Chicano theater and drama to a worldwide audience. His commitment to Chicano theater is deeply ingrained in the belief that theater is a great vehicle for sharing and conveying common ground and understanding. Through Huerta's dedication, the Chicano influence and experience is felt within the overall fabric of American society.

Further Reading

Cortés, Eladio, and Mirta Barrea-Maryls, eds. *Encyclopedia of Latin American Theatre.* Westport, Conn.: Greenwood Press, 2003.

Huerta, Jorge A., ed. *Necessary Theatre: Six Plays about the Chicano Experience.* Houston, Tex.: Arte Público Press, 1989.

Klam, Michael. "Hispanic Heritage Month—UCSD's Jorge Huerta "'Diversity Matters.'" *LaPrensa San Diego,* September 16, 2005, p. 1.

Ryan, Bryan, ed. *Hispanic Writers.* Detroit: Gale Research, 1991.

I

Idar, Jovita
(Jovita Idar de Juárez, Jovita Idar-Juárez, Jovita Juárez)
(1885–1942) *journalist, educator, editor, activist*

Jovita Idar is remembered as an extremely courageous journalist and activist. She wrote for her family's newspaper, *La Crónica,* and founded La Liga Femenil Mexcanista (the League of Mexican Women).

Born on January 7, 1885, in Laredo, Texas, Jovita Idar was the second of eight children of Jovita Vivero and Nicasio Clemente Idar. Jovita grew up in the U.S.-Mexican border town of Laredo during the years of growing frustration with Mexican president Porfirio Díaz. She witnessed two lynchings of fellow Mexican Americans and sought ways to help them. She earned a teaching certificate from the Holding Institute, a Methodist school, in 1903. She then taught Mexican children in Ojuelos; however, the deplorable conditions so frustrated Idar that she felt she would have a greater chance of improving and/or aiding Mexicans through writing and activism. She joined two of her brothers and her father at the family's newspaper, *La Crónica.* She wrote articles demanding equality for Mexicans. By 1910, she had a weekly column in which she supported the Mexican Revolution, vehemently opposed the brutalities of the Texas Rangers (the police force), and called for women to educate themselves and become independent from men. The Mexican Revolution of 1910 was an uprising of common people who overthrew the dictator, Díaz, and violence continued in Mexico through 1920.

In 1911, *La Crónica* formed the Gran Liga Mexicanista de Beneficencia y Protección (Grand Mexican League for Benefit and Protection), which urged lodge members of the Caballeros de Honor Order to hold the first Mexican congress. The league adopted the motto "Por la Raza y Para la Raza" ("For the Race and By the Race") with a primary mission of protecting Mexican Americans from the racist actions of Texas Rangers and other Anglos. Idar, as well as other women, participated in the congress, which also discussed social, labor, education, and economic matters. The meeting is considered the first attempt in Mexican-American history to organize a militant feminist social movement. As a result of the women's determination, in October 1911 the League of Mexican Women was formed. Idar became its first president and organized its principal effort, to provide education for poor children.

After an attack on Nuevo Laredo, Mexico, in 1913, Idar joined LEONOR VILLEGAS DE MAGNÓN and the Cruz Blanca, or White Cross, a medical relief team that treated the wounded forces of revolutionary leader Venustiano Carranza, whose forces were known as the Constitutional Army. Her father died the following year, and Idar took over control of *La Crónica.* She wrote a scathing article criticizing American president Woodrow Wilson's decision to deploy troops to the U.S.-Mexican border, where they incurred the wrath of the Texas Rangers. Four Rangers came to Idar's home to destroy her press equipment. Idar planted herself in the doorway and refused the officials entrance. The Rangers left, to the immense delight of the onlookers; however, they returned in the middle of the night and destroyed the presses, the linotype machine, and all of Idar's equipment and supplies.

Idar married Bartolo Juárez in 1917. The couple moved to the relative safety of San Antonio, where Idar became an active member of the Democratic Party. She continued to write, serving as an editor of *El Heraldo Cristiano,* a publication of the Rio Grande Conference of the Methodist Church. Education and community service remained important to Idar. She established a free kindergarten in 1920 and worked as an interpreter for Spanish-speaking patients in the county hospital until her death in 1946.

Further Reading

Berson, Robin Kadison. *Marching to a Different Drummer: Unrecognizable Heroes of American History.* Westport, Conn.: Greenwood Pres, 1994.

Gibson, Karen Bush. *Jovita Idar.* Hockessin, Del.: Mitchell Lane, 2002.

Kanellos, Nicolás, with Helvetia Martell. *Hispanic Periodicals in the United States: A Brief History and Comprehensive Bibliography.* Houston, Tex.: Arte Público Press, 2000.

Meier, Matt S., and Margo Gutierrez. *Encyclopedia of the Mexican American Civil Rights Movement.* Westport, Conn.: Greenwood Press, 2000.

Islas, Arturo

(1938–1991) *poet, essayist, novelist, short story writer, educator*

Arturo Islas is best known for his novel *The Rain God* and its sequel, *Migrant Souls.* The son of Arturo Islas and Jovita La Farga, he was born on May 24, 1938, in El Paso, Texas. During the Mexican Revolution, a violent period from approximately 1910 to 1920 when the people fought against the cruel dictatorship of Porfirio Díaz, Mexican troops killed Islas's paternal grandparents' first son. When one of the revolution's most infamous insurrectionists, Pancho Villa, advised Islas's grandfather to leave the country lest he face another tragedy, he and his wife, Crecenciana, moved to El Paso. They bore another son, who would be Islas's father. As a child, Islas spent many hours with his grandmother Crecenciana, who was pleased with her first grandson's light complexion and the fact that he spoke pure Castillian Spanish. He delved into literature from an early age and was thus able to escape his physical ailments, including polio.

One of the first Chicano professors, Arturo Islas also wrote frankly about racial, political, and sexual topics. *(Photo of Arturo Islas is reprinted with permission from the publisher [APP Archive Files] [Houston: Arte Público Press—University of Houston, © 2006])*

After graduating from El Paso High School in 1956, Islas received an Alfred P. Sloan Scholarship to study at Stanford University, where he earned a B.A. in literature with distinction in 1960, an M.A. in 1963, and a Ph.D. in 1971, the later degrees in English. He was awarded fellowships to support him through his schooling and taught literature courses at a local hospital and an adult school in San Francisco, despite undergoing three surgeries for intestinal cancer. In 1970, Islas was appointed to a tenure-track position at Stanford. He spent his academic career at Stanford, first as an assistant professor, 1971–76, then as an associate professor, 1976–86, and finally as a professor of American and Chicano literature, 1986–91.

Throughout his teaching career, Islas wrote essays, short stories, and poems that were published in a variety of publications. His work was noted for its sensitivity, insight, and openness. During the 1970s, he became active in the Chicano movement and began to explore his homosexuality. In 1976, he completed his first novel, originally entitled *Dia de los muertos/Day of the Dead.* The book, which depicts life for a Mexican family in a border town, was rejected for eight years before being published with a new title, *The Rain God,* in 1984 to critical acclaim. It was selected as one of the three best novels of 1984 by the Bay Area Book Reviewers Association and received the best fiction prize from the Border Regional Library Association in 1985 and the Southwest Book Award for fiction in 1986.

As a result of his success with *The Rain God,* Islas released the sequel, *Migrant Souls,* in 1990. In these works, Islas explores the imposed racial lines that separate good from bad, particularly between the Spanish aristocracy and humble nature of Indians. He also addresses themes of gender, patriarchy, and traditional views of homosexuality.

Cutting a flourishing writing career short, Islas died of AIDS-related pneumonia on February 15, 1991. *La Mollie and the King of Tears: A Novel* was published posthumously in 1996 and edited by Paul Skenazy. After Islas's death, 52 boxes of his unpublished fiction and nonfiction material were found. Frederick Luis Aldama edited the collection and published it as *Arturo Islas: The Uncollected Works* (2002). The following year, Aldama released *Dancing with Ghosts: A Critical Biography of Arturo Islas.* Islas played a pioneering role in bridging Anglo, Latin American, Chicano/a, and European storytelling styles and voices.

Further Reading

Aldama, Frederick Luis. *Dancing with Ghosts: A Critical Biography of Arturo Islas.* Berkeley: University of California Press, 2004.

Heide, Rick, ed. *Under the Fifth Sun: Latino Literature from California.* Santa Clara and Berkeley, Calif.: Santa Clara University/Heyday Books, 2002.

Lomelí, Francisco A., and Carl R. Shirley, eds. *Chicano Writers: Second Series.* Vol. 122. Detroit: Gale Research, 1992, pp. 197–203.

J

Jaramillo, Cleofas Martínez
(Cleofas Martínez, Cleofas M. Jaramillo)
(1878–1956) *novelist, poet, autobiographer, folklorist*

Author of four books, Cleofas Martínez Jaramillo wrote in a variety of genres and on many topics to preserve the Hispanic culture and customs of New Mexico. Cleofas Martínez was born on December 6, 1878, in Arroyo Hondo, New Mexico. She was one of seven children born to Julian Antonio, a businessman, and Mariana Lucero Martínez, both of whom belonged to pioneering families. (Originally the family surname was Martín, but it was later changed to Martínez.) Cleofas benefited from her father's shrewd business sense in mining, merchandising, and livestock. She enjoyed a comfortable childhood. Her mother often entertained her with stories. When she was nine, she began attending a convent school in Taos, New Mexico, where she was not permitted to speak Spanish—a rule she vehemently resented.

Upon graduation, Martínez attended Loretto Academy, a high school, in Santa Fe, New Mexico, where she happily and formally studied Spanish. Her cousin Venceslao Jaramillo began to court her while at the academy. He was a colonel and staff member for territorial governor MIGUEL A. OTERO. In 1889, she married Jaramillo. They enjoyed a honeymoon in Los Angeles, California, before settling in El Rito, New Mexico. Venceslao provided his wife with an extravagant lifestyle. He entered politics and owned a 33,000-acre sheep ranch, a store, and farmland. They had three children, two of whom died in infancy. Due to Venceslao's ailing health, the couple and their daughter, Angélica, moved to Denver, Colorado. Venceslao died in 1920. At 42, Jaramillo entered the business world of Santa Fe in an attempt to maintain her lifestyle. At the age of 17, Angélica was murdered. The loss of her daughter and husband affected Jaramillo deeply and seemed to parallel the cultural loss and longing she felt for an idealized bucolic past.

While grieving, Jaramillo immersed herself in the folklore and customs of New Mexico. In 1935, she read an article from *Holland's Magazine* on Spanish and Mexican cuisine. Believing the information to be deficient, she set about compiling traditional recipes. Writing in English to reach a wider audience, Jaramillo released *The Genuine New Mexico Tasty Recipes: Portales sabrosos* (1939). The book was rereleased as *The Genuine New Mexico Tasty Recipes: With Additional Materials on Traditional Hispano Food* in 1981. In an effort to preserve the quickly disappearing Hispanic culture, Jaramillo translated 25 of her mother's stories into English and released them as *Cuentos del hogar/Spanish Fairy Tales* (1939). Based on the same article in *Holland's Magazine,* Jaramillo was also inspired to found La Sociedad Folklórica in Santa Fe in an effort to preserve Hispanic culture.

Shadows of the Past (1941) recalls the Hispanic customs and traditions of the Southwest with a reverent, often nostalgic combination of school customs, domesticity, religion, witchcraft, food, and superstitions. Throughout the book, Jaramillo offers portraits of the women in her family, revealing an oasis of European culture surrounded by an ever-evolving modern world.

Romance of a Little Girl (1955) is an autobiographical account in which she laments her need to use English as a means to preserve her culture, of which the Spanish language plays a dominant role. Jaramillo died a year after its release. Her work along with that of other Hispanic women writers of the Southwest was largely forgotten until the Chicano movement. Although critic Raymond A. Paredes places Jaramillo in the "hacienda" mentality of authors, Tey Diana Rebolledo emphasizes the value and importance of the Hispanic women who wrote against oppression not only of the Anglo culture but the male-dominated Hispanic culture as well. Jaramillo's devotion to a vanishing culture preserved the traditions of the once-wealthy Hispanic society that would have otherwise been forgotten.

Further Reading

Lomelí, Francisco A., and Carl R. Shirley, eds. *Chicano Writers: Second Series.* Vol. 122. Detroit: Gale Research, 1992, pp. 154–158.

Peacock, Scot, ed. *Contemporary Authors.* Vol. 179. Detroit: Gale Research Group, 2000.

Rebolledo, Tey Diana, and Eliana S. Rivero. *Infinite Divisions: An Anthology of Chicana Literature.* Tucson: University of Arizona Press, 1993.

K

Kanellos, Nicolás

(1945–) editor, publisher, educator, literary critic, activist

Nicolás Kanellos cofounded the first Hispanic literary magazine, *Revista Chicano Riqueña* (later the *Americas Review*), and the first Hispanic publisher, Arte Público Press. The prestige and place Hispanic and Latino literature holds in the academic world and American literature as a whole were built in large part on Kanellos's dedication and persistence.

The son of Charles and Inés (de Choudens García) Kanellos, Nicolás Kanellos was born in New York City on January 31, 1945. His father was of Greek heritage, and his mother was Puerto Rican. During his youth, Puerto Ricans were the subject of intense racism and prejudice—from the media, within the school systems, and in the community at large. Latinos did not hold any position of authority in school or law; only in sports did Nicolás bear witness to the value of Latinos in America. However, during his yearly visits to Puerto Rico, he saw Puerto Ricans holding jobs of immense importance, such as lawyers, doctors, and government figures. In this way, he discovered that the American-held negative stereotypes of Puerto Ricans were not based on any innate inadequacy of Latinos but were merely opinions. Nicolás developed a "chip on his shoulder" and got into many fights in order to protect the honor of his people.

When Nicolás was nine, his family moved close to a large commercial book bindery in the warehouse district of Jersey City, New Jersey. Nicolás would pull the discarded, large printed sheets, known as signatures in the publishing industry, and create books of his own. He became an avid reader, supported by his father, who smuggled food from the restaurant where he worked and bartered it for books from the bindery workers. In this way, the Kanellos family acquired a near complete set of the *Encyclopedia of America.* Kanellos devoured these tomes and other collected books, such as the complete works of John Steinbeck, Ernest Hemingway, and Somerset Maugham.

During the 1950s, the immigration of Puerto Ricans into the United States was at its peak. Since Kanellos was bilingual, teachers often asked him to translate for the newest arrivals. His aunt Providencia García served as a major influence and example in Kanellos's life. García overcame gender and racial discrimination to develop the Latin division of Peer Southern Music Company (Peer International), to this day the largest Latin music publisher in the world, and became a primary influence in creating the Latin boom in music.

Kanellos gained a B.A. in Spanish literature from Fairleigh Dickinson University in 1966 and an M.A. in Romance languages from the University of Texas–Austin in 1968. He spent a year studying at the Universidad Nacional de México and another year at the University of Lisbon–Portugal. In 1970, he entered the Ph.D. program in Spanish and Portuguese literature at the University of Texas–Austin and earned his doctorate in 1974. While he did his graduate work, Kanellos became deeply involved in the Chicano movement. He worked in the Teatro Chicano de Austin, then moved to Gary, Indiana, where he founded *Revista Chicano Riqueña* (later the *American Review*) in 1972 and formed El Teatro de Desengaño del Pueblo (The People's Enlightenment Theater). He also taught Hispanic literature at Indiana University from 1971 to 1979.

In hopes of finding more funding for his publishing projects, Kanellos accepted a tenured faculty position at the University of Houston in 1979, where he opened the doors to Arte Público Press, the first modern-day Hispanic publishing house in the United States. Since then, Kanellos has written or edited *Mexican American Theater: Legacy and Reality* (1987); *Biographical Dictionary of Hispanic Literature in the United States: The Literature of Puerto Ricans, Puerto Rican Americans, Cuban Americans, and Other Hispanic Writers* (1989); *The Hispanic American Almanac: A Reference Work on Hispanics in the United States* (1993); *The Hispanic Almanac: From Columbus to Corporate America* (1994); *Chronology of Hispanic-American History: From Pre-Columbian Times to the Present* (coedited with Christelia Perez, 1995); *Hispanic Literary Companion* (1996); *Hispanic Periodicals in the United States, Origins to 1960: A Brief History and Comprehensive Bibliography* (2000); *Noche Buena: Hispanic American Christmas Stories* (2000); and *Herencia: An Anthology of Hispanic Literature of the United States* (coedited with Kenya Dworkin y Méndez, José B. Fernández, Erlinda González-Berry, Agnes Lugo-Ortiz, and Charles Tatum, 2004). *Herencia* is the first collection to feature the comprehensive works of Hispanic writing in the United States, covering writings from the 1500s to its publication.

He has also authored *Mexican American Theater: Then and Now* (1983), *Hispanic Theatre in the United States* (1984), *Two Centuries of Hispanic Theatre in the Southwest* (1985), *A History of Hispanic Theatre in the United States* (1990),

Nicolás Kanellos founded Arte Público Press, America's largest publisher of contemporary and recovered literature by U.S. Latino authors. *(Photo of Nicolás Kanellos is reprinted with permission from the publisher [APP Archive Files] [Houston: Arte Público Press—University of Houston, © 2006])*

Hispanic American Literature: A Brief Introduction and Anthology (1995), *Hispanic Firsts: 500 Years of Extraordinary Achievement* (1997), *Thirty Million Strong: Reclaiming the Hispanic Image in American Culture* (1998), and *Hispanic Literature of the United States: A Comprehensive Reference* (2004). He has contributed to journals such as *Hispania, Latin American Theater Review, Journal of Popular Culture,* and *Vista.*

In 1992, Kanellos launched the Recovering the U.S. Hispanic Literary Heritage program, which endeavors to locate, preserve, index, and publish Latino literary contributions from the colonial period to 1960. In 1994, Kanellos founded the Ph.D. program in Hispanic literature at the University of Houston and was awarded an endowed chair from the Brown Foundation. Concurrently, Arte Público Press developed Piñata Books, a children's division funded by a grant from the Mellon Foundation to publish children's books that depict Latino culture. Kanellos has received many honors, including a Hispanic Heritage Award for Literature (awarded by President Ronald Reagan in 1988), the American Library Association's Award for Best Reference Work (1993), and appointment to the National Council on the Humanities (by President Bill Clinton in 1994).

Kanellos is largely responsible for making Hispanic literature accessible to mainstream readers. He commented to Contemporary Authors Online about his perspective on his work: "As a publisher of Hispanic literature in the United States, I feel like a missionary who has to convert people to their own religion and identity. Hispanic culture has always been a part of the United States and its identity. People do not realize this because the publishing and intellectual establishment have kept it a secret while selling us on an old-world identity. . . . Arte Público Press intends to give back to the United States its many varied peoples."

Further Reading

Kanellos, Nicolás. *Noche Buena: Hispanic American Christmas Stories.* New York: Oxford University Press, 2000.

Meyer, Nicolas E. *Biographical Dictionary of Hispanic Americans.* New York: Facts On File, 1997.

Peacock, Scot, ed. *Contemporary Authors.* Detroit, Mich.: Gale Reasearch Group, 2002.

L

Landres, Marcela
(Marcela Acuria)
(1968–   ) *editor, activist, educator, publisher*

Marcela Landres, a dedicated editor and consultant, offers Latinos the resources as well as the advocacy they need to get their voices and experiences published and included as an integral aspect of American literature. Formerly an editor at Simon and Schuster, Landres is now an independent editorial consultant and publisher of *Latinidad*, a free career advice newsletter for Latino writers.

Marcela Acuria was born in New York City on September 15, 1968, to Olga and Julio Acuria, both Ecuadorean immigrants. Raised in the projects of Long Island City, in New York, Marcela led a sheltered life due to the protection of her father. As a child, she dreamed of becoming the first doctor in the family, primarily because it was her parents' wish. Her elementary school teachers liked her because she was a good student and well behaved, but they worried because she never spoke in class. As a youth, Marcela was painfully shy.

She turned to books, reading everything she could to expand her circumscribed universe. There was a little library a block from where she lived as a child. Each and every author she read as a child helped to influence and shape her world. She read voraciously, seeking any books that reflected her reality as a Latina growing up in the United States. The lack of anything she could truly relate to would later inspire her to help Latino writers get

published. In 1986, she married Richard Landres; The couple divorced in 1992. Landres attended Barnard College, where she studied English, graduating in 1994. Two years later, Landres attended the NYU Summer Publishing Institute. Not surprisingly, she was the only Latina in the class. There was a great deal of discussion about the success of African-American authors and books. Landres was perturbed at the lack of discussion about Latino authors and books. From that point on, she dedicated herself to helping Latino writers get published so that one day Latinos would no longer be absent from the discussion.

In 1996, Landres accepted a position at Simon and Schuster. She oversaw the award-winning Spanish-language imprint Libros en Español. While at Simon and Schuster she edited books by ANA NOGALES and YOLANDA NAVA. She began in earnest to teach at workshops at conferences and other locations across the nation, offering Latino writers the tools they needed to publish their works. She married Elliot Podhorzer in 1999.

In 2003, Landres left Simon and Schuster and became an independent editorial consultant, working with writers to provide developmental editing for manuscripts, critiques for book proposals, and strategic advice on how to launch and maintain a successful writing career. She specializes in helping Latino writers get published. To this end, she started a Web site and *Latinidad*, an online newsletter dedicated to helping Latino writers get published.

Marcela Landres created *Latinidad,* a newsletter dedicated to helping Latino authors promote their works. *(Shirley Miranda-Rodriguez)*

Landres recognizes the stereotyping inherent in the publishing industry and the need to label and market. Landres commented in a 2005 interview, "[F]or the most part as a child, no one ever says I want to grow up to be a great Latino writer. People just want to be great writers." She tells her clients that every writer must "aspire to greatness, but know that the publishing industry, the media, and even readers will likely label you a Latino writer. As with any challenge, embrace the label as an opportunity, and work it to your advantage."

Landres speaks frequently for organizations such as The Learning Annex, Columbia University, and the National Association of Latino Arts and Culture. She is a member of the Publishing Latino Voices for America Task Force for the Association of American Publishers, the Women's Media Group, and Las Comadres. Landres is one of the few Latina editors in book publishing.

Further Reading

Correa, AnaMaria. "Latina Experience: Visionary: Marcela Landres." *Para Mi* (May 2005): 22–24.

Harreld, Heather. "Profile of Simon & Schuster: Marcela Landres." Available online. URL: http://www.wordsmitten.com/marcela_interview.html. Downloaded on June 23, 2005.

Marcela Landres Web site. Available online. URL: http://www.marcelalandres.com.

Laviera, Tato
(Jesús Laviera Sánchez)
(1950–   ) *poet, playwright*

As a best-selling Latino poet in the United States, Tato Laviera is well known for creating the term *AmeRícan* and its unique spelling, which defines and declares a space for Puerto Rican sensibilities within the fabric of American identity. Laviera's poetry creates awareness of the unique role Puerto Rican people and their culture play in American society.

Jesús Laviera Sánchez was born on September 5, 1950, in Santurce, Puerto Rico. His father, a contractor, and his mother, who was known to be a very religious woman, raised him with a firm hand. Jesús moved with his mother to New York City in May 1960 when he was nine years old. At the time of the move, he spoke little English and possessed almost no understanding of American culture or traditions. Soon after arriving in the United States, a nun asked Jesús his name. He recalled that after his reply of "'Jesús Laviera Sánchez,' she said 'I could not be Jesús because I was black and didn't know any English.'" The school changed his name to *Abraham*, having a profound impact on him. At this point, he decided to become a writer and assume the nickname *Tato*, given to him by his brother Pablo. Despite his rocky beginning in the United States, Laviera graduated from high school in 1968 with honors.

Laviera attended Cornell University and Brooklyn College but did not graduate from either. Instead, he chose to work for the University of the Streets, an educational program that offered assistance to adults on New York City's Lower East Side. Laviera taught writing from 1970 to 1973 at Rutgers University's Livingston College. Later, he became involved with the university's Puerto Rican studies department. Deeply committed to community, Laviera worked as a social services administrator until the release of his first book, *La Carreta Made a U-Turn* (*The Oxcart Made a U-Turn*), a collection of poetry, in 1979. At this time, Laviera began to write plays. Beginning with *Olú Clemente* (1979), Laviera had several plays presented, although to date they have not been published. Laviera's plays include *Pinones* (1979), *La Chefa* (1981), *Here We Come* (1982), *Becoming Garcia* (1984), *AmeRícan* (1986), *The Base of Soul in Heaven's Café* (1989), *Lady Elizabeth* (1993), and *Can Pickers* (1995).

In 1980, President Jimmy Carter invited Laviera to the White House Gathering of Poets. The following year, Laviera released his second collection of poetry, entitled *Enclave,* which won the Before Columbus Foundation American Book Award. Verses in *Enclave* explore characters among the Nuyorican population. In his next collection of poems, *AmeRícan* (1985), Laviera introduces his term *AmeRícan,* which creates the space and validity to identify with one's origin, in this case Puerto Rican, without denouncing the host country of America. In this way, Laviera's poetry is praised and valued for its optimistic conviction and hope that American people will realize a higher consciousness of the country's varied and diverse population. His fourth book of poetry, *Mainstream Ethics* (1988), emphasizes unity, love, and joy in his Puerto Rican/Nuyorican/Latino inheritance, which he believes will eventually deconstruct mainstream prejudice and systems that fail people.

Throughout his poetry, Laviera expertly combines the oral traditions of Puerto Rican poets Juan Boria and Luis Palés Matos with Afro-Caribbean music. He is credited with promoting the Afro-Caribbean identity with particular attention to its rhythms. His poems contain a theatrical element that he emphasizes in his readings. At the Commons Lecture Hall at Calvin College, Laviera pointed to two principles in reading poetry: (1) "every word is a universe" and (2) the importance of pronunciation. He explains, "You have to say it correctly. By saying it correctly, you feel it. By you stretching it out, the poem becomes stronger. By you dancing it, the poem, the lines, take a life of its poem. By you putting form to it, the poem is yours and you live it." Laviera continues to perform his poetry and write full time.

Further Reading

Flores, Juan. "*La Carreta Made a U-Turn:* Puerto Rican Language and Culture in the United States." In *Divided Borders. Essays on Puerto Rican Identity.* Houston, Tex.: Arte Público Press, 1993, pp. 157–181.

Luis, William. *Dance Between Two Cultures: Latino Caribbean Literature Written in the United States.* Nashville, Tenn.: Vanderbilt University Press, 1997.

West-Durán, Alan. *Latino and Latina Writers, Volume II.* Detroit: Gale-Thomas, 2004, pp. 896–904.

Limón, Graciela
(1938–   ) *novelist, activist, educator*

Graciela Limón's novels, published two decades after the Chicano movement, have added a new perspective to patriarchal oppression and racial repression indicative of the Chicano culture. Born on August 2, 1938, in Los Angeles, California, Graciela Limón was the second of three children and the only girl of Jesús Limón and Altagracia Gómez Limón. Her father, originally from Sonora, Mexico, was a truck driver for the *Los*

Angeles Herald Express, and her mother, who was from Jalisco, Mexico, worked in a laundry facility. The expatriation of many Mexicans during the depression years separated Graciela from many of her family members on her mother's side. As a child, she often went to Guadalajara to visit her mother's relations. Graciela was an avid reader who enjoyed history and biographies of heroic women such as Joan of Arc. She attended Hammel Street School, St. Alphonsus School, and Bishop Conaty High School for Girls. She excelled in school and wanted to pursue higher education; however, she was steered toward vocational courses.

Social customs of a Latino immigrant family dictated that daughters do domestic work if they worked at all. Limón decided she would follow in the footsteps of the heroines she read about and a road of her own choosing. She saved her money and put herself through college and graduate school. She earned a B.A. in Spanish literature from Marymount College in Palos Verdes, California, in 1965; an M.A. in Spanish literature from the Universidad de las Américas in Mexico City in 1969; and a Ph.D. in Latin-American literature from the University of California–Los Angeles in 1975. She composed her dissertation on the Mexican writer Juan Rulfo, whose succinct yet beautiful prose captivated Limón.

Limón accepted a position as an assistant professor at Loyola Marymount University in Los Angeles, California, in 1969. She became an associate professor in 1975 and was granted full professorship and chair of the department of Chicano studies in 1980. Inspiration to write fiction grew from the classes she taught on the Spanish conquest of indigenous Mexico. Limón wanted to create an alternative that would give voice to the Mexican natives and not merely focus on the chronicles of the victors as the main narratives of the period. A year of intense research and study of the conquest of Mexico and its colonial period produced *María de Belén: The Autobiography of an Indian Woman* (1990). Limón's first book blends fiction, autobiography, and history.

From 1986 to 1991, Limón participated in peaceful yet dramatic demonstrations in protest of the U.S. involvement in El Salvador's civil war. She visited El Salvador with other Loyola Marymount representatives as part of an international gathering to honor the anniversary of the assassinations of six Jesuit priests, a female employee, and her daughter. Conversations with Salvadoran refugees at the church at La Placita in Los Angeles inspired her next book, *In Search of Bernabé* (1993). The manuscript won the University of California–Irvine (UCI) Chicano Literature Contest in 1991. UCI professor MARÍA HERRERA-SOBEK suggested Limón submit her work to Arte Público Press, which agreed to publish the book. *In Search of Bernabé* won the Before Columbus Foundation American Book Award, was a finalist for the *Los Angeles Times* Ard Seidenbaum Award for First Fiction, and was named a critic's choice by the *New York Times Book Review.* The book was praised particularly for its ability to suspend the tendency to automatically categorize people as good or bad.

The Memories of Ana Calderón (1994) is told in both the first and third person. The story follows Ana's choices for personal freedom even when that means turning her back on familial and cultural mores. When Limón decided to revise *María de Belén* for her new publisher, Arte Público Press, she found that the novel was, as she described in a 1998 interview "like lace—when one part is cut, it all falls apart." She decided to rewrite the entire novel. The resulting novel, *Song of the Hummingbird* (1996), reveals the life of Huitzitzilin, an aging former Aztec princess, through her last confession with a young priest. Throughout the novel, Huitzitzilin relates the details of the Spanish conquest with gory details and exquisite, profound sadness. The priest attempts to steer the woman away from her testimonial monologue and back to the traditional ritual of the Catholic confession. Her unrelenting outpouring eventually causes the priest to feel his humanity rise above his dogma.

Limón followed with *The Day of the Moon* (1999), which explores the belief that a person's worth can be determined by the color of his or her skin. Limón employs the Maya myth of reincarnation to lay the groundwork in *Erased Facts* (2001). *Left Alive* (2005) relates the tale of a young man who survived when his three siblings were murdered. Young Rafael Cota is willing to go to the edges of the world, including his own sanity, to defend his mother, the accused murderer.

Limón's work builds familial and cultural relationships first addressed by her literary predecessors who rose to fame during the height of the Chicano movement. Her breadth and skill in writing illustrates the obstacles a person faces to either establish or reinforce familial bonds, as well as the lengths a person will go to to deny aspects of his or her heritage. Limón is an integral voice helping to define and recreate multiculturalism for Latinos.

Further Reading

Castillo-Speed, Lillian, ed. *Latina: Women's Voices from the Borderlands.* New York: Touchstone, 1995.

Lomelí, Francisco A., and Carl R. Shirley, eds. *Dictionary of Literary Biography.* Vol. 209: *Chicano Writers, Third Series.* Detroit: Gale, 1999, pp. 127–132.

McCracken, Ellen. *New Latina Narrative: The Feminine Space of Postmodern Ethnicity.* Tucson: University of Arizona Press, 1999.

West-Durán, Alan. *Latino and Latina Writers, Volume II.* Detroit: Gale-Thomas, 2004, pp. 319–334.

Lopez, Josefina
(María Josefina López)
(1969–   ) *playwright, screenwriter, director, poet, activist*

At the age of 19, playwright Josefina Lopez wrote the successful and beloved *Real Women Have Curves,* which was produced, published, and adapted for the screen to national critical and audience acclaim. With more than 40 professional productions, she is one of the most widely produced Latina playwrights in the United States.

A great storyteller who inherited her gift from her mother, María Josefina López was born in Cerritos, San Luis Potosí, Mexico, on March 19, 1969. Lopez was the sixth of eight children born to Rosendo Z. and Catalina Perales López. When Josefina was five years old, her family moved to Boyle Heights, a community located outside Los Angeles, California. Josefina believed life would be blissful once she arrived in the City of Angels. However, her early years were fraught with overwhelming confusion about whether she was Mexican or American. She was undocumented and felt like an "alien." Lopez recalled in a 2005 interview, "[F]or 13 years I felt invisible and I yearned to be human."

When she was 12 years old, Josefina discovered her father was having an affair, one of several he had had over the years. She became outraged at how unjust life was for women, particularly Mexican-American women. Since Josefina was not allowed to outwardly express her anger toward her father, she channeled her frustration and other feelings into writing, which became her therapy. In 1984, she enthusiastically waited for the debut of *AKA Pablo,* the first television show about Mexican Americans, but when the series was cancelled after only six shows, López was highly disappointed. Later television shows perpetuated stereotypes and prejudices about Latinos, inciting López to write stories that revealed the truth about Latinos and women.

López found her writing muse in her mother, who would often enchant her daughter with suspenseful tales and unique perspectives that showed her how to view the world in an interesting way. However, it was Luis Valdez and his "acto" *La carpa de los Rasquachi* that would inspire López to become a playwright. She began writing plays at the age of 16 under the direction of several esteemed playwrights at the Los Angeles Theatre Center. From 1985 to 1988, she honed her writing craft at the Young Playwrights Lab.

In 1986, she saw Valdez's play *I Don't Have to Show You No Stinking Badges,* became inspired, and at age 17 wrote *Simply Maria or the American*

Josefina Lopez created a marketing trend by establishing a woman's right to validate herself based on her own parameters with her play and script *Real Women Have Curves. (Shane Sato)*

Dream, a play about an adolescent girl torn between accepting the customary subordinate role for a Mexican-American woman and becoming a modern, aspiring career woman. The decision of which role to choose is further complicated by Maria's loyalty to culture, traditions, and family. *Simply Maria* was a 1987 Young Playwrights Festival of New York semifinalist. It aired on KPBS in San Diego the following year and won the Public Television Local Program Award from the Corporation for Public Broadcasting, the Gold Award, the Media Award, and an Emmy.

In 1988, Lopez attended a workshop at the INTAR (International Arts Relations) Hispanic American Arts Center under the guidance of Maria Irene Fornes. She studied dramatic writing at New York University's Tisch School of the Arts and theater at the University of California–San Diego. Lopez wrote *Food for the Dead,* which continues to explore the ideas of independence and individual aspiration for women and goes further to investigate the secrets bound and hidden by archaic rules of society. Valdez's El Teatro Campesino produced and toured *Simply Maria* and *Food for the Dead* in 1989.

Lopez then set out to write *Real Women Have Curves,* her most successful and widely produced play to date. *Real Women Have Curves* exploits the social and cultural expectations of women whose bodies are valued over their hearts, minds, or spirits. During the 1990s, the play was wildly success-ful, appearing in theaters across the nation. Her honest approach to the unsung story of shame, frustration, and indignation over society's obsession with women's appearances created a devoted fan club for Lopez. The title of the play appeared on T-shirts and other marketing items as a declaration of independence from socially acceptable bodily forms. In 1993, Lopez received a B.A. in film and screenwriting from Columbia College in Chicago. Later that year, Lopez studied at the Warner Brothers Comedy Writing Workshop. She earned an M.F.A. in screenwriting from the University of California–Los Angeles. Lopez penned *Confessions of Women from East L.A.,* a play to challenge the "virgins, mothers, and whores" stereotypes Latinas are subjected to with the outlandish humor and the vibrant voices of East Los Angeles women. Lopez next wrote *Unconquered Spirits,* a feminist version of La Llorona, the ghost legend of the Wailing Woman. Both plays enjoyed successful tours and productions. In 2002, Lopez married Emmanuel Deleage, with whom she would have two children.

She cowrote the script of *Real Women Have Curves* with George LaVoo for HBO. The movie won the Audience Award and a Special Jury Award for Acting at the 2002 Sundance Film Festival and the Youth Prize at the 2002 San Sebastian International Film Festival. It was later released in movie theaters. In 2004, Lopez made her directorial debut with *ADD Me to the Party.* She extended her writing talents to television with shows such as *Living Single, Culture Clash,* and *The Latino Anthology Series.*

In 2002, Lopez opened Casa 0101, an art space with a mission to bring theater, filmmaking, and dance to her beloved Boyle Heights community. It is her hope that, "Casa 0101 will nurture future storytellers of Los Angeles who will someday transform the world." She moved to Paris, France, in 2005 for artistic reasons.

Inspired by anger and indignation to stand up for the underdog, Lopez knows how to infuse humor into the most sensitive and potentially over-sentimental issues. Lopez said in a 2005 interview, "[H]umor in a story that otherwise could easily be a drama or a tragedy gives the characters a certain degree of dignity, and it makes the audience bear or at least be entertained enough to listen to new truths that are sometimes too painful to accept." With dedication and fervor, Lopez writes stories with a strong devotion that has proven to empower and inspire women and Latinos.

Further Reading

Feyder, Linda, ed. *Shattering the Myth: Plays by Hispanic Women.* Houston, Tex.: Arte Público Press, 1992.

Herrera Hudson, Claudia. "Artist Hero: Josefina Lopez." Available online. URL: http://myhero. com/myhero/hero.asp?hero=Josefina_Lopez_ MAG. Downloaded on April 11, 2005.

Lomelí, Francisco A., and Carl R. Shirley, eds. *Chicano Writers: Third Series.* Vol. 209. Detroit: Gale Research, 1999, pp. 133–137.

Marvis, Barbara J., and Barbara Tidman. *Famous People of Hispanic Heritage.* Vol. 5. Baltimore, Md.: Mitchel Lane Publishers, 1996.

M

Mares, E. A.
(Ernesto Antonio Mares, Ernesto Mares, Tony Mares)
(1938–   ) poet, essayist, short story writer, playwright, educator

E. A. Mares has contributed to Chicano literature by creating images that seamlessly weave together history with prose and poetry. His words bear witness and pay tribute to the historic and contemporary lives of Hispanic New Mexicans.

The eldest of three sons of Ernesto Gustavo Mares and Rebecca Devine Mares, Ernesto Antonio Mares was born on May 17, 1938, in Albuquerque, New Mexico. His father's ancestors arrived in the United States via Mexico in the 18th century. Through this bloodline, Mares is the fifth grandnephew of the controversial 19th-century rebel priest Antonio José Martínez of Texas. Mares's predecessors also endured the fearful and humiliating process of being dispossessed of their ancestral lands near Raton, New Mexico. His mother's genealogy traces back to early Irish immigrants who eventually married into Hispanic families.

Mares's parents, like many Hispanics their age, had been heavily propagandized to denounce their Hispanic customs and language as necessary for survival and assimilation. Fortunately for the young Mares, his maternal grandmother, Rebecca García y Gutiérrez de Devine, had not succumbed to any pressure of the kind and insisted that her grandson speak Spanish. She played the greatest role in instilling Hispanic pride, traditions, and language in Ernesto.

Unlike some Hispanic writers, Mares does not feel a division between being Mexican and American. The primary division that he sensed as a child was a result of the divergent religious and spiritual beliefs held by his parents. His father, a railroad mechanic, was Protestant, and his mother, a secretary in a labor union, was Catholic. His parents encouraged education and logical thinking and were deeply involved in the Democratic Party. Many debates took place in the Mares household. From his parents' example, Ernesto learned that a person should engage the world on his or her individual terms and that it is not necessary to rely on an institution for learning.

Ernesto attended the San Felipe de Neri School in Old Town Albuquerque, where the missionary zeal of the young Sisters of Charity first initiated him into the ways of the dominant culture. Mares and a group of fellow students at St. Mary's High School did not agree with the institution's support of Senator Joseph McCarthy and were often browbeaten for their liberal views. Unrelenting, Mares sharpened his oratory skills on the debate team and secured a state championship in 1956. He became the editor of his high school paper, where he discovered an aptitude for journalistic work and developed the belief that it is, as he described it, "soul-satisfying to write."

Mares received a scholarship to attend Notre Dame. He did not enjoy his experience there and transferred after one year. He earned a B.A. in Spanish in 1960 from the University of New Mexico, where he studied with exiled Spanish novelist Ramón Sender and New Mexican author SABINE R. ULIBARRÍ. In 1962, he obtained an M.A. in Spanish from Florida State University. Mares began his illustrious teaching career in the history department at the University of Arkansas. He has since taught courses in Spanish, English, Southwest studies, and history or served as a visiting lecturer at Colorado College, the University of New Mexico, New Mexico Highlands University, and the University of North Texas–Denton.

In the late 1960s, Mares became interested in poetry. His poems and essays appeared in the prestigious and influential publication *Cuaderno,* the journal for Academia de la Nueva Raza (Academy of the New Chicano People) in Dixon, New Mexico. Unlike his contemporaries, Mares did not focus on creating a uniform Hispanic identity, but he instead created works that pointed out the danger of establishing a homogeny of Chicano ethnicity that would inherently disenfranchise those who did not meet its descriptions. Sentiments of this nature that also included acculturation and evolution can be found in his essay "El Lobo y El Coyote: Between Two Cultures" in the journal *Cuaderno* (1972). And yet Mares recognized the need to build on the foundation of history in "Myth and Reality" (1973), which reveals how unifying and compelling the central concept of Aztlán was to the Chicano movement as a whole. Mares's works have appeared in many regional and national journals and magazines. He gained a Ph.D. in history from the University of New Mexico in 1974.

In 1979, Mares's career as a playwright began with the Compañía de Teatro de Albuquerque's production of the successful bilingual comedy *Lola's Last Dance,* one of a trilogy of one-act New Mexican plays, which also included works by DENISE CHÁVEZ and RUDOLFO A. ANAYA. The production's success inspired Mares to collaborate regularly with the Compañía de Teatro de Albuquerque, assisting in Spanish-language adaptations of classic plays such as Arthur Miller's *View from the Bridge* (1955). The 1983 adaptation is set in the Barelas barrio of Albuquerque. Mares's plays include *New Mexico and the Multicultural Experience* (teleplay, 1981), *Padre Antonio Jose Martinez de Taos* (1983), *El Corrido de Joaquin Murieta* (1984), *Santa Fe Spirit* (musical, 1989), and *The Shepherd of Pan Duro* (1989). His chapbook *The Unicorn Poem,* released in 1980, weaves together history and myth. Chicano critic JUAN BRUCE-NOVOA noted, "Mares will work a series of overlayed metaphors: the map, the myth, the search, and the struggle for survival and freedom. His poem fills empty space with the silenced history of the Chicanos of New Mexico."

During the 1970s and 1980s, Mares traveled through New Mexico, Arizona, Texas, Nebraska, and Colorado to lead workshops, give lectures, read from his works, and perform his one-act play *I Returned and Saw Under the Sun: Padre Martínez of Taos.* He served as the poet in residence for the New Mexico Endowment for the Arts from 1976 to 1980. He released *Las Vegas, New Mexico: A Portrait,* with Alex Traube, in 1983 and published his play *I Returned and Saw Under the Sun: Padre Martínez of Taos* in 1989. From 1982 to 1987, he served as writer, producer, and performer during the Chautauqua Series for the New Mexico Endowment for the Humanities in addition to his duties as the curator of education for the Albuquerque Museum. During this time, he also served on many boards and programs for education, health, and Hispanic culture. In 1987, Mares and Carolyn Meyer, writer and author of numerous works of fiction and nonfiction for adolescents, were married.

Mares released *There Are Four Wounds, Miguel,* a trilobite poetry chapbook in 1994. A trilobite is an extinct marine anthropod from the Paleozoic period. Mares uses the term to reference ancestry. In 2001, Mares retired from teaching full time and was able to dedicate himself more fully to his poetry. He has served as the resident poet for several programs, including the New Mexico Poetry Jam, University of New Mexico's Taos Summer

Writer's Conference, National Hispanic Cultural Center Summer Writer's Conference, Southern Utah University Summer Poetry Institute, El País Writing Project, and University of Oklahoma Summer Program. He released *With the Eyes of a Raptor* in 2004 and a translation of *Casi toda la música,* by Ángel González, under the title *Almost All the Music* in 2006. He is currently at work on a book entitled *Resolana for a Dark New Age.*

Further Reading

Gonzales-Berry, Erlinda. *Paso por aquí: Critical Essays on the New Mexican Literary Tradition.* Albuquerque: University of New Mexico Press, 1989, pp. 267–296.

Heide, Rick, ed. *Under the Fifth Sun: Latino Literature from California.* Santa Clara and Berkeley, Calif.: Santa Clara University/Heyday Books, 2002.

Noyes, Stanley. "Notes on E. A. Mares; Poetry in New Mexico." *New Mexico Magazine* 61 (March 1983): 19.

Martí, José
(José Julián Martí Pérez)
(1853–1895) *journalist, poet, essayist, novelist, playwright, activist*

José Martí's essays established sentiment for Cuban independence from Spain, while his poetry inspired the Modernismo movement, a Spanish-American literary style that creates an exotic blend of visual symbolism to convey passion, harmony, and rhythm. Thus, he is called alternatively the Father of Cuban Independence and Father of the Modernismo.

José Julián Martí Pérez was born in the poor Paula neighborhood of Havana, Cuba, on January 28, 1853. His parents, Leonor Pérez and Mariano Martí, who met in Havana, were originally from Spain and proud of their Spanish inheritance. Martí, on the other hand, developed and maintained an allegiance to Cuba. This difference of nationalism proved to be discordant in the fam-

ily. At nine years old, José witnessed African slaves descending from a slave ship and only minutes later found a slave hanging from a nearby tree. At that moment, he vowed to fight for the rights of the oppressed. He attended San Anacleto School, Havana Middle School, and San Pablo School, affiliated with the High School of Havana. While in middle school, José came under the guidance of Cuban poet and patriot Rafael María Mendive, who encouraged José's Cuban national feelings and literary work.

Martí penned his first poem in 1868 at the beginning of the Ten Years' War, the first revolution of Cuba, upon the deportation of his mentor. *Abdala,* a dramatic poem, appeared in the only issue of *La Patria Libre* (January 1869) and was first produced in 1940, more than 70 years later. In October of that same year, Martí was arrested as a result of a letter he wrote claiming Cuban, rather than Spanish, nationality. He was sentenced to six years in prison and hard labor at the quarries of San Lázaro in Havana. While in prison, Martí expressed in letters to his mother his concern that his nationalism created pain for her. His entire life, although his filial allegiance would continue to clash with his desire to establish Cuban independence from Spain, Martí felt first and foremost a loyalty to defending the oppressed.

After one year of hard labor, Martí was deported to Spain. He recounts his departure from Cuba in the second chapter of his novel *Amistad funesta* (1885; Fatal friendship). He describes the inhumane conditions of prison life in "El presidio político en Cuba" (1871; "Political Prison in Cuba"). Upon his release in 1873, he continued his legal studies at the University of Zaragoza, where he obtained bachelor's degrees in law and in the humanities in 1874. During his three years in Spain, Martí wrote several essays in the Spanish press advocating the freedom of Cuba. In 1875, he moved to Mexico to reunite with his family. He wrote for the *Revista Universal* (Universal magazine), a liberal publication, and participated in gatherings of intellectuals. When

Porfirio Díaz took over as president of Mexico, the new regime was not friendly toward intellectuals; Martí, therefore, left for Guatemala. There he married Carmen Zayas Bazán, another Cuban exile, in 1877. Soon afterward, they visited Cuba to celebrate the end of the war but found that Martí was still considered disloyal and could not obtain work as a lawyer or teacher. His only son, Ismael, was born in 1878.

During this time in Cuba, the people were divided into three camps: Reformists (who favored autonomy, or home rule, under Spain), Annexationists (who sought to become part of the United States), and Separatists (who wanted true national independence). Martí firmly held the dangerous Separatist stance. He was again arrested in 1879 and exiled to Spain but escaped into France. He spent some time in New York City before traveling to Venezuela in 1881. He wrote for the prestigious *Revista Venezolana* until the local dictator, Antonio Guzmán, forced him to leave. Martí returned to New York, where he would spend the remainder of his life.

While in the United States, Martí wrote about the American definition of freedom of speech, efficiency, and educational opportunities. No longer tied solely to Cuba, Martí felt loyalty to the Americas and in his writings urged cooperation, unity, and independence for Cuba and Puerto Rico. In time, he began to write about the racism, materialism, and greed filling the hearts of many people in the United States. During the 1880s, Martí wrote for numerous publications and translated into Spanish the works of his favorite American authors, such as Walt Whitman and Ralph Waldo Emerson. He wrote four plays but is best known for his evocative essays and poetry. His first book of poetry, inspired by his son, *Ismaelillo* (1882; Little Ismael), is considered a landmark work and the first to establish the Modernismo style. *Versos sencillos* (1891; Simple Verses) is his best-known work and sung by heart in many Hispanic countries. Martí was well loved because his verses and prose spoke to the common man and woman.

José Martí was one of the first Hispanic journalists. *(Photo of José Martí is reprinted with permission from the publisher [APP Archive Files] [Houston: Arte Público Press—University of Houston, © 2006])*

Martí wrote voluminously about establishing Cuban independence. He helped define the political views that would shape the Partido Revolucionario Cubano, or Cuban Revolutionary Party, which was formed in 1892 and would eventually make Cuba an independent country. He upheld two points for the new party: abolish racism and resist American imperialism. In 1893, he wrote the Manifesto of the Cuban Revolutionary Party. He ordered the uprising in Cuba against Spain from New York and set sail for Cuba in January 1895. On May 19, 1895, he engaged in open combat against the Spanish forces and lost his life. To date, there are more than 200 book-length biographies written about Martí. His poetry, plays, essays, and novels have been collected in more the 70 volumes.

Further Reading

Allen, Esther, ed. *José Martí: Selected Writings.* New York: Penguin Books, 2002.

Lizaso, Felix. *Martí: Martyr of Cuban Independence.* Albuquerque: University of New Mexico Press, 1953.

Perez, Louis A., Jr. *Cuba Between Empires, 1878–1902.* Pittsburgh, Pa.: University of Pittsburgh Press, 1983.

Salgado, María A. *Dictionary of Literary Biography.* Vol. 290: *Modern Spanish American Poets, Second Series.* Detroit: Gale, 2004, pp. 196–209.

Martínez, Demetria
(Demetria, Louise Martínez)
(1960–) *novelist, poet, essayist, activist*

Demetria Martínez writes lyrical prose and refreshing poetry. She is best known for *Mother Tongue* (1994), a novel based on her experience with Salvadoran refugees.

The daughter of Dolores (Jaramillo), a teacher, and Theodore Martínez, the first Chicano elected to the Albuquerque school board, Demetria Louise Martínez was born on July 10, 1960, in Albuquerque, New Mexico. Demetria was a shy child who battled weight problems as a youth. She developed a deep sense of spirituality from her grandmother, who encouraged Demetria to read the Bible, and found an inner strength from writing in journals as a means of thwarting teenage depression. She found the Bible inspirational for writing poetry and discovered magic within the mundane as a practical and natural occurrence. Interwoven with her Catholic upbringing is an appreciation for the spirituality of the indigenous people of New Mexico. Her propensity to challenge authority and create change when needed came from her aunt and grandmother, who held positions in county offices.

Martínez took courses in religion and ethics at Princeton University's Woodrow Wilson School of Public and International Affairs. After four years of diligent studying, Martínez declared, "Life is too short to work at a job that requires hose, heels, and forty hours a week. Why settle for a career when one might have a calling?" After her graduation in 1982, she joined Sagrada Arts Studios, a Catholic artists' colony in Old Town Albuquerque. She spent six years at Sagrada, honing her poetry skills and working odd jobs, including part time as a reporter for the *National Catholic Reporter,* an independent progressive newsweekly, and as the religious writer for the *Albuquerque Journal.* About this time, she became interested in the sanctuary movement organized to protest U.S. policy toward Central American refugees. She wrote extensively on the sanctuary movement and the plight of Salvadoran refugees.

In 1986, a Lutheran minister invited Martínez to accompany him as he helped two pregnant Salvadoran women cross the U.S.-Mexican border. As far as she knew, the government of New Mexico sanctioned helping the two women as part of the sanctuary movement. However, the following year the U.S. attorney in New Mexico indicted both Martínez and the minister on charges of conspiracy against the U.S. government and aiding the transport of illegal aliens. She faced a penalty of 25 years in prison and $1.25 million in fines. Her poem "Nativity: For Two Salvadoran Women, 1986–1987" was used against her in the courts. The trial made national headlines, but she and the minister were eventually acquitted on the grounds of the First Amendment and the claim that the author had the right to research the sanctuary movement.

Martínez contributed her poetry, including "Nativity: For Two Salvadoran Women, 1986–1987," to *Three Times a Woman: Chicana Poetry* (1989), which she coedited with ALICIA GASPAR DE ALBA and MARÍA HERRERA-SOBEK. In 1990, Martínez joined the *National Catholic Reporter* full time, and for two years she covered controversial topics such as immigration and abortion. She became inspired to write her first novel while listening to a reading by SANDRA CISNEROS. *Mother Tongue* (1984), which won the Western States Award for Fiction, is based on the experience of assisting the Salvadoran refugees. The novel is the story of an exquisite romance between a New Mexican woman and an El Salvadoran refugee and is divided into five parts, each of which reveals a different perspective on the plight of Central American refugees. The title of the book refers to the culture and tradition that is inextricably bound to language.

Martínez explores themes of love, spirituality, the failure of political systems, and the power of forgiveness in self-actualization and transformation in her poetry collections *Breathing Between the Lines* (1997) and *The Devil's Workshop* (2002). *Confessions of a Berlitz Tape Chicana: Collected Columns,* released in 2005, is a collection of Martínez's essays. Martínez engages in activism with Enlace Comunitario, an immigrants' rights group that serves Spanish-speaking victims of domestic violence. She also teaches a workshop, "Writing for Social Change: Redream a Just World," with Anya Achtenberg. Martínez is an evocative writer whose imagery demonstrates a tremendous faith in the personal journey toward self-exploration and finding beauty in the mundane.

Further Reading

Gaspar de Alba, Alicia, María Herrera-Sobek, and Demetria Martínez, eds. *Three Times a Woman: Chicana Poetry.* Tempe, Ariz.: Bilingual Press/Editorial Bilingue, 1989.

Lomelí, Francisco A., and Carl R. Shirley, eds. *Chicano Writers: Third Series.* Vol. 209. Detroit: Gale Research, 1999, pp. 138–144.

Martínez, Demetria. *Breathing Between the Lines: Poems.* Camino del Sol series. Tucson: University of Arizona Press, 1997.

———. *Mother Tongue.* New York: One World/Ballantine, 1994.

Peacock, Scot. *Contemporary Authors.* Vol. 179. Detroit: Gale Research, 2000.

Martinez, Nina Marie
(1969–) *novelist*

Nina Marie Martinez gained literary recognition with *¡Caramba! A Tale Told in Turns of the Cards,* a delightful novel based in a fictional central valley town in California called Lava Landing. Nina Marie Martinez is the daughter of a Mexican-American migrant farmworker turned carpenter and a German-American homemaker. Born on March 19, 1969, in San Jose, California, Nina worked from an early age picking walnuts, prunes, and apricots alongside her father. By the age of nine, she had learned the carpentry trade from her father. She also learned, among many things, how to drive a truck, climb a roof, and balance 2-by-4 wooden beams or plywood on her head while walking. A great baseball fan, Nina dreamed of becoming an announcer for the San Francisco Giants.

Martinez attended six high schools in northern California while working at fast food restaurants before deciding to drop out altogether. She became a single mother at the age of 20 and stayed at home with her daughter for one year. She attended a series of community colleges beginning with Gavilán Community College in Gilroy, California, and supported herself by working for a legal firm and as a technical typist for a San Francisco Bay Area geologist. She transferred to the University of California–Santa Cruz in 1995, where she discovered her ability to write. Martinez supported herself and her daughter by selling vintage clothing in San Francisco, work clothes at migrant camps, and odds and ends at swap meets.

¡Caramba! A Tale Told in Turns of the Cards, her debut novel, published in 2003, boasts illustrations from the Mexican game of chance, Lotería, and is chock full of Mexican traditions. Critics nationwide adored *¡Caramba!,* as *Publisher Weekly* commented, "[An] effervescent, luminous debut. Although the novel has a slew of protagonists, readers first meet Natalie and Consuelo (Nat and Sway), two firecrackers with an 'ever growing

fascination with the wideness of the world' . . . Martínez, in a bubbly mix of English and Spanglish, draws on magical realism, kitschy humor and tongue-in-cheek clichés . . . but there's truth behind the zany humor . . . serious truth telling about love and happiness in life and death."

Martinez's writing is at once zany and meaningful. Her outlandish characters find themselves in dilemmas about identity and goodness. Martinez's own high cheekbones and dark looks, by-products of a mixed heritage, have often provoked questions about her ethnic identity. She commented in an interview with Tracey Vogel of *Metroactive* magazine, "[I]n a way, *¡Caramba!* is an answer to that question, for me . . . a connection to culture that's not just about language or religion, but about trying to find your home, even if it's just a fictional place."

¡Caramba! blurs together the bizarre with the ordinary in a seamless manner and represents an age of up-and-coming Latina authors. Ripe with rich details, Martinez's best writing may be yet to come. Still in love with baseball and vintage clothes, she is hard at work on her second novel.

Further Reading

Andriani, Lynn. "¿A Novel with Pictures? ¡Si Senor! Interview with Author Nina Marie Martinez." *Publishers Weekly* (February 16, 2004), 152.

Ciuraru, Carmela. "Review of *¡Caramba!*" *Washington Post Book World,* July 4, 2004, p. 8.

Martinez, Nina Marie. *¡Caramba! A Tale Told in Turns of the Cards.* New York: Knopf, 2004.

Martínez, Rubén
(Rubén Benjamin Martínez)
(1962–) *journalist, essayist, playwright, nonfiction writer, educator*

Rubén Martínez is an award-winning journalist who brings formerly unseen realities of migration and its effects on the family and community to the forefront of American consciousness with his journalism and books, including the acclaimed *Crossing Over: A Mexican Family on the Migrant Trail.* Combining politics with his writings, Martínez identifies himself as one of the Committed Generation, writers and artists who engage with social justice issues.

Rubén Benjamin Martínez was born on July 9, 1962, in Silver Lake, a neighborhood of Los Angeles, California. His grandparents spent years touring Mexico and the United States as opera and folk singers. Martínez's parents, Rubén Rodolfo Martínez, a Mexican-American lithographer and film buff, and Vilma Ruth Angulo Martínez, a Salvadoran psychologist and poet, inspired his creative abilities and gave him a love of road culture.

As a child, Rubén tested in the gifted range and was considered special, even brilliant, by his teachers. He believed he was meant to do something original and creative with his life and had dreams of being "an agent of history and bringing something beautiful into the world . . . a politician, a priest, a poet, a revolutionary. In some ways, I've been all of those, but on a much more modest scale than the child Ruben dreamt," as he stated in a 2005 interview.

Being brown in a mostly white environment formed Martínez's political nature. He encountered the dichotomy of a society in the early stages of accepting ethnic diversity. He ran into prejudice from some, while liberals offered gushy support. As a youth, Martínez's artistry was influenced by the Vietnam War, race riots, some friends' hippie parents, and the progressive politics and culture of the 1960s. Once out of high school, he worked as a forklift operator at his father's print shop and occasionally as a day laborer.

Martínez attended college at the University of California–Los Angeles until he decided to drop out after reading Jack Kerouac's *On the Road.* Martínez took to the road, appalling his parents. He created an education on his own terms from 1984 to 1990 as a road scholar, freelance writer, resident poet, and bookstore clerk. "The civil wars in Central America during the 1980s were my history major; the Beats and the Romantics were my English major; the Border Arts Workshop in Tijuana/ San Diego provided my performance studies major; rock 'n' roll was my music major; the *L.A. Weekly*, where I became a staff writer and later editor (from 1986 to 1993), was my journalism school," Martínez concluded in a 2005 interview.

Martínez worked from 1986 to 1993 as an artist in residence, conducting writing workshops at Los Angeles and neighboring schools sponsored by the California Poets-in-the-Schools program. From 1990 to 1991, Martínez taught writing at the Chino State Correctional Facility for Men. In 1992, he released his first book, *The Other Side: Notes from the New L.A., Mexico City and Beyond*, a collection of poetry and essays, to favorable acclaim.

Over the next few years, Martínez's writings began to garner the attention of academia. He received the Santa Monica Arts Council prize in poetry in 1986, a Fellowship in Literature from the California Arts Council in 1988, a University of California–Irvine prize in poetry in 1990, and a Greater Los Angeles Press Club Award of Excellence for coverage of the Rodney King beating investigation and its aftermath in 1992. He was also awarded the Freedom of Information Award from the American Civil Liberties Union in 1994 and an Emmy from the Academy of Television Arts and Sciences for hosting KCET-TV's *Life & Times* in 1995.

Martínez spent five years writing *Crossing Over* (2001), an enthralling and chilling account of Mexican immigration. The subject was the theme of conversations at the dinner table of Martínez family reunions. As the son and grandson of immigrants, Martínez recalled in a 2005 interview, "[T]he stories of how the Martínez family appeared in Los Angeles, California, is the essential political, historical, cultural and even spiritual basis of my life." He intended to incorporate all he could about immigration as it is perceived by Mexicans and Americans, including popular music, religion, art, literature, social community, and politics. In the end, Mar-

tínez focused on the Chavez family, who lost three of their sons as they attempted to cross the U.S.-Mexican border. Martínez's depiction and humanization of the Chavez family opened an insightful, poignant window into immigrant culture.

In 1997, Martínez, a performance artist as well as a writer, partnered with photographer Quique Avilés to lead a sequence of workshops in the Mount Pleasant barrio of Washington, D.C. The collective work included freestyle rap, the spoken word, music, and performance art techniques, which concluded in several performances at the GALA Hispanic Theatre. The same year, he composed and performed works with the musical groups Concrete Blonde and Los Illegals.

Rubén Martínez, hard-hitting journalist and thought-provoking author, addresses issues of social justice. *(Sehba Sarwar)*

Eastside Stories: Gang Life in East Los Angeles, a collaboration of photographs by award-winning photographer Joseph Rodriguez with text by Martínez, was published in 1998. Taking to the road once again, Martínez and Rodriguez traveled through the nation, creating *Virtual Migrant Dialogue* on the Internet with Mexican master photographer Pedro Meyer. The work documents the lives of migrant workers throughout America's heartland.

In 1999, *Poets & Writers* selected Martínez to lead literary workshops and public performances for youths from a largely Central American barrio of Los Angeles. Martínez conceived *Border Ballad,* a unique theatrical and musical solo show featuring narratives from modern immigrants against a surprising backdrop of rearranged Mexican and American folk music whereby the conceit lies in a brilliant form of role reversal. *Border Ballad* appeared in 2000 at the Mark Taper New Works Festival and the Audrey Skirball Theatre Project's Summer Festival. Martínez has appeared as a spoken word artist on MTV-Latino with Mexican rock heroes Maldita Vecindad y los Hijos del Quinto Patio.

Martínez was awarded the Loeb Fellowship at the graduate school of design at Harvard University from 2001 to 2002 and received a Lannan Foundation fellowship in nonfiction. He composed and performed works on The Roches' *Zero Church* album in 2002. Martínez became an associate professor in the creative writing program at the University of Houston in 2003. The following year, *Crossing Over* was the featured book for Books on the Bayou, Houston's citywide reading project. Martínez released *The New Americans* (2004), a collection of essays that explores the diverse experiences of five immigrant families who arrive in the United States from different countries. *The New Americans* serves as the companion book to the acclaimed PBS television series of the same name. In 2004, Martínez married Angela Garcia, a New Mexican native and Ph.D. candidate in anthropology at Harvard. They now live in northern New

Mexico, where she is working on her dissertation and he is researching his new book about race and class conflict in the American Southwest.

As global migration continues, Martínez will certainly use his diverse range of talents to record the voices of marginalized Chicano communities and immigration's effects on culture and traditions. He believes that eventually the United States and Mexico will begin to resemble each other. However, Martínez feels there is more than just a blending of cultures when it comes to migration; there is an element of discovering one's own humanity and place of belonging. In an interview, Martínez explained, "[T]he tragedy of the exile is feeling out of place anywhere in the world; the exile's redemption is realizing that the entire world is his home."

Further Reading

Castillo, Ana, ed. *Goddess of the Americas.* New York: Riverhead/Putnam, 1996.

Gómez-Peña, Guillermo, and Roberto Sifuentes. *Temple of Confessions: Mexican Beasts and Living Santos.* New York: PowerHouse Books, 1996.

González, Ray. *Currents from the Dancing River: Contemporary Latino Fiction, Nonfiction and Poetry.* San Diego: Harcourt Brace, 1994.

Martínez, Ruben. *The New Americans.* Available online. URL: http://zonezero.com/exposiciones/fotografos/newam/default.html. Downloaded on October 3, 2005.

O'Hearn, Claudine. *Half and Half: Writers on Growing Up Biracial/Bicultural.* New York: Pantheon, 1998.

Méndez, Miguel
(Miguel Méndez Morales)
(1930–   ) novelist, short story writer, poet, educator

Author of more than 50 works, Miguel Méndez is widely hailed as a leading writer in contemporary Chicano literature. He is well known for his contributions and ability to give voice to and portray the people occupying the American Southwest and Mexican borders.

One of five children of Francisco Méndez Cárdenas and María Morales, Miguel Méndez Morales was born on June 15, 1930, in Bisbee, Arizona. Due to the demands put on society by the Great Depression, thousands of Mexicans were repatriated to Mexico regardless of whether they were born in the United States. Only five months after his birth, Miguel and his family were deported, settling in El Claro, a government-owned farming community in Sonora, Mexico. From an early age, Miguel loved stories and literature. His parents entertained Miguel with stories of their youth and Native traditions of his Yaqui inheritance. Until his mother taught him to read, Miguel often begged her to read to him. He attended an elementary school until the sixth grade where the teachers were, as he recalled in an interview, "just as poor and needy as the community we lived in . . . but the teachers were so dedicated and human that I owe them the strong sense of responsibility they ingrained in me."

At 15 years old, Méndez left his home and moved to the Arizona-Sonora border. He found work as a fruit and vegetable picker and came into contact with a divergent mix of people. In 1946, Méndez abandoned the migrant life, settling in Tucson, Arizona, where he found work as a bricklayer. Despite the rigorous work and suffocating heat, Méndez recorded his experiences and the people he met, as well as incorporating the ways and means of the Yaqui into his writings. He penned his first novel at age 18, yet he was unsuccessful in finding a publisher.

In the 1960s, the Chicano movement reached Tucson. Méndez found that the philosophy and goals of the movement paralleled the themes of his writing. He submitted "Tata Casehua," an allegorical short story about the trials and tribulations of the Yaqui Indians, to *El Grito,* a Chicano literary journal. In 1968, after 22 years of writing, his first

story was published. His story was well received and led to an invitation to lecture at universities and literary organizations. A self-taught man and innately humble, Méndez found the transition to literary celebrity difficult. He became a teacher of Hispanic literature at Pima College in Tucson, in 1970.

Méndez writes in Spanish. His works have not been wholly translated into English but are praised among Spanish and Mexican critics. In his first novel, *Peregrinos de Aztlán* (1973), Méndez plays with language, exploring its nuances to reveal where different colloquialisms or dialects can merge to reflect a people as complex as the ones living the bicultural existence of the U.S.-Mexican border. Méndez intertwines baroque cultured Spanish, colloquial northwest Mexican rural Spanish, and the dialect of poor, working-class urban youths to create a kaleidoscope of experiences and perspectives paralleling the aristocratic Spanish gentry hacienda owners, Mexican storytellers, and the newest generation of Spanish, Mexican, and Indian hybrids of the region. Méndez uses an unwavering stream of consciousness style.

A selection of Méndez's writings include the following: *The Dream of Santa Maria De Las Piedras* (1989), *Que no mueran los sueños* (1991; So dreams won't die), *Miguel Méndez in Aztlán: Two Decades of Literary Production* (1995), *Los muertos también cuentan* (1995; The dead matter too), *From Labor to Letters: A Novel Autobiography* (1997), and *Río Santacruz* (1997; Santa Cruz River). In 1984, the University of Arizona awarded Méndez an honorary doctorate of letters, and in 1991, he garnered the Premio Nacional de Literatura Mexicana José Fuentes Mares. The Méndez's papers housed in the California Ethnic and Multicultural Archives in the Davidson Library at the University of California–Santa Barbara since 2004 confirm Méndez's status "as a lasting component of the Chicano canon," as described by Gary Keller of Bilingual Press/Editorial Bilingüe.

Further Reading

Lomelí, Francisco A., and Carl R. Shirley, eds. *Chicano Writers: First Series.* Vol. 82. Detroit: Gale Research, 1989, pp. 157–164.

Kanellos, Nicolás, et al., eds. *Herencia: The Anthology of Hispanic Literature in the United States.* New York: Oxford University Press, 2003, pp. 199–204.

Robinson, Cecil. *No Short Journeys: The Interplay of Cultures in the History and Literature of the Borderlands.* Tucson: University of Arizona Press, 1992.

Tardiff, Joseph C., and L. Mpho Mabunda, eds. *Dictionary of Hispanic Biography.* Detroit: Gale Research, 1996, pp. 542–544.

Milligan, Mary Guerrero
(Mary Frances Guerrero)
(1953–) *essayist, anthologist, short story writer, editor*

Editor, translator, and librarian Mary Guerrero Milligan cocreated *Daughters of the Fifth Sun: A Collection of Latina Fiction and Poetry* (1995), the first all-Latina anthology released by a New York publishing house. The eldest of five children, Mary Frances Guerrero was born on May 29, 1953, in Roswell, New Mexico, to Eloise Bustos and Andrew M. Guerrero, Jr. While Guerrero was still quite young, her family moved back to their hometown of San Antonio, Texas. Her mother told her captivating stories and stressed the importance of getting an education. True to her mother's desire for her, Guerrero developed a voracious appetite for books. When she was in middle school, Guerrero fell in love with libraries. At this tender age, she asked her school librarian for a job and was crushed when the librarian explained the amount of education required.

Guerrero attended elementary schools in San Antonio, spent a few years during junior high school in Waco, Texas, and returned to San Antonio to complete her high school education. She graduated from the University of North Texas with a B.A. in history and a minor in speech communication in 1975. She earned an M.S. in library and information science from the same institution in 1977. During college, she was active in early Chicano movement politics, including campaigns for La Raza Unida Party. At this time, she also began writing. Since graduation, she has been employed as a librarian, establishing exemplary library programs that have hosted well-established Chicana authors such as SANDRA CISNEROS and CARMEN TAFOLLA. In 1975, Guerrero married Bryce Milligan, with whom she would have two children, a son and a daughter. She adopted Milligan as her surname.

Milligan has written reviews for the *Albuquerque Journal,* the *San Antonio Express News,* and various literary magazines and small journals. She was also a regular essayist, translator, and interviewer for the multicultural literary journal *Pax: A Journal for Peace through Culture.* Throughout the 1980s and 1990s, Milligan developed one of the first annotated bibliographies of Latino children's literature. Various in-progress editions of this work were constantly requested by teachers and librarians from all over the Southwest until published reference works began to appear in this field.

The recipient of several writing awards, Milligan has several creative publications including a translation of a Mexican folktale in Naomi Shihab Nye's anthology *This Tree Is Older Than You Are,* a short story titled "Loteria" in *Blue Mesa Review* (spring 1993), and a short story and a one-act play published in the anthologies *Mujeres Grandes I* (1993) and *Mujeres Grandes II* (1995). Inés Hernandez-Tovar has accepted one of Milligan's essays for a forthcoming anthology of Tejana writing. Milligan is currently the chair of the South Texas region of the Texas Library Association and a member of the Texas Bluebonnet Award program committee.

In 1990, Milligan, her husband, and poet ANGELA DE HOYOS decided that Latino literature would not be in serious competition with the

1995, Milligan has been a consulting editor for Wings Press, a publisher specializing in Latino/a authors.

Further Reading

Milligan, Bryce, Mary Guerrero Milligan, and Angela de Hoyos, eds. *Daughters of the Fifth Sun: A Collection of Latina Fiction and Poetry.* New York: Riverhead Trade, 1996.

———. *¡Floricanto Sí! A Collection of Latina Poetry.* New York: Penguin, 1998.

Shihab Nye, Naomi. *This Tree Is Older Than You Are.* New York: Simon & Schuster, 1995.

In addition to her work as an editor at Wings Press, publisher of Latino and Chicano literature Mary Guerrero Milligan is also a librarian. *(Courtesy of the author)*

Mohr, Nicholasa
(Nicholasa Golpe)
(1938–   ) *young adult writer, poet, television writer, radio writer, children's writer, scriptwriter, short story writer, educator, novelist*

Nicholasa Mohr is the first Puerto Rican woman born on the U.S. mainland to write about her ethnic roots in New York City. In the literary world, she is best known for her young adult books.

Nicholasa Golpe was born on All Saint's Day, November 1, 1938, in Spanish Harlem, also known as El Barrio (The Neighborhood), a distinctly Puerto Rican enclave in Manhattan. Her parents, Pedro and Nicholasa (Rivera) Golpe immigrated to the United States from Puerto Rico during the Great Depression with their four children. Nicholasa was the last of three children born in New York City and the only girl. Her father died when she was eight years old. After his death, her mother gave Nicholasa some paper, pencils, and crayons to help the young girl cope with the loss of her father. She discovered she could create new worlds with pictures. Her mother, who instilled a great sense of self-worth in her daughter, encouraged Nicholasa's creativity. However, before Nicholasa reached high school, her mother passed away, and she moved in with an aunt who treated the orphaned girl with disdain and repulsion.

mainstream American canon unless it was published by major New York houses. This would enable professors and teachers to get the literature into their classrooms more easily. The three editors developed a prospectus for an all-Latina anthology entitled *Daughters of the Fifth Sun: A Collection of Latina Fiction and Poetry.* After 50 rejections and five years later, Putnam/Riverhead published the anthology in 1995. This was the first all-Latina anthology released by a New York publishing house. It spent three years on the New York Public Library's Best Books for the Teen Age list. The three editors followed it with *¡Floricanto Sí! A Collection of Latina Poetry* (1998). Since

Nicholasa Mohr has had the longest career as a creative writer for a Hispanic woman. *(Photo of Nicholasa Mohr is reprinted with permission from the publisher [APP Archive Files] [Houston: Arte Público Press—University of Houston, © 2006])*

money to visit Mexico afterward, where she studied the muralists and artists, such as Diego Rivera, Frida Kahlo, and José Clemente Orozco.

Upon her return to the United States, Golpe attended the New School for Social Research in New York City. It was there she met her future husband, Irwin Mohr. The couple married in 1957 and eventually had two sons, David and Jason. Mohr continued her artistic studies at the Brooklyn Museum Art School and the Pratt Center for Contemporary Printmaking. She worked as an art instructor in New York and New Jersey as well as an artist in residence with the New York City public schools.

By the early 1970s, Mohr enjoyed one-woman exhibits as a painter and work as an art agent. She was content with an artist's life, having no ambitions to become a writer, until a publisher pointed out the fact that no stories existed depicting the life of a young Puerto Rican in the United States. Remembering the void she felt in her own childhood without mirror images of her life to reflect upon in books, Mohr wrote 50 pages of autobiographical vignettes. The publisher turned down her work because he was hoping to read stories rife with terror, theft, and sensationalism. Mohr continued her work as an artist until Harper and Row requested she create an image for a book cover. Instead, she supplied them with her writings. Mohr was given a contract immediately, to which she responded by writing *Nilda* (1973).

Set during World War II, this autobiographical account of a poor Puerto Rican girl living in New York City captured the hearts of readers and critics. Mohr received immense praise for *Nilda* and was awarded the Outstanding Book Award in Juvenile Fiction from the *New York Times;* the Jane Addams Children's Book Award from the Jane Addams Peace Association; a citation of merit from the Society of Illustrators for *Nilda*'s book jacket design, which Mohr completed herself; and *School Library Journal*'s "Best of the Best 1966–1978" list in 1979. Based on the success of *Nilda,* Mohr felt compelled to write additional books. She won a

Despite her struggles and losses, Golpe was determined to pursue her artistic talents. She was able to endure the prejudices of her time and the hostility of her new home by remembering her mother's confidence in her. Golpe set her sights and vast determination on attending college. She was waylaid by a short-sighted counselor who believed Puerto Rican girls did not need formal education and were better suited for seamstress work. Disappointed yet inventive, Golpe enrolled in the Arts Students' League in New York, a college that offers fashion illustration classes, which would enable the burgeoning artist an opportunity to pursue drawing. Golpe worked through college, saving enough

MacDowell Colony writing fellowship in the summer of 1974.

Mohr filled a void in the marketplace with juvenile books that spoke to the experiences of young Latinos growing up in America. Her works include *El Bronx Remembered* (1975), *In Nueva York* (short stories, 1977), *Felita* (which she both wrote and illustrated, 1979), *All for the Better: A Story of El Barrio* (part of the Stories of America series, 1982), *Going Home* (sequel to *Felita*, 1986), *Isabel's New Mom* (1993), *The Magic Shell* (1994), *The Song of El Coquí, and Other Tales of Puerto Rico* (1995), and *Old Letivia and the Mountain of Sorrows/La vieja Letivia y el monte de los pesares* (1996).

Leaving the world of young adult readers, Mohr ventured into performance art with *Aquí y ahora* (teleplay, 1975), *Inside the Monster* (radio play, 1981), *Zoraida* (play, 1988), *I Never Even Seen My Father* (play, 1995), *Nilda* (play, 1999; based on her novel of the same name), *El Bronx Remembered* (play, 1999; based on the short stories "A New Window Display," "A Very Special Pet," and "Shoes for Hector").

Mohr expanded the boundaries of her writing and crafted works of adult fiction such as *Rituals of Survival: A Women's Portfolio* (1985), *In My Own Words* (1994), *Growing Up Inside the Sanctuary of My Imagination* (1994), *A Matter of Pride and Other Stories* (1997), and *Untitled Nicholasa Mohr* (1998). She also authored a screenplay with Ray Blanco, *The Artist*. She has contributed stories to textbooks and anthologies, including *The Ethnic American Woman: Problems, Protests, Lifestyles*. Her short stories have appeared in *Children's Digest*, *Scholastic Magazine*, and *Nuestro*.

Throughout her writing career, Mohr has served as a visiting lecturer at universities as well as an educator, librarian, and leader of student and community groups. She was the head creative writer and coproducer of the television series *Aquí y Ahora* (*Here and Now*), and a member of arts organizations, Film Video Arts, the New York State Developmental Disabilities Planning Council, the New Jersey State Council on the Arts, and the Young Filmmakers Foundation.

Mohr has received more than 20 honors and writing awards, including a Notable Trade Book Award, the American Book Award, and a lifetime achievement award from the National Congress of Puerto Rican Women. While entertaining her readers, Mohr uses her writing to mirror the cultural experiences shared by fellow Latinos and Latinas, with particular emphasis on Puerto Rican girls in New York City. At the same time, she introduces an in-depth look at the life and traditions of Hispanic Americans to a mainstream audience that she hopes will encourage readers of all ages and ethnicities to embrace and widen their perceptions of Latinos.

Further Reading

Luis, William, and Ann Gonzales, eds. *Dictionary of Literary Biography*. Vol. 145: *Modern Latin-American Fiction Writers, Second Series*. Detroit: Gale Group, 1994, pp. 170–177.

Miller, John C. "Nicholasa Mohr: Neorican Writing in Process." *Revista Interamericana* 9 (Winter 1980): 543–549.

West-Durán, Alan. *Latino and Latina Writers, Volume II*. Detroit: Gale-Thomas, 2004, pp. 905–916.

Mora, Pat
(Patricia Estella Mora)
(1942–) poet, essayist, children's writer, young adult writer, biographer, educator

Renowned for her healing and evocative prose and verse, Pat Mora is an award-winning writer of many disciplines. Her deep commitment to preserve cultural inheritance, advocate literacy, and reclaim women's strength has won her international recognition.

Born Patricia Estella Mora on January 19, 1942, she draws on her family for inspiration. Around 1916, both her maternal and paternal grandparents left Mexico during the violence that ensued after the Mexican Revolution. The Mexican Revolution of 1910 was an uprising of common folk who overthrew the dictator Porfirio Díaz. Both families endured harrowing crossings of the border and established homes in El Paso, Texas. Mora's parents, Raúl Antonio and Estela Delgado Mora, met there during the Great Depression and married in 1939. Mora and her three siblings, Cecelia, Stella, and Roy (later Antonio), delighted in the tales and antics of their great-aunt Ignacia (Nacha) Delgado, whom they nicknamed Tía Lobo (Aunt Wolf). Mora spoke Spanish with her grandmother and aunt but chose to hide her ethnicity at school. She would cringe when her father played mariachi music on the radio, seeking to assimilate and be like other American children. She attended St. Patrick's Catholic School and Loretto Academy, secretly wishing she would see something of her Mexican history or culture at school. Mora wrote years later, "One of the reasons that I write children's books is because I want Mexican culture and Mexican-American culture to be a part of our schools and libraries."

She was an avid reader, devouring comic books, mysteries, biographies, and poetry. Although she loved to read, Mora never thought of becoming a writer when she grew up. She wanted to be a nun and often would set up dining room chairs as pews and practice teaching. Mora's ambitions eventually changed to becoming a doctor and then a teacher by the time she reached college. She received a B.A. from Texas Western College (now the University of Texas–El Paso) in 1963. She married William H. Burnside, Jr., the summer following graduation. The couple have three children: William, Elizabeth, and Cecilia. Mora worked as an English and Spanish teacher in elementary and high schools from 1963 to 1966 before earning an M.A. in English from the University of Texas–El Paso in 1967. She lectured on English and communications part time at El Paso Community College from 1971 to 1978. Mora joined the faculty at the University of Texas–El Paso in 1979.

At nearly 40 years of age, Mora decided to make some changes. Instead of marking other people's writing, the time had come to pen her own words and experiences. She divorced her husband, took a position as assistant to the vice president of academic affairs at the university, and began writing seriously. She contributed to the *Revista Chicano Riqueña* and *Kikirikí/Children's Literature Anthology* (1981). In 1983, she hosted a radio program called *Voices: The Mexican-American in Perspective* and was granted a creative writing award from the National Association for Chicano Studies. The following year, she married Vernon Lee Scarborough, an archaeologist and professor, and released her first poetry collection, *Chants* (1984).

In 1986, Mora released another book of poetry, *Borders,* which garnered the Southwest Book Award. In these poems, Mora explores the cultural, social, political, and emotional borders that separate and define the individual. This volume reflects on the perspective she gained when traveling to Cuba, India, and Pakistan to create a forum for healing relationships with people, land, and culture in 1986. She also received a Kellogg national fellowship to study national and international issues of cultural conservation. She served as the director of the museum at the University of Texas–El Paso for one year before, in 1989, devoting herself full time to being a writer and speaker. When Scarborough was hired as an anthropology professor at the University of Cincinnati, Mora and her husband relocated there. Mora published her third poetry collection, *Communion,* in 1991.

Mora released her first children's book in 1992. *A Birthday Basket for Tía* explores intergenerational relationships and is based on the love she felt for and from her Tía Lobo. Critics and readers alike raved about this book. Mora followed her initial success with 19 additional children's books, some of which are bilingual or are offered in Spanish. Her children's work includes: *The Desert Is My Mother: El desierto es mi madre* (1994), *Listen to the Desert: Oye al desierto* (1994), *Pablo's Tree*

(1994), *The Gift of the Poinsettia: El regalo de la flor de Noche Buena* (1995), *Tomás and the Library Lady* (1997), *The Rainbow Tulip* (1999), *The Night the Moon Fell: A Maya Myth* (2000), *The Bakery Lady/La señora de la panderia* (2001), *Lore to Mamá: A Celebration of Mothers* (2001), *The Race of Toad and Deer* (2001), *A Library for Juana: The World of Sor Juana Inés* (2002), *Maria Paints the Hills* (2002), *Doña Flor: A Tall Tale about a Giant Woman with a Great Big Heart* (2005), and *The Song of Francis and the Animals* (2005). Mora has received 23 awards and honors for her children's books, including the Southwest Book Award and the Teachers' Choice award from the International Reading Association.

After her entry into the world of children's books, Mora wrote a series of essays called *Nepantla* (1993). *Nepantla* is a Nahuatl word meaning the "land of the middle." Mora believes great possibilities exist within this space between worlds. She writes, "I am a child of the border, the land corridor bordered by two countries." A border person, she views herself as the bridge between different perspectives and cultures with the responsibility, challenge, and talents to forge mutual understanding. Mora was awarded a National Endowment for the Arts Creative Writing Fellowship in 1994. She has received eight literary awards, six awards for her adult books, and three awards for her young adult books. Mora published *Agua Santa: Holy Water* (1995), a book of poetry that evokes Mexican-American mythology, culture, and history.

In 1997, Mora deepened her commitment to children and literacy when she successfully lobbied to establish April 30 as El Día de los Niños/El Día de los Libros (The Day of the Children/The Day of the Books), a national day dedicated to the celebration of children and literacy. That same year, she released a book of poetry, *Aunt Carmen's Book of Practical Saints* (1997), and a memoir, *House of Houses* (1997). In her memoir, Mora weaves together the voices of her ancestors to reveal stories of oppression, survival, and sometimes triumph.

In 1999, Mora served as the Carruthers Chair Distinguished Visiting Professor at the University of New Mexico. The following year, Mora and her siblings established the Estela and Raúl Mora Award. In 2002, Mora received the Civitella Ranieri Fellowship from Umbria, Italy. Deeply affected by the desert, shamanic imagery, and the spirituality of Mother Earth, Mora is sometimes called a regional or feminist writer. In *Horn Book,* Mora wrote in 1990 about supporting and establishing pride in cultural inheritance and being a woman: "I will try to write to correct these images of worth. I take pride in being a Hispanic writer. I will continue to write and to struggle to say what no other writer can say in quite the same way." Mora imparts healing, love, and community into her writings and her projects, profoundly reminding her readers of the value of connection and relationships.

Further Reading

Fox, Linda C. "From Chants to Borders to Communion: Pat Mora's Poetic Journey to Nepantla." *Bilingual Review/Revista Bilingue* 21, no. 3 (1996): 219–230.

Kanellos, Nicolás, et al., eds. *Herencia: The Anthology of Hispanic Literature in the United States.* New York: Oxford University Press, 2003, pp. 329–330.

Kristovic, Jelena, ed. *Hispanic Literature Criticism.* Detroit: Gale Research, 1994.

Mora, Pat. *House of Houses.* Boston: Beacon Press, 1997.

Tardiff, Joseph C., and L. Mpho Mabunda, eds. *Dictionary of Hispanic Biography.* Detroit: Gale Research, 1996, pp. 575–577.

Moraga, Cherríe

(1952–   ) *poet, essayist, short story writer, playwright, anthologist, activist, educator*

An essential voice in world literature, Cherríe Moraga broke the silence that imprisoned many people, particularly women, on the basis of racial, gender, sexual, and class prejudice with the publication of

This Bridge Called My Back, an anthology of essays, poems, and short stories by women of color that she coedited with Gloria Anzaldúa. Moraga, an award-winning author, is well known for her courageous and polemical writing.

Cherríe Moraga was born in Whittier, California, on September 25, 1952. She inherited the features of her Mexican-American mother, Elvira Moraga, and the fair skin of her Anglo father, Joseph Lawrence. Self-described as *la güera,* or "the fair-skinned girl," Moraga was able to "pass" as white and avoid discrimination. However, Moraga found that denying her cultural heritage and accessing the advantages of the dominant race had its consequences, for in the process she lost a piece of her identity, particularly her Chicana heritage. While she was young, the family moved around frequently, finally settling in San Gabriel, California. Moraga grew up listening to her mother's extended family animatedly recount stories in vivid detail with a fluid mix of Spanish and English that lured her into the world of oral storytelling. Moraga picked up Spanish phrases and words but did not become fluent in the language.

Moraga attended Immaculate Heart College in Los Angeles, earning a B.A. in English in 1974. Attracted to art, she did not allow herself the luxury of pursuing her interest so that she could stay on track and become the teacher she felt she must be. After graduation, Moraga taught English at a small private high school for two years before she took a writing course at the Women's Building in Los Angeles. She loved writing, even though her first writings were somewhat stilted, lacking the conviction that became her most beloved and recognizable attribute. She was in her mid-20s when the burning desire to declare her lesbianism collided with her fervor to write matters of the heart. On her journey, Moraga found much more than she expected. "When I finally lifted the lid to my lesbianism, a profound connection with my mother reawakened in me. It wasn't until I acknowledged and confronted my own lesbianism in the flesh, that my heartfelt identification with and empathy

for my mother's oppression—due to being poor, uneducated, and Chicana—was realized," she is often quoted for saying. Her first poetry revealed her secrets in lesbian love poems. These writings were criticized by fellow writers for small, ordinary vocabulary and the belief that no one would accept a lesbian affair. However, Moraga remained true to her inner voice.

In 1977, she moved to San Francisco to allow herself the opportunity to see if she could make it as a writer and the permission to fully express herself as a lesbian. She shared her poetry with working-class lesbian poet Judy Grain, who encouraged Moraga "to do what nobody else can do, which is to write exactly from your own voice, the voices you heard growing up." With renewed confidence and vigor, Moraga enrolled in San Francisco State University to study feminist writing, a combination of creative writing and feminist literature. She met Anzaldúa, who suggested she and Moraga create an anthology together focused on how women of color deal with the suppression of their voices and experiences. Moraga's advisers agreed to accept the manuscript as her master's thesis, and thus *This Bridge Called My Back: Writings by Radical Women of Color* came into being. When they could not find a publisher who would accept the book, Moraga cofounded Kitchen Table/Women of Color Press and published the book in 1981.

A divergent collection of poems, essays, and short stories, *This Bridge Called My Back* inspired women of different nationalities to put aside differences and celebrate similarities and strength while exposing innermost experiences with visceral honesty. Moraga's contribution to the book includes two poems and her infamous essay called "La Güera." *This Bridge Called My Back* made a tremendous impact. It won the Before Columbus Foundation American Book Award in 1986; virtually every feminist publication in the United States reviewed it; colleges and universities across the nation include it in either Chicano-Latin studies or feminist curricula; and the book is credited for bringing to light the unfortunate and crippling racism among women during the height of the women's movement.

In 1983, Moraga released *Loving in the War Years: Lo que nunca pasó por sus labios* (What never passed her lips), a collection of poetry and prose that explores self-acceptance based on the multi-faceted experiences of being a woman, Chicana, and lesbian. In the same year, Moraga edited *Cuentos: Stories by Latinos.* Moraga then tried her hand at writing plays. Her plays from the 1980s include *La extranjera* (1985; The foreign woman), *Giving Up the Ghost: Teatro in Two Acts* (1986), *Shadow of a Man* (1988), and *Heroes and Saints* (1989).

In 1992, at age 40, Moraga decided she wanted to have a baby. She captured her intimate thoughts through diary entries during her pregnancy and the precarious early months of her son's life in *Waiting in the Wings: Portrait of a Queer Mother* (1997). In 1993, Moraga combined editing skills with Norma Alarcón and ANA CASTILLO to create *The Sexuality of Latinas,* a collaboration of 37 contributors exploring sexuality through poetry, essays, fiction, and artwork. That same year, she released her own collection of radical poetry and prose, *The Last Generation,* which seamlessly weaves Spanish and English in a call to transcend archaic political positions toward sexuality, race, art, nationalism, and gender.

From 1991 to 1997, Moraga was the playwright in residence at Brava Theatre Center of San Francisco, during which time she wrote numerous plays, including *Heart of the Earth: A Popol Vuh Story* (1994), *Circle in the Dirt* (1995), and *Watsonville: Some Place Not Here* (1995), which won the 1995 Fund for New American Plays Award from the Kennedy Center for the Performing Arts. Additional plays by Moraga include *Who Killed Yolanda Saldívar?* (2000), *The Hungry Woman: A Mexican Medea* (2002), and *Waiting for Da God?* (2004).

In 2002, *This Bridge Called My Back* was rereleased, featuring the artwork of 17 women artists. *Loving in the War Years* also enjoyed a 20th-anniversary rerelease in 2003. Moraga has taught literature, writing, and women's studies at universities across the nation. She has received numerous awards, including the Will Glickman Prize, the Drama-logue and Critic Circles Awards, and the PEN West Award. Frequently anthologized and requested as a lecturer, Moraga currently serves as the artist in residence in the department of drama and the department of Spanish and Portuguese at Stanford University. Moraga is a prolific, profound writer, whose willingness and dedication to a candid and intelligent approach to taboo subjects have created the possibility of societal transformation and overall acceptance.

Further Reading

Feyder, Linda, ed. *Shattering the Myth: Plays by Hispanic Women.* Houston, Tex.: Arte Público Press, 1992.

Lomelí, Francisco A., and Carl R. Shirley, eds. *Chicano Writers: First Series.* Vol. 82. Detroit: Gale Research, 1989, pp. 165–177.

Moraga, Cherríe, and Gloria Anzaldúa, eds. *This Bridge Called My Back.* Berkeley, Calif.: Third Woman Press, 1984.

Novas, Himilce. *The Hispanic 100: A Ranking of the Latino Men and Women Who Have Most Influenced American Thought and Culture.* New York: Citadel Press, 1995.

Yarbro-Bejarano, Yvonne. *The Wounded Heart: Writing on Cherríe Moraga.* Houston: University of Texas Press, 2001.

Morales, Alejandro
(Alejandro Dennis Morales)
(1944–   ) *novelist, essayist, short story writer, educator*

Alejandro Morales is a leading figure in Chicano literature best known for his novel *The Brick People.* He is praised for his seamless blending of history, literature, and theory in what has been termed *histographic metafiction.*

Alejandro Dennis Morales was born on October 14, 1944, in Montebello, California. Both his parents, Delfino Morales Martínez and Juana Contreras Ramírez, were originally from Guanajuato, Mexico. Morales grew up in the East Los Angeles barrio of the Simons Brick Company. Although his parents played a pivotal role in influencing Morales, it was a family friend, Vicente Lemus, who encouraged Morales to read. Morales often sought the advice of the old gentleman, whom he affectionately called El Comradito. Morales also found encouragement from junior high and high school teachers who guided him toward literature and writing. In fact, some of his high school journal writings served as inspiration and foundation

Alejandro Morales wrote one of the first books to depict the gritty life on the barrio streets. *(Photo of Alejandro Morales is reprinted with permission from the publisher [APP Archive Files] [Houston: Arte Público Press—University of Houston, © 2006])*

for his first novel, *Caras viejas y vino nuevo* (1975; *Old Faces and New Wine*).

After graduating from Montebello High School in 1963, Morales became involved with gangs, drugs, and alcohol. He served a short time in the Los Angeles County jail and then decided to channel his feelings and confusion into writing. He earned an associate's degree in 1965 from East Los Angeles College and then transferred to California State University–Los Angeles. In 1967, Morales graduated with a bachelor's degree in Spanish and married H. Rohde Teaze, with whom he would have two children. Upon graduation, Morales taught at Claremont High School for one year. He and his wife then moved to New Jersey, where Morales enrolled at Rutgers University. He earned a master's in 1973 and a doctorate in 1975 in Spanish, both from Rutgers. By his third year in graduate school, Morales had developed a keen interest in medieval history. However, under the direction of a professor, he decided to focus on the burgeoning world of Chicano literature. As a groundbreaking influence in a new field of study, Morales wrote one of the first doctoral dissertations on Mexican-American literature in the United States. While in school, he became active in the Chicano movement, participating at the Floricanto, a festival dedicated to promoting the Chicano experience through literature.

In 1975, Morales accepted a teaching position in the Spanish department at the University of California–Irvine, where he continues to teach. After many attempts to get his first book published, the novel finally was released by a Mexican publisher in 1975. Written entirely in Spanish, *Caras viejas y vino nuevo* was a finalist in a contest sponsored by Mexican Press. It was translated into English by Max Martinez under the title *Old Faces and New Wine* in 1981 and translated a second time by Francisco A. Lomelí as *Barrio on the Edge* in 1997. Originally, the book was seen as erotic and vulgar, given the explicit depiction of life in the barrio; today, Morales's work is praised for its visceral, authentic, and unapologetic style. It is one of the first published works to include Spanglish, a combination of Spanish and English.

Morales based his second novel, *La verdad sin voz* (1979), on the life of an Anglo physician in Mathis, Texas. This work was later translated into English under the title *Death of an Anglo* (1988). Serendipitously, although Morales invented the people and details from his imagination, he later discovered much of his creation closely paralleled actual events and real people.

Reto en el paraíso (1982; *Defiance in Paradise*) explores the effects of Manifest Destiny on the lives of dispossessed Californio landowners. A Californio was a Spanish-speaking inhabitant of Alta California, originally a colony of Spain and later Mexico prior to its annexation by the United States after the U.S.-Mexican War. Californios include European settlers from Spain and Mexico, mestizos, local Native Americans who adopted Spanish culture and religion, and their present-day descendants. *The Brick People* (1988) is a biographical novel based on the lives of his mother and father. Morales interviewed scores of people from his old neighborhood who had worked at the Simons Brick Factory to compile a sociological biography suffused with magic realism. *The Rag Doll Plagues* (1993) takes a hard yet surreal look at three rampant diseases and the havoc they wreaked on colonial Mexico, present-day Mexico, and a fictional, mid-21st-century technocratic city known as LAMAS and created by combining Los Angeles and Mexico. From the late 1980s to the early 1990s, Morales reviewed books for the *Los Angeles Times.*

Waiting to Happen (2002) represents Morales's first novel in a heterotopian trilogy. A place where differences meet, heterotopia is the space that exists between utopia, a conceived space, and eutopia, or real space. The book blends narrative modalities of myth, history, and detective novel styles. The second book in the trilogy, *The Place of the White Heron,* is under consideration for publication. *Pequeña nación* (2004; Small nation) contains two short stories and a novella. *The Captain of All These Men of Death* was released in 2006.

Morales is currently at work on a book set in the 1920s and focused on the Los Angeles River and its bridges. He continues to give readings and lectures and teaches at the University of California–Irvine in the Chicano studies department. He has been awarded a Ford Foundation fellowship, ITT International fellowship, National Endowment for the Arts grant, California Council of Arts grant, Mellon Foundation grant, and MEXUS grant. Morales's short stories and numerous articles have had a significant impact on Chicano literature. His works appear in English, Spanish, Dutch, and French translations. Morales's poetic use of language, deep understanding of Mexican-American culture, and the important effect place and environment have on the developing human psyche have secured his position as an integral brick in the foundation of Latino literature.

Further Reading

Heide, Rick, ed. *Under the Fifth Sun: Latino Literature From California.* Santa Clara, Calif.: Santa Clara University; and Berkeley: Heyday Books, 2002.

Lomelí, Francisco A., and Donaldo W. Urioste. *Chicano Perspectives in Literature: A Critical and Annotated Bibliography.* Albuquerque: Pajarito Publications, 1976.

Palacios, José Antonio Gurpegui. *Alejandro Morales: Fiction Past, Present, Future Perfect.* Tempe, Ariz.: Bilingual Review Press, 1996.

Morales, Ed
(Edward Morales)
(1962–) *journalist, nonfiction writer*

Through sensitivity and tenacity, Ed Morales encourages his readers to think in a circular, evolving way rather than a restrictive, potentially dangerous linear or black-and-white mode of thinking and reacting. He is well known for his contributions and articles in the *Village Voice,* as well as for his two books, *Living in Spanglish: The Search for Latino Identity in America* and *The Latin Beat: The Rhythms and Roots of Latin Music, from Bossa Nova to Salsa and Beyond.*

A colorful mix of many cultures, languages, and attitudes surrounded Ed as a child. Born and raised in the Bronx in New York City, Edward Morales entered the world on June 16, 1962, the child of Zolio and Maria Morales, both of Puerto Rican descent. Inspired by the multiethnic diversity of his childhood, he wanted to write and capture the kaleidoscope of people and cultures. Ed wrote for the school paper at the Bronx High School of Science.

Morales attended Brandeis University in Massachusetts, where he graduated with a double major in sociology and philosophy in 1982. He directed a program for high school dropouts encouraging students to stay in school from 1982 to 1983. Although he did manage to reach some kids, he eventually became frustrated by the program's few success stories. Concurrently, from 1982 to 1984, he took political economy and anthropology classes at the New School for Social Research in New York.

In 1986, Morales began freelance writing, with a short story appearing in the prestigious *Between C & D,* one of the most influential literary magazines of the New York City downtown scene in the 1980s. From 1987 to 1994, Morales wrote primarily for the *Village Voice,* covering how the Latino and Latin American communities were affected by a variety of subjects, from politics to pop culture. In 1992, he received a grant from the Jerome Foundation to travel to study Latino theater groups around the country. Through this work he was able to ascertain the differences, as well as the similarities, that Latinos from different countries possess. He covered the Puerto Rican Film Festival for three years, which enabled him to interact with Latin Americans in an environment that organically encouraged amity. He also traveled to Mexico to cover rock bands. Morales

wrote and performed his poetry at New York's Lower East Side Nuyorican Poets Cafe. His poetry appeared in *Iguana Dreams* (1992), *Aloud* (1993), and *Boricuas: Influential Puerto Rican Writings— An Anthology* (1995). In 1994, he was informally chosen by MIGUEL ALGARÍN and fellow writer Bob Holman as one of 10 poets to tour the nation and perform poetry.

In 1995, Morales became a staff writer at the *Village Voice,* where he continued to cover the Latino community. Morales joined *Newsday* in 2001. His freelance work has appeared in *Rolling Stone, Entertainment Weekly, Vibe, Details, Spin,* the *New York Times,* the *Miami Herald,* and the *Los Angeles Times.* In 2003, Morales released two books, *Living in Spanglish: The Search for Latino Identity in America* and *The Latin Beat: The Rhythms and Roots of Latin Music, from Bossa Nova to Salsa and Beyond. Living in Spanglish* is a pioneering effort to unify Latinos under the notion of their differences. The book reminds Latino readers of their shared history and similar foundations while establishing authenticity, comfort, and a sense of camaraderie for generations of people who include ethnic diversity as part of their identity as an American. *The Latin Beat* uses music as a means to show how the many segments of Latin cultures blend together to create a hybrid of what it means to be Latino/a in the United States. He currently writes a Latin music column for *Newsday* and has completed his third book, *Latin in Manhattan.* Morales contributes to society with a constant call to allow evolution of thought to form individual and cultural identity. He was the Revson Fellow for the 2006–07 academic year at Columbia University. This one-year program of study will allow him to work with other fellows and work toward "the future of New York City."

Further Reading

Landau, Saul. "Mixed Messages." *Washington Post,* March 24, 2002, p. BW03.

Morales, Ed. *Living in Spanglish: The Search for Latino Identity in America.* New York: St. Martin's Press. 2003.

Poey, Delia. *Iguana Dreams: New Latino Fiction.* New York: Perennial, 1992.

Moran, Julio
(1956–) *journalist*

Julio Moran has long been a guiding presence in representing Latinos in journalism. He is the executive director of the California Chicano News Media Association (CCNMA) and three-time winner of the Pulitzer Prize for excellence in journalism.

Julio Moran was born on July 5, 1956, to Julio and Genoveva Morán, both from Mexico. Moran, the family's third child, was the first one born in Los Angeles, California. His older brother and sister were born in Mexico. Later fueled by the misrepresentation of people of color in the American media, Moran, however, was not affected by this discrepancy as he grew up in predominantly Latino neighborhoods in the San Fernando Valley. He later lived in a housing project that was predominantly African American.

On August 29, 1970, when Moran was just 14 years old, 20,000 Chicanos took to the streets to protest the Vietnam War and the fact that Chicanos were being killed in numbers disproportionate to the general population. Known as the Chicano Moratorium, the tragic events of the day proved to be monumental in the life of young Moran. The police reacted with violence to the antiwar protesters, killing RUBÉN SALAZAR, a journalist for the *Los Angeles Times.* Moran stated in a 2005 interview, "That demonstration and Rubén's death showed that Latinos still had a long way to improve conditions, Rubén also showed that the media could have an influence in bringing about change." As a child, Moran knew he wanted to write. He began in high school as a sports writer. His high school

journalism teacher, Helen Aragon, helped instill confidence in Moran that he could be a successful journalist.

He graduated from San Fernando High School, still writing about sports. He went straight to Pepperdine University in Malibu, California. When Moran started college at Pepperdine, whose student body was composed predominantly of white and wealthy kids, he began to see the cultural and economic differences not so evident in his childhood. Most of his white classmates knew Latinos only as maids and gardeners. As Pepperdine is a small, conservative Christian college, he was constantly forced to deal with issues of race.

In his sophomore year of college, Moran realized the tribulations that people of color faced were not being reported. He commented in a 2005 interview about this oversight, "I realized that if I didn't cover them no one would." During his last semester of school, Moran interned at the *Los Angeles Times,* where he met FRANK DEL OLMO. Del Olmo had grown in the same neighborhood as Moran, and Moran found him an inspiring mentor. As Moran stated, "Del Olmo proved that you can be a first-rate journalist without denying your Latino heritage and he fought to improve the hiring and coverage of Latinos." Moran graduated from Pepperdine in 1978 with a B.A. in journalism and history and with a mission to help change journalism to include and fairly represent all people.

Moran's first job in journalism was as a reporter for the *Los Angeles Herald-Examiner* in 1978. A year later, he worked at the *San Fernando Sun,* also as a reporter. Moran then moved on to work as an editor with *Nuestro* magazine in New York from 1979 to 1981. He got a call from the *Los Angeles Times* and worked as a reporter for the paper from 1981 to 1995. Moran received the first of three Pulitzer Prizes in 1983 for a series about how Latinos were leaving Catholicism and converting to Protestant denominations. He was on the city staff that won the Pulitzer Prize for its coverage of the Los Angeles riots in 1992 and the Northridge earthquake in 1994.

In 1996, Moran earned a certificate from the Maynard Institute for Journalism Education Management Training Center at Northwestern University. In 1997, he became the executive director of CCNMA, a title he held until 2005. In 1998, Moran became a professor at the University of Southern California Annenberg School of Journalism, teaching newswriting and reporting. Helping young Latinos achieve their goals of becoming professional journalists inspires him most today. He teaches and has always exemplified that being accurate and inclusive denotes good journalism.

Further Reading

Moran, Julio. "Latinos Renewing Bonds with Religion." *Los Angeles Times,* August 8, 1983.
"A Reporters Take Online." Available online. URL: http://malagigi.cddc.vt.edu/pipermail/icernet/2003-December/002691.html. Downloaded on June 27, 2005.

Moreno, Sylvia
(1953–   ) *journalist*

A multitalented writer, Sylvia Moreno is a pioneering Latina journalist in the United States dedicated to helping her readers find the commonality they share with the world's people. First-generation Mexican American Sylvia Moreno was one of six children of Abraham and Julia Resendez Moreno. Moreno was born on September 27, 1953, in Brownsville, Texas, a U.S.-Mexico border town. All her extended family lived in Mexico, creating a void in support and making assimilation into American culture more compelling for the Moreno children. Primarily self-educated, Moreno's parents encouraged and expected their children to achieve higher education. Motivated by her parents' aspirations, Moreno enrolled in advanced placement classes. She enjoyed writing from an early age, entering writing contests in junior high school and

writing and editing her high school paper. In her senior year, Moreno's English teacher, James Ericson, introduced American and European literature, classical music, and art to his students. That, for Moreno, partly served as the impetus later for her to leave the isolation of a border town to travel the world, experience other cultures, and live in other parts of the United States.

Moreno studied journalism at the University of Texas–Austin. Within two weeks of graduating in 1975, she went to work for United Press International (UPI) in Austin, covering the Texas legislature. She also reported and edited for UPI in Kansas City and Dallas for nearly two years, with the exception of a summer internship she served at *Newsday* on Long Island, New York. Moreno joined *Newsday* full time in 1977. For 16 years, she reported on a variety of beats and topics on Long Island for *Newsday* and in New York City for *New York Newsday,* including local politics and government, education, religion, social services, and immigration. During her tenure, she was also a member of the *New York Newsday* special projects team and worked as an editor on Long Island for two and a half years.

At the beginning of her journalism career and for the next decade, Moreno was the sole Latino professional, male or female, in the newsrooms in which she worked. To gain support and a sense of camaraderie, she joined the National Association of Hispanic Journalists (NAHJ) in 1985 and served as a board member from 1989 to 1991. Moreno helped train aspiring minority reporters and editors during three summers at two campuses of the Institute for Journalism Education (now known as the Maynard Institute).

Moreno subsequently covered the Texas legislature and state politics in the Austin bureau of the *Dallas Morning News* from 1993 to 1997. She joined the *Washington Post* in September 1997 to work as a metro reporter, covering local news in northern Virginia. A year and a half later, she began covering the District of Columbia, also for the metro section. In June 2004, she became the

Award-winning Sylvia Moreno is a renowned journalist who writes for the *Washington Post. (Courtesy of the author)*

Southwest bureau chief for the *Post,* based, once again, in Austin. Four of the five years, from 2000 to 2004, Moreno codirected a high school writing program geared toward minority students that was cosponsored by the *Washington Post* and NAHJ. (The program is now also cosponsored by the Asian American Journalist Association.) Moreno encouraged students to use their understanding and knowledge of minority communities to broaden sensitivity to those cultures in the mainstream population.

Moreno is particularly interested in writing human interest articles and has been able to use her unique cultural perspective to develop in-depth stories on the Latino community. In general, she finds prejudice is rooted in ignorance. Moreno

strives to help her readers see the basic human thread that connects all people. "The more you get to know others, the less barriers you have," she said in a 2005 interview. Moreno has won several journalism awards, including a Publisher's Award from *Newsday* and two Front Page Awards from the New York Newswomen's Club.

Further Reading

Moreno, Sylvia. "Suspected CBS Source Is Well-Regarded Texan Democrat, Lives Among GOP Voters." *Washington Post,* September 17, 2004, p. A5.
———. "Trail Offers a Look at Washington's Black Heritage." *Washington Post,* December 21, 2003, p. A11.
———. "Watergate Papers Go Public: University of Texas to Unveil Woodward Bernstein Collection." *Washington Post,* February 4, 2005, p. A3.

Morton, Carlos
(Charles Morton)
(1947–) *playwright, educator*

A groundbreaking force in establishing Latino theater as an essential and integral part of American theater, Carlos Morton has had more than 100 theatrical productions, both in the United States and abroad. His professional credits include the San Francisco Mime Troupe, the New York Shakespeare Festival, the Denver Center Theatre, La Compañía Nacional de México, the Puerto Rican Traveling Theatre, and the Arizona Theatre Company. He has also written for Columbia Pictures Television and Fox Television, as well as authored three radio plays in Spanish for the Mexico's Secretariat of Foreign Relations and the Mexican Institute of Radio.

A vagabond traveler by nature and nurture, Charles Morton was born in Chicago, Illinois, on October 15, 1947, to Helen Lopez and Ciro Morton. A third-generation Latino, Morton is part Cuban and part Mexican, getting most of his cultural inheritance from his Mexican roots. His father was in the military and, consequently, moved his family every two years or so from the American Midwest to Latin American countries, such as Panama or Ecuador, and then back to Illinois, Indiana, or Michigan. At the age of five, Charles lived for a short time in Juaréz, Mexico, with his grandmother, where he got his first taste of a border city and the fluidity of culture. He then reunited with his parents, and they spent five years in Panama. His mother often took him, his brother, and his sisters to see all-day Spanish-language films with stars such as Pedro Infante. His mother's love of the theater, music, and storytelling created an admiration in Charles for live art.

Charles was a joker in school, an extrovert due to moving around so much. He learned how to make friends easily and just as easily to break ties when necessary. Morton began writing short stories in high school, writing for the school paper in Battle Creek, Michigan, where he graduated. He dreamed of becoming a news reporter, like the fictional Clark Kent, sans the cape. At the age of 17, Morton moved to Chicago and went to work as a copy boy for the *Daily News, City News Bureau,* and the *Chicago Tribune.* At this time, he toed the straight line for the most part—rather collegiate. He attended Morton Junior College and took classes at the famous Second City, an improvisational comedy club, where he practiced dramatic readings and learned how to invoke comedy in his writings.

In 1968, Morton got a job as a gofer with Peter Jennings's crew to cover the Democratic National Convention in Chicago. The police assaulted them with tear gas, prompting Morton to change his opinion of authorities whom he no longer blindly trusted. He read Timothy Leary and the works of early beatniks such as Jack Kerouac and dropped out of school. Rebellious, Morton moved to El Paso, Texas, in 1970. In search of his identity and as a way of rediscovering his roots, he changed his name to Carlos. When his grandfather, Carlos Perez, came to America, he had quickly discovered the inequality Mexicans faced and had changed his last name to Morton and found work. Morton, in turn, Hispanicized his name as a statement of his bicultural existence and conscious effort to declare his Latino identity.

In El Paso, Morton discovered the Movimiento Estudiantil Chicano de Aztlán (MEChA), an organization and movement that strives for self-determination of the Raza—Chicano race—by raising political, social, and cultural awareness. With the support of MEChA, Morton, along with others including his mentor and friend Jorge Huerta, worked tirelessly to implement Chicano studies at major universities throughout the nation. At this time, Morton also became acquainted with El Teatro Campesino, founded by Luis Valdez, and thereafter became completely impassioned by theater. In 1972, Morton left for Mexico on a quest to rediscover the Spanish language, hitchhiking or traveling by bus to the deep recesses of his ancestral land. He returned to the States and graduated with a B.A. in English from the University of Texas–Houston in 1975. By this time, he had published articles, poems, and plays. His first play, *El jardín,* was produced at the University of Iowa in 1975.

In the mid-1970s, Morton found himself working in New York City as a cabdriver. Huerta encouraged Morton to attend graduate school on a fellowship program that included only two playwrights. Morton moved to Cardiff-by-the-Sea, California, where he attended the University of California–San Diego (UCSD), graduating in 1979 with an M.F.A. in drama. He met and fell in love with Azalea Marin at UCSD. That same year, he won the Mina Shaughnessy Scholarship from the Fund for the Improvement of Postsecondary Education, Washington, D.C. Morton married Azalea in 1981 and soon moved again. He served as a part-time lecturer at the University of California–Berkeley from 1980 to 1981, and from this point on, Morton became a prolific playwright, averaging about two to three plays in production a year. Of his many plays, *The Many Deaths of Danny Rosales* and *Johnny Tenorio* are produced most often.

Morton won first prize in the National Latino Playwriting Contest from the New York Shakespeare Festival in 1986. One year later, he earned a Ph.D. in drama from the University of Texas–Austin. At this time, he taught speech and drama at Laredo Junior College then became an assistant professor of drama at the University of Texas–El Paso. His plays continued to be produced, and he continued to win awards and honors such as second prize in the James Baldwin Playwriting Contest and Fulbright Lecturer at the National Autonomos University of Mexico.

Morton next moved to Riverside, California, to settle down for his longest stint of 11 years. He taught drama at the University of California–Riverside. He also served as interim director for the University of California Institute for Mexico and the United States (UC MEXUS), as well as a director at the Study Abroad Center for San José de Costa Rica, University of California. His second book, *Johnny Tenorio and Other Plays,* was released in 1992. His next book was *The Fickle Finger of Lady Death* (1996), an English-language translation of four plays by contemporary Mexican playwrights. He won another first prize in the National Hispanic Playwriting Contest, Arizona Theatre Company (1995).

Common themes found in his plays are global as well as private in nature. He speaks of justice, racism, poverty, and exploitation, imploring his audiences and readers to consider the plight of all humankind. As a proponent of didactic theater, Morton strives to entertain while he educates. He successfully weaves outlandish humor into potent messages so they find a home in the heart and soul. Morton commented in a 2005 interview that he tells his students or would-be playwrights, "[I]f you have an axe to grind, write an essay; to tell a story, you must have a message, a purpose, and laughter."

He has been described by Chicana scholar Kat Avila, as "a guardian angel of Latino theater directors and producers" willing to help the new Chicano generation find its place in theater. Morton simply sees his support of fellow dramatists as part of being a professor and contributor to the community. In 1999, Morton was inducted into the Writers of the Pass in El Paso, Texas, and released his fourth book, *Rancho Hollywood y otras obras del teatro chicano,* (1999), a Spanish-language collection of his plays.

Morton is currently the director of the Center for Chicano Studies and professor of dramatic arts at University of California–Santa Barbara, where he teaches classes in playwriting, U.S. Latino theater, and Latin American theater. His latest work, *Dreaming on a Sunday in the Alameda and Other Plays (Chicana & Chicano Visions of the Americas),* released in 2004, brings to life characters from a mural painted by Diego Rivera.

Further Reading

Cortés, Eladio, and Mirta Barrea-Maryls, eds. *Encyclopedia of Latin American Theatre.* Westport, Conn.: Greenwood Press, 2003.

Heide, Rick, ed. *Under the Fifth Sun: Latino Literature from California.* Santa Clara and Berkeley, Calif.: Santa Clara University/Heyday Books, 2002.

Ryan, Bryan, ed. *Hispanic Literature: A Selection of Sketches from Contemporary Authors.* Detroit: Gale Research, 1991.

Muñoz, Elías Miguel
(1954–) *poet, novelist, playwright, short story writer, literary critic, educator*

Elías Miguel Muñoz's vast and varied writings represent the growing trend in Latino literature to move beyond generalizations and stereotypes. His work is groundbreaking in its inclusion and open-minded, piercing approach to such taboo subjects as homosexuality and issues such as Western greed, consumption, and parallels between communism and capitalism.

The eldest of two sons of Elías and Úrsula Muñoz, Elías Miguel Muñoz was born on September 29, 1954, in Ciego de Ávila, Cuba. Elías enjoyed a pastoral childhood. He grew up in a barrio where children of diverse sociological and economical backgrounds played together either visiting the beach or gathering around the Muñoz family television. However, living under Fidel Castro's Communist regime offered extremes. Even as a young child, Elías sensed the uncertainty of the future. Neighbors were like family members, yet every neighborhood had a government informant who led the Committee for the Defense of the Revolution and who kept a vigilant eye on all barrio activities. Elías wrote his first short story, entitled "Oasis," at age 13. The story tells how he and a friend were forced to sever their friendship because they lived on opposite ends of the political spectrum.

As Muñoz and his brother reached their teen years, their parents devised a plan to get their sons out of the country to avoid the draft requiring 16-year-old male citizens to join the Cuban military service. At the age of 14 Muñoz and his 10-year-old brother found themselves at their father's second cousin's home in Madrid, Spain, in the dead of winter. Accustomed to a sheltered, pampered life in Cuba, Muñoz found the adjustment to life in Madrid to be a shocking contrast, which he called in a 2005 interview "both scary and dramatic." Within a year, Muñoz's parents secured passage for themselves and their sons to the United States, and the family was reunited in Gardena, California, in May 1969.

Muñoz disliked California, finding it unwelcoming and lifeless. During his initial integration into American culture, Muñoz stuck adamantly to his Hispanic roots, creating a microcosm of Cuba by socializing primarily with cousins and other Cuban immigrants. Slowly, he became friends with Latinos of other backgrounds and eventually befriended some Anglo Americans. He adopted the name *Mike* for a short time before realizing he could not escape the nationality that formed the foundation for much of his sensibilities.

Upon high school graduation, Muñoz attended El Camino College, earning an A.A. At El Camino, he tutored in English and Spanish and discovered an aptitude for teaching. He obtained a B.A. in Spanish and French from California State University–Dominguez Hills in 1976 and an M.A. in Spanish and Latin-American literature from the University of California–Irvine (UCI) in 1979. Throughout his college career, Muñoz wrote for himself, despite dissuasion from teachers and arguments with his father, who did not deem writing a viable activity for a young man and considered the act a waste of time. Regardless of the obstacles, Muñoz continued to hone his writing craft and won the Del Amo Foundation Scholarship, which allowed him to study in Madrid from 1976 to 1977. He found support for writing from a professor while in the doctoral program at UCI, where he earned a Ph.D. in Spanish and American literature in 1984.

In 1984, Muñoz began a five-year teaching career at Wichita State University (WSU) in Wichita, Kansas, and released his first book, *Los viajes de Orlando Cachumbambé (Orlando's Seesaw)*. In the book, which is written entirely in Spanish, the protagonist immigrates to the United States from Cuba and attempts to forsake his homeland for his new country. However, Cuban culture consistently influences his inner dialogue and serves as the pivotal point of reference for categorizing new experiences, memories, and self-identity. While in Wichita, Muñoz met and dated Karen Christian, a graduate student at WSU. The couple parted ways for several years, yet rejoined and married in 1993. They have two daughters.

Muñoz's doctoral dissertation, "El discurso utópico de la sexualidad en Manuel Puig," became a book with the same title in 1987. The book addresses sexual role-playing and identity performance as integral to life's transformational processes. *Desde esta orilla: Poesía cubana del exilio* (1988; *From this Shore: Cuban Poetry of Exile*) is a scholarly book on Cuban diaspora poetry. The term *diaspora* refers to people or an ethnic population forced or induced to leave their traditional ethnic homelands, becoming dispersed throughout other parts of the world, and the ensuing developments in their dispersal and culture.

Muñoz released *Crazy Love* in 1989. The novel deals with the prejudices and stereotypes placed upon homosexual and bisexual people. In this case, the Cuban father and grandmother attempt to control and enforce their rigid demands of what is acceptable machismo, or dominantly male, behavior of the novel's protagonist, Julian. Muñoz adapted this novel into the successful play *The L.A. Scene,* which premiered and ran off Broadway in New York City in 1990.

In 1989, Muñoz published two books of poetry, *En estas tierras/In This Land* and *No fue posible el sol* (1989; *The Impossible Sun*). That same year, he was selected to participate in a writing workshop at the Sundance Film Institute in Utah, which was organized by American actor and film producer Robert Redford and directed by Nobel Prize winner and acclaimed Colombian writer Gabriel García Márquez. Among the participants were screenwriter José Rivera and fiction writer HELENA MARIA VIRAMONTES. The workshop proved to be transformational for Muñoz. Although he was up for tenure at Wichita State University, Muñoz left his teaching post to dedicate himself to writing full time. He led workshops, gave readings, and wrote smaller pieces for publication in magazines and journals—all in pursuit of the dream to tell stories as his primary means of living. The fruits of his labor materialized in *The Greatest Performance* (1991), a lyrical novel hailed by critics as the first fictional work to deal with the impact of AIDS in the Latino community. Muñoz stated in a 2005 interview, "*The Greatest Performance* made me a writer." In this innovative story, Muñoz weaves together themes of exile, memory, and reconciliation to deconstruct the crushing effects of patriarchy on a developing psyche.

Muñoz wrote three books for the McGraw-Hill StoryTeller's Series, which include *Viajes fantásticos* (1994; *Fantastic Journeys*), *Ladrón de la mente* (1995; *Mind Thief*), and *Isla de luz* (2001; *Island of Light*). These archetypical stories combine

Cuban-American writer Elías Miguel Muñoz breaks traditional boundaries with his explorations of taboo topics. *(Photo of Elías Miguel Muñoz is reprinted with permission from the publisher [APP Archive Files] [Houston: Arte Público Press—University of Houston, © 2006])*

themes of love, magic, the flexible continuum of time, and betrayal with the use of popular genre formulas such as the romance novel and the science-fiction thriller to examine sexual and cultural stereotypes.

Brand New Memory (1998) features Cuban-American adolescent Gina, born and raised in southern California, who is forced to reconsider her bucolic imaginings of what a childhood in Cuba may have been like when her grandmother pays a visit. It has become part of high school curricula across the nation. In 2006, Muñoz released a novel, *Vida mía* (*This Life of Mine*), published in Spain.

A poet at heart, Muñoz uses his writing to exploit exclusionary tactics of patriarchal societies and the atrocious effects the conservative, yet typical, veneration of machismo has on homosexuals, bisexuals, subjugated women, and men who must conform to its rigid standards. Muñoz's books are populated by characters who find themselves ostracized by their family and culture. Deeply ensconced in the parallel universes of writing and creating worlds, both real and imagined, and his daily life as a father, husband, and friend, Muñoz finds that writing is like life. He said in a 2005 interview, "[I]t teaches you to be in the moment. You hold a vision and just hope it becomes something strong and meaningful."

Further Reading
Heide, Rick, ed. *Under the Fifth Sun: Latino Literature from California*. Santa Clara and Berkeley, Calif.: Santa Clara University/Heyday Books, 2002.

Muñoz, Elías Miguel. *Brand New Memory*. Houston, Tex.: Arte Público Press, 1998.

West-Durán, Alan. *Latino and Latina Writers, Volume II*. Detroit: Gale-Thomas, 2004, pp. 681–697.

N

Nava, Yolanda
(Yolanda Margot Nava)
(1944–) *journalist, folklorist, educator*

Emmy Award–winning journalist and author Yolanda Nava cofounded the first television station in the United States owned and operated by Mexican-American women. Yolanda Margot Nava comes from a long line of industrious, community-oriented people. Her maternal grandfather, a carpenter and draftsman, left revolution-torn Mexico in 1914 for Arizona. He built 20 schools in southern Arizona before moving his family to Ventura, California. When the Great Depression hit, Nava's mother needed a new source of faith. She found solace in Christian Science, a religion she would raise her daughter in. Nava was born in Los Angeles, California, on November 23, 1944, to Roberto and Consuelo Chavira Sepulveda Nava. A tight-knit Mexican family and social structure surrounded Nava. Concurrently, the Christian Science teachings gave her a faith and understanding that if she kept her vision on a larger sense of purpose, she would be guided through a life filled with gratifying experiences. Nava has always enjoyed writing, a penchant she inherited from her trilingual father, who was an avid reader and a columnist at *La Opinión.* Her parents divorced when Yolanda was eight. She lived with her mother and felt a void in her life for an intellectual presence.

Nava attended John Marshall High School in Los Angeles, graduating in 1962. She received a B.A. in 1967 from the University of California–Los Angeles and her teaching credentials from California State University–Northridge in 1968. Nava taught high school for two years and junior college for one year before becoming a counselor at the United Way in 1970. During the early 1970s, Nava actively participated in the Movimiento Estudiantil Chicano de Aztlán (MEChA), an organization that raises political, social, and cultural awareness about the Chicano experience. She also worked with an organization active with various community education programs and as a freelance anchor/news reporter for a mix of programs, including news, religion, public affairs, and a live daily talk show. In 1972, she hosted a weekly public affairs program on NBC called *Impacto!* that covered issues of concern to Mexican Americans living in Los Angeles.

Nava moved to Sacramento and served as an anchor/news reporter for KTXL-TV from 1977 to 1979 and for KXTV from 1979 to 1981. In 1983, Nava cofounded Ponce Nicasio Broadcasting, Inc., the first television station owned and operated by Mexican-American women. She served as the station's vice president until 1996. Nava became the segment producer and host for *Saturday,* a public affairs show for NBC in Los Angeles. Concurrently, Nava wrote, reported, produced, and edited the weekly West Coast segment for La Raza Productions called *Latin Tempo.* She earned an Emmy and another Emmy nomination during her three-year stint at CBS as a news reporter and host from 1987 to 1990. Nava changed courses to write

Yolanda Nava is an Emmy Award–winning broadcast journalist and author. *(Courtesy of the author)*

Famous Latinos Share Real-Life Stories, Time-Tested Dichos, Favorite Folktales, and Inspiring Words of Wisdom (2000) takes off on the simple response that beans, *frijoles* in Spanish, could impart strength and tenacity. The book features personal stories from many successful Latinos, including author ISABEL ALLENDE, and is categorized into 14 virtues. It garnered the Latino Literary Hall of Fame's 2001 Best Self-help Book Award and the IRWIN Award for Best Non-Fiction Campaign from Book Publicist of southern California. Nava is featured in the Writer's Corner, the official site of the Christian Science Publishing Society (www.spirituality.com). In 2001, she was selected as one of five Key Latino Leaders in California by the state department of education and participated in a statewide campaign to encourage people to enter the teaching profession. From 2001 to 2003, Nava served as a consultant and chair on the board of directors of the Christian Science Publishing Society. In 2003, she became involved with the department of cultural affairs for the state of New Mexico, a post she currently serves.

Further Reading

Hinojosa, Maria. "Yolanda Nava." Available online. URL: http://www.latinusa.org/program/lusapgm410.html. Downloaded on April 6, 2006.

Martinez, Diana. "Latino Chicken Soup." *Hispanic Magazine* (September 2000), 16–20.

Nava, Yolanda. *It's All in the Frijoles: 100 Famous Latinos Share Real-Life Stories, Time-Tested Dichos, Favorite Folktales, and Inspiring Words of Wisdom.* New York: Fireside, 2000.

Wilson, Reggie. "Review *It's All in the Frijoles. Now Read This* (September 2001), 4.

speeches for Los Angeles city supervisor Michael D. Antonovich from 1991 to 1993. Her interests and concerns for education prompted a six-year stint as the communications consultant for the Los Angeles school district at the division of adult and career education. In 1998, Nava returned to broadcast journalism to host KCET's *Life & Times Tonight,* a nightly local newscast.

Then personal tragedy struck when Nava's mother became terminally ill. At her mother's bedside, Nava asked what had made her so strong. Consuelo replied, "Beans, beans made me strong!" Her mother's audacious reply and her imparted *dichos,* or traditional "sayings," led Nava to write an article about her mother in her weekly column for Eastern Group Publications. She met with FRANK DEL OLMO of the *Los Angeles Times,* who subsequently reprinted the article in the paper. Literary agent Betsy Amster saw the article and encouraged Nava to expand on the concept of *dichos* to create a book. *It's All in the Frijoles: 100*

Navarro, Mireya
(1957–) *journalist, educator*

New York Times reporter Mireya Navarro was one of 15 writers of *Race in America,* the 2001 Pulitzer Prize winner for national reporting. Navarro was born on

May 17, 1957, in San Juan, Puerto Rico, the eldest of two girls of Dinorah and Rafael Navarro. As a child, Mireya never dreamed of becoming a writer. She enrolled at the University of Puerto Rico intending to become a premed student. It was not until she watched the movie *All the President's Men* that she considered writing as a career. Navarro transferred to George Washington University in Washington, D.C., in 1976 to study journalism. She visited home each summer and did not truly set roots in America until her college graduation in 1979. Although she encountered the usual American stereotypes of Latin Americans, the narrow-mindedness of others had little effect in the shaping of her individuality or sense of self.

After graduation, Navarro joined the *San Francisco Examiner,* where she wrote in a variety of capacities including for the city and business sections, trial courts, and as a reporter in Mexico and Nicaragua. In the mid-1980s, she attended the Summer Program for Minority Journalists at the Maynard Institute. One of her professors, Eileen Shanahan, vastly influenced Navarro. Shanahan mentored Navarro on gender relations in journalism and the realm of ethics and gave her sound career advice. While in the San Francisco Bay Area, Navarro taught journalism at San Francisco City College.

In 1989, Navarro accepted a position at the *New York Times.* In the beginning of her career she covered mainly news-oriented topics such as AIDs, prisons, race relations, and Latino culture. Throughout the 1990s, she served as an adjunct professor for the Columbia Graduate School of Journalism. From 1994 to 1999, she worked as the Miami bureau chief and was able to provide a Latino perspective on contemporary news issues. In 1999, Navarro accepted a position with the *New York Times* to become the life and style writer for the Los Angeles area. With this position, the rigidity necessary in straight news reporting took a back seat to a freer style of writing, laced with a livelier, colloquial form. The result is a more textured body of work for Navarro.

Navarro is perfectly placed to affect the shift from compartmentalizing individuals into boxes of conformity to a more open-ended approach to people and topics. Fueled by her fascination with how America divides itself into ethnic groups, her stories and journalistic style offer Americans an opportunity to constantly reevaluate personal opinions. Navarro stated her goal as a journalist in a 2005 interview is to "do stories no one would think of and put fresh voices in the paper. I strive for originality in story choice and to add to the conversation, rather than repeat what is already being said." Navarro is a provocative writer whose efforts implore the nation to abolish rote, pack mentality and to think and act on a truly individual and case-by-case basis.

Further Reading

Columbia Graduate School of Journalism. "Yolanda Navarro." Available online. URL: http://www.jrn. columbia.edu/faculty/navarro.asp. Downloaded on May 25, 2005.

Navarro, Mireya. "Latinos Are Choosing to Have Smaller Families." *New York Times,* December 2004, p. A5.

———. "Rediscovering Rita. (Rita Moreno, actriz puertorriqueña) (Rita Moreno, Puerto Rican actress)." *Latina* (November 1998), pp. 35–38.

Niggli, Josephina
(Josefina Maria Niggli)
(1910–1983) *novelist, children's book writer, playwright, short story writer, screenwriter, nonfiction writer*

Although a playwright, Josephina Niggli is best known for her novel *Mexican Village,* the first Mexican-American book to reach the mainstream American audience.

An only child, Josephina Maria Niggli was born in Monterrey, Nuevo León, Mexico, on July 13, 1910. Her father, Frederick Ferdinand Niggli, whose Swiss and Alsatian ancestors immigrated to Texas in 1836, had moved to Mexico in 1893 and found a job as the manager of a cement plant in the village of Hidalgo. Her mother, Goldie (Morgan)

Niggli, was a violinist of French, Irish, and German descent. The Mexican Revolution, which brought about a great upheaval as the insurrectionists fought Porfirio Díaz, the country's dictator, broke out the year Niggli was born. Three years later the Mexican president, Francisco Madero, was assassinated. With less than an hour's notice, three-year-old Niggli and her parents moved to San Antonio, Texas. In an effort to secure her safety, her mother home-schooled Niggli throughout her primary education. Niggli then enrolled in Main Avenue High School.

Niggli entered the College of the Incarnate Word in San Antonio at age 15, where she discovered a love of writing. Supported by Dr. Roehl, head of the English department, Niggli submitted a short story and won second place in a contest held by *Ladies' Home Journal* and the National Catholic College Poetry Contest. Her work was published in other magazines, such as *Mexican Life* and *Collier's.* She wrote successful radio plays for the local radio station KTSA that ranged from lighthearted comedy to historical drama. Her father financed the publication of a collection of her poems under the title *Mexican Silhouettes* (1928). After Niggli received a B.A. in philosophy with a history minor in 1931, she studied playwriting with Coates Gwynne, director of the San Antonio Little Theatre.

Four years later, Niggli decided to continue her education at the University of North Carolina at Chapel Hill. She joined the Carolina Playmakers, where she wrote, directed, designed costumes, and acted in the folk-oriented plays that were the company's forte. From 1935 to 1939, Niggli wrote her best plays, which include *Tooth or Shave, The Cry of Dolores, The Red Velvet Goat, Azteca, Sunday Costs Five Pesos, Soldadera,* and *The Singing Valley.* Her plays appeared in various anthologies: *The Carolina Play-Book* (1936), *The Best One-Act-Plays of 1938,* and *Contemporary One-Act Plays* (1938). In 1938, Niggli edited her own anthology, *Mexican Folk Plays.* With the support of two fellowships in dramaturgy from the Rockefeller Foundation, Niggli wrote *Miracle at Blaise* and *The Ring of General Macías.*

In 1945, Niggli released *Mexican Village,* a classic portrayal of life in small-town Mexico. This collection of 10 interrelated stories was translated into several languages, adapted as a screenplay titled *Sombrero,* and won the Mayflower Association of North Carolina's award for the best book written during the previous year by a North Carolinian. Niggli wrote *Pointers on Playwriting* in 1945; *Pointers on Radio Writing* in 1946; her first novel, *Step Down, Elder Brother* in 1947; and a children's book, *Miracle for Mexice,* in 1964.

From 1942 to 1944, Niggli taught radio script writing and production at the University of North Carolina. She was awarded another fellowship in 1950 at the Abbey Theatre in Dublin, Ireland. In 1956, she received a fellowship to study at the Old Vic School in Bristol, England. That same year, she joined the Western Carolina University faculty as a director of drama and journalism instructor, remaining there until her retirement in 1975.

Niggli died on December 17, 1983, at the age of 73. She stands as one of the most influential Mexican-American authors of the 20th century. Her visceral depiction of Mexican tradition, life, and customs paved the path for contemporary Chicano literary awareness.

Further Reading

Dvorkin, Joseph Henry. "Josefina Niggli." *Voices from the Gaps.* Available online. URL: http://voices.cla.umn.edu/vg/Bios/entries/niggli_josephina.html. Downloaded on May 15, 2005.

Spearman, Walter. *The Carolina Playmakers: The First Fifty Years.* Chapel Hill: University of North Carolina Press, 1970.

Telgen, Diane, and Jim Kamp. *Notable Hispanic American Women.* Detroit: Thompson Gale, 1993.

Nogales, Ana
(Ana Ledwin, Ana Ledwin Nogales, Dr. Nogales)
(1951–   ) *journalist, nonfiction writer*

Ana Nogales is an essential voice, pioneer, and force addressing the specific needs of Latinos in personal relationships through her books, journalistic work, and clinical psychology practice. Featured in several magazines and television and radio shows, Nogales is one of the most beloved Latino doctors and relationship writers in the United States.

Ana Ledwin was born on June 26, 1951, to Roberto and Ester Ledwin in Buenos Aires, Argentina. Her parents' influence has colored and inspired her life's work. She took the best from both parents—learning to dream with the power of illimitable possibilities from her father and the value of hard work and tenacity from her mother.

Ana went to the same school, Normal Numero Uno, from kindergarten through high school. Growing up with the same people gave her solidarity and a sense of peace. Timid and shy as a child, it was her seventh grade teacher, Susana, who inspired Ana's confidence and helped her see herself as special. Another turning point in Nogales's life came when she decided to drop out of school at the tender age of 15. Her mother insisted she get a job. At Ledwin's first job interview, her prospective employer informed her that she would be required to do whatever he wanted. He gave her a look that suggested the position's tasks would include far more than making coffee. Ledwin promptly returned to high school. She went on to college, earning a degree in psychology from John F. Kennedy College in Argentina in 1979.

Over the next several years, she married, adopting her husband's name, gave birth to a daughter, Eleonora; got a license in psychology; built a private practice; and was an instructor and director of psychology at Instituto Uriburu in Buenos Aires. Nogales divorced and moved to the United States with Eleonora in 1979. In the United States, the possibilities seemed endless. In 1982, Nogales completed a master's and doctoral degree combination in psychology at United States International University, San Diego. She then opened a private practice in Los Angeles, Orange, and Riverside Counties, supervising a clinical program for 15 professionals in mental health in 1982. Her media career began at the Spanish language cable network Univision, where she hosted a regular weekly seg-

ment, *Ella y él* (Girl and guy) with Enrique Garatas. The show discussed the particular needs and interests of communication and relationships particular to the Latin experience. At this point she became known as "Dr. Nogales." She remarried and gave birth to two daughters, Gabriela and Natalie.

In 1990, Nogales began writing a column, which she continues to do, for *La Opinión,* the nation's largest Spanish-language newspaper. From 1992 to 1995, she hosted her own psychology show, and from 1996 to 1998, she hosted her own television show, *Aquí Entre Nos* (Just between us), dedicated to helping callers resolve personal problems with practical advice. The board of supervisors of Los Angeles County commended the program for its outstanding service to the people of the County of Los Angeles. Her compassion and wisdom established her as a household name throughout the Latino community.

Ana Nogales is best known as Dr. Nogales and for her relationship work and writings specific to Latino issues. *(Courtesy of the author)*

The overwhelming popularity and success of Nogales's radio and television shows inspired her to produce a series of self-help audio cassettes called Auto-Ayuda Psicológica. The tapes address many of the topics that are discussed during her radio and television appearances, such as "Combating Depression," "Managing Anxiety," and "Understanding the Opposite Sex." In 1999, she founded Casa de la Familia, a nonprofit organization established for victims of such crimes as rape, sexual assault, child sexual and physical abuse, and domestic violence. She serves as the clinical director for the organization.

In addition to her contributions to *La Opinión,* Nogales writes a monthly column in the national magazine *Para Todos.* Nogales was an online columnist for the international Spanish-language Web site Salud.com, as well as for SoloEllas.com, a bilingual Spanish/English Web site for Latinas. Nogales also writes for the Pfizer Laboratories Newsletter about intimacy and relationship issues.

Numerous press and magazines articles began applauding the work of Nogales throughout the 1990s. One article in particular caught the attention of a publisher who asked Nogales to write a book. Nogales teamed up with Laura Bellotti to write *Dr. Nogales' Book of Love and Sex* (1998), the first book ever to address the specific needs and idiosyncrasies of Latino couples.

Five years later, her next book, *Latina Power: Using the Seven Strengths You Already Have to Create the Success You Deserve* (2003), was warmly received by critics and the Latino community. This book outlines seven traits women innately have, namely: 1) *espíritu creativo* (creative spirit), 2) the *aguantadora*'s (survivor's) passionate determination, 3) the *comadre*'s (girlfriend's) networking ability, 4) the *diplomática*'s (diplomat's) discretion, 5) the *atrevida*'s (risktaker's) courage, 6) the *malabarista*'s (multitasker's) balance, and 7) *reina*'s (the diva's) confidence. The book offers as examples the journeys of successful and amazing women, including ISABEL ALLENDE. Each chapter features an interactive element, including a quiz to determine how strong each attribute is in the reader's own personality, plus exercises to reinforce each trait. Filled with the personal stories of successful Latinas, *Latina Power* inspires readers to vigorously pursue their own dreams.

In 2004, Nogales received the Paloma Award from the organization FLA (Future Leaders of America) for her "inspirational leadership serving the community" and the mentorship award from the organization Dialogue On Diversity for "career contributions, through writing, teaching, and counseling, to healthy family and social adjustment throughout American society."

Nogales has been featured at workshops and conferences all over the United States, including at the Omega Institute, as well as in Mexico City, Guadalajara, and Buenos Aires. Most recently, Nogales helped start a local Las Comadres, a support group for Latinas, in Orange County, where she currently resides.

Further Reading

Mendoza, Sylvia. *The Book of Latina Women: 150 Vidas of Passion, Strength, and Success.* Avon, Mass.: Adams Media, 2004.

Nogales, Ana. *Latina Power: Using the Seven Strengths You Already Have to Create the Success You Deserve.* New York: Fireside, 2003.

Telgen, Diane, and Jim Kamp. *Notable Hispanic American Women.* Detroit: Thompson Gale, 1993.

O

Otero, Miguel A.
(Miguel Antonio Otero, Jr.,
Miguel A. Otero, Jr.)
(1859–1944)   *autobiographer, biographer*

Miguel A. Otero's autobiographical trilogy, a first-hand account of the American frontier during the last half of the 19th century, stands as one of the most significant and worthy antecedents of Latino writings. Miguel A. Otero was the son of Miguel Antonio Otero (1829–82), businessman, Greek and Latin professor, and secretary and three-time delegate to the U.S. Congress (1855, 1857, and 1859) from the territory of New Mexico, and Mary Josephine Blackwood, a southern-bred Anglo. Otero was born on October 17, 1859, in St. Louis, Missouri, the second of four children. When he was seven years old, Miguel and his brother were sent to a boarding school in Topeka, Kansas, where they experienced frightening conditions. Otero recalled, "The school proved to be a detestable place and its horrors are still fresh in my memory. I can only compare my experiences at the frontier boarding school with those which Dickens relates in *Oliver Twist*."

The affluent Otero family moved freely throughout the Midwest and the Southwest, living in Kansas, Missouri, Colorado, Arizona, and New Mexico. Otero held great affection for frontier life, where he met such legendary figures as James Butler "Wild Bill" Hickok, "Buffalo Bill" Cody, "Calamity Jane," and William H. Bonney, who became infamous as "Billy the Kid." Otero considered the famous Wild Bill to be "one of the most perfect specimens of manhood I have ever seen . . . He often took my brother and myself on buffalo hunts." Otero also met and grew to admire Colonel Jose Francisco Chaves, whom he would later meet with on a regular basis.

Otero left the frontier to attend college, first at St. Louis University and then at Notre Dame, where he was trained in business administration. After college, Otero joined his father's firm as an accountant. He worked at the San Miguel National Bank in Las Vegas, New Mexico, from 1880 to 1885, while also serving as the treasurer for the city of Las Vegas. In 1886, he was elected probate clerk of San Miguel County. Two years later, he married Caroline Virginia Emmett, with whom he had a son in 1891, Miguel Antonio III, who died shortly after birth. Miguel Antonio IV was born the next year, soon followed by their daughter, Elizabeth. When President William McKinley named Otero governor of the territory of New Mexico in 1897, Otero became the first Hispanic to be appointed governor of a Southwest territory. In the nine years of his gubernatorial term, Otero named Colonel Chaves superintendent of public instruction for two separate terms (1901 and 1903) and helped President Theodore Roosevelt organize the Rough Riders. Otero was so deeply moved by the 1904 assassination of his friend Colonel Chaves that he eventually wrote *Colonel Jose Francisco Chaves, 1833–1924,* which was published by the Historical Society of New Mexico in 1926. Otero married

Maud Paine Frost in 1913. He wrote *Conquistadores of Spain and Buccaneers of England, France and Holland* (1925) and served on many boards until his retirement in 1934.

Based on the encouragement of friends, Otero began writing his memoirs after his retirement. Otero released *My Life on the Frontier, 1864–1882* (1935) as the first volume of what would become his autobiographical trilogy. The first volume reveals in vivid detail his mother's stories of the Old West, observations about frontier life from the point of view of a boy and then of a young man, and descriptions of local people, such as Bonney, Hickok, and Cody. Otero supported his memories with quotes from newspapers of the period. The following year, he released *The Real Billy the Kid: With New Light on the Lincoln County War* (1936). Otero recalled, "I was just one month older than Billy. I liked the Kid very much. In looking back to my first meeting with Billy the Kid, my impressions were most favorable and I can honestly say that he was a man more sinned against than sinning."

His second autobiographical volume, *My Life on the Frontier, 1882–1897* (1939), is peppered with personal experiences, such as a failed assassination attempt on his life, as well as newspaper and book quotations and territorial matters, such as land grants, politics, and frontier problems. *My Nine Years as Governor of the Territory of New Mexico, 1897–1906* (1940) is the last volume of Otero's autobiography. In it, he gives a detailed account of his administration during his two terms as governor.

Otero died on August 7, 1944, in Santa Fe, New Mexico. *Otero: An Autobiographical Trilogy,* containing the three volumes he wrote, was rereleased posthumously in 1974. *The Real Billy the Kid* was reprinted in 1998. The University of New Mexico has compiled papers and photographs of Otero in the Miguel A. Otero Collection.

Further Reading

Kanellos, Nicolás, et al., eds. *Herencia: The Anthology of Hispanic Literature in the United States.* New York: Oxford University Press, 2003, pp. 120–122.

Lomelí, Francisco A., and Carl R. Shirley, eds. *Chicano Writers: First Series.* Detroit: Gale Research, 1989, pp. 189–193.

Meier, Matt S., Conchita Franco Serri, and Richard A. Garcia. *Notable Latino Americans: A Biographical Dictionary.* Westport, Conn.: Greenwood Press, 1997.

Moquin, Wayne. "Governor Miguel A. Otero's Plea for New Mexican Statehood." In *A Documentary History of the Mexican American.* New York: Bantam, 1972, pp. 324–327.

Twitchell, Ralph Emerson. *The Leading Facts of New Mexican History.* Albuquerque, N. Mex.: Horn and Wallace, 1963, pp. 309–310.

Otero, Nina
(Maria Adelina Isabel Emilia Otero, Nina Otero-Warren)
(1881-1965) *nonfiction writer, activist*

Activist and leader in the suffragist movement, Nina Otero also captured the quickly fading pastoral life led by Spanish gentry in *Old Spain in Our Southwest* (1936). This book offers a key component for understanding what American expansionism meant to the Spanish aristocracy.

Maria Adelina Isabel Emilia (Nina) Otero was born on October 23, 1881, in Las Lunas, New Mexico. (Some sources indicate La Constancia, New Mexico, as her birthplace.) Her parents, Eloisa Luna and Manuel Basilio Otero, both claimed heritage from Spanish conquistadores, tracing their lineage to 11th-century Spain. Nina's early year were spent in a pastoral environment along the Rio Grande. The advent of the railroad into her hometown brought an influx of Anglos, commerce, and a change of life that Otero would later record in her writings. From 1892 to 1894, Otero was educated at Marysville College of the Sacred Hearts, a finishing school located in St. Louis, Missouri. When she was 16, Otero moved with her family to Santa Fe, New Mexico, where her uncle (some reports say cousin) MIGUEL A. OTERO was the territorial governor of New Mexico. She married Lieutenant Rawsom Warren in 1908. Although they were only married for one year, Otero often used her married name, Otero-Warren.

Upon her mother's death, Otero raised her younger siblings and some of their children. Her matronly responsibilities did not keep her from becoming involved in social, political, and economic issues. By 1914, Otero joined the suffragist campaign in New Mexico, providing leadership in the Congressional Union for Women Suffrage (later known as the National Women's Party). From 1917 to 1929, she served as the Santa Fe superintendent of instruction, chair of the state board of health, and other positions of esteem and advocacy for the American Red Cross, New Mexico State Council of Defense in the First Judicial District, New Mexico's Republican Women's Organization, as well as inspector of Indian services for the Department of the Interior and interpreter and liaison officer with the Pueblo Land Board. She ran unsuccessfully as the Republican Party nominee for the U.S. House of Representatives in 1922.

In the late 1920s, Otero purchased 1,257 acres of land outside Santa Fe with her friend Mamie Meadors. They called the homestead Las Dos (The Two) and offered the land as a sanctuary for writers, artists, and intellectuals. Las Dos, which overlooked the Sangre de Cristo and Jemez mountain ranges, inspired Otero to write about her childhood at the family's hacienda in Las Lunas. *Old Spain in Our Southwest* (1936) is divided into five sections: "The Wind in the Mountains," "An Old Spanish Hacienda," "Day by Day," "A Little History," and "Songs and Stories." The first section offers first-person reflections about an unstoppable storm that makes the narrator feel out of place in an environment she once called home. The following three sections consist of memories, anecdotes, and historical accounts that bring to life the culture and mores of the old Spanish heritage, including the feudal relationship. The last section includes vignettes and folktales, many of which were contributed by schoolchildren via a contest Otero sponsored while superintendent. After the publication of her book, Otero returned to civil administration and entrepreneurial and educational endeavors until her death in January 1965. Otero's writings firmly record and legitimize the resiliency of the Hispanic people and their indispensable influence on and position in American society.

Further Reading

Kanellos, Nicolás, et al., eds. *Herencia: The Anthology of Hispanic Literature in the United States.* New York: Oxford University Press, 2003, pp. 188–190.

Robelledo, Tey Diana. *Women Signing in the Snow: Cultural Analysis of Chicana Literature.* Tucson: University of Arizona Press, 1995.

Ruiz, Vicki L. *From Out of the Shadows: Mexican Women in Twentieth Century America.* New York: Oxford University Press. 1998.

Whaley, Charlotte. *Nina Otero-Warren of Santa Fe.* Albuquerque: University of New Mexico Press, 1994.

P

Paredes, Américo
(Américo Paredes Manzano)
(1915–1999) *essayist, short story writer, folklorist, novelist, poet, educator, activist*

Américo Paredes is considered one of the most influential forebears of Chicano literature, folklore, and ballads. His work as a folklorist established the importance and permanence of the Mexican-American ballad, while his visionary and diverse writings provided a foundational base for the style and sensibility of Chicano literature.

Américo Paredes Manzano was born on September 3, 1915, in Brownsville, Texas, to Justo and Clotilde Manzano-Vidal Paredes. His namesake was Amerigo Vespucci, the 16th-century Italian mapmaker who gave his name to the Western Hemisphere. Paredes's patriarchal ancestors settled in the Texas-Mexico region in the 1700s when it was part of the Spanish territory known as Nuevo Santander. Paredes's family enjoyed the ranchero life. As a youth, the burgeoning writer sat around campfires with his father and other men who worked the land to hear folktales, myths, and other stories. He also enjoyed music and studied the piano and guitar. Paredes wrote poetry while attending Brownsville High School. Despite being discouraged by a teacher who assumed Mexican Americans did not aspire to attend college, Paredes persevered until he found a sympathetic mentor.

With talent and determination, he won a statewide poetry contest and was admitted to Brownsville Junior College. In addition to his classes, Paredes worked as a writer, translator, and proofreader for the *Brownsville Herald*. The *Herald* published his articles and poetry in both their Spanish and English editions. Most of Paredes's earliest works were composed in English. However, beginning in 1932, he consciously expressed his deepest feelings in Spanish, in essence helping create the mixture of Spanish and English known as Spanglish, which is so prevalent in modern Chicano writings. Between 1936 and 1940, his poetry appeared in "Los lunes literarios" (Literary Mondays), a literary section of the newspaper *La Prensa* of San Antonio. He published *Cantos de adolescencia* (Songs of adolescence), a collection of poetry, in 1937. His first published work showed the influence of the romantic Spanish poet Gustavo Adolfo Bécquer. He worked for a brief time with Pan American. In 1939, Paredes married Consuelo Silva, a singer. The couple had one son before divorcing shortly thereafter.

During World War II, Paredes worked as a reporter for *Stars & Stripes* in Japan. While serving as an administrator for the International Red Cross, Paredes met his second wife, Amelia Sidzu Nagamine, a woman of Japanese-Uruguayan descent. After the war, the couple settled in Austin, Texas, and married in 1948. Paredes had four children with Amelia: Américo Jr., Alan, Vincente, and Julia. In 1950, Paredes enrolled at the University of Texas. He graduated in 1951 summa cum laude with a B.A. in English and philosophy. He gained an M.A. in English in 1953 and a Ph.D. in English in 1956. Paredes began teaching at the University of Texas, rising to a professorship in 1965. As an educator and activist, Paredes made significant contributions to Chicano/Mexican-American studies. Although the academic environment was not welcoming to Mexican-American scholars or the subject of their heritage, Paredes would change that. In 1957, he organized the folkloric archives; in 1967, he founded the university's Center for Intercultural Studies of Folklore and Ethnomusicology; and in 1970, he established the Mexican-American studies program at the University of Texas. He directed the Center for Mexican American Studies from 1970 to 1972.

Paredes spent many dedicated years traveling the lower Rio Grande border, collecting Mexican-American *corridos* (ballads), folktales, and legends. He found particular inspiration from the story of Gregorio Cortez, a folk hero who evaded capture by U.S. law officials until he turned himself in and was consequently and tragically killed. According to Texan law enforcement, Cortez was a criminal, whereas folks across the Texas-Mexico border had quite a different version of the story. Paredes interviewed Valeriano Cortez, a son of Gregorio Cortez, to reconstruct the hero's legend for posterity. Paredes discovered that Gregorio Cortez and his brother had an altercation with Texan sheriffs who were looking for a horse thief. Due to faulty translations, Cortez's brother was shot. The sheriff then tried to arrest Cortez, who shot him in self-defense. Cortez fled knowing he would not receive a fair trial and successfully avoided capture for 10 days despite the fact that hundreds of men pursued him. Tragically, the people of the area were tortured, jailed, and killed for assisting Cortez until he turned himself in to avoid further suffering by his people.

Based on his intensive research, Paredes wrote *With a Pistol in His Hand* (1958). The book inspired a movie adaptation, written by VICTOR VILLASEÑOR, called *The Ballad of Gregorio Cortez* (1982). The book and movie underscored and brought to light the horrid maltreatment Mexican Americans have received at the hands of Anglo Americans.

With Joseph Castle, he published *Folk Music of Mexico: Book for the Guitar No. 671* (1966). From 1968 to 1973, Paredes served as the editor of the influential *Journal of American Folklore*. In 1970, Paredes released a collection of folktales entitled *Folktales of Mexico*. The book contains 85 tales divided into five categories: "Legendary Tales," "Animal Tales," "Ordinary Tales," "Jokes and Anecdotes," and "Formula Tales." His collection of essays in *The Urban Experience and Folk Traditions* (1971) demonstrates his knowledge of folklore of five different U.S. regions. In 1972, Paredes released *Toward New Perspectives in Folklore* with Richard Bauman and one of the earliest anthologies of Chicano authors called *Mexican-American Authors,* coedited with Raymund Paredes. The anthology offers an overview of 20th-century Chicano literature.

A Texas-Mexican Cancionero: Folksongs of the Lower Border appeared in 1976 and features a comprehensive anthology and study of traditional songs in the border area. The 66 songs appear with their original lyrics, English translations, and the melody line. The book includes five song categories: "Old Songs from Colonial Days," "Songs of Border Conflicts," "Songs for Special Occasions," "Romantic and Comic Songs," and "The Pocho Appears." Paredes's book *Humanidad: Essays in Honor of George I. Sánchez* (1977) demonstrates Paredes's contributions to the field of education and humanities. The essays, which deal with bilingualism, biculturalism, the presence of the Spanish language in the American Southwest, Chicano history, and the works of Mexican intellectuals, feature the works of Paredes and nine other distinguished scholars, including ERNESTO GALARZA, the Chicano social scientist, historian, author, and educator.

Paredes's creative work continued well into his 70s. Because his earlier works were so visionary in nature, many of them were not published until decades after they were written. With the arrival of the University of Houston's Arte Público

Press, much of Paredes's writings were finally published. These works include *George Washington Gómez: A Mexicotexan Novel* (1990), *Between Two Worlds* (poetry, 1991), *Uncle Remus con chile* (a children's book, 1993), *Folklore and Culture on the Texas-Mexican Border* (edited by Richard Bauman, 1993), *The Hammon and the Beans and Other Stories* (short stories, 1994), and *The Shadow* (1998). He became a professor emeritus for the University of Texas in 1985.

He was awarded a Guggenheim fellowship (1962), Charles Frankel Prize from the National Endowment for the Humanities (1989), and the Order of the Aztec Eagle from the government of Mexico (1990). The latter is the highest award given to noncitizens for preserving Mexican culture. In 1995, San Antonio–born folksinger Tish Hinojosa composed a *corrido* for Paredes called "With a Pen in His Hand." Paredes died on May 5, 1999, leaving behind a legacy rich with culture, tradition, and most of all folklore.

Further Reading

Jackson, Bruce, Michael Taft, and Harvey S. Axelrod, eds. *The Centennial Index: One Hundred Years of the Journal of American Folklore.* Washington, D.C.: American Folklore Society, 1988.

Kanellos, Nicolás, et al., eds *Herencia: The Anthology of Hispanic Literature in the United States.* New York: Oxford University Press, 2003, pp. 170–174.

Lomelí, Francisco A., and Carl R. Shirley, eds. *Dictionary of Literary Biography* Vol. 209: *Chicano Writers, Third Series.* Detroit: Gale Group, 1999, pp. 182–193.

Ryan, Bryan, ed. *Hispanic Writers.* Detroit: Gale, 1991.

Paredez, Deborah
(Deborah Ann Paredez)
(1970–) *poet, educator*

Deborah Paredez represents a new generation of contemporary Latina poets who, building on the foundation of Chicano movement poets and writers, have the freedom to introduce through their verses and prose the vast complexities that face modern Latinos. Playing a pivotal role in Chicano literature, Paredez is noted for her courage to explore the complex issues facing modern Latinos.

The elder of two children of Consuelo and Gilberto Villarreal, Deborah Ann Paredez was born on December 19, 1970, in San Antonio, Texas. Her mother's Mexican ancestors have lived in Texas since the 1730s, while her father was a comparatively recent immigrant, originally from northern Mexico. Paredez grew up in a predominantly white, working-class neighborhood in San Antonio. Throughout her childhood she vacillated from wanting to claim her Mexican inheritance to maintaining an ambivalent stance toward her ethnicity. Her home vibrated with Mexican culture, including music, food, and the inclusive sensibilities Latinos maintain regarding what constitutes a family. Being positioned between the Anglo and Latina perspective gave Paredez a double consciousness, or vision of the world in which she was a participant and observer of both cultures.

She did not learn the Spanish language at home. Rather, her parents spoke Spanish whenever they did not want Paredez or her younger brother to understand what they were saying. The loss of the Spanish language had long affected the Paredez family. Paredez's maternal grandmother, Stella Salinas, had worked at Kelly Air Force Base during World War II. As the secretary, she was responsible for typing letters instituting the policy that forbade employees to speak Spanish. The oppressive means the U.S. government employed to force assimilation continued with her father, who was drafted into military service during the Vietnam War shortly after signing his citizenship papers. The atrocities of war and the prejudicial tactics the U.S. government employed to place Latinos in disproportionate numbers at the war's front lines resulted in a silence about Vietnam that pervaded Paredez's early years.

The Vietnam War so influenced Paredez that her first poem carried a strong antiwar sentiment. She had found a means to give voice to the unspeakable. Her sixth-grade teacher at Kruger Middle School, Carmen Barerra, noticed Deborah's potential and insisted she be tested for the advanced English program. She passed and was admitted into Julie Bathke's advanced English class and thus began a long-standing mentor/friendship. Bathke and Paredez met regularly throughout the budding poet's years at Kruger Junior High School and Douglas MacArthur High School. The teacher's presentation of a democratic array of poetry collections instilled openness within Paredez to accept and seek out a variety of inspirational sources for her writing.

As a young adult, Paredez was keenly aware of the social responsibilities she felt humankind needed to embrace. She leaned toward progressive politics with the notion that inclusiveness and art could create the world that the 1970s had prepared her for and had yet to materialize. She knew she wanted to be part of the arts and that it would be a constant vocation if not her profession. She engaged in writing as a solitary practice and theater work to be part of a community. Paredez attended Trinity University, securing a B.A. in English with an emphasis in dramatic literature in 1993. She edited the college's literary magazine and continued to hone her writing through class assignments and individual pursuits.

During the 1990s, Paredez held various jobs, from working in flower shops to teaching summer arts camps and serving as the assistant literary director at the Guadalupe Cultural Arts Center in west San Antonio, one of the oldest Latino arts centers in the nation. She also conducted workshops for at-risk young women to help draw out their talents through poetry and performance.

Paredez's poetry saw publication beginning in the mid-1990s. Her poems have appeared in *Daughters of the Fifth Sun: A Collection of U.S. Latina Fiction and Poetry* (1995), *This Promiscuous Light* (1996), and *¡Floricanto Sí! A Collection of Latina Poetry* (1998). Paredez taught in the department of drama and film at Vassar College from 2000 to 2003. Her book of poetry *This Side of Skin* (2002) emerged primarily as a series of meditations on grief that revisited the Orpheus and Eurydice myth. In 2002, she received the Alfredo Cisneros del Moral Foundation Writing Award, founded by SANDRA CISNEROS, and earned a Ph.D. from the interdisciplinary theater and drama program at Northwestern University. She joined the department of theater and dance and the Center for Mexican American Studies at the University of Texas–Austin in 2003. Her research and courses often investigate the symbiotic relationship between art and politics. Paredez holds a particular interest in U.S. Latina/o performance and popular culture. Her articles "Remembering Selena, Remembering Latinidad" (*Theatre Journal,* 2002) and "Becoming Selena, Becoming Latina" (*Mexicanas in Transnational Context,* forthcoming) comprise part of her current manuscript about the career and afterlife of the Tejana performer Selena Quintanilla Perez. She currently resides in Austin with her husband, Frank Guridy, a Nuyorican–Dominican Republic historian whom she married in 2004. Her next project will focus on arts activism among communities of color in the Bronx and is tentatively titled *Emerging Latino/a Poets.*

Paredez has written about her own work, "I have learned about small measures of redemption and illumination that reside in the Williams-ean object: a drawerful of stockings in a widower's bedroom or snow melting from the eaves in the Bronx. Most recently, my work has directed me, as the poem 'October' suggests, to those places beyond death, where, as Marie Howe writes, the living 'are gripped by a cherishing so deep.' The poems continue to offer these unexpected arrivals and I work to leave the door ajar."

Further Reading

Milligan, Bryce, Mary Guerrero Milligan, and Angela de Hoyos, eds. *Daughters of the Fifth Sun: A Collection of U.S. Latina Fiction and Poetry.* New York: Riverhead Trade, 1996.

————. ¡Floricanto Sí! A Collection of Poetry. New York: Penguin, 1998.

Paredez, Deborah. This Side of Skin. San Antonio: Wings Press, 2002.

Pietri, Pedro
(1944–2004) *poet, playwright*

Best known for his epic poem *Puerto Rican Obituary*, Pedro Pietri helped found the Nuyorican Poet's Cafe, establish the prestige of the Nuyorican movement in literature, and create the popularity of poetry slams. Son of Francisco and Petra (Aponte) Pietri, Pedro Pietri was born on March 21, 1944, in Ponce, Puerto Rico. A couple of years after his birth, his father moved to Spanish Harlem in New York City, ahead of his wife and children, and began work as a dishwasher at the St. Regis Hotel. The rest of the family followed in 1947, when Pedro was three years old. Operation Boostrap, a U.S. project to industrialize the formerly agricultural Puerto Rico in the early 1950s, forced vast numbers of Puerto Ricans to leave their homeland. The surplus of Puerto Ricans who relocated to New York fell under extreme prejudice. Pietri felt this deeply; however, he found inspiration through his aunt, who often recited poetry and on occasion put on theatrical plays in the local church.

Pietri began writing poems while enrolled in Haaven High School. Soon after graduation, Pietri was drafted into the army and served in the Vietnam War. Upon his discharge from the army, Pietri joined the Young Lords, a Puerto Rican civil rights activist group. In the late 1960s, Pietri gave himself the title Reverendo de la Iglesia de la Madre de Tomates (Reverend of the Church of the Mother of Tomatoes). He first read his renowned poem *Puerto Rican Obituary*, in 1969. The poem, which was published in 1973 along with other poems in the book of the same name, tells about the unrealized dreams of five Puerto Ricans who immigrate to New York City hoping for a better way of life. Powerful and evocative, particularly when performed rather than merely read, Pietri's *Puerto Rican Obituary* invigorated the Nuyorican (New York Puerto Rican) movement and has been translated into more than 20 languages. It is credited and favored for its portrayal of the Puerto Rican experience in New York and imbued with as much emotion and loyalty from Nuyoricans as RODOLFO GONZALES's poem *I Am Joaquín/Yo Soy Joaquín* held for Chicanos fighting for their rights during the Chicano movement.

About the time *Obituary* saw publication, Pietri helped MIGUEL ALGARÍN and MIGUEL PIÑERO form the Nuyorican Poet's Cafe, a center on the Lower East Side of New York City for poets and other artists to share their work. With an innate ability to speak the truth plainly, Pietri became a strong voice for Puerto Ricans. He released three more collections of poetry, *The Blue and the Gray* (1975), *Invisible Poetry* (1979), and *Traffic Violations* (1983). His poetry contains bitterness, frankness, and absurd humor on the page and burst into life when he gave his performances. His entire demeanor took on the message of his verses. Pietri demanded alertness from his listeners. He called for them to wake up and live vibrant lives, not confined mundane existences. He consistently dressed in black because he had attended so many funerals for friends and families that he figured he might as well be prepared. A commanding presence, he was known to sing "The Spanglish National Anthem" in public and hand out simulated "Puerto Rican passports."

Pietri married Phyllis Nancy Wallach, a teacher and translator, on March 3, 1978. He sustained a living through teaching creative writing, receiving a series of grants, and publishing his writings, including his plays. He wrote more than 23 plays, not all of which have been published. However, many are archived at the Billy Rose Theatre Collection. His plays that saw production include *Lewlulu* (1976), *What Goes Up Must Come Down* (1976), *The Living-Room* (1978), *Dead Heroes Have*

No Feelings (1978), *Appearing in Person Tonight—Your Mother* (1978), *Jesus Is Leaving* (1978), *The Masses Are Asses* (1984), *Mondo Mambo/A Mambo Rap Sodi* (1990), and *Act One and Only* (2001). *The Masses Are Asses* and was translated into Spanish and published as *Las masas son crasa* in 1997. *Illusions of a Revolving Door: Plays, Teatro,* a collection of his plays, was released in 1992.

Pietri has been widely anthologized. His work has appeared in *Aloud: Voices from the Nuyorican Poets Café* (1994), *The Outlaw Bible of American Poetry* (2000), and *The Prentice Hall Anthology of Latino Literature* (2002), among many others. In 2003, Pietri was diagnosed with stomach cancer in a Bronx hospital. He went to Mexico to receive an alternative holistic treatment for a year. On March 3, 2004, Pedro died en route from Mexico to New York.

Further Reading

Beltrán, Raymond R. "There Was Never No Tomorrow: Nuyorican Pedro Pietri in His Own Words." Available online. URL: http://www.calacapress.com/pedropietri-laprensa.html. Downloaded on March 23, 2005.

Marzan, Julio, ed. *Inventing a Word: An Anthology of Twentieth-Century Puerto Rican Poetry.* New York: Columbia University Press, 1980.

West-Durán, Alan. *Latino and Latina Writers, Volume II.* Detroit: Gale-Thomas, 2004, pp. 935–950.

Pimentel, O. Ricardo
(Oscar Ricardo Pimentel)
(1953–   ) *journalist, novelist*

O. Ricardo Pimentel is a pioneering force in print journalism with an eye to social justice and a drive to achieve fairness, accuracy, and balance in the newsroom. As a leader in his industry, Pimentel has served on the boards of the California Chicano News Media Association (CCNMA) and the National Association of Hispanic Journalists (NAHJ).

Born on May 21, 1953, in San Bernardino, California, and raised there as well, Oscar Ricardo Pimentel is the youngest of three boys of Rodolfo and Maria Pimentel. He regards his parents as being the primary influences in his life. Both his parents emigrated from Mexico, spoke English and Spanish, and regaled Pimentel and his brothers with stories of their childhood, instilling in him a sense of pride in his Mexican heritage. From his mother, he learned about the Catholic faith and gained sensitivity for others and respect for the need for justice and fairness. His father read voraciously and taught himself to read and write in English. He often took his sons to the library, where Pimentel fell in love with the written word and fed his growing curiosity. He acquired the skills from his father and the heart from his mother to become an excellent journalist. In junior high school, he joined his school newspaper.

After graduating from San Bernardino High School in 1971, Pimentel enrolled in San Diego State University. He sold his motorcycle for the first month's rent, took out a small loan, and worked odd jobs to earn money for his many school expenses. Although his efforts were valiant, Pimentel had to quit college. He enlisted in the U.S. Navy, enrolling in the Defense Information School to learn the basics of journalism. He graduated in 1973 and afterward helped produce news releases out of Guam, Hawaii, and Antarctica. When he left the navy, Pimentel was disillusioned with journalism. In time, he learned the stories he had written for the military contained a myopic point of view and that what he was really disillusioned with was propaganda. He enrolled in Humboldt University to study communications. He missed writing and decided to transfer to Fresno University, where he could study journalism. While there, he wrote for the college newspaper and *La Voz de Aztlán*. He graduated with a B.A. in 1980.

Pimentel's first job was as a reporter for the *Sun* in San Bernardino. After four months, he got an offer he could not refuse from the *Fresno Bee*. He met Larry Romero and Luis Galvan, veteran Latino journalists, who encouraged him to use his cultural knowledge to show other dimensions of Latinos rather than the victim or suspect stereotypes most of America had come to know. He worked at the newspaper for two years before becoming a reporter at the *San Diego Union* for one year. In 1983, he accepted a position at the *Sacramento Bee* and married Laura Thomason. The couple would have two children, Noah and Emily. In 1985, the parent company of the *Sacramento Bee,* McClatchy Newspapers, promoted Pimentel to Washington, D.C., correspondent. In this position he covered policy, Congress, and the Supreme Court.

Throughout the 1990s, Pimentel worked in management positions for the *Fresno Bee, Stockton Record, Tucson Citizen, Sun,* and *Arizona Republic.* He released *The House with Two Doors* (1997), a novel based on the Vietnam era, which explores the clash between machismo and *marianismo* (the self-sacrificing role of women). In 1999, Pimentel wrote a column on public policy with an emphasis on Latino affairs at the *Arizona Republic.* The column became nationally syndicated, appearing in more than 100 newspapers. His articles put a human face on Latinos and redefined the demons created by small-minded individuals. Pimentel is a tenacious, dedicated writer who seeks to establish sensitivity for culture and the effects of politics on all humans through his journalistic efforts and books.

Pimentel remarked in a 2005 interview that he "was a bit astounded at the level of animosity that immigration could stir." His second novel, *Voices from the River* (2001), is based on the experiences of his mother and uncle as they immigrated to the United States in the 1940s. In 2004, Pimentel accepted a position at the *Milwaukee Sentinel* and stands as one of the leading Latino editors in print journalism.

Further Reading

Arizona State University. "Ricardo Pimentel." Available online. URL: http://www.asu.edu/ clas/justice/events/Seeking_Justice/series_03/ ricardo_pimentel.htm. Downloaded on April 1, 2005.

Chihak, Michael. "Columnists Raise Hackles, Awareness." *Tucson Citizen,* May 24, 2004. Available online. URL: http://www.tucsoncitizen.com/ news/opinion/051504b7_chihak. Downloaded on April 28, 2006.

Ha, Tran. "Room at the Top?" *Poynteronline.* Available online. URL: http://www.poynter.org/content/ content_view.asp?id=14561&sid=47. Downloaded on April 15, 2005.

Pineda, Cecile
(1932–) *novelist, playwright, short story writer, poet, essayist, educator*

Cecile Pineda defies classification with her ever-evolving, transformational work. She is well known for challenging the propensity of humankind to judge, criticize, and ostracize with stories that concurrently suggest and lead to the redemption of a supportive society and allied world community.

The only child of Emilio Rosendo Pineda Galván and Marthe-Alice Henriod, Cecile Pineda was born in Harlem in New York City on September 24, 1932. During her father's emigration journey from Mexico during the Mexican Revolution, he used the name Ernesto Pratt to avoid discrimination. The Mexican Revolution of 1910 was a popular uprising to overthrow the dictator Porfirio Díaz. Violence continued throughout Mexico until 1920. Accustomed to an educated and privileged existence in Mexico and fluent in nine languages, Emilio pursued an education at Columbia University and taught Romance languages at City College in New York. Pineda's mother, an austere and aloof woman, came from a French-Swiss middle-class home. Pineda found solace and comfort in her godmother, Jane E. Brown, who instilled in her a love of peasant culture and deep appreciation for art, myth, folklore, literature, and theater.

As a child, Cecile felt isolated. She attended Corpus Christi, a parochial school with a progressive agenda taught by Dominican nuns. She excelled at Marymount High School and thus earned a full scholarship to Barnard College, from which she graduated in 1954, with honors, majoring in English with a theater minor. In 1966, she married Felix Leneman, with whom she would have two sons but would later divorce. Pineda moved to San Francisco in the late 1960s. She studied theater at San Francisco State University, earning a master's degree in theater in 1970.

In 1969, Pineda formed the Theatre of Man, a highly experimental theater, that featured many of Pineda's adaptations, including *Murder in the Cathedral* (1969), *Stoneground* (1974) and *The Trial* (1975), as well as the original plays *Vision of the Book of Job* (1970), *After Eurydice* (1972), *Medea: A Legend for the Theater* (1976), *Threesomes: A Clown Play* (1977), *Time/Piece* (1978), and *Goya* (1979). Pineda worked in several vast and varied capacities at the Theatre of Man, which she described in a 1995 interview as a "poet's theater, concerning itself with creating a theatrical language based on archetype, myth, symbol, and dream. Some of my thematic explorations focused on sexual role expectation, totalitarianism, the problem of evil, and the dread of postmodern existence. My training in the craft of writing was acquired by doing." Due to financial restraints, Pineda was forced to close her theater in 1981. The same year, her mother passed away, and her beloved godmother fell ill and eventually died.

Faced with the degeneration of her marriage and the loss of two matriarchs and her theater, Pineda recognized the need to create an entirely new support system. Pineda stated that the time had come to "reinvent a new identity for myself before I could forge another community. I have always looked for family outside traditional ways." She embarked on the path of a novelist, thereby creating a community that helped her connect the fragmented parts of herself and the society she saw as broken yet salvageable.

Pineda's debut novel, *Face* (1984), was inspired by the true story of a man whose fall from a cliff results in a cataclysmic disfiguration that alienates him from society. In a parallel of spiritual transformation, the protagonist reconstructs his face and learns to establish his identity based on his own needs rather than the reflections, assumptions, and opinions of others. By reclaiming his self-image, the main character triumphs not only through his courage and self-redemption but also through the process of forgiving those who alienated him. *Face* won the Commonwealth Club of California Gold Medal and the Sue Kaufman Prize, awarded by the American Academy and Institute of Arts and Letters; it was also nominated for the American Book Award for a first work. Pineda later adapted *Face* into a screenplay, which was optioned by Rubicon Films.

Pineda followed with *Frieze* (1986), a novel that spins the story of a slave forced to create 120 stone panels, each depicting a scene from the life of Buddha. With lyrical language, the novelist explores the power and potential of free will and spiritual devotion as the protagonist evolves from an unwilling victim to one in charge of his own destiny and use of his creative powers. Written with the assistance of a National Endowment Fiction Fellowship, *The Love Queen of the Amazon* (1992) takes a hard look at sexual and social restrictions. Pineda weaves a touch of magic realism into this thrilling and suspenseful story that follows Ana Magdalena's entrepreneurial journey to self-empowerment. *Fishflight: A Dream of Childhood* (2001) is a nonfiction memoir regaled for its poetic prose. Pineda once again changes tactics with her novel *Bardo99* (2000), in which she delves into the world of comedy and the absurd. Told from an androgynous guard's point of view, *Redoubt: A Mononovel* (2004) explores the themes of socialization, gender, and sexuality.

Pineda's career also includes many stints as an educator and teacher. She has served as a creative writer in residence at many institutions, among them the University of San Antonio (1986),

Saidapet University in Madras, India (1987), the University of California–Berkeley (1989), California College of Arts and Crafts in Oakland (1987–92), San Francisco State University (1992–93), San Jose State University (1991–94), and Bennington College in Vermont (1995). She taught creative writing in the English department at San Diego State University from 1995 to 1999 and was appointed visiting writer at Mills College from 1999 through 2000.

Pineda is a valued contributor to Latina letters based on her ability to deeply situate her readers in despair and yet, with a wise pen, open a world of hope and possibility. Her work is appreciated for its originality and insightful sensitivity to the complexities that plague modern society.

Further Reading

Horno-Delgado Asuncion, et al., eds. *Breaking Boundaries: Latina Writings and Critical Readings.* Amherst: University of Massachusetts Press, 1989.

Johnson, David E. "Face Value: An Essay on Cecile Pineda's *Face.*" *Americas Review* 19 (Summer 1991): 73–93.

Lomelí, Francisco A., and Carl R. Shirley, eds. *Chicano Writers: Third Series.* Vol. 209. Detroit: Gale Research, 1999, pp. 202–211.

Pineda, Cecile. *Face.* San Antonio, Tex.: Wings Press, 2003.

Piñero, Miguel
(Mike Piñero)
(1946–1988) *playwright, poet, anthologist*

Considered one of the most important and primary Puerto Rican playwrights to gain mainstream attention, Miguel Piñero is best known for the play *Short Eyes.* He is also credited for founding the Nuyorican Poet's Cafe in New York City with Miguel Algarín and Pedro Pietri.

One of four children of Miguel Angel Gómez Ramos and Adelina Piñero (some reports have the surnames reversed), Miguel Piñero was born on December 19, 1946, in Gurabo, Puerto Rico. The family moved to New York's Lower East Side when Miguel was four years old. Within a few years, Piñero's father abandoned his family, forcing them to live on the streets until Piñero's mother, who was pregnant at the time, could secure work. Piñero turned to drugs and crime at an early age. He spent time in juvenile detention centers and as a result achieved only a seventh-grade education. By the time of his third incarceration in the New York prison system, Piñero was 24 and serving time at the infamous Sing Sing Prison. He decided to improve his life. He obtained his G.E.D. and joined Clay Stevenson's theater workshop, writing and acting about life on the streets as he knew it and had experienced it.

Piñero began to write *Short Eyes: The Killing of a Sex Offender by the Inmates of the House of Detention Awaiting Trial,* completing the play after he was released on parole in July 1973. The play reveals the brutal realties of prison life in which a child molester is murdered by fellow inmates. Upon his release, Piñero found a mentor in director Marvin Felix Camillo at New York City's Riverside Church. Together they formed the theatrical group known as The Family, which consisted of former drug addicts and ex-convicts. The group first performed the play in January 1974 at the Theater of the Riverside Church (where Piñero later became playwright in residence). Gaining success, the play moved to Joseph Papp's Public Theater and the Vivian Beaumont Theater at Lincoln Center in New York City. The play received critical and popular acclaim in addition to the New York Drama Critics Award for Best American Play, an Obie Award, and a Drama Desk Award. Piñero adapted *Short Eyes* into a screenplay that was made into a film in 1977.

Suddenly, Piñero found himself thrust into the limelight. Prestigious universities such as Princeton University, Rutgers University, and the Pratt Institute called upon him to give lectures. Yet he felt uncomfortable and unqualified for the position. He returned to the community he knew, opening up his house to offer encouragement and support to young Puerto Rican artists, or "Nuyoricans," from his own neighborhood. In this vein, he and Algarín opened the Nuyorican Poet's Cafe, a center for performance and visual art that is still in operation today. Piñero formed 15 young hustlers from Times Square into a theater group to perform his one-act play *Subculture,* which was about New York's harsh teenage lifestyle. He ventured into poetry, offering poems for the book he coedited with Algarín entitled *Nuyorican Poets: An Anthology of Puerto Rican Words and Feelings* (1975).

In 1977, Piñero married Juanita Lovette Rameize, but they divorced two years later, soon after they adopted a son, Ismael Castro. Piñero then moved to Los Angeles and founded the One Act Theatre Festival, where his play *Guntower* was performed. Despite the success and respect his work gained, Piñero could not escape the familiar magnetism street life held for him. He was arrested a couple of times in the 1970s. All his plays echo the gritty marginalized experiences of drug users, prostitutes, and convicts. He wrote the plays *Eulogy for a Small Time Thief* (1977) and *The Sun Always Shines for the Cool* (1978). He returned to New York City in the early 1980s to teach creative writing at Rutgers University. His collection of poems *La Bodega Sold Dreams* was published in 1980. He wrote the play *Midnight Moon at the Greasy Spoon* (1981). In 1982, he received a Guggenheim fellowship for writing. He published a trilogy that included *Eulogy for a Small Time Thief, Midnight Moon at the Greasy Spoon,* and *The Sun Always Shines for the Cool* in 1984. He released *Outrageous One Act Plays* in 1986, a collection featuring *Paper Toilet, Cold Beer, The Guntower, Irving, Sideshow,* and *Tap Dancing and Bruce Lee Kicks.*

Piñero also found success in acting. He appeared on the television shows *Miami Vice, Baretta,* and *Kojak.* He wrote an episode for *Baretta* and one for *Miami Vice.* His acting credits in film include *Times Square* (1980), *Fort Apache, The Bronx* (1981), *Breathless* (1983), *Exposed* (1983), *Deal of the Century* (1983), *Alphabet City* (1984),

and *Pick-Up Artist* (1987). His roles, like his writing, tended to reflect his real-life experiences, as he often portrayed a criminal.

Piñero died June 17, 1988, at the age of 41 from cirrhosis of the liver. At the time of his death, he was writing *Every Form of Refuge Has Its Price,* a play set in the intensive care unit of a hospital. More than 10 years after his death, Benjamin Bratt portrayed Piñero in a film, simply titled *Piñero.*

Further Reading

Vorlicky, Robert. *Act Like a Man: Challenging Masculinities in American Drama.* Ann Arbor: University of Michigan Press, 1995, pp. 133–154.
West-Durán, Alan. *Latino and Latina Writers, Volume II.* Detroit: Gale-Thomas, 2004, pp. 951–970.
Wheatley, Christopher. *Dictionary of Literary Biography.* Vol. 266: *Twentieth-Century American Dramatists, Fourth Series.* Detroit: Gale Group, 2002, pp. 238–244.

Ponce, Mary Helen
(Mary Elena Ponce, Merrihelen Ponce)
(1938–) *autobiographer, anthologist, educator, short story writer, novelist, educator*

Mary Helen Ponce is best known for her novel *The Wedding.* Her writings are noted for their honesty and realistic depiction of life for Mexican-American women in southern California in the 1940s and 1950s.

The youngest of seven daughters and three sons, Mary Elena Ponce was born in Pacoima, California, on January 24, 1938. Her parents, Tranquillo and Vincenta (Solis) Ponce, raised their children in Pacoima. Ponce describes her happy childhood in a San Fernando barrio in this excerpt from an unpublished story: "We feared few things in the barrio. We knew everyone; everyone knew us. We belonged. We had family: parents, sisters, brothers, tías, tíos, abuelitos and padrinos [aunts, uncles, grandparents, and godparents]. Our's was a secure world. We were free to play in the streets, climb trees, and snitch fruit off a neighbor's tree without fear. The poverty of our homes, lack of education, and jobs, was something our parents and older siblings worried over. For us, the younger generation, there was only the security of community: la iglesia [the church], la escuela [the school], la tienda de Don Jesús [Don Jesus's grocery store]."

Ponce's older sisters played an influential role in her life, encouraging her to develop multiple talents. One of her sisters introduced Ponce to literature with a subscription to the Book of the Month Club. Her earliest teachers changed her name to *Mary Helen* because it was easier for them to pro-

Mary Helen Ponce was one of the first writers to depict life for Mexican-American women in the 1950s. *(Photo of Mary Helen Ponce is reprinted with permission from the publisher [APP Archive Files] [Houston: Arte Público Press—University of Houston, © 2006])*

nounce. Ponce found too many other girls had the same name, so for a brief time she changed her name to *Merrihelen*. After high school, Ponce married. She chose to stay home to raise her four children: Joseph, Ana, Mark, and Ralph. When her youngest child entered kindergarten, Ponce enrolled in California State University–Northridge. She earned a B.A. in Mexican-American studies with a minor in anthropology in 1978 and earned an M.A. in Mexican-American studies with a minor in women's studies in 1980. Ponce obtained a second M.A. in history in 1984 from the University of California–Los Angeles (UCLA).

In the early 1980s, Ponce began to devote much time to creative writing. Her short stories and essays were published in *La Opinión,* the largest Spanish-language newspaper in southern California, as well as literary magazines and journals, particularly in the Southwest. She published *Recuerdo: Short Stories of the Barrio* in 1983. From 1982 to 1987, Ponce taught Chicano studies at UCLA. She presented her writings, which often combined history and literature, at many universities, including UCLA, the University of New Mexico, and the Colegio de México in Mexico City.

Ponce used an autobiographical, first-person narration for her first novel, *The Wedding* (1989). Set in the San Fernando Valley in a neighborhood quite similar to the author's childhood barrio, Ponce explores the protagonist's thoughts, dreams, and hopes that lead up to her pending wedding. In 1987, she released *Taking Control,* a collection of short stories that depicts the struggles of Mexican-American women. The author changed her original perspective that her characters were victims of their situations to the status of everyday heroines, who, despite overwhelming odds, took control of their lives and made decisions of empowerment. Ponce's memories of her childhood in Pacoima, are vividly depicted in *Hoyt Street: An Autobiography* (1993, and 2006). She studied for a doctorate at the University of New Mexico in American studies and earned her Ph.D. in 1995.

Further Reading

Heide, Rick, ed. *Under the Fifth Sun: Latino Literature from California.* Santa Clara and Berkeley, Calif.: Santa Clara University/Heyday Books, 2002.

Lomelí, Francisco A., and Carl R. Shirley, eds. *Chicano Writers: Second Series*, Vol. 122. Detroit: Gale Research, 1992, pp. 197–203.

Ponce, Mary Helen. *Hoyt Street: An Autobiography.* Albquerque: University of New Mexico Press, 2006.

Portillo Trambley, Estela
(Estela Portillo)
(1927–1998) *playwright, poet, short story writer, novelist, educator*

Known for her mythical characters and themes and a declaration for emancipation for women and all who are oppressed, Estela Portillo Trambley is considered the first Chicana to publish a collection of fiction and to write a musical comedy. Estela Portillo was born in El Paso, Texas, on January 16, 1927 (some reports incorrectly indicate her birth year as 1936). She was one of four children of Delfina Fierro, a piano teacher from Chihuahua, Mexico, and Francisco Portillo, a railroad mechanic from Jalisco, Mexico. Estela lived primarily with her grandparents in the Segundo Barrio of El Paso, until they died when she was 12 and she returned to live with her parents. Portillo primarily spoke Spanish at home. She recalled images from her childhood in an interview with JUAN BRUCE-NOVOA in *Chicano Authors: Inquiry by Interview:* "I would watch sunlight continuing itself on adobe walls; the silences in early afternoon had a mysterious splendor. We were poor. I am still poor, *pero la pobreza nunca derriba el espíritu* [but poverty never defeats the spirit]."

Rooted in Nahuatl spirituality, this belief in the endurance and strength of the human spirit would braid its way throughout much of her later writings. Portillo discovered her love and talent for writing at an early age. During high school, she wrote for the school paper and won a poetry prize.

She furthered her studies at the College of Mines (now part of the University of Texas–El Paso [UTEP]), obtaining a B.A. and an M.A., both in English. She married Robert Trambley in 1947, with whom she would have five daughters and one son. Portillo Trambley accepted a post to teach English at El Paso Technical High School, which she held for several years, and from 1959 to 1966, she served as head of the English department.

Upon her only son's death, Portillo Trambley immersed herself in writing. Although her work from this time has never been published, it served as the spiritual and formidable groundwork for the writer's sense of self-understanding. In 1968, she wrote her first play to be produced by a bilingual theater group at UTEP, and although the writer claimed this initial play was "the most atrocious play that you could ever imagine," she admitted that "the bug bit [her]."

A friend sent Portillo Trambley's *The Day of the Swallows* to *El Grito*, an influential Chicano literary magazine, which published her play. Chicano theater scholar JORGE HUERTA commented about the *The Day of the Swallows,* "Ms. Portillo has created beautifully developed characters that require careful study and analysis in order to achieve their proper representation on the stage." *The Day of the Swallows,* which explores the restrictive roles placed on women, won the 1972 Quinto Sol Award and is considered by some to be her best work.

The following year, Portillo Trambley quit teaching to host a two-hour talk show on the El Paso radio station KIZZ. Often discussing controversial topics, she was later invited to direct a semiweekly cultural television program called *Cumbres* (Peaks). Throughout the 1970s, Portillo Trambley wrote plays that differed from the political *actos,* or "sketches," created by the prolific and influential playwright LUIS VALDEZ. Her plays focused on relationships and had a three-act structure, often following the hero's journey, as outlined in the renowned author and intellectual orator Joseph Campbell's book *The Hero with a Thousand Faces* (1949). Her protagonists were usually women struggling to establish autonomy in mundane reality with enough strength left over to question the state of their spiritual and emotional sensibilities. *Morality Play* (1974) represents the first musical created by a Chicana and shows the victory of human faith, hope, and charity over the dehumanizing influences of those in power. Portillo Trambley contributed to *We Are Chicano,* which was first produced in 1974. *Black Light* (1975), second-place winner in the Hispanic-American Playwrights' Competition at the New York Shakespeare Festival, explores the search for a balance between indigenous roots and the modern world. *El hombre cosmico* (The cosmic man) was first produced at Chamizal National Theatre in 1975.

Portillo Trambley ventured into editing with *Chicanas en literatura y arte* (*Chicana women in literature and art*) in 1974. The following year she published *Rain of Scorpions and Other Stories* (1975), which consists of nine short stories and a novella. Continuing with her theme of the universal search for meaning and truth, her characters in this latest collection begin to understand the connection among all life, in particular the idea that vitality, genesis of life, and happiness is found within. She returned to playwriting with *Sun Images . . . Los amores de Don Estufas* (1976), a musical comedy that entertains while it weaves the tales of those seeking their fortunes by crossing the U.S.-Mexican border. *Isabel and the Dancing Bear* was initially staged in 1977. *The Labyrinth of Love: Sor Juana Inés de la Cruz* (1979), performed at University Playhouse, is a historical play about 17th-century Mexican writer, intellectual, and nun of the title. Some critics and readers find Portillo Trambley's use of powerful imagery overwhelming, while others appreciate her innovative approach to familiar topics in Chicano literature.

Portillo Trambley released her first novel, *Trini,* in 1983. *Trini,* an evocative coming-of-age story, touches on themes of economic security and independence, family separation, connection to an indigenous past, and woman's search and declaration for autonomy in a sexist culture. *Trini*

was released in 2005 with a foreword by HELENA MARIA VIRAMONTES. She published *Sor Juana and Other Plays* in 1983.

Throughout the 1990s, Portillo Trambley worked as a teacher for homebound children with physical, emotional, and learning problems. She served as a visiting professor at the University of California–Riverside, and in 1995 she held the presidential chair in creative writing at the University of California–Davis. After battling cancer, Portillo Trambley died on December 28, 1998. She is remembered for her unwavering conviction in the triumph of the human spirit over oppression.

Further Reading

Lomelí, Francisco A., and Carl R. Shirley, eds. *Chicano Writers: Third Series, Vol. 209.* Detroit: Gale Research, 1999, pp. 212–222.

Portillo Trambley, Estela. *Trini.* New York: Feminist Press, 2005.

Ryan, Bryan, ed. *Hispanic Writers.* Detroit: Gale Research, 1991.

Vallejos, Tomas. "Estela Portillo Trambley's Fictive Search for Paradise." *Frontiers: A Journal of Women Studies* 5, no. 2 (summer 1980): 54–58.

Prida, Dolores
(1943–) *playwright, poet, essayist, television writer, screenwriter, journalist, editor*

Known for her use of satire, absurdity, and music to ease into Latino/a issues of immigration, assimilation, gender oppression, and other serious topics, Dolores Prida is celebrated as one of the most widely produced Latina playwrights. The eldest of three children of Manuel and Dolores Prieta Prida, Dolores Prida was born on September 5, 1943, in the small town of Cabairíen, Cuba. As a young child, she was a voracious reader and eventually turned to writing poems and short stories. Her father proved to have an incurable case of wanderlust and infidelity that Prida would later use as models of machismo behavior in her writing. Her father did not agree with Fidel Castro's politics and left the island in 1959. Dolores, her mother, and her two siblings followed, arriving in Miami, Florida, in 1961. The family soon moved to New York, where Prida gained employment at Schraffts, a well-known restaurant chain. She quickly moved up the corporate ladder, eventually becoming an administrator and editor of the company newsletter. While working, she studied Spanish-American literature at Hunter College from 1965 to 1969. She left college and her job to accept a one-year position with Collier-Macmillan International as a foreign correspondent. During the 1960s, Prida honed her poetry and became part of the Nueva Sangre (New Blood) movement.

Throughout the 1970s and 1980s, Prida developed her objective writing skills at various journalistic and editorial jobs. She served as an editor for Simon and Schuster's *International Dictionary,* the Spanish-language daily newspaper *El Tiempo,* and *Nuestro* magazine. She also worked as the information services director for the National Puerto Rican Forum, served as the London and New York correspondent for *Vision* magazine, and worked as the publication director for the Association of Hispanic Arts. In 1976, Prida joined the Teatro Popular and witnessed for the first time a live performance.

Prida made her debut on the theatrical scene with *Beautiful Señoritas* in 1977. This play employs outlandish characters and humor to exploit the impossible image Latin women are supposed to uphold and established the trademarks that would continue to characterize Prida's work: the use of Spanish or an amalgam of Spanish and English, combination of song and dance, and satire and humor by which to make observational comments on society. *Coser y cantar: A One-Act Bilingual Fantasy for Two Women* (1981) explores the dual personalities, one who has adapted to the new world and the other who holds tenaciously to old customs, a fight for control in the minds of most immigrants. *Coser y cantar* means "to sew and to sing."

Dolores Prida is one of the most widely produced Latina playwrights, known for her ability to infuse humor into serious subjects. *(Photo of Dolores Prida is reprinted with permission from the publisher [APP Archive Files] [Houston: Arte Público Press—University of Houston, © 2006])*

She collaborated with other playwrights and wrote for groups such as the Theater Duo in New York and Puerto Rican Traveling Theatre. Plays of this era include *Pantallas: Comedia apocalíptica en un acto* (1986; *Screens: An Apocalyptic Comedy in One Act*), *Botánica* (1990), and *Savings: A Musical Fable* (1991). An anthology of her plays containing *Beautiful Señoritas, Coser y cantar, Savings, Pantallas,* and *Botánica* was published under the title *Beautiful Señoritas & Other Plays* in 1991. Prida received an honorary degree from Holyoke College in 1989 and visiting professorships at Dartmouth College (1995), the University of Michigan (1997), and Hunter College (1998). She continued to write for print as well, contributing articles for *Latina* magazine, which was launched in 1996.

In 1998, Prida won a playwriting competition sponsored by the Federal National Mortgage Association, known as Fannie Mae, which instead of pursuing traditional advertising campaigns had launched a search for plays that addressed Hispanic home ownership in the United States. Prida's submission, *Casa propia: Ópera sin música en dos actos (A Home of One's Own: An Opera Without Music in Two Acts),* was the winning entry. Prida's latest play is *Four Guys Named José and una Mujer Named María* (2000). Prida has won several awards and fellowships, including an INTAR (International Arts Relations)/Ford Foundation Playwright in Residence award, Cintas Fellowship Award for Literature, Creative Public Service Award for Playwriting, the Manhattan Borough President's Excellence in Arts Award, and the Urban Stages Achievement Award.

Further Reading

Henderson, Ashyia. *Contemporary Hispanic Biography.* Vol. 3. Detroit: Gale Group, 2003.

Kanellos, Nicolás, ed. *Biographical Dictionary of Hispanic Literature in the United States.* Westport, Conn.: Greenwood Press, 1989, pp. 244–249.

West-Durán, Alan. *Latino and Latina Writers, Volume II.* Detroit: Gale-Thomas, 2004, pp. 737–747.

R

Ramos, Jorge
(1958–) journalist, nonfiction writer, memoirist

Considered one of the most influential Latinos in America, Jorge Ramos has authored seven books and coanchors the evening news for Univision, the largest Spanish-speaking network in the United States. He writes a weekly column for more than 40 newspapers in the United States and Latin America and offers daily radio commentary broadcast on dozens of radio stations.

The eldest of five children, Jorge Ramos was born in Mexico City on March 16, 1958, to Lourdes and Jorge Ramos. As a young child he enjoyed track and field and played soccer. He dreamed of competing in the Olympics but due to an injury was forced to give up his dream of becoming a professional athlete. Eventually, he turned to writing and playing the guitar. During his teen years, Ramos rebelled against the strict Mexican traditions. He broke from organized religion, particularly the Catholic Church, and formed his own agnostic, practical form of spirituality. He also began to recognize the secondary role women played in Mexican society.

Ramos attended Ibero-American University in Mexico City, where he gained a B.A. in communications. His thesis explored the role women played in Mexican media. At his first job for XEW, the longest-running radio station in Mexico, Ramos became a specialist in international affairs. He soon discovered that many of his fellow journalists were paid to alter their stories to fit the needs of the government and other organizations. When his own journalistic work was tagged for rewriting, Ramos refused to read the revision, which had lost all of its objectivity and instead glorified the Partido Revolucionario Institucional (PRI), the political party that wielded hegemonic power in Mexico—under a succession of names—for more than 70 years. Ramos resigned, declaring in his letter of resignation, "what was asked of me goes against my honesty, principles, and professionalism . . . having done it would have been an assault on the most simple and clear idea of what journalism is: a search for the truth." Six months later, Ramos was accepted into a journalism program at the University of California–Los Angeles. He sold his car, withdrew his life savings, and left Mexico on January 2, 1983.

Ramos's decision to leave was not soley based on censorship, though it was a major factor; he had also become frustrated by the confines of a rigidly traditional society and the ineptitude of the Mexican government. He sought a life of his own choosing. He worked as a waiter and in a theater, where he befriended novelist MARÍA AMPARO ESCANDÓN, and her husband, Benito Martínez-Creel. In 1984, journalist Pete Moraga gave Ramos his first opportunity in American media at KMEX for Canal 34. The following year, Ramos moved to Miami to work on a show called *Mundo Latino* (Latin world). In 1986, at the age of 28, he became the youngest national anchorperson in the history of American television when hired by Noticierio SIN, which later became Univision. That same year, he met and later married Gina Montaner, with whom he would have one daughter, Paola, and eventually divorce. Ramos remarried and had a son, Nicolás.

Early in his career, Ramos was told he must lose his Mexican accent, and although he tried, this bit of his heritage proved indelible. Ramos turned his accent into an advantage, and instead of thwarting his success, his accent helps him stand out among other reporters. Ramos skyrocketed into Spanish-language news and media. Noted for his courage and integrity, Ramos maintains a journalistic eye in reporting that, while serving an important purpose, did not give voice to the passion and opinions inspired by covering the world's biggest events, interviews with major political and arts figures, and inside information to which he has become privy. Ever resourceful, Ramos began to write books in the late 1990s. He has thus far written *Detrás de la Máscara* (1998; Behind the mask), *Lo que vi* (1999; What I saw), *La Otra Cara de América* (2000; *The Other Face of America*), *A la Caza del León* (2001; The lion hunt), *No Borders: A Journalist's Search for Home* (2002; *Atravesando fronteras*), *The Latino Wave: How Hispanics Will Choose the Next President* (2004; *La ola latina*), and *Dying to Cross: The Worst Immigrant Tragedy in American History* (2005; *Morir en el Intento*). *The Other Face of America* became a Spanish-language best seller, and *No Borders* provides a biographical and inspirational look into the journalist's life.

In 1999, Ramos established Becas de Periodismo, a scholarship program promoted by the Latin American Center of Periodismo (CELAP). In 2002, he created the first book club on Hispanic television, *Despierta Leyendo* (Wake up reading), which is seen once a month on Univision's morning television program. Ramos reaches an audience of 40 million people in the United States and 13 Latin American countries with his Univision newscast. He has won 19 awards and honors, including an Emmy.

Further Reading

Henderson, Ashyia. *Contemporary Hispanic Biography*. Vol. 2. Detroit: Gale Group, 2002.

Padgett, Tim. "Jorge Ramos: The Man of the News Hour." Time.com. Available online. URL: http://www.time.com/time/nation/article/ 0,8599,1093648,00.html. Posted on August 13, 2005.

Ramos, Jorge. *No Borders: A Journalist's Search for Home*. New York: Rayo, 2003.

Ramos, Manuel
(Manuel Anthony Ramos)
(1948–) *novelist, short story writer, poet, essayist, educator*

Manuel Ramos is considered one of the best Latino mystery writers. His novels weave together thrilling elements with a measure of social awareness.

The eldest of three sons, Manuel Anthony Ramos was born on March 6, 1948, in Florence, Colorado. Ramos's large and extensive family taught by example the value and importance of preserving and fighting for the rights and dignity of the common people. His paternal grandfather served alongside the insurrectionist Pancho Villa, who attempted to overthrow the cruel dictator Porfirio Díaz during the Mexican Revolution, which lasted from 1910 to 1920. His father, Henry Ramos, a native of Zacatecas, Mexico, served as director of a training school for the International Laborers Union. His mother, Emma, was born and raised in a Colorado mining town, where her father worked as a coal miner.

Supported by his parents' encouragement to read, Ramos spent many hours at the local library. He recalled in a 2005 interview, "I loved to read and that place took me far away from the small town. I read every kind of book they had and developed an admiration for crime fiction and mysteries, as well as the concept of a novel . . . the more I read the more I knew I wanted to be able to write stories that others would want to read." His love of a good story grew with the wild and fantastic tales spun by his grandparents.

Ramos began writing character sketches of his relatives while he attended Florence Junior High School. He further honed his craft at Florence High School, where he took creative writing classes. While Ramos was a teenager, his family moved to Colorado Springs, where he graduated from Harrison High School. He attended Colorado State University (CSU), where he gained a B.A. with honors in political science in 1970. While in college, he raised social awareness during the Chicano movement by helping to organize the first Mexican-American student group at CSU in 1968, which they called the Mexican American Committee for Equality (MACE). However, it eventually became the United Mexican American Students (UMAS). The group made several demands on the university for increased enrollment of Chicano students, more relevant courses, and more diverse faculty. The demands resulted in a program at CSU, continuing to this day, that recruits minority students and provides scholarship help and tutoring assistance.

After gaining a law degree from the University of Colorado in 1973, Ramos went into private practice in northern California with another Chicano attorney. He worked for the Denver legal services program and served as a legal services attorney and the deputy director and litigation director for the Legal Aid Society of Metropolitan Denver. Over the years, he has reviewed books for a number of different outlets, including *Bloomsbury Review, Denver Post,* and KUVO, a public radio station in Denver. He has also taught classes in Chicano literature at the Metropolitan State College of Denver.

Ramos married Florence Hernandez on September 23, 1983. The couple have one son, Diego. By the mid- to late 1980s, Ramos's short stories and poetry saw publication in a variety of magazines, anthologies, and collections. He received a Chicano/Latino Literary Contest Award from the University of California–Irvine in 1991. *The Ballad of Rocky Ruiz* (1993) introduces Luis Montez, a Chicano lawyer momentarily disillusioned by his beloved ideals that have not yet materialized. By using the victories and shortcomings of the Chicano movement as a backdrop, the novel examines the social division between those who are political and socially well connected and those who live on society's fringes. His debut book won the Colorado Book Award and was nominated for an Edgar Allan Poe Award by the Mystery Writers of America in the category of best first novel.

In *The Ballad of Gato Guerrero* (1994), Ramos follows the investigative work of Luis Montez. In *The Last Client of Luis Montez* (1996), *Blues for the Buffalo* (1997), and *Brown on Brown* (2003), Ramos continues to follow Luis Montez. *Moony's Road to Hell* (2002) introduces Denver private investigator Danny "Moony" Mora, who engages on a quest that involves Mora's old enemy lawyer and reaches back to the Chicano movement of the 1970s. In all cases, Ramos's novels effectively deal with social issues while spinning tales of suspense and action. His characters are well rounded and portray the resiliency and hope of Chicano people.

Further Reading

Heide, Rick, ed. *Under the Fifth Sun: Latino Literature from California.* Santa Clara and Berkeley, Calif.: Santa Clara University/Heyday Books, 2002.

Lomelí, Francisco A., and Carl R. Shirley, eds. *Dictionary of Literary Biography* Vol. 209: *Chicano Writers, Third Series.* Detroit: Gale Group, 1999, pp. 232–235.

Rothstein, Betsy. "The Haunting, Mysterious Words of Manuel Ramos." *El Semanario,* July 29, 1993, p. 12.

Rechy, John
(John Francisco Rechy)

(1934–   ) *novelist, essayist, playwright, short story writer, activist, educator*

An explosive and multitalented author of 14 books, two plays, and numerous essays and short stories, John Rechy is the recipient of two coveted lifetime achievement awards: PEN-USA-West's 1997 Lifetime Achievement Award and the Publishing Triangle's William Whitehead Award for Lifetime Achievement. He is perhaps best known for his graphic yet sensitive portrayal of a homosexual perspective and life.

The youngest of five children of Guadalupe Flores and Roberto Sixto Rechy, John Francisco Rechy was born on March 10, 1934, in El Paso, Texas. Of Scottish and Mexican heritage, Rechy grew up during the Great Depression. He was raised on stories of Mexico (both parents left during the Mexican Revolution), Catholicism, and a healthy dose of nonconformity. The Mexican Revolution of 1910 was an uprising of common folk who overthrew the dictator Porfirio Díaz, yet violence continued throughout Mexico until 1920. Rechy had a very tense and angry relationship with his father, which juxtaposed his loving, deep bond with his mother. His natural sensitivity and ability to empathize filtered into childhood acting before he directed his attention to writing. At age 17, Rechy penned a historical novel called *Time on Wings* and edited his college paper at Texas Western College (now University of Texas–El Paso). He was removed from the paper because, as Rechy wrote, "I had turned it into a 'radical' literary periodical." After earning a B.A. in English in 1952, Rechy enlisted in the U.S. Army.

Following his military service, Rechy moved to New York City with $20 in his pocket, a dream to study with Pearl Buck, and the intention to take graduate classes at Columbia University. Columbia rejected his admission, leaving Rechy uncertain about his future. Serendipitously, he met a merchant marine who suggested Rechy could make quick money hustling in Times Square. Thus, Rechy began his career as a male prostitute, concurrently attending creative writing classes at the New School for Social Research. Rechy recorded his hustling experiences in letters to a friend, who encouraged Rechy to adapt his letters into fiction. *Evergreen Review* first printed his short stories.

Rechy's first book, *City of Night* (1963), reveals the exploits of a male prostitute with explicit honesty. Initial reviews criticized the book; however, it became an international best seller. It was translated into several languages, is now taught in contemporary literature courses throughout the country, and is often called a "modern classic." Rechy did not promote the book, instead choosing to protect his private life. He began body building, an activity he continues to enjoy. He spent some time in the Caribbean before returning to El Paso. Together, Rechy and his mother visited Los Angeles in 1965, where Rechy engaged once again in copious sex—this time in a park filled with a range of characters. On the road back to Texas, Rechy penned *Numbers* (1967), about a homosexual who, like Rechy, finds a vast array of lovers in a park while dealing with the ravages of time.

Back in El Paso, Rechy attempted to give his aging mother everything he thought she wanted or needed. Rechy wrote, "With money from my books, I would try to make up for all her years of poverty and sacrifice, the demands I and the rest of my family had placed on her love." From these trying times came *This Day's Death* (1969), a book about a man who attempts to understand how to cope with his mother's decline, and *Vampires* (1971), a novel that as Rechy explains, is "an exotic creation . . . about opulent decay and corruption as beautiful wealthy guests gather in an island mansion to play out a pageant of confessions and judgments."

On October 9, 1970, Rechy's mother died. Rechy was thrown into deep despair, finding refuge in heavy drugs. To help assuage his grief, he wrote *The Fourth Angel* (1972), about a teenager who cannot deal with his mother's death. Rechy's new books did not sell well, and having spent much of his money, he returned to hustling the streets of Los Angeles to earn a living during the early 1970s. Occidental College invited Rechy to be a guest writer, and he was able to channel his return to the streets into *Sexual Outlaw: A Documentary* (1977). With the release of the new book, Rechy decided to become more public and advocate gay rights in what he called "a conscious decision to not hold back." Although this book was initially reviewed on content over form, eventually the *San Francisco Chronicle Book Review* included *Sexual Outlaw* on its list of the 100 best nonfiction books of the century.

Rushes (1979) is a dark account of one night in a leather and western bar. Paralleling the sexual exploitations are symbols of Catholicism. *Bodies and Souls* (1983) explores the lives of a mixed array of Los Angeles's disenfranchised "angels." Rechy then turned his talents to playwriting. From 1986 to 1987, his play *Tigers Wild* was performed off Broadway at Playhouse 91. His one-act play *Momma As She Became—But Not As She Was* (1978) has been performed throughout the country and Europe and has been widely anthologized.

In 1988, Rechy released *Marilyn's Daughter,* a novel that follows a young woman's search to uncover whether she is truly the child of Marilyn Monroe and Robert Kennedy. Critics hailed Rechy's originality and literary style in the novel. Rechy recalled the influences of his Mexican heritage to pen *The Miraculous Day of Amalia Gomez* (1991). The book is a celebration of the human spirit and endurance and is widely used in Chicano studies programs across the nation. *Our Lady of Babylon* (1996) presents the nightly sojourns of an 18th-century lady who dreams about prominent yet disgraced women, such as Eve, Magdalene, and La Malinche. A clairvoyant tells the protagonist that her dreams, which reveal the misjudgments and rare strengths of these women, are in fact memories.

The release of *The Coming of the Night* (1999), the sequel to *City of Night,* was met with great enthusiasm and appeared as number two on the *Los Angeles Times*'s best-seller list. In 2000, Rechy released a CD-ROM of his life and works— *Memories and Desire: The Worlds of John Rechy.* In 2003, Rechy published *The Life and Adventures of Lyle Clemens. Publishers Weekly* commented, "This distinctly American novel is ultimately about the search for love and redemption, about the ideal of 'amazing grace' from the old song that serves as a touchstone for Lyle. It's a comic tour de force and, at the same time, a truly heartfelt book." *Beneath the Skin* (2004) is a collection of four decades' worth of essays.

Rechy's writings have appeared in *The Nation, Los Angeles Times Books, Washington Post Book World, The Saturday Review, New York Times Book Review, San Francisco Chronicle, Philadelphia Inquirer, Dallas Morning News, London Magazine, Evergreen Review, New York* magazine, *The Advocate, Mother Jones, Premiere,* and many other national publications. He has been nominated twice for the *Los Angeles Times* Book Awards Body of Work designation. He has received a fellowship from the National Endowment for the Arts and Phi Kappa Phi and Longview Foundation awards for his fiction. He has lectured at Harvard University, Yale University, Duke University, the University of California–Los Angeles, Occidental College, the University of Northern Illinois, and Columbia University, among other academic institutions. He currently teaches film and creative writing at the University of Southern California. The brilliance of Rechy's writing is not only based on his craftsmanship and mastery of storytelling but also the courage and sensitivity with which he presents the humanity of the forgotten souls of society.

Further Reading

Birken, Lawrence. "Desire and Death: The Early Fiction of John Rechy." *Western Humanities Review* 51 (Summer 1997): 236–245.

Bruce-Novoa, Juan. "In Search of the Honest Outlaw: John Rechy." *Minority Voices* 3, no. 1 (1979): 37–45.

Pérez-Torres, Rafael. "The Ambiguous Outlaw: John Rechy and Complicitous Homotextuality." In *Fictions of Masculinity, Crossing Cultures, Crossing Sexualities*. Edited by Peter F. Murphy. New York: New York University Press, 1994, pp. 204–225.

West-Durán, Alan. *Latino and Latina Writers, Volume II*. Detroit: Gale-Thomas, 2004, pp. 405–421.

Ríos, Alberto

(1952–) *poet, short story writer, educator*

Alberto Ríos established himself as a preeminent poet when he received the Academy of American Poets' Walt Whitman Award for *Whispering to Fool the Wind* (1982). He became a voice to follow in the footsteps of his Chicano forebears who pioneered the highly esteemed position poets held during the height of the Chicano movement.

The son of a British mother, Agnes Fogg Ríos, and a Mexican father, Alberto Álvaro Ríos, Alberto Ríos was born on September 18, 1952, in the border town of Nogales, Arizona. His first language was Spanish; however, like other Latinos, Alberto was forced to give up his native language in school. As a result, by the time he reached junior high school Ríos could no longer speak Spanish. This loss of language inspired the youth to create a third language that he incorporated into his poetry written on the back pages of his school notebooks, which he called "mildly rebellious, abstract poems." Ríos continued writing poetry in high school and college. He earned a B.A. with honors in English and creative writing in 1974 from the University of Arizona. He gained another B.A. in psychology the following year from the same college. Ríos then enrolled in law school at the University of Arizona but quit after a year to enroll in the M.F.A. program in creative writing. In 1979, he received an M.F.A. and released a chapbook entitled *Elk Heads on the Wall*. That same year, he married Maria Guadalupe Barron, with whom he would have one son, Joaquin.

In 1980, the National Endowment for the Arts granted Ríos a fellowship in creative writing.

Ríos released *Sleeping on Fists* in 1981. However, it was the next book, *Whispering to Fool the Wind* (1982), that would canonize Ríos's work into the sanctioned halls of Chicano letters forever. The fervor of the Chicano movement had subsided, and through the debris rose the poetic genius of Ríos with his unique imagery, invented language, and magic realism in both prose and poetry alike. What impressed critics most about Ríos's work was his ability to combine the immediacy of oral storytelling into the written word. In 1982, Ríos joined the faculty of Arizona State University (ASU) as an assistant professor. He became an associate professor in 1985, accepted a full professorship in 1989, and was honored as regents' professor of English in 1994. He continues to teach English at ASU.

Throughout his teaching career, Ríos has continued to delight his readers with *The Iguana Killer: Twelve Stories of the Heart* (1984), *Five Indiscretions* (1985), *The Lime Orchard Woman* (1988), *The Warrington Poems* (1989), *Teodoro Luna's Two Kisses* (1990), *Pig Cookies and Other Stories* (1995), *The Curtain of Trees: Stories* (1999), *Capirotada: A Nogales Memoir* (written with his father, 1999), *The Smallest Muscle in the Human Body* (2002), and *Theatre of the Night* (2006). Ríos is the recipient of numerous awards, and his work has been included in more than 175 national and international literary anthologies. His work is regularly taught in schools across the nation and has been adapted to dance and both classical and popular music.

Further Reading

Heide, Rick, ed. *Under the Fifth Sun: Latino Literature from California*. Santa Clara and Berkeley, Calif.: Santa Clara University/Heyday Books, 2002.

Lomelí, Francisco A., and Carl R. Shirley, eds. *Chicano Writers: Second Series*. Vol. 122. Detroit: Gale Research, 1992, pp. 220–224.

Ríos, Alberto, and Alberto Álvaro Ríos. *Capirotada: A Nogales Memoir*. Albuquerque: University of New Mexico Press, 1999.

Rivera, Geraldo
(Gerald Michael Riviera, Gerald Miguel Rivera, Gerald Rivera)
(1943–) *journalist, autobiographer*

Internationally known for his tabloid television hosting, Geraldo Rivera's journalistic work reveals a man concerned with empowering the voiceless, improving the human condition, and obtaining justice and understanding for all cultures. The second of five children, Gerald Michael Rivera was born on July 3 (some reports say July 4), 1943, to Allen Cruz and Lillian Friedman Rivera, in Brooklyn, New York. They were a likely target of prejudice due to the fact that Allen is a full-blooded Puerto Rican and Lillian is of East European Jewish ancestry. To avoid discrimination, the family often misspelled their name as Riviera. However, Geraldo's parents never fully explained to him why they misspelled his surname. They moved to Long Island, New York, when Gerald was about 10 years old.

After graduating from West Babylon High School, Rivera served in the U.S. Merchant Marine for two years. He met Linda Coblentz while enrolled at the University of Arizona in the mid-1960s. They married in 1965 but divorced soon afterward. After gaining a B.S. in 1965, Rivera attended Brooklyn Law School, earning his J.D. in 1969. While completing postgraduate studies at the University of Pennsylvania as a Smith Fellow, Rivera worked in poverty law, serving as the public spokesman for the Young Lords, a Puerto Rican activist group at the height of the Chicano movement. Rivera appeared on New York television, gaining the attention of a WABC executive. ABC offered Rivera a reporter position. However, according to *Exposing Myself* (1991), an autobiography Rivera cowrote with Daniel Paisner, his name was not considered exotic enough; hence, with promptings during his interview, Geraldo Rivera was born.

Rivera accepted a position on ABC's Eyewitness News Team after taking a crash course in broadcast journalism at Columbia University. Initially, he covered human interest stories until a chance meeting with a suicidal heroin addict inspired the story "Drug Crisis in East Harlem." His career in motion, Rivera married Edie, the daughter of author Kurt Vonnegut, Jr., in 1970. Rivera exposed the deplorable conditions of Willowbrook State School for the Mentally Retarded, a mental institution on Staten Island in New York in 1972. The enormous public outcry forced the government to return $25 million in funding to New York's mental health budget. For the next four years, Rivera covered drug-addicted newborns, migrant farmworkers, the elderly, and homosexuals. Admittedly due to infidelity, Rivera and Edie divorced in 1975. One year later, he wed Sherryl Raymond, a marriage that produced one child and lasted eight years. In 1976, he joined ABC's *Good Morning America,* where he covered a mix of sensational stories and celebrities.

Yearning for more substantial work, Rivera accepted a position as special correspondent for ABC's newly launched *20/20* program in 1978. Rivera immersed himself in hard-hitting news and investigative reporting, including "The Elvis Cover-Up," the most well-watched episode of a television series of 1979. In 1985, Rivera vehemently defended a story that romantically linked Marilyn Monroe with John F. Kennedy and his brother Robert. He voiced his frustration at the network for dropping the story to a syndicated columnist and as a result lost his job. With an exorbitant standard of living and no means of supporting it, Rivera accepted the syndicated engagement to host "The Mystery of Al Capone's Vault" for *Entertainment Tonight* in 1986. Although anticlimactic in that the vault revealed nothing, the show garnered unprecedented viewership. In 1987, Rivera married C. C. Dyer, with whom he would have two children, and launched the *Geraldo Show.* The show presented sensational subjects and controversial topics. He made international headlines when his nose was broken in a fight between show guests—a black activist and a neo-Nazi. In an effort to cover a higher caliber of journalism, Rivera began the *Two Rivers Times,* a weekly newspaper, and began to produce and host *Rivera Live,* a late night call-in show in 1994. He joined NBC, working for them from 1997 to 2001, until he became a war correspondent for Fox News Channel. In 2000, he and Dyer divorced, and in 2003, Rivera married Erica Michelle Levy. Widely misunderstood and often criticized for overt emotions and sensational tendencies, Rivera is a passionate, tenacious journalist who has been honored with more than 150 awards, including 10 Emmys.

Further Reading

Mazurkiewicz, Margaret. *Contemporary Authors.* Detroit: Gale, 2002.

Meier, Matt S., Conchita Franco Serri, and Richard A. Garcia. *Notable Latino Americans: A Biographical Dictionary.* Westport, Conn.: Greenwood Press, 1997, pp. 314–316.

Rivera, Geraldo, with Daniel Paisner. *Exposing Myself.* New York: Bantam, 1991.

Rivera, Tomás

(1935–1984) *poet, novelist, essayist, short story writer, educator*

Sometimes referred to as the father of Chicano literature, Tomás Rivera is one of the most influential voices to come out of the Chicano literary boom of the 1970s. His first book, *. . y no se lo tragó la tierra/ . . and the Earth Did Not Devour Him,* is widely hailed as the benchmark of Chicano literature.

Tomás Rivera was born on December 22, 1935, in Crystal City, Texas. The son of Mexican immigrants Florencio Rivera and Josefa Hernández, Rivera called Texas his home but lived the life of a migrant worker. He and his family traveled as far as Iowa, Wisconsin, North Dakota, Michigan, and Minnesota to work the fields as day laborers. As a result of the traveling, Rivera's schooling was constantly interrupted. Initially, he attended barrio schools where he learned to read and write in Spanish. He spoke Spanish at home and learned English at the age of nine while attending public school in Texas. Each year, the family would leave around mid-April, the beginning of the harvest season, and return after the final harvest in early November. Encouraged by his father and maternal grandfather to obtain an education, Rivera arranged his high school curriculum around the agricultural calendar.

Rivera spent one year at Southwest Texas Junior College in San Marcos, Texas, while still earning a living as a farm laborer. He transferred to Southwest Texas State College (now University), graduating with a B.A. in English in 1958. After graduating, he began teaching at an elementary school. He married Concepcion Garza in 1958, and in 1964 he earned an M.A. in education administration with minors in English and Spanish. Upon graduation, Rivera returned to Southwest Texas Junior College to lecture in English, French, and Spanish. He then moved to Oklahoma to attend the University of Oklahoma–Norman, where he simultaneously earned a Ph.D. in Romance languages and another M.A. in Spanish literature in 1969. Upon graduation, Rivera accepted a post as an associate professor of Spanish at Sam Houston University in Huntsville, Texas.

Rivera released *. . . y no se lo tragó la tierra/ . . . and the Earth Did Not Devour Him,* which won the Quinto Sol award, in 1971. Based on personal experiences, this tome in the Latino literary canon presents a series of stream-of-consciousness vignettes in a nonlinear format. The anonymous child-narrator reflects on the lives of migrant workers in the late 1940s and early 1950s. Rolando Hinojosa-Smith translated this work, which was originally published in Spanish, into English as *This Migrant Earth* in 1985. It was released as a movie under the title *And the Earth Did Not Swallow Him* in 1999. Rivera published a collection of poetry entitled *Always and Other Poems* in 1973.

Writing with vitality, artistry, and deep respect for the human condition, Rivera contributed poems to *El quetzal emplumece* (1976), as well as poems and essays to a number of journals and magazines. His work is cited in several anthologies. Rivera also wrote *Chicano Literature: A Dynamic Intimacy and The Harvest/La cosecha.* JUAN BRUCE-NOVOA commented on Rivera's writings, "What Rivera achieves is the evocation of an environment with a minimum of words, and within that environment the migratory farmworkers move with dignity, strength, and resilience."

Rivera accepted a full professorship in Spanish at the University of Texas–San Antonio. He became the chairman of the foreign language department in 1973 and was also named dean of the College of Multidisciplinary Studies. Three years later, he became vice chancellor and executive vice president at the University of Texas–El Paso. In 1979, Rivera once again made history when the University of California–Riverside offered him the office of chancellor, making him the first Hispanic to hold a University of California chancellor post. Dedicated to education and the betterment of Latino communities, Rivera served on many boards, including the Ford Foundation and the Carnegie Foundation for the Advancement of Teaching. President Jimmy Carter named Rivera to the board of foreign scholarship (Fulbright program). He was also awarded several honorary doctoral degrees.

Rivera was at work on the novel *La casa grande del pueblo* when he died of a heart attack at the age of 49 on May 16, 1984. Rivera devoted his life to opening doors to higher education and to the writing and publishing world for Mexican Americans and fellow Latinos. Rivera's dedication and memory remain strong in centers of research and service, from the Tomás Rivera Policy Institute to local libraries that were established and dedicated in his name.

Tomás Rivera is considered the father of contemporary Chicano literature. *(Photo of Tomás Rivera is reprinted with permission from the publisher [APP Archive Files] [Houston: Arte Público Press—University of Houston, © 2006])*

Further Reading

Kanellos, Nicolás, et al., eds. *Herencia: The Anthology of Hispanic Literature in the United States.* New York: Oxford University Press, 2003, pp. 301–303.

Meier, Matt S., Conchita Franco Serri, and Richard A. Garcia. *Notable Latino Americans: A Biographical Dictionary.* Westport, Conn.: Greenwood Press, 1997, pp. 317–319.

Rivera, Tomás, and Julian Olivares, eds. *Tomás Rivera: The Complete Works.* 2d ed. Houston: Arte Público Press, 1998.

Tardiff, Joseph C., and L. Mpho Mabunda, eds. *Dictionary of Hispanic Biography.* Detroit: Gale Research, 1996, pp. 748–749.

Rodríguez, Luis J.
(Luis Javier Rodríguez)

(1954–) autobiographer, poet, short story writer, children's book writer, essayist, activist

Luis J. Rodríguez is best known for *Always Running: La Vida Loca, Gang Days in L.A.,* which received a *Chicago Sun-Times* First Prose Book Award and a Carl Sandburg Literary Award for Non-Fiction, and was chosen for *Choice* Magazine's Outstanding Academic Books List; as a *New York Times Book Review* Notable Book, and as a 1994 New York Public Library Book for the Teen Age. Author of prose, poetry, short stories, essays, and children's books, Rodríguez is a vital community leader who uses his experience and garnered wisdom to teach and inspire youth, convicted persons, and fellow writers.

Proud of his indigenous Mexika/Raramuri descent, Luis Javier Rodríguez was born to Alfonso and María Estela (Jiménez) Rodríguez on July 9, 1954, in El Paso, Texas. For the first two years of his life, he lived in Juárez, Mexico. The Rodríguez family then moved to the Watts community of Los Angeles, where they lived until relocating to the San Gabriel Valley in 1962. Rodríguez has one brother, Jose Rene, two sisters, Ana Virginia and Gloria Estela, and three half siblings, Seni, Mario, and Alberto.

Luis fell in with a gang by age 11 and began using drugs at age 12. Acutely aware of the injustice that surrounded him as the target of harassment by police and Anglo children, Luis took part in many school walkouts against prejudice in the education system. Frustrated by the lack of change, he dropped out of high school at age 15. Rodríguez was kicked out of his home but eventually was allowed to live in the garage. Heavily involved with gang life, he still found time to write verses and immerse himself in books. Rodríguez found solace when he read. As he explained to Aaron Cohen in a 1995 interview, "I would kind of go inside and hide myself in books, and not have to worry about the yelling and screaming, and bullets flying." An activist from early on, Rodríguez participated with the 1968 East Los Angeles School Blowouts, the Chicano Moratorium in August 1970, and other protests demanding Latino equal rights.

By the time he was 19, Rodríguez faced a six-year prison term, was hooked on drugs, had lost 25 of his friends due to violence, and had been arrested for a variety of crimes, including stealing, rioting, fighting, attempted murder, and assaulting a police officer. Letters of support from the community helped lessen his conviction to a shorter county jail term. Capturing his experiences in verse, Rodríguez later submitted his poetry to contests and won a Quinto Sol Literary Award of $250 and a trip to Berkeley, California. Determined to honor the community that believed in him, Rodríguez quit drugs and the gang life, finished high school, and channeled his artistry into painting several murals in his community. He joined the Movimiento Estudiantil Chicano de Aztlán (MEChA), an organization that raises political, social, and cultural awareness about the Chicano experience, and attended a few college courses before quitting school to work full time. During the 1970s Rodríguez worked as a steel mill worker, truck driver, school bus driver, carpenter, and foundry worker. In 1974, he married Camila Martinez, who gave birth to their son, Ramiro, in 1975, and daughter, Andrea, in 1977.

In the early 1980s, Rodríguez served as the director of the Los Angeles Latino Writers Association as well as working as a public affairs associate, a reporter-photographer for seven East Los Angeles weekly newspapers, a daily newspaper reporter, and a radio programmer. He and Camila divorced in 1979. He married Paulette Donalson in 1982, although they divorced a couple of years later. In 1985, Rodríguez moved to Chicago, where he became the editor of the *People's Tribune,* a weekly revolutionary newspaper. He covered labor, poverty, homelessness, health care, and prison issues. Rodríguez became active in the growing Chicago poetry scene. In 1988, he married Maria Trinidad (Trini) Cardenas and began work in the publications department of the archdiocese of Chicago. On the weekends, he worked as a news writer and reporter for WMAQ-AM. The following year, 1989, Rodríguez formed Tia Chucha Press, a publisher dedicated to promoting emerging, socially conscious poets and, through it, published his first collection of poems known as *Poems Across the Pavement.* This volume of poetry explores life on the streets, cultural alienation, and racial relations. Well aware of the needs of the community, Rodríguez cofounded the Chicago's Guild Complex, one of the Midwest's largest literary arts organizations.

In the 1990s, he wrote freelance articles for prominent publications such as *U.S. News & World Report, The Nation,* the *Chicago Tribune,* the *Los Angeles Times,* and others. He also conducted workshops in schools, prisons, juvenile facilities, community centers, and homeless shelters. Rodríguez released his second collection of poetry, *The Concrete River,* in 1991, which won a PEN West/Josephine Miles Award for Literary Excellence.

In 1993, Rodríguez published the highly controversial *Always Running: La Vida Loca, Gang Days in L.A.* GARY SOTO, reporting for the *New York Times,* stated in his review, "Rodríguez' account of his coming of age is vivid, raw, fierce, and fearless. Here's truth no television set burning night and day, could ever begin to offer." Rodríguez wrote *Always Running* as a memoir, although he commented he "synthesized events and reorganized the material so that it would work as literature, but still maintain the truth and reality of the situation." Some school districts banned *Always Running,* believing the book's intense imagery and straightforward language would encourage violence. However, Rodríguez's intentions in writing the book were to educate young men and women, including Ramiro, his then 15-year-old son, of the realities and brutalities of gang life, definitely not to glorify it. After *Always Running* was released,

Rodríguez quit his jobs to focus his efforts on promoting his book. Many of his works were translated into Spanish, allowing him to travel extensively on behalf of the books' promotions and his message of hope and survival.

During the mid-1990s, Rodríguez returned to his indigenous roots. He participated in Native American spiritual ceremonies, studied with a variety of teachers and mentors, visited areas of his own native heritage, and cofounded Youth Struggling for Survival, an organization dedicated to helping gang and nongang youth find true power and inner strength using Native wisdom. He also helped start Rock A Mole (rhymes with *guacamole*) Productions, which produces music and art festivals. Trini and Rodríguez added two sons to the family, Ruben, born in 1988, and Luis, in 1994. In 1998, Rodríguez released his first children's book, *América Is Her Name (Le llaman América),* which won the Paterson Books for Young People Book Award and the *Skipping Stones* magazine Honor Award and was included on the Bank Street List of Best Children's Books. He also published *Trochemoche: New Poems,* which won *ForeWord* magazine's Silver Award for Poetry Book of the Year. *It Doesn't Have to Be This Way: A Barrio Story (No tiene que ser así: Una historia del barrio),* a bilingual children's book released in 1999, garnered the Parents' Choice Approved Winner for Children's Books, *Skipping Stones* magazine's Honor Award for Multicultural and International Literature, and the Americas Award Commended Title for Best Book for Children.

Rodríguez returned to Los Angeles in 2000. In May 2001, Rodríguez, along with 50 individuals from around the world, was honored as an Unsung Hero of Compassion by the Dalai Lama. In December of that same year, Rodríguez, Trini, and partner Enrique Sanchez opened Tia Chucha's Café Cultural, a bookstore, coffee shop, performance space, art gallery, and computer center in Sylmar, California. Rodríguez also released *Hearts and Hands: Creating Community in Violent*

Well-known author and owner of Tia Chucha Café Cultural, Luis J. Rodríguez stands outside his home in southern California. *(Greg Bojorquez)*

Times that same busy year. The following year, he started Dos Manos Records with musician Ernie Perez to produce his first CD of poetry and music called *My Name's Not Rodríguez*. He also published a collection of short stories known as *The Republic of East L.A.: Stories,* winner of Short Story Collection 2003 PEN Oakland Josephine Miles Book Award and inclusion on the *Los Angeles Times'* Best Books of the West and a Book Sense selection.

In 2005, Rodríguez released two books—a book of poetry, *My Nature Is Hunger: New & Selected Poems, 1989–2004,* and *Music of the Mill: A Novel.* During his career, Rodríguez has received a Sundance Institute Art Writers Fellowship, a Lila Wallace–*Reader's Digest* Writers' Award, a Lannan Fellowship for Poetry, a Hispanic Heritage Award for Literature, a National Association for Poetry Therapy Public Service Award, a California Arts Council Fellowship, an Illinois Author of

the Year Award, and several Illinois Arts Council fellowships.

Rodríguez's writing talents vary and have been recognized in many genres; however, Rodríguez considers himself first a poet. He stated in a 2005 interview, "[P]oetry is the springboard for everything that I want to write." Through Rodríguez's poetry, readers and critics alike clearly hear his message, as commented *World Literature Today:* "In all Rodríguez' poems, the sense of place is palpable and becomes essentially a fully developed voice in and of itself." It is not only through his verses that the raw tenderness of Rodríguez's compassion and dedication to society and community emerges, but also in his efforts to serve and lead.

Further Reading

Cohen, Aaron. "An Interview with Luis J. Rodríguez." *Poets & Writers Magazine* (January/February 1995): 50–55.

Heide, Rick, ed. *Under the Fifth Sun: Latino Literature from California.* Santa Clara and Berkeley, Calif.: Santa Clara University/Heyday Books, 2002.

Rodríguez, Luis J. *Always Running: La Vida Loca, Gang Days in L.A.* Willimantic, Conn.: Curbstone Press, 1993.

Sullivan, Patrick. "Class War: Luis Rodríguez Casts a Skeptical Eye on Attempts to Ban His Autobiography." *Sonoma County Independent,* February 4–10, 1999, pp. 21–22.

Tardiff, Joseph C., and L. Mpho Mabunda, eds. *Dictionary of Hispanic Biography.* Detroit: Gale Research, 1996, pp. 759–760.

Rodríguez, Richard
(Ricardo Rodríguez)
(1944–) poet, journalist, editor, nonfiction writer, memoirist, essayist

Richard Rodríguez is best known for his autobiography, *Hunger of Memory: The Education of Richard Rodríquez.* This book received an unprecedented 50 reviews by mainstream and Latino literary journals, popular magazines, and prestigious daily papers.

The son of Victoria Moran, a clerk-typist, and Leopoldo Rodríguez, a dental technician, Ricardo Rodríguez was born on July 31, 1944, in San Francisco, California. His parents had both recently emigrated from Mexico and met in the United States. He moved with his family to Sacramento, California, at the age of three. By the time he was six years old, he had noticed the deep impact of language on his level of comfort and sense of self. He was reassured by the Spanish spoken at home yet increasingly felt pressure to learn English in the public sectors despite the fact that he was afraid of the guttural sounds of the English language. His parents bought a home on the edge of a middle-class Anglo-American neighborhood. Ricardo attended a private Catholic school where he was forced to speak only English. This development of a public self divided him from the intimate bond he held with his family, particularly his parents, who primarily spoke Spanish. Ricardo became known as Richard and proved to be an excellent student.

After graduating from Bishop Armstrong High School, Rodríguez received a B.A. in English from Stanford University in 1967. Through his education, Rodríguez began to sense an alienation from his cultural roots. He spent a summer working in construction, believing that if he worked with his hands as a bracero, literally "one who works with his arms," he would better understand and commiserate with his fellow Mexican Americans. After a few short months, Rodríguez concluded that although he may have a dark complexion, he could never be like his fellow workers: Education had changed that. In fact, he realized he had idealized hard labor as those in the English Renaissance, the focus of his studies, had romanticized pastoral life. Rodríguez moved to New York, where he obtained an M.A. in religious studies from Columbia University in 1969. He returned to California and enrolled in the Ph.D. program in English language and literature at the University of California–Berkeley. Alienated from the struggles of most Chicanos, Rodríguez did not participate in the political activism for Chicano rights during his college education. As a minority graduate student, Rodríguez was awarded a Fulbright fellowship (1972–73) and a National Endowment for the Humanities fellowship (1976–77). By the mid-1970s, Rodríguez felt a growing disparity in receiving the benefits of affirmative action when he himself was no longer a minority but a fully assimilated and acculturated member of mainstream society. He therefore declined the several university teaching positions offered to him and refused to submit his dissertation. In 1981, Rodríguez left higher education to pursue an independent writing career.

Rodríguez released *Hunger of Memory: The Education of Richard Rodríguez* in 1982. His controversial opinions on affirmative action and bilingual education resulted in more critical reviews than most other Mexican-American authors had received. Rodríguez's book upset Chicano idealists, who called for solidarity. However, even some Latino critics praised Rodríguez for his unique combination of lyrical and highly rhetorical style with journalistic prose. Presented in a nontraditional style, this autobiographical collection of essays won favorable attention from right-wing politicians, who felt they had found their minority spokesperson despite the fact that Rodríguez proposed the main problem of affirmative action was not its existence, but its emphasis on race rather than on socioeconomic class. Rodríguez openly disagreed with the current traditions of bilingual education. He stated his opinions in an interview with *Publisher's Weekly:* "[P]ublic educators in a public schoolroom have an obligation to teach a public language. Public language isn't just English or Spanish or any other formal language. It is the language of public society, the language that people outside that public sector resist. For Mexican-Americans it is the language of *los gringos*. For Appalachian children who speak a fractured English or Black children in a ghetto, the problem is the same it seems to me. . . . My argument has always been that the imperative is to get children away from those languages that increase their sense of alienation from the public society."

Throughout the 1980s, Rodríguez honed his journalistic skills, contributing to *Harper's, U.S. News & World Report,* and the *Los Angeles Times Sunday Perspective.* He also worked as an editor for Pacific News Service. Imbuing more of this journalistic approach, Rodríguez released *Days of Obligation: An Argument with My Mexican Father* in 1992. The book, which was selected as a finalist for the Pulitzer Prize in 1993, deals with racial and cultural identification and homosexuality in Latino cultures. In 1992, he won an Emmy Award for his short historical piece "Pearl Harbor Anniversary." In 1997, Rodriguez received the George Foster Peabody Award for his essays on American life as part of the PBS *News Hour with Jim Lehrer.* His awards include the Frankel Medal from the National Endowment for the Humanities and the International Journalism Award from the World Affairs Council of California. His latest work, *Brown: An Erotic History of the Americas* (2002), explores the symbiotic way Hispanic and American cultures influence each other. The title also represents the growing darkening of the American fabric with the mixing of cultures.

Further Reading

Browdy de Hernandez, Jennifer. "Postcolonial Blues: Ambivalence and Alienation in the Autobiographies of Richard Rodriguez and V. S. Naipaul." *AutoBiography Studies* 12 (Fall 1997): 151–165.

Marquez, Antonio C. "Richard Rodriguez's *Hunger of Memory* and New Perspectives on Ethnic Autobiography." In *Teaching American Ethnic Literatures: Nineteen Essays.* Edited by John R. Maitino. Albuquerque: University of New Mexico Press, 1996, pp. 237–254.

Meier, Matt S., Conchita Franco Serri, and Richard A. Garcia. *Notable Latino Americans: A Biographical Dictionary.* Westport, Conn.: Greenwood Press, 1997.

West-Durán, Alan. *Latino and Latina Writers, Volume II.* Detroit: Gale-Thomas, 2004, pp. 455–476.

Rojas, Arnold
(A. R. Rojas)
(1896–1988) *essayist, folklorist, novelist*

Arnold Rojas is known for giving the best and most distinct narrative of the vaqueros' life and sensibilities. Vaqueros are cowboys who worked the lands of the southwestern United States.

Arnold Rojas was born on September 25, 1896 (one source says 1899), in Pasadena, California. His family had immigrated to the United States from western Mexico in the 1820s. His Indian ancestors were the fierce Yaqui and Maya, while his Spanish inheritance came from Sephardic Jews who migrated to the Americas to escape the Inquisition. After his parents died in 1902, Arnold lived in an orphanage in San Luis Obispo, California. He received a third-grade education. When he was 12, Arnold ran away to the San Joaquin Valley, where he could pursue his dream of becoming a vaquero.

He worked on the ranches of the valley, learning the subtle distinctions that would make him a true Mexican-American vaquero and not a traditional American cowboy. He lived with an uncle during his teens. He loved to read the works of Mark Twain, Charles Dickens, O. Henry, and Arthur Conan Doyle but preferred oral storytelling. He listened to and memorized the campfire stories of fellow vaqueros. In 1935, Rojas opened a stable, which he kept in operation until 1950.

Following World War II, Rojas was named the chairman of a rodeo sponsored by the American Legion post in Bakersfield, California, then the center of the San Joaquin's cattle industry. He approached Jim Day, editor of the *Bakersfield Californian,* seeking publicity for the rodeo. Day suggested that Rojas write the publicity piece. Rojas composed thumbnail character sketches of several old vaqueros whom he planned to honor at the rodeo. Upon publication in Day's column, "Pipefuls," in the *Bakersfield Californian,* Ralph F. Kreiser, a local historian, encouraged Rojas to continue recording his stories. Soon after, Rojas's vaquero tales appeared regularly in the newspaper and the local historical society's newsletter under Rojas's own byline.

Noted California historian Monsignor James Culleton fell in love with Rojas's work and agreed to publish the collected stories and vignettes. Rojas released *California Vaqueros* (1953), *Lore of the California Vaqueros* (1958), *Last of the Vaqueros* (1960), *The Vaquero* (1964), *Bits, Bitting, and Spanish Horses; The Chief Rojas Fact Book about Successful Horse Training and the Proper Use of Equipment* (1970), *These Were the Vaqueros: Collected Works of Arnold R. Rojas* (1974), and *Vaqueros and Buckeroos* (1979). Rojas's writings are considered to be the preeminent works about the life of a vaquero. His style was rather folkloric, more a recording or oral storytelling than perfection of the written word. However, this unbridled mannerism that speaks directly to the characters is exactly what he sought to portray. With loving attention to the appeal of the freedom of wide open spaces and dedication to his horse above all, Rojas captured an essential character in the history of the southwestern United States.

Rojas died on September 8, 1988. Some of his papers are held in the Historical Collection of Kern County, Beale Memorial Library, Bakersfield, California.

Further Reading

Haslam, Gerald. "California's Last Vaquero." *Western American Literature* 21 (August 1986): 123–130.

Heide, Rick, ed. *Under the Fifth Sun: Latino Literature from California.* Santa Clara and Berkeley, Calif.: Santa Clara University/Heyday Books, 2002.

Lomelí, Francisco A., and Carl R. Shirley, eds. *Dictionary of Literary Biography, Chicano Writers, First Series.* Vol 82. Detroit: Gale Group, 1989, pp. 217–220.

Ruiz, Vicki L.
(Vicki Lynn Mercer, Vicki Lynn Ruiz)
(1955–   ) nonfiction book writer, folklorist, literary critic, educator

Vicki L. Ruiz's extensive research unfolds in sensitive yet incisive books that document the experiences of Mexican Americans, particularly unions and women of the early 20th century. Her most valued contribution to Chicano letters rests in her ability to give tangible facts and create a picture for contemporary readers so that they might understand the trials and tribulations Latinos have faced, thereby granting additional value to the successes they have experienced.

Vicki Lynn Mercer was born in Atlanta, Georgia, on May 21, 1955, to Robert Mercer and Ermina Ruiz. Her paternal grandparents disapproved of their son's choice to marry a Hispanic woman and, therefore, disowned him. Vicki absorbed the stories her mother and maternal grandmother told around the kitchen table. She listened attentively to tales about her ancestors who worked in Colorado coal mines and beet fields, how they immigrated to the United States during the Mexican Revolution, and how her grandfather was once an active member of the Industrial Workers of the World (19th-century radical union). The Mexican Revolution of 1910 was an uprising of common folk who overthrew the dictator Porfirio Díaz, and violence continued throughout Mexico until 1920. Mercer's parents did not like television and instead encouraged Vicki and her sister to read and do well in school. Vicki spent many hours reading in the local book mobile.

Vicki spent her early childhood in Florida, where her father owned a large sport fishing boat that required frequent moving up and down the state coast. When Vicki was in eighth grade, her mother insisted that the family settle down in Panama City, Florida. Unfortunately, in this small town that Vicki half-affectionately dubbed the "Redneck Riviera," she experienced a certain amount of racial prejudice. After high school, she attended Gulf

Vicki L. Ruiz is a well-respected historian and educator in addition to being a successful author. *(Photo by Yuen Lin/Vicki Ruiz)*

Coast Community College and graduated with an A.S. in 1975. She transferred to Florida State University, securing a B.A. in science, summa cum laude, in 1977. She wanted to become a high school teacher until one of her professors convinced her to pursue a graduate degree. She applied to Stanford University, where Professor Al Camarillo supported her application and provided mentorship throughout her college experience. Camarillo introduced her to union activist Luisa Moreno and the history of the women's cannery union. After gaining an M.A. in history from Stanford University in 1978, she visited Moreno in Guadalajara, Mexico. The following year, Mercer married Jerry Ruiz, with whom she would have two sons, Miguel and Dan-

iel, and later divorce in 1990. Inspired by Moreno to research the cannery workers, Ruiz wrote her dissertation on the plight of Mexican-American cannery workers and the formation of their union. She gained a Ph.D. in history from Stanford University in 1982, and in 1987 her dissertation was published as *Cannery Women, Cannery Lives: Mexican Women, Unionization, and the California Food Processing Industry, 1939–1950.*

Ruiz began teaching Chicano literature, history, and women's studies at many universities, including the University of California–Davis, the Claremont Graduate School, the University of Texas–El Paso, and Arizona State University (ASU). In 2001, she became a professor of history and Chicano/Latino studies at the University of California–Irvine (UCI). She is currently teaching at UCI.

Throughout her teaching career, Ruiz continued to research Mexican women's history. She has written books that document personal experiences that she learned about through extensive interviews. She coedited *Women on the U.S.-Mexico Border: Responses to Change* (with Susan Tiano, 1987), *Western Women: Their Land, Their Lives* (with Lillian Schlissel and Janice Monk, 1988), *Unequal Sisters: A Multicultural Reader in U.S. Women's History* (with Ellen Carol DuBois, 1990) and *Women in the West: A Guide to Manuscript Sources* (with Susan Armitage, Helen Bannan, and Katherine Morrissey, 1991). She has also written *From Out of the Shadows: Mexican Women in Twentieth-Century America* (1998), *Las obreras: Chicana Politics of Work and Family* (2000), *Created Equal: A Social and Political History of the United States* (coauthored with Jacqueline Jones, Peter Wood, Elaine T. May, and Thomas Borstelmann, 2003), and *Latina Legacies: Identity, Biography, and Community* (coedited with Virginia Sánchez Korrol, 2005).

Of these works, perhaps her best known is *From Out of the Shadows.* Ruiz explains in this book, "I want the reader to imagine what it was like to be a woman in the 1930s—to recognize the opportunities available to Mexican women in the

U.S. and, very importantly, what was beyond their grasp. Here is a question of providing an understanding of what decisions they could make within the parameters of their world, of considering the structural elements in their lives (deportation, repatriation, poverty) as well their possibilities and aspirations. In what ways did education and popular culture feed their dreams?"

Ruiz married Victor Becerra in 1992. She recently completed *American Dreaming, Global Realities: Re-Thinking U.S. Immigration History* with Donna R. Gabaccia and *Latinas in the United States: A Historical Encyclopedia,* coedited with Sánchez Korrol. The latter project was funded by grants from the Ford Foundation and the National Endowment for the Humanities.

Ruiz has received numerous awards, including a Critics Choice Award from the Educational Studies Association in 1991 for her work as coeditor of *Unequal Sisters: A Multicultural Reader in U.S. Women's History.* That same year, the National Women's Political Caucus presented Ruiz with a Distinguished Achievement Award for her first book. In 1992, she earned the Chicana/Latina Research Project Scholar Award. Ruiz was honored in 1994 with a Community Service Award from the Chicano/Latino studies department at California State University–Long Beach. During her career at the University of California–Davis, she received an Outstanding Faculty Award and an Honored Faculty Award. She also received the 2001 ASU College of Liberal Arts and Sciences Distinguished Faculty Award, 2001 Distinguished Mentorship Award from ASU Faculty Women Association, 2001 Outstanding Achievement and Contribution Award from the ASU Commission on the Status of Women, and the Humanities Associates Teaching Award from UCI. She and her coeditor Sánchez Korrol were named Women of the Year in Education by *Latina* magazine and received a 21 Leaders for the 21st Century Award. Ruiz was chosen by President Bill Clinton as a presidential recess appointment for the National Humanities Council.

Further Reading

Palmisano, Joseph M. *Notable Hispanic American Women, Book 2.* Detroit: Gale Research, 1998, pp. 158–164.

Ruiz, Vicki L. *From Out of the Shadows: Mexican Women in Twentieth-Century America.* New York: Oxford University Press, 1998.

Scanlon, Jennifer, and Sharon Cosner. *American Women Historians, 1700s–1900s: A Biographical Dictionary.* Westport, Conn.: Greenwood Press, 1996.

Ruiz de Burton, María Amparo
(María del Amparo Ruiz Arango, H. S. Burton, Mrs. H. S. Burton, C. Loyal)
(1832–1895) *novelist, poet, playwright*

María Amparo Ruiz de Burton is the first Mexican-American woman known to have written two novels in English. Few accounts of life in California before U.S. annexation exist, making the works of Ruiz de Burton an integral element to understanding the ideological history of the Southwest.

María del Amparo Ruiz Arango was born into an aristocratic family on July 3, 1832 (some accounts say 1835), in Loreto, Baja California, Mexico. She was the granddaughter of José Manuel Ruiz, governor (1822–25) of the state of Baja California, Mexico, and commander of the Mexican northern frontier, and the daughter of Isabel Ruiz Maytorena. Her father's identity remains unclear. The family enjoyed the comforts of the wealthy and the spoils of the vast land tract they owned on the Baja California Peninsula (located south of present-day California) until the U.S.-Mexican War. In July 1847, La Paz, Baja California, surrendered to the United States, and plans were made for the United States to claim Baja California as well as Alta California, as U.S. territory.

Ruiz Arango met Captain Henry S. Burton when he arrived in La Paz in 1847 to take possession of Baja California. Insurrections in cities along the Baja peninsula delayed complete command until after the 1848 Treaty of Guadalupe

Hidalgo was signed, which returned Baja California to Mexico and granted Alta California and the rest of what would become the Southwest to the United States. The treaty promised residents of Baja California U.S. citizenship and rights if they settled in the United States. Ruiz Arango left with her mother, her sister, and 480 refugees by boat to Monterey, California. Despite their differences, Ruiz Arango and Captain Burton had fallen in love. He accompanied her to Monterey, where they were wed in 1849. Their love affair was recounted by Winifred Davidson in the *San Diego Union* and the *Los Angeles Times* circa 1930 and is

María Amparo Ruiz de Burton wrote the only known fictional account of California history from the position of the dispossessed Californios. *(Photo of María Amparo Ruiz de Burton is reprinted with permission from the publisher [APP Archive Files] [Houston: Arte Público Press—University of Houston, © 2006])*

also captured in Hubert Howe Bancroft's *California Pastoral* (1888). The early California song "The Maid of Monterey" is believed to have been written about Ruiz de Burton.

Ruiz de Burton quickly mastered English. After some time in northern California, Burton was ordered to San Diego. Ruiz de Burton and her husband purchased the Jamul Ranch near San Diego, California, in 1853, where they lived for six years. During this time, she wrote and produced a five-act stage adaptation of *Don Quixote* (the play was published in 1876). Several years later, when the outbreak of the Civil War became imminent, Burton was transferred to the East Coast. Ruiz de Burton moved gracefully through the elite social circles and established powerful friendships, such as with Mary Todd Lincoln. Access to social gatherings made Ruiz de Burton privy to the inner workings of the military and political arenas. In 1859, Burton died of malarial fever, leaving Ruiz de Burton widowed with two children, Nellie and Harry.

She returned to California in 1870 to find that portions of the Jamul Ranch had been sold to pay her husband's debt and that 15 American squatters, each claiming 160-acre homesteads, were living on her property. In 1851, Congress had passed the California Land Act, which considered all Mexican land grants public domain until the owners could verify the legitimacy of land titles. Ruiz de Burton thus began a variety of business ventures to secure her family's financial stability and was forced to engage in several legal battles to maintain her land.

Fueled by the injustice and overwhelming ethnocentricity rampant within the American government, Ruiz de Burton began writing in the early 1870s. Her first novel, *Who Would Have Thought It?* (1872), inspired by her 10-year stay on the East Coast, reveals the greed, hypocrisy, racism, and moral depravity of Northern abolitionists, politicians, and clergymen. Unlike other Hispanic writers of the time, Ruiz de Burton does not merely focus on the ways and means of Hispanic people, but first and foremost she challenges Anglo society's assumption that all upper-class Mexicans would want to be white, as well as questions the future benefit and impact of U.S. expansionism on all Americans. Woven throughout the satirical look at U.S. politics, the author portrays a love story of an unlikely pair from opposing sides of the political and racial divide. Given the controversial content, the book was published with no author credited and is listed in the Library of Congress under *H. S. Burton* and *Mrs. Henry S. Burton.*

The Squatter and the Don (1885) is a novel based on Ruiz de Burton's experiences in the reclamation of her land, which also serves to parallel the trials of many Californio landowners who lost their land due to the California Land Act of 1851. Californios are of Spanish and/or Mexican descent and lived in California before it became a state of the United States. The book was printed with the pseudonym *C. Loyal,* referring to *Ciudadano Leal,* or "loyal citizen." This historical romance is the first to portray the point of view of the vanquished Californios, who, as the author describes them, once stood proud, almost heroic, yet became destitute and politically marginalized after California became a U.S. state. Ruiz de Burton continues to allude to the loss of culture and way of life for all Americans with the rapid growth of the railroad and the corporate monopolies developing throughout the nation. Although the author attempts to consider the welfare of all Americans, she still holds negative stereotypes of American Indians, African Americans, Chinese, and Jewish people.

Ruiz de Burton continued to fight for her land until her dying day, which came on August 12, 1895. Like many Spanish and Mexican landowners, she died impoverished, never even knowing that her grandfather had bequeathed the land in Baja California to her. *The Squatter and the Don* was translated into English and released in 1997. Ruiz de Burton was the first to speak for the conquered Californios. She denounced the deceitful means the U.S. government used to possess the land and bring about the Californios' financial ruin, and with intelligent foresight, she opposed

U.S. capitalist development. The recovery of Ruiz de Burton's books restores cultural and racial pride to descendants of Californios, as well as offers a first-person account of the consequences of Manifest Destiny and expansionism for some people.

Further Reading
Crawford, Kathleen. "María Amparo Ruiz Burton: The General's Lady." *Journal of San Diego History* 30 (1984): 207–208.

Goldman, Anne E. "*The Squatter and the Don* by María Amparo Ruiz de Burton." *MELUS* 19 (1994): 129–131.

Harris, Sharon M. *Dictionary of Literary Biography,* Vol. 221: *American Women Prose Writers, 1870–1920.* Detroit: Gale Group, 2000, pp. 310–316.

Kanellos, Nicolás, et al., eds. *Herencia: The Anthology of Hispanic Literature in the United States.* New York: Oxford University Press, 2003, pp. 123–129.

Lomelí, Francisco A. and, Carl R. Shirley, eds. *Chicano Writers: First Series.* Vol. 89. Detroit: Gale Research, 1989, pp. 251–255.

Ryan, Pam Muñoz
(Pamela Bell)
(1951–   ) *children's book writer, young adult writer*

Pam Muñoz Ryan, a prolific writer of picture books and books for middle school readers, has been granted more than 50 awards and honors. She is best known for *Esperanza Rising* (2000), a fictional tale that parallels her Mexican grandmother's immigration to California.

Pamela Bell was born on December 25, 1951, in Bakersfield, California. She is the eldest of three daughters of Esperanza Muñoz Bell, as well as the eldest of 23 cousins on her mother's side. Her large, gregarious family boasts a wealth of ethnic backgrounds, which include Spanish, Mexican, Basque, and Italian. On the weekends, Pamela enjoyed her grandmothers' cooking. From her maternal grandmother Pamela tasted traditional Mexican fare

indicative of the family's native town, Aguascali-
entes, Mexico, and from her paternal grandmother,
she was treated to southern cuisine typical of her
Oklahoman heritage.

Books intrigued Pamela at an early age. She
spent many days escaping the heat of her hometown in the air-conditioned library. She attended
McKinley and Jefferson Elementary Schools
and Washington Junior High School, where she
became the editor of the school's newspaper. Upon
graduation from Bakersfield High School in 1969,
she enrolled at San Diego State University, earning
a bachelor's degree in child development in 1974.
Immediately after college, Bell landed her first job
as the Red Cross Coordinator for the Vietnamese
and Cambodian refugee playschools at the U.S.
military relocation camp at Camp Pendleton,
California. She married Jim Ryan in 1975.

From 1975 to 1978, Ryan put her bilingual
skills to work for the Escondido Unified School
District as a bilingual teacher in the Head Start
program. When her first child was born, Ryan
decided to leave teaching to stay home and raise
her family. In time, she would give birth to three
other children. In the early 1980s, Ryan went back
to school to get a master's degree in education.
After turning in an assignment, a professor asked
her if she had ever considered professional writing,
thus planting that possibility in her mind. Coinci-
dentally, within a few weeks, Doris Jasinek, a colleague, asked Ryan to coauthor a book with her.
Ryan cowrote three Food for Thought gift books:
A Family Is a Circle of People Who Love You (1988),
How to Build a House of Hearts (1988), and *Falling
in Fun Again* (1990) with Jasinek.

Ryan then tried her hand at writing for the
children's market. After submitting work on her
own for several years and receiving many rejections,
she hired a literary agent, and her work began to be
read. *One Hundred Is a Family* (1994), a children's
picture book, celebrates the many shapes and sizes
that constitute a family and received excellent
reviews. *The Flag We Love,* a patriotic dedication
to the American flag, followed in 1996. They were

followed by *The Crayon Counting Book* (1996),
California Here We Come (1997), and *Armadillos
Sleep in Dugouts: And Other Places Animals Live*
(1997). Ryan wrote for the Doug series, based on
Jim Jenkins's cartoon character, with *Doug Counts
Down* (1998), *Doug's Treasure Hunt* (1998), and
Funnie Family Vacation (1999).

Ryan's first book to achieve widespread critical acclaim was written for middle school readers. *Riding Freedom* (1999) is based on the true
story of Charlotte "Charley" Darkey Parkhurst, a
19th-century American woman who lived her life
disguised as a man so she could be a stagecoach
driver. *Riding Freedom* won several notable awards,
including the Willa Cather Award and the California Young Reader Medal.

While reading an adult book about famous
American women, Ryan came across an article
that mentioned an evening in 1933 when Amelia
Earhart took Eleanor Roosevelt on her first night-
time flight over Washington, D.C. *Amelia and
Eleanor Go for a Ride* (1999) commemorates that
event. This book earned Ryan eight awards and
honors, including the American Library Association Notable Book Award.

Esperanza Rising (2000) is based loosely on
her grandmother's emigration from Mexico in the
1930s. Esperanza enjoyed wealth and privilege
until her father's sudden death, which forced her
and her mother to flee Mexico. They found work
in California's migrant labor camps, where they
endured discrimination, poverty, and long days of
difficult manual labor. Ryan employed her writing skills to weave fiction and imagination into
this enchanting book. She was awarded the Pura
Belpré Award, given biennially by the American
Library Association, which honors a Latino or
Latina writer or illustrator whose work best portrays, affirms, and celebrates the Latino cultural
experience in an outstanding work of literature for
children and youths.

When Marian Sang (2002) pays tribute to
Marian Anderson, a singer best known for her historic concert on the steps of the Lincoln Memorial

in 1939, which was attended by 75,000 people. *Becoming Naomi León* (2005) was inspired by a Oaxacan festival. Ryan recalled on her Web site, "I came across a one-line reference to the Night of the Radishes. The event sounded so magical I knew I had to see it. In 1997, on the 100th anniversary of La Noche de los Rabanos, I visited the romantic and mysterious Oaxaca City, a feast of colors, tastes, pageantry, and festivals. When I began writing Naomi's story she evolved into a soap carver, my imagination rushed me back to Oaxaca. Or was it Oaxaca's spell that first mesmerized me, and inspired the lioness, Naomi León?" *Becoming Naomi León* received many awards, including the Tomás Rivera Mexican American Children's Book Award and the American Booksellers' Association Book of the Year Honor.

Although Ryan has received much attention for her books targeted at older readers, she enjoys writing for younger children as well. Additional picture books include *A Pinky Is a Baby Mouse* (1999), *Hello Ocean* (2001), *Mice and Beans* (2001), *Mud Is Cake* (2002), *How Do You Raise a Raisin?* (2002), *A Box of Friends* (2002), *There Was No Snow on Christmas Eve* (2005), and *Nacho and Lolita* (2005).

Ryan's books have found audiences from several markets. *Becoming Naomi León, When Marian Sang,* and *Esperanza Rising* have been adapted into audio books. *Riding Freedom, Esperanza Rising, Becoming Naomi León, The Flag We Love, California Here We Come, Hello Ocean,* and *Mice and Beans* have all been translated into Spanish. Ryan's contribution to children's literature extends beyond her cultural heritage to include readers of all backgrounds. She has written six books for a Japanese publisher. After writing the books in English, they were translated into Japanese specifically for the children's literature market in Japan. Ryan's short stories for young adults have appeared in several anthologies, including *First Crossing: Stories About*

Award-winning author Pam Muñoz Ryan is a prolific writer for the children's and young adult markets. *(Steve Thanos Photography)*

Teen Immigrants (2004), and *Friends: Stories About New Friends, Old Friends, and Unexpectedly True Friends* (2005).

Further Reading

Abbey, Cherie D. *Biography Today Author Series: Profiles of People of Interest to Young Readers*. Vol. 12. Holmes, Pa.: Omnigraphics, 2003.

McMahon, Thomas. *Authors and Artists for Young Adults*. Vol. 47. Detroit: Gale, 2002, pp. 189–196.

Rockman, Connie. *Ninth Book of Junior Authors and Illustrators*. Bronx, N.Y.: H. W. Wilson, 2005.

S

Salas, Floyd
(Floyd Francis Salas)
(1931–) *poet, novelist, short story writer, autobiographer, educator*

Floyd Salas is a controversial author whose works have depicted underground worlds, from the 1960s drug scene in counterculture Berkeley, California, to forbidden love affairs in 19th-century California. The third of five children of Edward and Anita Sanchez Salas, Floyd Francis Salas was born on January 24, 1931, in Walsenburg, Colorado. Both his paternal and maternal ancestral lines trace back to Spanish explorers of the 16th century, including Francisco Vásquez de Coronado and Ponce de León. Floyd contracted whooping cough soon after his birth, which instead of making him weaker appeared to make him stronger, as he never had a typical childhood cold after his recovery. His father taught him to read comic strips when he was five years old. While in second grade at Ebert Elementary School in Denver, Colorado, the teachers noted Floyd's intelligence and developed an individual curriculum for him. Then the family moved to the Shasta Dam area in northern California in June 1939, and Floyd experienced the isolation of trying to fit into his new environment. He found solace in the many books and magazines in his home. However, having descended from a line of boxers, Floyd was not solely relegated to the solitude of a bookworm. He earned the respect and friendship of athletes by winning every schoolyard fight.

In 1943, Salas beloved mother died. Salas grew temporarily blind in one eye after his mother's death. His older brothers left to fight in World War II, and the Salas family fell apart. He attended six high schools and was arrested five times for fighting. Eventually, Salas found work at the Oakland Public Library at age 15 and allowed literature to reform the broken pieces of his life. He married Velva Daryl Harris in 1949. The couple had one son, Gregory Francis, and divorced in 1970. Salas attended the California College of Arts and Crafts (1950–54) and Oakland Junior College (1955–56). In 1956, his cousin introduced Salas to the boxing coach at the University of California–Berkeley. Impressed by Salas, the coach awarded him the first boxing scholarship to the university. Salas was awarded the Rockefeller Creative Scholarship at the Centro Mexicano de Escritores in Mexico City in 1958. Salas earned a B.A. in 1963 and an M.A. in 1965, both from the University of California–Berkeley. Throughout his college career, Salas dabbled in drugs and felt the constant pressure of police surveillance.

In 1966, Salas began his career as a teacher at San Francisco State University. He has since taught writing, English, or boxing at Peralta College for Non-Traditional Studies, the University of California–Berkeley, Foothill College, the University of San Francisco, and Sonoma State University.

Boxer and writer Floyd Salas founded the Oakland affiliate of the International Association of Poets, Playwrights, Editors, Essayists and Novelists (PEN). *(Photo of Floyd Salas is reprinted with permission from the publisher [APP Archive Files] [Houston: Arte Público Press— University of Houston, © 2006])*

Salas released his first novel, *Tattoo the Wicked Cross,* in 1967. This book about the harsh life within the juvenile detention system received mostly favorable reviews, although some critics felt the book was a bit excessive at times. *What Now My Love* (1970) is a short novel about hippies and the drug culture. *Lay My Body on the Line* (1978) explores student uprisings in San Francisco in the late 1960s. Salas married Virginia Ann Staley in 1979, but the couple divorced in 1981. During his writing career, a series of fellowships supplemented his income. Salas released *Buffalo Nickel* (1992), a

memoir; *State of Emergency* (1996), a novel; and a book of love poems entitled *Color of My Living Heart* (1996). Salas also contributed to *I Write What I Want* (1974), *Word Hustlers* (1976), *To Build a Fire* (1977), and *Stories and Poems from Close to Home* (1986). Salas began teaching novel writing in the M.A. program at the University of San Francisco in 1996, a post he currently holds. Salas is considered a prominent writer whose absolute conviction to the truth, emotions, and vibrancy is felt in all his works.

Further Reading

Heide, Rick, ed. *Under the Fifth Sun: Latino Literature from California.* Santa Clara and Berkeley, Calif.: Santa Clara University/Heyday Books, 2002.

Lomelí, Francisco A., and Carl R. Shirley, eds. *Dictionary of Literary Biography, Chicano Writers, First Series.* Vol. 82. Detroit: Gale Group, 1989, pp. 230–234.

Salas, Floyd. *Buffalo Nickel.* Houston, Tex.: Arte Público Press, 1992.

Salazar, Rubén
(1928–1970) *journalist, activist*

The most influential and prominent Latino journalist of his time, Rubén Salazar courageously took on corrupt authorities and systems with an unquenchable thirst to represent his people and create demands for social justice and reform. His untimely death at the Chicano Moratorium made him the quintessential martyr of the Chicano movement.

Rubén Salazar was born on March 3, 1928, in Juárez, Mexico, a border town across the Rio Grande from El Paso, Texas. The year after his birth, he moved with his parents, Luz Chávez and Salvador Salazar, to El Paso. He attended Lamar High School, gained U.S. citizenship in 1949, and entered the U.S. Army the following year. He served two years in the military.

Salazar earned a B.A. in journalism from Texas Western University (now the University of Texas–El Paso) in 1954. During his last two years at the university, he worked for E. M. Pooley at the *El Paso Herald-Post*. Pooley admired Salazar's writing and his inclination to seek out hard-hitting investigative reporting. Salazar and Pooley agreed Salazar should pose as a vagrant, go to jail, and record the conditions he found. Salazar's exposé based on his incarceration awoke the community to the deplorable sanitation and cruel treatment Mexican Americans received while imprisoned. After receiving his degree, Salazar worked at the *Press Democrat* for three years before accepting a reportorial position at the *San Francisco News*.

In 1959, Salazar joined the *Los Angeles Times*. After covering general assignments, Salazar noticed that he received more bylines when he wrote articles about the Mexican-American community. His rising esteem earned him a position as a foreign correspondent in the Dominican Republic, then Vietnam in 1965. Salazar grew anxious to spend time at home with his wife and their three children. He wanted to cover the growing tension mounting in the Chicano communities of Los Angeles. But after his stint in Vietnam, the *Times* sent him to Mexico City, where he served as the bureau chief for Central America, Mexico, and the Caribbean. He reported on the military slaughter of students in Mexico City.

Salazar returned to California in January 1969 and wrote a column covering the Chicano movement and Mexican-American communities of the Los Angeles area. His intelligent craftsmanship in writing articles scrutinized police brutality, exposed illegal procedures, and eventually incurred the wrath of the Los Angeles Police Department (LAPD). Late in 1969, Salazar accepted a position as news director at KMEX-TV, which he fulfilled concurrently with writing his *Times* column. He was reportedly under investigation by the LAPD and FBI, who both pressured Salazar to tone down his intense examination of their organizations.

On August 29, 1970, approximately 20,000 Latino men, women, and children marched six miles to Laguna Park in East Los Angeles. Known as the Chicano Moratorium, the marchers protested the Vietnam War and the disproportionate number of Latinos being killed on the front lines. Salazar was there with his crew to cover the events. The demonstration, which began peacefully, turned to panic and confusion. A few demonstrators threw rocks and bottles, and the police responded by attacking the entire crowd. While Salazar and his crew took a break in the Silver Dollar Bar, police officers stormed into the bar, claiming that they were looking for a murder suspect. The officials refused to allow anyone to leave. A policeman released a tear gas projectile that struck Salazar and killed him. Witnesses claimed the policeman's act was unwarranted, but the police were never charged with any wrongdoing in the incident.

Salazar's premature and suspicious death caused a major uproar in the Chicano community. The legendary folksinger-composer Lalo Guerrero commemorated Salazar with the *corrido* "El 29 de Agosto," which describes the events of the Chicano Moratorium and was quite effective in rallying the saddened and outraged Chicanos to unite with greater force and momentum. Salazar's tragic death became an instant symbol of police abuse and of the failure of the American justice system to provide Latinos with fair and equal treatment. An intelligent, level-headed, and articulate voice for social change and a hope for the future, Salazar was posthumously awarded a Robert F. Kennedy Journalism Award the year after his death. Salazar's legacy as an indomitable, relentless advocate for Mexican Americans' rights was further established when Laguna Park in Los Angeles was renamed Salazar Park and a library in Santa Rosa was also bestowed with his name.

Further Reading

Martínez, Al. *Rising Voices: Profiles of Hispano-American Lives.* New York: New American Library, 1974.

Meier, Matt S., Conchita Franco Serri, and Richard A. Garcia. *Notable Latino Americans: A Biographical Dictionary.* Westport, Conn.: Greenwood Press, 1997, pp. 345–347.

Salazar, Sally. "Rubén Salazar: The Man Not the Myth." *Press Democrat,* August 29, 1980, p. B, 6.

Sotomayor, Frank, and Magdalena Beltrán-del Olmo. *Frank del Olmo: Commentaries on His Times.* Los Angeles: *Los Angeles Times,* 2005.

Salinas, Luis Omar
(Omar Salinas)
(1937–   ) *poet, educator*

Luis Omar Salinas is best known for creating extraordinary imagery and for his collection of poems entitled *Crazy Gypsy.* The son of Olivia Treviño and Rosendo Valdez Salinas, Luis Omar Salinas was born on June 27, 1937, in Robstown, Texas. Shortly after his birth, the family moved to Monterrey, Mexico, where his father opened a grocery store. Tragically, his mother died of tuberculosis when Luis was four years old. His father returned with his children to Robstown and after a few months decided he was unable to raise his children alone. Luis's sister, Irma, moved to their aunt Anitas's home, and Luis went to live with his aunt and uncle Oralia and Alfredo Salinas, who lived in Texas and whom he would come to consider his parents. Luis moved with his new family to San Francisco, California, while in elementary school. They also lived in Fresno and in Bakersfield, California. Luis was a paperboy, a Boy Scout, and a member of his high school football and wrestling teams. He helped with his uncle's business and worked in the fields during the summer.

Salinas earned an associate's degree from Bakersfield Junior College in 1958. He moved to East Los Angles and studied literature and drama at California State College–Los Angeles. He suffered a mental breakdown, which delayed his education for a couple of years and besieged him through the 1960s, and returned to college in 1963. Two years later, he took a creative writing course from poet Henri Coulette, who was very impressed with the "literary sophistication of [Salinas's] surrealist poems" as quoted from an unpublished letter. Salinas transferred to California State College–Fresno and studied under Professors Philip Levine, Robert Mezey, and Peter Everwine. He taught Chicano studies at the university and found camaraderie with other Chicano poets, including LEONARD ADAME, GARY SOTO, Ernesto Trejo, and Jon Veinberg. Eventually, they were known as the Fresno School of Poets.

Salinas released his first collection of poems, *Crazy Gypsy,* in 1970 to critical and commercial acclaim, and Salinas was invited to read his poetry throughout the nation. Poems from this book are often anthologized for their unusual imagery and stark re-creation of loneliness and alienation. He compiled an anthology of Chicano writers under the title *From the Barrio* in 1973. Three years later, his poetry was collected in *Entrance: 4 Chicano Poets,* along with the works of Adame, Soto, and Trejo.

Salinas explored the polar extremes of emotion in his second collection of poems, *Afternoon of the Unreal* (1980). *Prelude to Darkness* (1981) is a collection of love poems with melodramatic overtures. *Darkness under the Tress/Walking behind the Spanish* (1982) is considered the finest collection of Salinas's work. Continuing with lyrical and vastly imaginative verses, Salinas released *The Sadness of Days: New and Selected Poems* (1987), *Follower of the Dusk* (Flume Chapbook series, 1991), *Sometimes Mysteriously* (1997), *Greatest Hits, 1969–1996* (Greatest Hits series, 2002), and *Elegy for Desire* (2005). Salinas is known as a sensitive, intuitive poet, and his work has been largely anthologized and given various awards.

Further Reading
Boyle, T. C., August Wilson, and Jay Parini. *American Writers: A Collection of Literary Biographies: Supplement VIII.* Detroit: Charles Scribner's Son, 2001.

Heide, Rick, ed. *Under the Fifth Sun: Latino Literature from California.* Santa Clara and Berkeley, Calif.: Santa Clara University/Heyday Books, 2002.

Lomelí, Francisco A., and Carl R. Shirley, eds. *Chicano Writers: First Series.* Vol. 82. Detroit: Gale Research, 1989, pp. 234–238.

Salinas, Maria Elena
(1954–   ) *journalist, nonfiction writer*

Perhaps the most well-known Hispanic female journalist, Maria Elena Salinas has won three Emmys in her two decades of commitment to informing the Hispanic population about news events on a local and international level. Maria Elena Salinas was born on December 30, 1954, in Los Angeles, California, the youngest of three girls of Maria de Luz and Jose Luis Cordero Salinas. When she was one year old, she moved with her family to Mexico City. When Maria was in the third grade, the family moved back to Los Angeles, settling in the South Central section of the city, which was a predominately African-American neighborhood. At St. Vincent's Elementary School, Maria was one of the only students who spoke Spanish. The complete immersion in American culture forced her to learn English quickly, which she was fortunately able to do.

Salinas was influenced by her mother's strong work ethic and ability to harmoniously integrate her role as a mother with her work as a seamstress. As a child, Maria dreamed of becoming a dancer or a fashion designer, the latter vocational desire a result of her mother and older sister's penchant for sewing. Another of Maria's dreams was to become a mother, a dream that would not be fulfilled until much later than she expected. At the age of 14, Maria began working in a sweatshop in the garment district. She gave much of her earnings to her parents to help pay the rent and fund her tuition at her high school. Salinas attended East Los Angeles College to study marketing and merchandising, concurrently working at the Metropolitan Theatre selling hot dogs. Through her industrious nature, she was quickly promoted to the ticket office. She also worked for Azteca Films, a film distributor, and lived a brief time in Mexico. When she won the Miss Mexico of Los Angeles beauty pageant, she decided to turn her attention to the beauty and fashion industry.

Salinas worked for a beauty school from 1977 to 1979 where Mexican-American women, particularly recent immigrants, could take lessons to build self-confidence. Salinas taught classes on culture, social etiquette, and beauty. Her work was quite successful, enabling her to open her own franchise, which she operated for nearly three years. During this time, she served as a master of ceremonies for several fund-raisers and cultural and community events. She entered the world of journalism through radio, working for Radio Express and Radio America.

In 1981, Salinas hosted a public affairs show for KMEX-34 television in Los Angeles. Despite her tenacity, Salinas grew so nervous prior to her first telecast that she contracted laryngitis for two weeks. Salinas approached her journalism career with the unremitting effort she gave to all her endeavors. In 1982, Salinas became a founding member of the National Association of Hispanic Journalists (NAHJ). She took classes on broadcast journalism at the University of California–Los Angeles to expand her knowledge. However, she did not graduate, a fact that would bother her for years to come. Her shyness crept into press conferences, preventing her from asking questions for one year. Eventually, Salinas overcame her initial timidity and began to cover the Hispanic community with her usual innate fervor. She hosted *Los Angeles Ahora* for KMEX, making a great impact on the local Mexican-American community by providing resource information for a variety of needs. Salinas took her responsibility to report the issues of Latinos quite seriously. Her efforts and dedication paid off in 1987, when she was promoted to anchor. Salinas became viscerally aware of the disenfranchisement felt by Hispanics when she attempted to report Mexican Americans' opinions on an upcoming election. Instead of finding informed citizens, she discovered many of the people were uninformed about the election and the candidates. From that point on, Salinas pioneered several efforts to encourage Latinos to vote and get U.S. citizenship. To this end, she works with the National Association of Latino Elected and Appointed Officials. Salinas has also been quite instrumental in education. She has worked with the U.S. Departments of Health and Education on issues ranging from the importance of immunization for young children, to the risks of heart disease, as well as parental involvement in education. Her commitment to education led her to establish the Maria Elena Salinas Scholarship for Excellence in Spanish-language News, which is administered by the NAHJ and awards two $5,000 scholarships to promising journalism students.

In 1991, Salinas married Eliott Rodriguez, a news anchor for WFOR-TV (CBS 4) in Miami, with whom she has had two daughters, Julia Alexandra and Gabriela Maria. Although Salinas wanted to be like her mother, in retrospect she found that she had actually acquired many of her father's characteristics. After his death on August 6, 1985, she discovered he had once been a Catholic priest. His social agenda and dedication to serve humankind had seeped into her consciousness and provided a guiding force for her work in journalism and many of her endeavors. She wrote about the process of this discovery in *Yo soy la hija de mi padre: una vida sin secretos/I Am My Father's Daughter: Living a Life Without Secrets* (2006).

In addition to three Emmys, Salinas has been honored as the Journalist of the Year by Hispanic Media 100 and received the first International Scholar award from Emory University's Goizueta Business School, which also named her a distinguished dean's speaker. Other recognition has come in the form of a Striving for Excellence Award and Lifetime Achievement Award from the Broadcasting Training Program, the Superior Achievement Award from the National Association

Anchor for Univision and syndicated news columnist Maria Elena Salinas is one of the most recognized and awarded Hispanic broadcast journalists. *(Univision)*

of Hispanic Publications, a Lifetime Achievement Award from the California Chicano News Media Association, and the Gift of Hope Award from the Women's Hope Fund. Throughout the years, Salinas has interviewed more world leaders, dictators, and political figures than any other female journalist. Currently, Salinas cohosts *Aquí y Ahora* and writes a syndicated bilingual column for Univision that is widely distributed through King's Feature syndication.

Further Reading

Castellón, Eduardo, ed. "Maria Elena Salinas: She Gives Voice to Those Without a Voice."

Eco-Latino, March 2003. Available online. URL: http://www.ecolatino.com/en/stories/030103/new_mesalinasengrljh.shtml. Downloaded on April 28, 2006.

Mendoza, Sylvia. *The Book of Latina Women: 150 Vidas of Passion, Strength, and Success.* Avon, Mass.: Adams Media, 2004.

Salinas, Maria Elena, with Liz Balmaseda. *Yo Soy la Hija de Mi Padre: Una Vida Sin Secretos/I Am My Father's Daughter: Living a Life Without Secrets.* New York: Rayo, 2005.

Savio, Anita. "Forget the Pope and Sub-Comandante Marcos, the real story is Maria Elena Salinas Miami, Florida—television reporter and journalist— Entrevista." *Latino Leaders: The National Magazine of the Successful American Latino* (February/March 2002): 46–50.

Sanchez, Marcela
(Ana Marcela Sanchez)
(1967–) *journalist*

Marcela Sanchez covers Washington, D.C., with an eye on Latin America in her bilingual weekly column *Desde Washington.* Her reporting keeps issues that affect Latin Americans at the forefront of the minds of *Washington Post* readers.

Ana Marcela Sanchez was born on January 30, 1967, in Bogotá, Colombia. Her parents, Julio and Inés Fonseca Sánchez, were music enthusiasts and wrote about music trends and its impact. The power of words, whether in song or literature, inspired Sanchez. Her mother, who was university educated and a source of strength and inspiration, often read to Sanchez and her older brother. Sanchez loved to read, regularly accessing her parent's rich library for books on a variety of subjects. Her exposure to literary diversity combined with an innate ability to recognize the value in opposing sides of an issue made Sanchez an excellent mediator. From an early age, she believed a clearer understanding of disparate points of view was crucial to solving problems, both big and small. At 13 years old, she had a flash

of understanding that her moderator skills would best be put to use as a journalist.

For Sanchez, the English language was the doorway to reporting issues of importance to a wider audience with greater impact. Through a Rotary Club program, she lived for one year in New York City as a high school exchange student. When she came to the United States, she did not speak a word of English. Sanchez joined the high school paper and immediately began testing her ability to translate the written word from Spanish to English. She applied to American universities, and although she was accepted to a few, her parents could not afford the tuition. Financial aid was difficult to come by for foreign students. Sanchez therefore returned to her native country. She studied journalism at Externado University in Bogotá, graduating in 1989 with a B.A. As journalism was a new subject in Colombia, Sanchez and her parents felt she would get a more comprehensive education in the United States. They found a way to support Sanchez, and she was able to return to the United States and study at the University of North Dakota. She received an M.A. with a major in communications and a minor in economics in 1993. While at North Dakota, she met her future husband, Philip Bender, whom she married in 1996.

At that time, the U.S. government allowed foreign students a one-year visa following graduation. Sanchez needed to secure a position that would begin her career as a Latin American correspondent in the United States within that period. She had written two articles in English for the *Grand Forks Herald* while in school. She needed clips written in Spanish to prove she was capable of being a bilingual writer. In 1993, Sanchez and Bender moved to Washington, D.C., where Sanchez joined *El Tiempo Latino,* the largest Spanish weekly in the Washington metropolitan area. She began as a staff writer, serving in this capacity until she became an assistant editor and in 1996 the foreign correspondent for Colombia. Sanchez began to diversify her writing, working for many companies concurrently. From 1994 to 1998, Sanchez served as the Washington correspondent for *El Tiempo,* a major daily newspaper in Colombia. From 1997 to 1999, she contributed to the Colombia television newscasts *En Vivo* and *QAP.* The famous Colombian writer Gabriel García Márquez began *QAP* as an outlet to report issues typically repressed by most Colombian broadcasters. In 1999, the Colombian government closed down the station, presenting Sanchez with her first encounter with censorship.

Sanchez also joined the *Washington Post* in 1997. She continued covering foreign affairs, writing for *El Espectador,* another Colombia daily, from 1998 to 2000. Sanchez started her column *Desde Washington* in 2000. She currently reports from the White House, Capitol Hill, the State Department, the Pentagon, and the government's multilateral organizations. Sanchez commented in a 2005 interview, "There is so much more to Washington than right or wrong, good or bad. Decisions are often made for reasons that are not immediately apparent to outsiders. It's my hope to explain the gray areas and offer insight that gives my readers a subtler understanding of this town."

When she speaks in journalism classes, she encourages others to stay persistent and not expect instant gratification. Sanchez has had a clear vision since an early age. She has accomplished her goal of representing both sides of an issue. However, now her work is on a larger scale, reminding Americans of their neighbors south of the Rio Grande. Sanchez continues to allow her mediator skills to guide her writing. She said in a 2005 interview that she sees herself "more as a Latin American journalist covering Washington then as a Washington journalist covering Latin American affairs." Sanchez commented in a 2005 interview, "I offer a pan-Latin perspective that draws from my experience of covering Washington first as a Latin American correspondent and now as a reporter at the *Washington Post.*" Sanchez is an essential voice creating a bridge of understanding between the United States and Latin America.

Further Reading

Washington Post Readers Group. "Marcela Sanchez." Available online. URL: http://www.postwritersgroup.com/sanchez.htm. Downloaded on March 28, 2005.

Sanchez, Marcela. "Immigration Is Not the Only Problem." *Washington Post,* May 26, 2005.

———. "Judiciaries Gone Wild." *Washington Post,* April 14, 2005.

Sánchez, Ricardo
(1941–1995) *poet, essayist, short story writer, screenwriter*

Ricardo Sánchez gained prominence as an inspirational poet during the Chicano movement, a time of grassroots activism that inspired a cultural and literary explosion and demanded social reform. Ricardo Sánchez, the youngest of 13 children of Pedro Lucero and Adelina Gallegos Sánchez, was born on March 29, 1941, in El Paso, Texas. He grew up in a rough area of El Paso known as Barrio del Diablo (Devil's Neighborhood). As a child, he experienced racism and few opportunities that inspired him. He dropped out of high school, joined the army for a brief time, and served two imprisonments (paroled in 1963 and again in 1969). He married Maria Teresa Silva on November 28, 1964, with whom he would have four children. Upon release from prison, he gained his high school equivalency in 1969. Sánchez opened Mictla Publications in 1971 and released his first book, *Obras* (Works). In it, Sánchez offers strong images of barrio life in a stream-of-consciousness style with verse and prose in English, Spanish, and Chicano barrio and prison slang. That same year, he contributed to and coedited with Abelardo Delgado *Los cuatro* (The four) and wrote *Canto y grito mi liberacion/The Liberatión of a Chicano Mind* and *Mano a mano* (Hand to hand).

Sánchez became involved with academics at the University of Texas–El Paso in 1971. He served as a consultant, writer, lecturer, or instructor at a number of universities and community colleges in Massachusetts, Texas, New Mexico, Wisconsin, Utah, and Washington. Sponsored by Ford Foundation grants, Sánchez earned a Ph.D. in American studies and cultural linguistic theory at Union Graduate School in Yellow Springs, Ohio, in 1974. He released *Hechizospells: Poetry/Stories/Vignettes/Articles/ Notes on the Human Condition of Chicanos & Pícaros, Words & Hopes within Soulmind* in 1976. He spent the 1977 scholastic year as visiting professor and lecturer for the Spanish-Speaking Outreach Institute at the University of Wisconsin, Milwaukee. *Milhuas Blues and Gritos Norteños* (1980) is a result of his time spent in Milwaukee. In September 1978, Sánchez attended the One World Poetry Festival in Amsterdam, Netherlands, an international event drawing poets from all continents. *Amsterdam cantos y poemas pistos* (Amsterdam songs and drunken poems) of 1983 records through detailed poetry the preparations, impressions, impact, and aftermath of the event. He also wrote a screenplay, *Entelequia,* which was directed by Juan Salazar in 1979.

Sánchez spent the 1980s and 1990s in various positions serving local communities and ensuring education on health, Chicano culture, and literature, including founding and managing the Poets of Tejas Reading Series and Paperbacks y Mas, directing Poetry Tejas International, and founding the Canto al Pueblo (Chant to the People) festivals. His writings after his visit to Amsterdam are marked with more maturity and less violent imagery. He released *Brown Bear and Honey Madnesses: Alaskan Cruising Poems* (1982), *Selected Poems* (1985), *Eagle-Visioned—Feathered Adobes: Poems* (1990), and *American Journeys: Jornadas americanas* (1994). Although Sánchez's writing had mellowed, he still wrote in a spontaneous, unrepentant, sometimes forceful voice. He gave lectures and read his work across the nation, invigorating his audiences. Sánchez died of cancer on September 3, 1995, in El Paso. *The Loves of Ricardo,* a collection of poetry, was released posthumously in 1997.

Further Reading

Bruce-Novoa, Juan. "A Voice Against Silence: Ricardo Sánchez." In *Chicano Poetry: A Response to Chaos.* Austin: University of Texas Press, 1982, pp. 151–159.

Candelaria, Cordelia. "Abelardo Delgado and Ricardo Sánchez." In *Chicano Poetry: A Critical Introduction.* Westport, Conn.: Greenwood Press, 1984, pp. 50–58.

Dr Ricardo Sánchez Web site. Available online. URL: http://www.dr-ricardo-sanchez.com.

Lopez, Miguel R. *Chicano Timespace: The Poetry and Politics of Ricardo Sánchez.* College Station: Texas A & M University Press, 2000.

Santiago, Esmeralda
(1948–) *memoirist, screenwriter, novelist, editor*

Esmeralda Santiago is a brilliant writer most celebrated for her debut book and coming-of-age memoir, *When I Was Puerto Rican.* Her candid portrayal of life for an immigrant is laced with humor, honesty, and humanity.

The eldest child of Pablo Santiago Diaz, a poet and carpenter, and Ramona Santiago, a factory worker, Esmeralda Santiago was born May 17, 1948, in Villa Palmeras, Santurce, Puerto Rico. Her father vacillated in and out of his family's home, often leaving Esmeralda, her siblings, and their mother unprotected and without provisions. Esmeralda constantly moved throughout her childhood, forcing her to define herself from a place within, rather than an external place called home. She enjoyed the time she spent in the country village of Macún and disliked the time she spent in the city of San Juan, the capital of Puerto Rico. Her mother finally decided to leave her common-law husband (they were never officially married) and move with her children, of which there were eventually 11, to New York City.

The transition and acculturation to the United States proved difficult for Santiago. She was 13 years old when the family moved to New York and immediately discovered the box created for persons of Latin heritage. When document forms and Americans labeled Santiago Hispanic she began to feel the loss of her Puerto Ricanness. In an attempt to fit in, Esmeralda devoured the English language so quickly she was able to translate for her mother and other neighbors who could speak only Spanish. Within two years, she was admitted into New York City's Performing Arts High School, where she majored in drama and dance. She left her mother's home when she was 21 and began a love affair with a domineering Turkish man far older than herself. During this time, she sporadically attended community colleges. She gained a full scholarship to Harvard University and thus began the long trek back to herself and self-confidence that would allow her to leave her abusive boyfriend. Upon graduating from Harvard University with a B.A. in film production, magna cum laude, in 1976, Santiago returned to Puerto Rico.

Santiago stayed only a brief time in Puerto Rico. She soon discovered that she no longer belonged in Puerto Rico, any more than she could seamlessly fit into American culture. She is often quoted for her observation, "My Spanish was rusty, my gaze too direct, my personality too assertive for a Puerto Rican woman." Santiago returned to New York City, where she met Frank Cantor. Together they started Cantomedia, a documentary film and media production company, in 1977, which they continue to operate. They were married the following year and eventually had two children. Santiago wrote documentary and educational scripts for their company. She took a writing course from Martin Robbins, whose encouragement led Santiago to write essays that were eventually printed by the *Christian Science Monitor, Boston Globe,* and *New York Times.* Santiago earned an M.F.A. in fiction from Sarah Lawrence College in 1992.

Merloyd Lawrence, an editor who had her own imprint at Addison-Wesley, now owned by Pearson Education, discovered a personal essay written by Santiago in the *Radcliffe Quarterly.* Lawrence reviewed Santiago's other writings and asked her to write a memoir. *When I Was Puerto Rican* (1993) captures Santiago's childhood in Puerto Rico in 15 chapters or vignettes. The author effectively uses metaphors such as a guava to describe her nostalgia for a lost homeland. She also incorporates Spanish and English to help the reader understand the space between two worlds, which can either be the United States and Puerto Rico, the wealthy and the poor, or man and woman.

Defining identity continued as a theme in her first novel, *América's Dream* (1996). In this work, Santiago draws on stories she heard from Spanish-speaking nannies at New York parks where she took her children. Santiago's protagonist yearns to rise above her station and get out from underneath the oppressive patriarchal rules her husband demands. *Almost a Woman* (1998) builds on Santiago's first memoir to recount her adaptation to American society. The book received such high levels of critical and public acclaim that Santiago adapted it into a screenplay for PBS's *Masterpiece Theatre.* The show, which aired in 2001, was awarded a George Foster Peabody Award for excellence in broadcasting. Santiago collaborated with Joie Davidow in the collections *Las Christmas: Favorite Latino Authors Share Their Holiday Memories* (1998) and *Las Mamis: Favorite Latino Authors Remember Their Mothers* (2000).

Santiago's third memoir, *The Turkish Lover* (2004), deals directly with the hollow life she led while entangled with her controlling Turkish boyfriend and her struggle for liberation. Her books have been translated into Spanish. It was selected a BookSense recommendation for September 2004 and appeared on several best of 2004 lists. Santiago released her first children's book in 2005 under the title *A Doll for Navidades.* In addition to her many awards and literary credits, Santiago is active in community-based programs for adolescents and was one of the founders of a shelter for battered women and their children. She promotes literature, the arts, and libraries. Her community activism was cited when she received a Girl

Scouts of America National Woman of Distinction Award in March 2002. Santiago has earned honorary doctors of letters from Trinity University, Pace University, and Metropolitan College.

Further Reading

Esmeralda Sanchez Web site. Available online. URL: http://www:esmeraldasantiago.com.

Hernandez, Carmen. *Puerto Rican Voices in English: Interviews with Writers*. Westport, Conn. 1997, pp. 157–169.

Puleo, Gus. "Dance Between Two Cultures: Latino Caribbean Literature Written in the United States." *Hispanic Review* 67 (1999): 407–411.

West-Durán, Alan. *Latino and Latina Writers, Volume II*. Detroit: Gale-Thomas, 2004, pp. 985–1002.

Serrano, Nina

(1934–) *poet, filmmaker, educator, activist*

Nina Serrano created support networks for the Chicano literary community within the Chicano movement. She is a founding member of Third World Communications and the activist group Pocho Che Collective (later known as the San Francisco Mission Poets).

Nina Serrano was born on September 1, 1934, in the Bronx, New York. Her father, a Colombian emigrant, and her eastern European mother worked long hours in restaurants and cafeterias in Manhattan. They often put Nina under the care of their friend Augustín Polo Arroyo, whom young Nina often called Uncle Paul. Uncle Paul mainly spoke Spanish and introduced Nina to the world of art. He took her to see ballet, opera, vaudeville, museums, and theater. Since the bulk of her conversational ability was in Spanish, school authorities placed Nina in speech-correction classes to eliminate her accent. At the age of 14, Nina Serrano entered a public school for performing arts, where she studied theater.

After graduating from high school, Serrano looked for work on Broadway to no avail. She married in 1953 and accompanied her husband to the University of Wisconsin. Two years later, she gave birth to a son, Greg, and enrolled at the University of Wisconsin to study speech and drama. While there, she became involved in the Civil Rights and peace movements and served as president for the Student Peace Union. As part of her presidency, she visited England, Russia, and China and was also able to study theater while abroad. Her daughter, Valerie, was born in 1958. Serrano visited Cuba and Mexico and was devastated by the poverty she witnessed, which completely negated the picturesque stories she had been told. Spurred to introduce the Midwest town of Madison, Wisconsin, to other cultures, Serrano began working in an experimental school where she introduced multicultural magazines.

Ready for a different lifestyle, Serrano and her family moved to San Francisco, California, in 1961. She produced children's programs at KPFA, served as the director for a San Francisco mime group, and also became involved with European repertory drama. Serrano traveled extensively, visiting Cuba, Chile, Mexico, Uruguay, Guatemala, Puerto Rico, and Nicaragua. She experimented with filmmaking and playwriting. In 1972, Serrano became actively involved with the Chicano movement. She worked for a bilingual radio station, produced *Reflecciones de Raza* (Race reflections), and later created a wealth of television programs, including a Latin-American history program on KPSA in Berkeley. She was a contributing editor to *Tin-Tan,* a short-lived quarterly published by Editorial Pocho-Che.

In 1980, Serrano published *Heart Songs: The Collected Poems of Nina Serrano (1969–1979).* Serrano's poetry highlighted her higher ambitions for the Chicano movement. Rather than primarily focusing on lifting the oppression of one people, she believed that "the Chicano Movement embodies in it the need for world peace, cultural exchange, and understanding, as well as the burning desire for a more just and democratic society." She wrote the screenplay, *La ofrenda: Days of the*

Dead, which was produced in 1986. She continues to write poetry.

Further Reading

Harvey, Nick, ed. *Mark in Time, Portraits and Poetry/ San Francisco.* San Francisco: Glide, 1971, p. 107.

Heide, Rick, ed. *Under the Fifth Sun: Latino Literature from California.* Santa Clara and Berkeley, Calif.: Santa Clara University/Heyday Books, 2002.

Lomelí, Francisco A., and Carl R. Shirley, eds. *Chicano Writers: Second Series.* Vol. 122. Detroit: Gale Research, 1999, pp. 255–259.

Serrano, Nina. *Heart Songs: The Collected Poems of Nina Serrano (1969–1979).* San Francisco: Pocho-Che, 1980.

Serros, Michele
(Michele Marie Serros)
(1966-   ) *poet, short story writer, young adult writer, children's writer, television writer*

Hailed by *Newsweek* in 2001 as "one of the top young women to watch for in the new century," Michele Serros burst on the literary scene with the refreshingly hip *Chicana Falsa: And Other Stories of Death, Identity, and Oxnard.* This collection of poetry and short stories is now required reading in many high school and Chicano and Latin-American studies departments at major universities across the country. Frequently anthologized, her natural wit and poignant observations have earned Serros a long-standing position in the annals of Latino literature.

Michele Marie Serros is the second child of Beatrice Ruiz Serros and George Serros, her primary role models. A fourth-generation Californian, Serros was born in Oxnard, California, on February 10, 1966. Michele's parents divorced when she was 11—at the time a source of embarrassment and confusion for her. Not knowing where else to turn, Michele wrote to her favorite author, Judy Blume, for answers to her questions and relief from her pain. Blume suggested she use writing as an outlet

for her emotions. Serros remains a devoted diarist and has kept every one she has written since she was a preteen. Daily writing became quite therapeutic as a means to express feelings that bubbled inside—oftentimes curing the stomachaches caused by her repressed emotions. When she had problems getting her writing published, her sister suggested she could change her name to Michael Hill (a male and Anglo twist on the original) to become more accepted, but assimilation would not fit the bill.

Serros kept her name and brazenly read her poetry, three poems to be exact, at coffeehouses or anywhere she could. She went to school at Santa Monica College and worked part time at a frame shop. In 1991, Serros's mother became quite ill and fell into a coma. During a brief remission, Serros was granted a beautiful inspiring interlude with her mother before Beatrice fell back into a coma. A few days later, her mother died, creating a void in the 25-year-old Serros.

To earn the school credits she needed, Serros went abroad for additional studies, a total immersion in Mexican culture, and to learn Spanish. Through ironic twists and with sharp humor, she turned her experiences into inspiration for her short stories. In 1993, she returned home and soon afterward was asked to help out at a Chicana writers' conference, where she thought she was being invited to share her poetry. Much to her chagrin, Serros discovered they wanted her to serve brunch. Serros conveyed her displeasure, and the organizer quickly offered Serros the prospect of reading her poetry at an open mike reading. The incident invoked such passion in Serros that during her reading she spoke with vulnerable ardor and furor, an emotion and bravado that caught the attention of a publisher who asked her if she had committed her poetry to a book. She had not, but that was not going to stop her.

Serros went to work polishing her poems and stories into a book she called *Chicana Falsa: And Other Stories of Death, Identity, and Oxnard.* Lalo Press picked up the book for publication but soon went bankrupt and became unable to market,

Michele Serros is known for her sardonic and witty writing. *(Marie Gregorio-Oviedo)*

distribute, or sell it. Serros reacted by using her books as furniture until she got the nerve to sell them wherever she could. She ran into problems selling them without an ISBN until Sisterhood Bookstore in Westwood, California, initiated her first real order—for 15 books.

A year later, Serros was invited to be a road poet, touring nationally with Lollapalooza, reading her work to stadium crowds of 25,000. Her creative talents were put to use when she created a sock puppet of sorts, doused it in nostalgic 1980s and 1990s teen perfume, and called it "Grunge on a Stick." The quirky little item quickly became an underground best seller.

In 1997, Serros released selected stories from *Chicana Falsa* as a spoken word CD. She had sold thousands of books on her own, and after three years, her efforts to promote and sell her book paid off. Riverhead Books published *Chicana Falsa* in 1998, and it became an instant

hit. Her poetry was selected to appear on buses in New York City. She had not yet completed her degree in Chicana/o studies when professors began using *Chicana Falsa* in classrooms at the University of California–Los Angeles. Serros was on her way; "A young sassy writer whose brilliant weapon is her humor," as described by SANDRA CISNEROS.

Serros's work is a window into a life caught between two cultures, a blend of the old and the new. Serros merely expresses her experience with as much insight and humor as possible. She commented in a 2005 interview, "I like any poems that use natural, raw language and that you can tell the poet is taking a risk of 'exposing' her/himself. I find that very courageous." Serros's latest collection of fiction, *How to Be a Chicana Role Model,* was published in July 2000 and was on the *Los Angeles Times's* best-seller list.

Serros moved to New York City and began to work as a commentator for National Public Radio (*Morning Edition, Weekend All Things Considered*). She has been a featured contributor to the *Los Angeles Times'* children's fiction section. Serros spent 2002 living in Los Angeles and writing for the ABC television sitcom *The George Lopez Show.* "An opportunity," she said, "that hopefully with my contribution opens the door for a wider representation of Latinos in the mass media."

Serros captures and crafts 1970s and 1980s pop culture with the ethnic disparities of growing up Chicana in southern California in her poetry, short stories, journalism, and books. She has spoken at more than 35 universities, including some of the most prestigious in the country, and at more than 30 organizations in promotion of literacy, Latin-American pride, and women empowerment. Currently living in New York City, Serros released *Honey Blond Chica,* a young adult novel in 2006 and continues to speak at high schools, correctional facilities, and universities across the country.

Further Reading

Heide, Rick, ed. *Under the Fifth Sun: Latino Literature from California.* Santa Clara and Berkeley, Calif.: Santa Clara University/Heyday Books, 2002.

Serros, Michele. *How to Be a Chicana Role Model.* New York: Riverhead Books, 2000.

Stavans, Ilan. *Wáchale! Poetry and Prose about Growing Up Latino in America.* Peru, Ill.: Cricket Books, 2001.

Soto, Gary

(1952–   ) *poet, essayist, young adult writer, children's book writer, short story writer, playwright, biographer*

Raw and provocative, Gary Soto's poems have enthralled thousands of readers, won many awards, and given the world insight into the pain of loneliness and separation. Soto's writing talents began with poetry and over the years have extended to more than 30 acclaimed short stories, biographies, essays, young adult novels, picture books, and plays.

Gary Soto was born into poverty on April 12, 1952, to Manuel and Angie (Treviño) Soto. Born and raised in Fresno, California, where redlining kept his family confined to Mexican-American neighborhoods, he did not expect much from life. His grandparents had emigrated from Mexico, and his parents were day laborers on the farms of the San Joaquin Valley or factory workers when the crops had been harvested. When Gary was five years old, his father was killed in a roofing accident. Eventually, his mother remarried. However, that did little to change their economic status. Much of his family spoke Spanish though Soto was not formally taught the language, and they did not prize education or reading. He learned discipline through a school military club called the Cadets. Soto recalled in a 1995 issue of *Ploughshares,* a literary journal, the grim realities of his childhood: "one of the aspirations was that if we stayed out of

prison, we would be fine. As long as we did that, there was a reason to be proud."

After graduating from high school in 1970, Soto enrolled in Fresno State College, majoring in geography, mainly to avoid the draft for the Vietnam War. He happened upon an anthology, *The New American Poetry,* edited by Donald Allen, and became hooked by Edward Field's poem "Unwanted." In this poem, Soto discovered his feelings of alienation not only were felt by him or Mexican Americans but could be called a "human pain," something universal. He transferred to California State University–Fresno, studied poetry in earnest under the tutelage of poet Philip Levine, and began to get excellent grades. He fell in with fellow poets LEONARD ADAME, LUIS OMAR SALINAS, Ernesto Trejo, and Jon Veinberg. Eventually they became known as the Fresno School of Poets. Soto graduated magna cum laude in 1974 with a degree in English. A year out of school, he married Japanese-American Carolyn Sadako Oda, his college sweetheart, who continues to support and inspire Soto's writing.

At a time when his fellow Latinos addressed the Chicano movement and other contemporary political issues, Soto turned his focus inward. By exploring the depths of his feelings, the unrequited desires of his youth, violence, and poverty, he found that he could touch a chord in his readers and thereby make the connection he longed for. His technique proved to be a well-rewarded tactic. In 1975, Soto was awarded the Academy of American Poets Prize and the *Discovery*-Nation Award, and in 1976, he received the United States Award of the International Poetry Forum and the University of California–Irvine's Chicano Contest Literary Prize. That same year, Soto earned an M.F.A. in creative writing from the University of California–Irvine, was honored as graduate student of the year in humanities, and served as a visiting writer at San Diego State University.

Soto released his first book of poems, *The Elements of San Joaquin,* in 1977. This collection of poems, which paints a bleak picture of migrant life, was well received by critics. The same year, Soto took a teaching position at the University of California–Berkeley in the English department and was awarded the Bess Hokin Prize from *Poetry* magazine. He received a Guggenheim Fellowship in 1979 and spent the year in Mexico writing. His poetry has been published in several well-respected journals and literary magazines, such *The Nation, Ploughshares,* the *Iowa Review, Poetry,* and the *New Yorker.* Soto found a powerful voice with his writing and began to generate a steady stream of books, including *The Tale of Sunlight* (1978), *Father Is a Pillow Tied to a Balloon* (1980), and *Where Sparrows Work Hard* (1981).

During the 1980s, Soto published three books of essays, self-labeled "narrative recollections": *Living Up the Street, Small Faces,* and *Lesser Evils: Ten Quartets.* Writing prose gave Soto a sense of freedom. "I felt I could be louder, more direct, also sloppier, whereas with poetry, I believed you had to control your statement, not be so obvious," Soto commented in *Ploughshares.* Within his prose collections, Soto gained an objective perspective on his childhood, enabling him to find humor and joy amid the hardships of growing up in the barrio. He released another collection of poetry, *Who Will Know Us? New Poems,* in 1985.

As his audience grew, Soto began to receive fan letters from Mexican-American teenagers, which inspired him to write children's and young adult books. In 1990, he released *Baseball in April,* which won the Beatty Award and was recognized as one of the American Library Association's "Best Book for Young Adults." He then released another young adult book, *A Summer Life* (1991); a collection of poetry for young readers, *Neighborhood Odes* (1992); and a short story collection for young adults, *Local News* (1993). He retired from teaching in 1993 to devote himself to writing full time. Soto published a young adult novel, *Jesse* (1994), and *New & Selected Poems* and *Canto familiar* (both in 1995) before trying a new venture. His first picture book, *Too Many Tamales* (1996), received a starred

review from *Booklist* and was hailed by the magazine as "a joyful success."

He continues to write every day, adding to his list of published works in a wide variety of genres. His picture books include *Chato's Kitchen* (1997), *Snapshots from a Wedding* (1998), *Old Man and His Door* (1998), *Chato and the Party Animals* (2000), and *If the Shoe Fits* (2002). The books Soto has written for middle school readers are *The Cat's Meow* (1997), *The Skirt* (1997), and *Marisol* (2004), the latter of which is part of the American Girl series. Marisol is also offered as a doll, the first Mexican-American doll sold by American Girl. As a playwright, Soto released *Novio Boy: A Play* in 1997 and *Nerdlandia: A Play* in 1999. *Junior College* (1997), *Poetry Lover* (2001), *Fearless Fernie* (2002), *One Kind of Faith* (2003), and *World's Apart: Traveling with Fernie and Me* (2005) are all poetry books that continue to reveal Soto's sharp, sardonic wit. *Buried Onions* (1997) was a highly successful young adult novel, followed by the young adult novels *Nickel and Dimes* (2000) and *The Afterlife* (2003), a *Buried Onion* sequel. In 1998, Soto published *Petty Crimes,* a short story collection. He followed with three novels for readers ages eight to 14: *Pacific Crossing* (1999), *Taking Sides* (2003), and *Crazy Weekend* (2003). Soto released a book of essays entitled *The Effects of Knut Hamson on a Fresno Boy* in 2000. A strong believer in and supporter of the United Farmworkers Union, Soto published two biographies about the organization's leaders, *Jesse de la Cruz: A Profile of a United Farm Worker* (2002) and *César Chávez: A Hero for Everyone* (2005). He has also produced three short films for Mexican-American children.

As many writers do, Soto has been known to wonder about the quality of his writing. Soto recalled in the *Ploughshare* article printed in spring 1995 a game he would often play with his wife, Carolyn: "I would be working on a book of poems, and I'd say to her, 'Do you like this?' and she would nod her head. I would decide, more or less, which poems to save by how many nods she gave me. But I'd be so nervous, waiting for her reaction.

I'd think, 'Oh my God, maybe I'm a fraud, maybe this woman's going to call the Bureau of Consumer Fraud on me.' I have to keep reminding myself that after all these books over all these years, I must be doing something right."

Indeed, his writings have amassed an extraordinary audience, with well over half a million copies of his books sold. In addition to receiving fellowships from the Guggenheim Foundation, the National Endowment for the Arts, and the California Arts Council, Soto is the recipient of the American Book Award from the Before Columbus Foundation, the Andrew Carnegie Medal from the American Library Association, the PEN Center West Award, and the Levinson Award for Poetry.

Further Reading

D'Evelyn, Tom. "Soto's Poetry: Unpretentious Language of the Heart." *Christian Science Monitor* 77 (March 6, 1985): 19–20.

Kristovic, Jelena, ed. *Hispanic Literature Criticism.* Detroit: Gale Research, 1994.

Novas, Himilce. *The Hispanic 100: A Ranking of the Latino Men and Women Who Have Most Influenced American Thought and Culture.* New York: Citadel Press, 1995.

Tardiff, Joseph C., and L. Mpho Mabunda, eds. *Dictionary of Hispanic Biography.* Detroit: Gale Research, 1996, pp. 865–867.

Torres, Hector. "Gary Soto: Overview." In *Reference Guide to American Literature.* 3d ed. Edited by Jim Kamp. Detroit: St. James Press, 1994.

West-Durán, Alan. *Latino and Latina Writers, Volume I.* Detroit: Gale-Thomas, 2004, pp. 475–490.

Sotomayor, Frank O.
(Frank Ortega Sotomayor)
(1943–   ) *journalist*

Award-winning journalist Frank O. Sotomayor has been at the forefront of efforts to bring greater ethnic diversity to the nation's print media. Sotomayor was instrumental in the development of the California Chicano News Media Association (CCNMA), the National Association of Hispanic Journalists (NAHJ), the Institute for Journalistic Education, and the Minority Editorial Training Program (METPRO)—organizations with different missions yet a common goal of encouraging and supporting the complete and accurate representation of minorities in America's media.

Born and raised in the Hollywood barrio, a low-income neighborhood of Tucson, Arizona, Frank Ortega Sotomayor was surrounded by a loving family. The youngest of five children, he was born on May 20, 1943, to Amelia Ortega, a homemaker, and Florencio Sotomayor, a hotel gardener. Sotomayor's parents stressed the importance of a good education. He excelled in his studies at his predominately Mexican-American schools and was perceived as a student leader by his peers, teachers, and principals.

Sotomayor dreamed of becoming a professional athlete but lacked the necessary skills. Instead, he would become a journalist, initially specializing in sports. As a 10th grader, he wrote a book report that garnered the attention of one of his teachers, who encouraged Sotomayor to write for the high school paper. He did so and immediately found he possessed talent and a penchant for the reporting, discovery, and challenge of writing inherent in journalism. He was particularly fond of the idea that many people would read his words and that he could perhaps influence policies and perceptions. He began work at age 17 for the *Arizona Daily Star* in Tucson as a sports reporter and copy editor.

Continuing to live at home, he studied journalism and served as an editor for his college paper at the University of Arizona. There, Sotomayor met and fell in love with Meri Finnerty, a fellow journalism student. He was named outstanding male graduate in 1966 and reported that summer from Peru for U.S. papers. He earned an M.A. in communications from Stanford University the following year, where he and other Chicano students helped to begin a recruiting effort to boost the enrollment of Latinos. In summer 1968, Soto-mayor and Finnerty married.

After being drafted into the U.S. Army, Soto-mayor worked as a news editor and reporter at the military newspaper *Pacific Stars and Stripes* in Tokyo, Japan. In 1970, Sotomayor began his *L.A. Times* career as a foreign desk editor. Two years later, he assisted in the incorporation of the nation's first minority journalist organization, the CCMNA, with *Times* colleague FRANK DEL OLMO and other Latinos. In 1974, Sotomayor and Finnerty wrote "Para los Niños—For the Children," a report published by the U.S. Commission on Civil Rights about educational problems and opportunities for Mexican Americans.

Sotomayor taught at Columbia University in a summer program designed to introduce minorities to the field of journalism. The program lost funding after 1974, but, undeterred, faculty members, including Robert Maynard and Sotomayor, took steps to establish the Summer Program for Minority Journalists at the University of California–Berkeley. The Summer Program later became the Institute for Journalism Education (now known as the Maynard Institute). Sotomayor served as the first director for the institute's editing program at the University of Arizona.

By the late 1970s, Sotomayor and del Olmo began in earnest to recommend the hiring of Latino writers at the *Los Angeles Times.* Many of their recommended candidates were hired, improving the newsroom's ethnic diversity and providing additional staff to produce a groundbreaking reporting project. Sotomayor and JORGE RAMOS were

Frank Sotomayor gives a speech at a National Association of Hispanic Journalists event. *(Monica Almeida)*

coeditors of a 1983 Latino series that consisted of 27 articles that ran over a three-week period. The project received the 1984 Pulitzer Prize for Public Services, print journalism's highest honor. Not only were Latinos able to initiate, create, and produce the entire series, but the articles offered accurate and complete portrayals of Latinos in southern California—some from a personal perspective.

As a CCNMA vice president in 1980, Sotomayor helped establish the Journalism Opportunity Conference. It continues to operate as the largest job fair for minority journalists on the West Coast. When his boss at the *Times* decided to establish Minority Editorial Training Program (METPRO) to train minorities through hands-on experience, Sotomayor provided advice based on his summer program experience. In 1982, Sotomayor served on a planning committee for a national meeting of Latino journalists, which led to the formation of the NAHJ.

Sotomayor served as the editor of *Nuestro Tiempo,* a *Times* bilingual section that covers the Latino community in Los Angeles, from 1989 to 1993 and then returned to his position as assistant city editor. In 2000, he became assistant MET-PRO director and editorial chair of the *Times* Student Journalism Program.

He received the Centennial Achievement Award from the University of Arizona in 1998 and in 2002 was inducted into the NAHJ Hall of Fame. In February 2004, the world of journalism was struck a heavy blow when del Olmo died of a heart attack. Sotomayor and Magdalena Beltrán–del Olmo, the pioneering journalist's wife, spent the following months collecting and organizing columns written by del Olmo. Together they coedited *Frank del Olmo: Commentaries on His Times,* a book published by the *Los Angeles Times.*

In an age when print media is consolidating under conglomerate parent companies, Sotomayor's dedication to establishing ethnically diverse newsrooms that better empathize, understand, and articulate the needs and concerns of ethnic communities is vitally important. Sotomayor's mentoring, writing, and influence help to educate and inform the dominant culture of the splendor in America's rich diversity.

Further Reading

Sotomayor, Frank, and Magdalena Beltrán-del Olmo. *Frank del Olmo: Commentaries on His Times.* Los Angeles: *Los Angeles Times,* 2005.

Torres, Joseph. "NAHJ Inducts Del Olmo, Sotomayor, Gutierrez and Espinosa into Hall of Fame." Available online. URL: http://www.nahj.org/release/2002/pr061702.html. Downloaded on June 2, 2005.

University of Arizona, Dean of Students. "Frank Sotomayo." Available online. URL: http://dos.web.arizona.edu/alumnifriends/alumni.html#frank_sotomayor. Downloaded on May 25, 2005.

Suárez, Virgil
(1962–   ) *poet, novelist, short story writer, essayist, educator, anthologist*

Hailed as a leading spokesperson for his generation of Cuban Americans, Virgil Suárez's prose and poetry speaks to the experience of the exile and the difficulty of acclimatization to life and culture in the United States. His writing is praised for his direct yet cinematic style.

The only son of Virgilio Rafael, a pattern cutter, and Oneida Lopez-Rodriguez Suárez, a seamstress, Virgil Suárez was born on January 29, 1962, in Havana, Cuba. He enjoyed an idyllic childhood in Arroyo Naranjo, a Havana suburb where, he recalled in a 2005 interview, "days were spent amongst the tropical creatures, flora and fauna, and Caribbean people of great resilience." Isabel, his paternal grandmother, served as an instrumental figure in his development not only as a writer but also as a lover of the written word. A schoolteacher all her life, she read to Suárez from the Harvard University Press edition of *One Thousand and One*

Virgil Suárez is a gifted and celebrated writer of many different genres. *(© 2006 Virgil Suárez)*

Arabian Nights. She inculcated a great sense of and need for storytelling in the budding writer.

Suárez immigrated through Spain to the United States in the early 1970s. On the very first day of school at Henry T. Gage Junior High in Huntington Park, California, he was forced after gym class to strip naked and shower with 300 other kids. He recalled in a 2005 interview "being so lost and confused that I slipped and fell on the dirty tiles of the shower. I remember getting back up with a great roar of kids laughing all around me. To this day I believe it was a sort of a breached birth, a nightmare that still haunts me." He played soccer with Mexicans who had recently immigrated and often encountered violence and

prejudice. School proved an interminable horrific experience for Suárez. He sought solace in reading and dreamed of being a painter or an artist. However, his talents did not extend to the visual arts, so he turned to writing poetry at about the age of 14 to express his creativity. He returned to Cuba nearly every summer to visit with relatives.

Suárez received a B.A. in creative writing in 1984 from California State University–Long Beach. He earned an M.F.A. in creative writing in 1987 from Louisiana State University. Upon graduation, he embarked on a long teaching career, which has included the following schools: Miami-Dade Community College, Florida International University, Louisiana State University–Baton Rouge, Florida State University–Tallahassee, and the University of Miami–Coral Gables.

Suárez's first novel, *Latin Jazz* (1989), chronicles the experiences of a Cuban-American family in Los Angeles by switching among the narrative perspectives of each family member. Critics raved about Suárez's debut work. He married Delia Poey in 1990, with whom he would have two children. *The Cutter* (1991) brings to light a young sugarcane cutter's desperate attempts to leave Cuba and join his family in the United States. *Welcome to the Oasis and Other Stories* (1992) vividly evokes the Latino experience in a collection of six stories. *Havana Thursdays* (1995) reveals how a family's infrastructure crumbles and the women rebuild themselves when the patriarch dies. *Going Under: A Cuban-American Fable* (1996) follows the reawakening of a Cuban American temporarily lost in the materialism of the American dream. Suárez draws on his memories to inform the stories, essays, and poems collected in *Spared Angola: Memories from a Cuban-American Childhood* (1997). *Infinite Refuge* (2002) offers a poignant and raw portrayal of how the mass exodus from Cuba and its subsequent separation, culture shock, and disintegration of family have affected people's lives.

Suárez's books of poetry include *You Come Singing* (1998), *Garabato Poems* (1999), *In the Republic of Longing: Poems* (1999), *Palm Crows*

(2001), *Banyan: Poems* (2001), *Guide to the Blue Tongue: Poems* (2002), and *90 Miles: Selected and New Poems* (2005). The verses in these collections are at once meditative, confessional, and political. They speak to the heart of the immigrant, the exile, and anyone lost in the marginalized pockets of mainstream society.

Suárez's essays, stories, and poems have appeared in a vast number of literary journals and reviews, including *Ploughshares, Prairie Schooner, Colorado Review, Southern Review, Massachusetts Review, American Literary Review, American Voice,* and *North American Review.* He is also an active book reviewer for the *Los Angeles Times,* the *Miami Herald,* the *Philadelphia Inquirer,* and the *Tallahassee Democrat.* He has edited the following anthologies: *Iguana Dreams: New Latino Fiction* (with Poey, 1992), *Paper Dance: Fifty Latino Poets* (with Victor Hernandez Cruz and Leroy V. Quintana, 1995), and *Little Havana Blues: A Cuban-American Literature Anthology* (with Poey, 1996). Suárez's books edited with Ryan G. Van Cleave are *American Diaspora: Poetry of Displacement* (2001), *Like Thunder: Poets Respond to Violence in America* (2002), *Vespers: Contemporary American Poems of Religion and Spirituality* (2003), and *Red, White, and Blues: Poets on the Promise of America* (2004).

Suárez received an award for best American poetry from the National Endowment for the Arts and the Latino Heritage Award from the Book Seller's Association for *Banyan.* He teaches creative writing and Latino/a literature courses at Florida State University. Currently, Suárez writes primarily poetry, although he will occasionally pen a short story. The author stated that the process of writing "has made [him] a better person, and it's allowed [him] to understand [his] human condition a bit better, though it is always a struggle." Driven to preserve the culture of his childhood, he stated in a 2005 interview, "I want to write to leave a record not only of how I lived, but how a community of immigrants lived." His prolific volume of writing captures his intention perfectly.

Further Reading
Kanellos, Nicolás, et al., eds. *Herencia: The Anthology of Hispanic Literature in the United States.* New York: Oxford University Press, 2003, pp. 496–498.

Suárez, Virgil. *Spared Angola: Memories from a Cuban-American Childhood.* Houston, Tex.: Arte Público Press, 1998.

West-Durán, Alan. *Latino and Latina Writers, Volume II.* Detroit: Thomas-Gale, 2004, pp. 747–762.

T

Tafolla, Carmen
(1951–) *poet, short story writer, essayist, educator*

Credited as one of the first women to use code-switching, a style of writing that alternates between Spanish and English, Carmen Tafolla creates poetry that lends itself beautifully to both performance art and the written word. Born on July 29, 1951, in a West Side barrio of San Antonio, Texas, Carmen Tafolla is the second daughter of Mariano Tafolla, Jr., a Mexican-American sailor and mechanic whose family had lived in the Southwest since the 1600s, and Maria Duarte, who was born on a Hawaiian plantation to migrant workers from Spain. As a young child, Carmen absorbed the stories told by her beloved grandmothers and barrio elders. By the time she was eight, Carmen began experimenting with poetry. She wanted to travel the world and explore other cultures and languages. Despite the fact that her church forbade dancing, Carmen loved dance, art, and drama. Drawn to anything Mexican or Spanish because of the repressive no-Spanish rules of her school, she also delighted in dreams of writing.

Carmen's early education was spent exclusively in Chicano schools until she was awarded a scholarship to a private high school. Throughout her young adult years, Tafolla read Spanish-language and Latin-American authors, whom she admired for their freshness, directness, and courage to break from the expectations and proprieties of tradition.

By the 1970s, she was swept away by Chicano authors such as ALURISTA, TOMÁS RIVERA, and LUIS OMAR SALINAS. She earned a B.A. in Spanish and French in 1972 and an M.A. in education the following year, both from Austin College in Sherman, Texas, while teaching French to high school students. She started teaching at the college level in 1973, when she became director of the Mexican American Studies Center at Texas Lutheran College in Seguin, Texas, a position she held from 1973 to 1975 and from 1978 to 1979.

The literary world came to know her works in 1975 when she shared her poetry at the second Floricanto Chicano literary festival, held that year in Austin, Texas. She not only popularized code-switching and gave distinct voices and texture to archetypes of the barrio but also introduced strong female characters formerly unknown in the male-dominated field of Chicano literature. At this point, Tafolla developed a talent for speaking in public with a unique blend of nonconformist techniques such as poems, accents, and dramatic anecdotes. In addition to her creative publications, she continued her academic writings, such as the two chapters in 1976 in *The Spanish Speaking Church in the U.S.* Her first book, *Get Your Tortillas Together,* coauthored with Reyes Cárdenas and Cecilio Garcia-Camarillo, was also released that year. Her poetry began to be published frequently in literary magazines, textbooks, and periodicals, including *Caracol,* and in 1978 she finished a nonfiction book on racism, sexism, and Chicana women entitled *To*

Split a Human: Mitos, machos y la mujer chicana (released in 1985). After a year as head writer for a bilingual television series for the station KLRN, she married Chicano scholar Ernesto Bernal in 1979, and between them they have five children: two teenagers Ernesto brought to the family, two children they bore, and one adopted. She earned a doctorate in bilingual education from the University of Texas–Austin in 1982.

In 1983, Tafolla and her family moved to California, where she taught women's studies at California State University–Fresno. That same year, she released a collection of poems entitled *Curandera.* The strong matrilineal sensibilities and indomitable spirit of the personas she introduces in this publication illustrate the influence matriarchs hold for her. She recalled in a 2006 interview, "I admired Aurora Santos, the 84-year-old barrio resident, who 'schooled' me in long and eloquent university-quality lectures about culture, heritage, the history of the West-Side barrios, and living the clean life of the 'Indio.' I admired my grandmother, who told many stories of her life, and told me to someday 'Put them in a book.'"

In 1985, Tafolla contributed her works to *Five Poets from Aztlán,* and the following year, she and her family moved to Flagstaff, Arizona. She won first prize in poetry from the University of California–Irvine for *Sonnets to Human Beings* in 1987. While giving a presentation to the Hispanic Educators Association in Las Vegas, Nevada, in 1990, Tafolla delivered a dramatic performance known as "With Our Very Own Names," in which she introduced seven characters with different voices, appearances, and identities. This performance, now called "My Heart Speaks a Different Language," boasts a changing nine characters (out of a selection of more than 30) and has been performed by Tafolla more than 600 times. That same year, she left university teaching and administration and was able to dedicate herself to writing full time.

Tafolla published many children's books, often in textbooks and readers, since the 1980s,

including *Minnie the Mambo Mosquito* in 1990, *The Dog Who Wanted To Be a Tiger* in 1996, and *Take a Bite* in 1997. In the year 2000, she published the popular bilingual *Baby Coyote and the Old Woman.* She released another book of poetry in 2004 entitled *Sonnets and Salsa.* Tafolla is one of the most highly anthologized Chicana authors and has received many awards and honors, including the first annual Art of Peace Award in 1999 and recognition by the National Association for Chicano Studies for writing that "gives voice to our peoples." She has completed a movie script coauthored with filmmaker Sylvia Morales for a feature-length film, a comedy entitled *REAL MEN . . . and Other Miracles. The Holy Tortilla and a Pot of Beans: A Collection of Stories* and a collagist autobiography, *The Colors of Words: Between the Borders of a Writer's Life,* are

Southwest poet Carmen Tafolla speaks directly to the issues facing Mexican Americans. *(Courtesy of the author)*

scheduled for release in 2007. Some of her works are archived at the University of Texas Benson Latin American Collection.

Tafolla's poetry is featured in a moving exhibit called "Rebozos y Voces," with 15 original paintings by Catalina Garate. This exhibit, which has toured throughout the Southwest, speaks to the universal experiences of womanhood, told through the *rebozos* (shawls) and the voices of the rural Mexican indigenous woman. Through her performance art and books, Tafolla succeeds in creating poetry authentic to and with the strength of the human voice.

Further Reading

Carmen Tafolla Web site. Available online. URL: http://www.carmentafolla.com

Lomelí, Francisco A., and Carl R. Shirley, eds. *Dictionary of Literary Biography, Chicano Writers, First Series*. Vol. 82. Detroit: Gale Group, 1989, pp. 257–260.

Rodriguez, Alfonso, and Santiago Daydí-Tolson, eds. *Five Poets of Aztlán*. Binghamton, N.Y.: Bilingual/ Editorial Bilingüe, 1985.

Woinowski, Beth, Aaron Bianco, and Maria Zavialova. "Carmen Tafolla." Available online. URL: http://voices.cla.umn.edu/vg/Bios/entries/tafolla_carmen.html. Downloaded on April 28, 2006.

Thomas, Piri
(John Peter Thomas, John "Piri" Thomas)
(1928–) *autobiographer, poet, essayist, short story writer, activist*

Piri Thomas's searing autobiographical account of life in a barrio, *Down These Mean Streets,* had such a powerful effect on literature that it served as the essential impetus for a generation of Nuyorican writers. With his memoir, Thomas introduced the term *barrio,* the effect of racism from the oppressed perspective, and the poverty of the marginalized to mainstream American society.

John Peter Thomas was the firstborn and beloved child of Dolores Montañez, a Puerto Rican immigrant, and Juan Thomas. His father was originally from Cuba but had lived in Puerto Rico before moving to New York City, where he met and married Montañez in 1927. Thomas was born a year later, on September 30, 1928. He has dark skin, like his father, whereas his siblings inherited their mother's lighter skin color. As many people assumed Thomas was black, he felt the constant sting of racism and stereotyping in the community called Spanish Harlem that he lived in. But even more overwhelming was the racism he felt in his own family. Thomas distinctly felt his father preferred his lighter-skinned children. Thomas found solace and inspiration in the love he shared with his mother, who affectionately called him "Piri," which is derived from *espíritu,* or "spirit." Thomas also had the luck of finding a mentor in an English teacher who encouraged his writing.

In 1944, when the family moved to Babylon, Long Island, the pressure of prejudice increased to such a volume that Thomas left home at 16, returning to Spanish Harlem. He strongly preferred to live on his own rather than endure the hate of the Long Island community and his frustration and anger at his family, who were so willing to assimilate into the Anglo culture. While on his own, Thomas turned to drugs and petty crimes. He traveled to the Deep South in a quest to ascertain whether he should remain true to his Puerto Rican heritage or just give in and accept his status and identity as a black man, as everyone assumed him to be. Still in doubt about his identity, Thomas joined the U.S. Merchant Marine and traveled through the West Indies, South America, and Europe. Upon his return, he became addicted to heroin and began committing armed robberies to earn a living. He was arrested in 1950 for his crimes and sentenced to 15 years in prison.

Thomas wrote in earnest while in prison. He became infatuated with the strength and faith of the Muslim people, even studying the religion. During his seven-year prison term, Thomas earned his G.E.D. Upon being paroled at age 28, he lived with his aunt, Angelista. He left the Muslim religion and adopted the Pentecostal Christian faith inspired by his aunt. While attending church, he met Daniela Calo, whom he married in 1958, had two children with, but later divorced. He also began to work in prison and drug rehabilitation programs in New York. He had completed his memoirs while in prison, but the entire manuscript was accidentally destroyed. In 1962, Thomas received a Louis M. Rabinowitz Foundation grant to rewrite his memoirs. *Down These Mean Streets* (1967), Thomas's memoir, contains a mix of dialects the author developed in Spanish Harlem. This groundbreaking work shook the literary world to its foundation with its honest, haunting, and gut-wrenching look into the lives of the disenfranchised. The autobiographical account is considered a forerunner for the Nuyorican (New York Puerto Rican) movement, as it gave inspiration and credibility to the experiences of Puerto Ricans struggling in the United States. It is considered a classic and was released with a new introduction by the author in 1997.

Thomas received a Lever Brothers community service award in 1967. He released his second autobiographical work as *Savior, Savior Hold My Hand* in 1972. While this book did not receive the same overwhelming praise as his debut work, critics still found Thomas's writing cracking with passion and possessing the ability to draw readers in with lyrical imagery. *Seven Long Times* (1975) is the third in his autobiographical series. *Stories from El Barrio* (1980) was geared for young readers.

Thomas has also penned powerful poetry and helped to pioneer interest in spoken word poetry. A selection of his best poetry include: "A First Night at El Sing Sing," "Born Anew at Each A.M.," "Cara de Palo Thoughts," "Fire Water," "If in the Moment of Passing," "I Have Seen," "Love Is a Sharing," "My World," "No More Trumpets of Despair," "Sermon from the Ghettos," "Softly, Puerto Rican, You Ain't Alone," "The Eyes of My Heart," "The Formed Faces of All," "The Tombs," and "What Is the Thick Black Line?" Thomas distributed his

Piri Thomas is one of the most significant Nuyorican writers and is quite adept at performing his poetry. *(Photo of John Peter "Piri" Thomas is reprinted with permission from the publisher [APP Archive Files] [Houston: Arte Público Press—University of Houston, © 2006])*

poetry along with Latino salsa/jazz and gospel music in the release of *Sounds of the Streets* (1994). In *No Mo' Barrio Blues* (1996), Thomas recorded readings of his poetry to the beat of original Latin jazz, rhythm, blues, and Caribbean music.

Thomas released *Por estas calles bravas,* a Spanish translation of his first memoirs, in 1998. In 2004, the Public Broadcasting Service aired *Every Child Is Born a Poet: The Life and Works of Piri Thomas.* The program delves into drama and poetry to show Thomas in action as he performs his poetry. It discusses Nuyorican literature, traces Thomas's path from childhood to manhood, and includes provocative mixed-media artwork. Thomas currently resides in California with his wife, Suzanne Dod Thomas. He is at work on a book entitled *A Matter of Dignity,* the sequel to *Down These Mean Streets.* He continues to speak at universities and schools and in communities throughout the United States.

Further Reading

Hernández, Carmen Dolores. "They Have Forced Us to Be Universal." Interview with Piri Thomas. Available online. URL: http://www.cheverote.com/reviews/hernandezinterview.html. Downloaded on April 14, 2006.

Mohr, Eugene V. *The Nuyorican Experience: Literature of the Puerto Rican Minority.* Westport, Conn.: Greenwood, 1982.

Rodriguez de Laguna, Asela. "Piri Thomas' *Down These Mean Streets*: Writing as a Nuyorican/Puerto Rican Strategy for Survival." In *U.S. Latino Literature: A Critical Guide for Students and Teachers.* Edited by Harold Augenbraum and Margarite Fernandez Olmos. Westport, Conn.: Greenwood, 2000, pp. 21–29.

Wald, Gayle. *Crossing the Line: Racial Passing in Twentieth-Century U.S. Literature and Culture.* Durham, N.C.: Duke University Press, 2000.

U

Ulibarrí, Sabine R.
(Sabine Reyes Ulibarrí)
(1919–2003) *poet, essayist, short story writer, educator*

Sabine R. Ulibarrí is best known for his short stories, particularly the collection entitled *Tierra Amarilla,* and his combination of *costumbrismo,* or regional writing, with magic realism. Ulibarrí's family takes pride in their long tradition of being New Mexican residents. The eldest child of Sabiniano and Simonita Ulibarrí, Sabine Reyes Ulibarrí was born on September 21, 1919, in Tierra Amarilla, a small village nestled at the base of the Sangre de Cristo Mountains of northern New Mexico. Ulibarrí took great delight in the rugged terrain of his homeland and found strength in his large family, particularly his grandmother. His parents were both college graduates and instilled the value of education in their children. Ulibarrí was an insatiable reader from an early age. He performed well academically in high school yet by that age had developed an autonomous and liberal nature that provoked him to question the strict rules imposed by the midwestern nuns who ran the school. During his studies at the University of New Mexico, Ulibarrí taught in the Rio Arriba County schools and at the Spanish-American Normal School. In 1942, Ulibarrí married María Concepción and joined the U.S. Army. He flew 35 missions as a gunman during World War II, earning the Distinguished Flying Cross.

After the war, Ulibarrí continued his studies at the University of New Mexico with the help of the G.I. Bill. He graduated in 1947 with a bachelor's degree in English and Spanish. He began work in the department of Romance languages at the University of New Mexico and, in 1949, completed his master's degree in Spanish. He left teaching for a brief time to pursue a doctorate, which he received from the University of California–Los Angeles in 1958, the same year his son, Carlos, was born. His dissertation on the Spanish poet Juan Ramón Jiménez (1881–1958) was published in Madrid in 1962. Ulibarrí returned to teaching and enjoyed many professional accomplishments and rewards for his service to education. In fact, his first published works focus on the educational system. These include *Spanish for the First Grade* (1957) and *Fun Learning Elementary Spanish,* Volume 1 (1963) and Volume 2 (1965).

Ulibarrí employed bold imagery in his collection of poetry entitled *Al cielo se sube a pie* (1961; *One gets to heaven on foot*). He gained recognition for his collection of short stories *Tierra Amarilla: Cuentos de Nuevo México,* originally published in Ecuador in 1964 and published as *Tierra Amarilla: Stories of New Mexico* in 1971 by the University of New Mexico Press. This collection of short stories invokes the *costumbrismo* style of depicting everyday manners, customs, people, and the environment of Ulibarrí's New Mexican hometown. *Costumbrismo* originated during the 16th- and 17th-century Golden Age of Spanish literature. It enjoyed popularity in the first half of the 19th century.

Ulibarrí followed with another book of poetry, *Amor y Ecuador* (1966; *Love and Ecuador*) and *El alma de la raza* (The soul of the [Chicano] race) in 1971 in support of the Chicano movement. Additional works include *Mi abuela fumaba puros y otros cuentos de Tierra Amarilla/My Grandma Smoked Cigars and Other Stories of Tierra Amarilla* (1977), *Primeros encuentros/First Encounters* (parallel text in English and Spanish, 1982), *El gobernador Glu Glu* (1988), *El condor, and Other Stories* (parallel text in English and Spanish, 1989), *Kissing Cousins: 1000 Words Common to Spanish and English* (1991), *Flow of the River: Corre el río* (1992), *Suenos/Dreams* (1994), and *Mayhem Was Our Business/Memorias de un veterano* (1997). Ulibarrí died of cancer on January 4, 2003. His most significant contribution to Chicano literature is his ability to evoke the fierce beauty of the Hispanic New Mexican region and its people without being confined by its boundaries.

Further Reading

Duke dos Santos, Maria, and Patricia De la Fuente, eds. *Sabine R. Ulibarri: Critical Essays.* Albuquerque: University of New Mexico Press, 1995.

Kanellos, Nicolás, et al., eds. *Herencia: The Anthology of Hispanic Literature in the United States.* New York: Oxford University Press, 2003, pp. 296–300.

Lomelí, Francisco A., and Carl R. Shirley, eds. *Chicano Writers: First Series.* Vol. 82. Detroit: Gale Research, 1989, pp. 260–267.

Urista, Alberto Baltazar   *See* ALURISTA

Urrea, Luis Alberto
(Lou Alberto Urrea)
(1955–   ) *poet, novelist, short story writer, essayist, educator, folklorist*

Luis Alberto Urrea, a talented and diverse writer of many genres, is best known for his trilogy depicting life on the United States–Mexico border. One of six children of Alberto Urrea Murray, from Rosario, Sinaloa, Mexico, and Phyllis Dashiell, originally from New York City, Luis Alberto Urrea was born on August 20, 1955, in Tijuana, Mexico. Urrea was registered with the U.S. government as a U.S. citizen born abroad and was thereby able to circumvent any issues with the Immigration and Naturalization Service when he moved with his family to San Diego, California. Luis's childhood neighborhood, which was frightening and violent, left a haunting impression on him that would later affect much of his writing. Both his parents worked full time, leaving Luis in the care of a Mexican nanny who taught him Spanish as his first language.

Luis struggled with his health as a young child, contracting tuberculosis, German measles, and scarlet fever. Due to his sicknesses, it became difficult to find care for him. Eventually, his parents left him in the care of his godparents, Abelino and Rosario García. From his godparents, Luis learned to trust and believe in the possibility of love. Until he entered the first grade, Luis spent most of his days with the Garcías. He particularly found comfort and in fact healing from his godmother, the most important person in his life, who used her skill with herbs and in the kitchen to bolster Luis's sense of self-worth and his health.

Luis attended St. Jude's Academy, a Catholic school where corporal punishment was the norm. Urrea decided he wanted to become a priest. His father disapproved, considering anyone who did not desire a woman to be weak and launched a violent campaign to toughen up his son. In 1976, the family moved to Clairemont, where Luis attended Whittier Elementary, Marston Junior High School, and Clairemont (Ridgemont) High School. While in high school, Urrea penned his first book, *I See the Wind the Blindman Cried.* During his schooling, he Americanized his name, becoming Lou for the sake of assimilating. When he enrolled in the University of California–San Diego in 1973, Urrea reclaimed his birth name and developed a firmer sense of his own identity. During college, he wrote lyrics for San Diego rock band Harlequin, produced plays with a theater troupe called ReBirth, and wrote *Frozen Moments* (1977), which was funded by a grant from the university dean.

Upon graduation in 1977, Urrea worked with the missionary group Spectrum Ministries and Pastor Von in Tijuana. These experiences laid the basis for *Across the Wire: Life and Times on the Mexican Border.* Urrea sent the book to every major publisher, who in turn rejected his work. In 1978, he became a teacher's aide for Cesar Gonzales at Mesa College. With the help of ALURISTA, Urrea's work began to see publication in various literary magazines and local periodicals such as the *San Diego Reader,* which published excerpts from *Across the Wire.*

In 1982, Urrea accepted a position to teach expository writing and fiction workshops at Harvard University until 1986. He served as an associate professor of liberal arts at Massachusetts Bay Community College from 1986 to 1990. Urrea married in 1987 and three years later moved with his wife to Colorado. In 1991, Urrea joined with the Chicano theater scholar and director JORGE HUERTA and his Teatro Máscara Mágica to write, rehearse, stage, produce, and tour a full-stage play in six weeks. The play, *Un puño de tierra/A Handful of Dust,* was directed by Jose Luis Valenzuela and based on the opening chapter of *Across the Wire,* titled "Sifting Through the Trash." Urrea never gave up on *Across the Wire,* and his determination was rewarded in 1993 when the book was finally published, the same year he divorced.

Urrea became a full-time writer in 1994. Although he is an accomplished and awarded poet and novelist, his best-known works and contributions to Chicano literature and culture lie in his border trilogy, which includes *Across the Wire, By the Lake of Sleeping Children: The Secret Life of the Mexican Border* (1996), and *Nobody's Son: Notes from an American Life,* a memoir published in

1998. His novels include *In Search of Snow* (1994), *The Devil's Highway* (2004), and *The Hummingbird's Daughter* (2005). His poetry has been collected in *The Fever of Being* (1994) and *Ghost Sickness* (1997). Additional works include *A World of Turtles: A Literary Celebration* (1997), *Wandering Time: Western Notebooks* (1999), and *Six Kinds of Sky: A Collection of Short Fiction* (2002). Urrea's writings have been featured in several anthologies and literary magazines.

Urrea was inducted into the Latino Literature Hall of Fame for *Vatos* and has received the American Book Award from the Before Columbus Foundation for *Nobody's Son,* Book of the Year by *ForeWord* magazine for *Six Kinds of Sky,* New York Times Notable Book and the Christopher Award for *Across the Wire,* Western States Book Award and Colorado Center for the Book Award for *The Fever of Being,* Best American Poetry Selection for

Luis Alberto Urrea made the national best-seller list with *Hummingbird's Daughter,* a fictional account based on the life of folk hero and healer Teresa Urrea. *(© Nina Subin)*

Ghost Sickness, and Lannan Foundation Award for nonfiction and Pulitzer Prize nomination for *The Devil's Highway.*

Further Reading

Heide, Rick, ed. *Under the Fifth Sun: Latino Literature from California.* Santa Clara and Berkeley, Calif.: Santa Clara University/Heyday Books, 2002.

Lomelí, Francisco A., and Carl R. Shirley, eds. *Dictionary of Literary Biography*, Vol. 209: *Chicano Writers, Third Series.* Detroit: Gale Group, 1999, pp. 269–274.

Urrea, Luis Alberto. *Nobody's Son: Notes from an American Life.* Tucson: University of Arizona Press, 1998.

V

Valdes-Rodriguez, Alisa
(Alisa Valdes)
(1969–) *journalist, novelist*

Alisa Valdes-Rodriguez popularized a new genre, "chick lit" for a Latina audience. She was named one of the top 25 Hispanics by *Hispanic Business* magazine and *Time* magazine and Woman of the Year by *Latina* magazine. With her best-selling book, *The Dirty Girls Social Club,* she defied stereotypes and brought Latina culture into the mainstream without a strict adherence to the cultural means and ways many Latinas identify for themselves.

Alisa Valdes was born in Albuquerque, New Mexico, on February 28, 1969, to Nelson P. Valdes, a professor of sociology who emigrated from Havana, Cuba, at age 15, and Maxine Conant, a poet whose diverse family tree includes Salem, Massachusetts, founding fathers as well as Spanish, Portuguese, and Irish ancestors. At four years old, Alisa moved with her parents and older brother to Glasgow, Scotland. A year later, the Valdes family returned to the United States, settling in New Orleans, Louisiana. Mardi Gras greatly pleased Alisa, who believed the festivities celebrated her birthday since it coincided with the all-city party. In her usual tongue-in-cheek manner, Valdes attributes this connection to the beginning of her narcissism.

In 1977, Alisa moved with her family back to Albuquerque, where she would spend the rest of her childhood. She played the saxophone and excelled in sports, academics, and dance. As she enjoyed writing from an early age, both parents encouraged Valdes to enter an English honors class at Del Norte High School. Somewhat subversive, Valdes submitted a baroque paragraph instead of an expository paragraph as requested for an assignment. Her English teacher publicly criticized her work and immediately demoted Alisa to remedial English. Instead of allowing this humiliation to destroy her self-esteem or diminish her love of writing, Valdes used it to liberate herself from the confines of pedantic writing. She graduated from high school in 1987.

Valdes's conviction to develop her inner voice was further challenged while at Berklee College of Music, where she studied tenor saxophone from 1987 to 1992. In 1992, Valdes wrote an article about the blatant sexism she encountered from school officials. The *Boston Globe* printed the article, which resulted in a change in the school's policies. That summer, Valdes performed as a house saxophonist on a cruise ship. Upon graduation from Berklee, Valdes pursued higher education at the Columbia School of Journalism, obtaining a master's degree in 1994. She then accepted a position as a staff writer for the *Boston Globe.* In 1997, Valdes married Patrick Jason Rodriguez, with whom she would have a son.

Valdes-Rodriguez moved to southern California to work at the *Los Angeles Times* in 1998. Despite the well-paying job and prestige at the *Times,* Valdes-Rodriguez did not like Los Angeles culture. In 2000, she and her family moved to Albuquerque, where Valdes-Rodriguez wrote for the *Albuquerque Tribune.* Frustrated with the stereotypical portrayal of Latino/as in books and print journalism, Valdes-Rodriguez e-mailed Robert Crais, one of her favorite authors, to ask for his advice. Crais encouraged Valdes-Rodriguez to write the book she wanted to read. Thus inspired and supported, Valdes-Rodriguez set out to write *The Dirty Girls Social Club.* Valdes-Rodriguez also drew inspiration from Zoe Valdes, a Parisian writer from Cuba whom Valdes-Rodriguez said in a 2005 interview she admired for her "quick, funny writing that focused on the things I, as a writer and human being, valued most: irreverence, sarcasm, lack of pedantry, and flawed universal humanity."

The Dirty Girls Social Club, released in 2003, quickly became a national best seller, opening up a new genre to Latinas in the fast-paced world of "chick lit." With hip, irreverent prose, Valdes-Rodriguez introduces six college friends who call themselves *sucias,* translated as "dirty girls." The book begins six years after the women have graduated from college and follows the young women as their antics wholeheartedly embrace life, celebrate friendship, and abolish archaic stereotypes. After the book's release, *Latina* magazine named Valdes-Rodriguez one of the top 11 women of the year, and *Hispanic Business* magazine named her one of the 100 most influential Hispanics in the United States. The great success of the book provoked the interest of Jennifer Lopez, who, along with Laura Ziskin, purchased the option to make a movie based on the book. Their option expired in 2004. In 2005, Valdes-Rodriguez began her own television and film production company called Dirty Girls Production. She intends to make an independent film based on her book.

Playing with Boys (2004) follows the adventures of three very different women living in Los Angeles as they seek love and success. With two literary sensations and a vast readership, Valdes released *Make Him Look Good* (2006); *Haters,* a

young adult novel (2006); and *Goodbye Suckerville* (forthcoming in 2007). She contributed to *Girls' Night In* (2004), *Girls' Night Out* (2006), and *Maybe Baby* (2006).

Further Reading

Miranda, Carolina A. "Alisa Valdes-Rodriguez: The Godmother of Chica Lit." *Time,* August 13, 2005. Available online: URL: http://www.time.com/time/nation/article/0,8599,1093632,00.html. Downloaded on April 10, 2006.

Scribner, Amy. "Latina friendships and foibles" Available online. URL: http://www.bookpage.com/0305bp/fiction/dirty_girls.html. Downloaded on October 20, 2005.

Smith, Dinitia. "A Novel's Latinas Defy Clichés." *New York Times,* April 24, 2003, p. E1.

Valdez, Luis
(Luis Miguel Valdez)
(1940–) *playwright, director, screenwriter, activist*

Considered the father of Chicano theater, Luis Valdez made his widespread and significant impact with the founding of El Teatro Campesino, a touring farmworkers' theater troupe, and by creating *Zoot Suit,* the first play written and produced by a Mexican American ever to appear on Broadway. Valdez has long been deeply affected by family, love for *la raza,* the Chicano race—and appreciation for the historical culture.

Born on June 26, 1940, in Delano, California, Luis Miguel Valdez was the second of 10 children. He joined his parents, Armida and Francisco Valdez, in the fields at age six, following the crops throughout central California. He attended many schools before the family settled in San Jose, California, where he graduated from high school. His early interests in puppet shows inspired and fueled his pursuit of theater at San Jose State College (now University), to which he won a scholarship in 1960. He won a writing contest for *The Theft* (ca. 1961) and had his first play, *The Shrunken Head of Pancho Villa,* produced in 1963. He graduated with a B.A. in English in 1964.

After college, Valdez joined the highly political San Francisco Mime Troupe. The group used "agit-prop" (agitation and propaganda) theater as well as Italian commedia dell'arte to voice their protests against the Vietnam War and other causes. The following year, 1965, Valdez returned to Delano to assist and support César Chávez in his efforts to unionize farmworkers. Valdez combined his theater knowledge, folklore, and mime troupe experience to create El Teatro Campesino (The Peasant Theater) and the *acto* (a short, dramatic sketch or skit). Initially performed on flatbed trucks in the fields of Delano, the *actos* dramatized the plight of the farmhands with slapstick humor, satire, role reversal, allegorical strategies, and straightforward language "to present a clear and concise social or political message" writes historian NICOLÁS KANELLOS.

Now an integral genre of Chicano theater, *actos* are flexible enough that members of the troupe can incorporate idiosyncrasies, dialect, or personal experiences to capture the essence of their community. The immediate result was a highly successful unification of Latinos. El Teatro Campesino did not wait for the people to come to it; it went to the people and thus pioneered a grassroots theater movement. In 1967, Valdez took his troupe on the road to reach more Latinos and explore Chicano themes beyond migrant concerns, including *corridos* (ballads) and religious themes. Valdez's works from this period include *Las dos caras del patroncito* (1965; *The two faces of the owner*), *La Quinta Temporada* (1966; *The fifth season*), *Los Vendidos* (1967; *The Sellouts*), *La conquista de México* (1968; *The conquest of Mexico*), *The Militants* (1969), *No saco nada de la escuela* (1969; *I don't get anything out of school*), *Huelguistas* (1970; *Strikers*), *Vietnam Campesino* (1970; *Vietnam peasant*), *Dark Root of a Scream* (1971), and *Soldado Razo* (1971; *The soldier race*).

The most celebrated and well-known Latino playwright, Luis Valdez became successful by performing on truck flatbeds during the unionization of Latino farmworkers. *(Photo of Luis Valdez is reprinted with permission from the publisher [APP Archive Files] [Houston: Arte Público Press— University of Houston, © 2006]*

Valdez won an Obie in 1968, an Emmy in 1973, and Los Angeles Drama Critics awards in 1969, 1972, and 1978. He formed a Chicano cultural center in Del Ray, California, in 1967, which was eventually moved to San Juan Bautista, California. Named El Centro Campesino Cultural (The Peasant Cultural Center), the theater and the cultural center became a fully professional production company in 1971. Valdez's national recognition and the success of Chicano theater created a swell of new theaters throughout the country.

In 1978, he wrote, directed, and produced *Zoot Suit,* a play based on the 1942 Los Angeles Sleepy Lagoon murder case. Staged in Los Angeles, *Zoot Suit* was wildly successful for two years, moving to Broadway in 1979. Although it was not well received by New York reviewers or theater goers, it marked a turning point for Latinos in that it was the first play by a Mexican American ever to be staged on Broadway. In 1981, Valdez wrote and directed *Bandido* (Bandit). *Zoot Suit* was adapted as a film in 1982. That same year, El Teatro Campesino staged *Corridos,* a play later adapted into a video production for the Corporation for Public Broadcasting in 1987. *I Don't Have to Show You No Stinking Badges* ran successfully in the Los Angeles Theatre Center in 1986. However, his greatest crossover success to the mainstream arrived with the 1987 hit film *La Bamba,* which Valdez wrote and directed, about Mexican-American rock star Ritchie Valens. Through the 1990s, Valdez produced and sometimes directed television shows and films.

Valdez has taught theater at several universities and holds honorary doctorates from San Jose State, the University of Santa Clara, Columbia College of Chicago, and the California Institute of the Arts. Although he has been criticized for his portrayal of women and perpetuating Mexican stereotypes, he has remained true to *la raza*, and his contribution to Chicano theater is regarded as fathomless.

Further Reading

Cortés, Eladio, and Mirta Barrea-Maryls, eds. *Encyclopedia of Latin American Theatre.* Westport, Conn.: Greenwood Press, 2003.

Harper, Hillard. "The Evolution of Valdez and El Teatro Campesino." *Los Angeles Times,* October 15, 1984, sec. 6, p. 1.

Meier, Matt S., Conchita Franco Serri, and Richard A. Garcia. *Notable Latino Americans: A Biographical Dictionary.* Westport, Conn.: Greenwood Press, 1997, pp. 392–394.

Novas, Himilce. *The Hispanic 100: A Ranking of the Latino Men and Women Who Have Most Influenced American Thought and Culture.* New York: Citadel Press, 1995.

Varela, Félix
(Félix Francisco José María de la Concepción Varela y Morales)
(1788–1853) *journalist, editor, activist*

Cuban exile Félix Varela began one of the first Spanish-language newspapers in the United States. Son of Francisco Varela, a Spanish military officer, and Josepha de Morales, Félix Francisco José María de la Concepción Varela y Morales was born on November 20, 1788, in Havana, Cuba. After his father died when Félix was young, his maternal uncle, Bartolomé Morales, governor of Saint Augustine, Florida, watched over the young boy. Varela was enraptured by spiritual matters and possessed a great love of languages and philosophy. He attended College and Seminary of San Carlos in Havana and was ordained a priest in 1811. Upon graduation, Varela was given the chair of philosophy at the college, where he also taught physics, chemistry, Latin, and rhetoric. Varela was an exceptional teacher who modernized the college's curriculum and introduced philosophy as an integral part of common life.

Varela authored numerous Spanish-language philosophical brochures and books from 1811 to 1820. *Las lecciones de filosófia* (four volumes, 1818–20; Lessons of philosophy) is considered his most important work because it inspired the masses to demand personal rights. He studied music and played the violin and took part in the proceedings of the Royal Patriotic Society of Havana. Varela was among the first to publicly speak out against the traditional scholasticism that had dominated Spanish thought for centuries. He employed natural science, the use of reason, and theories proven in the laboratory to provide the foundation for his method of teaching and deduction.

His simple, clear lectures drew large crowds of liberal-minded fellow countrymen and -women. Varela taught a course on the new constitution, which would establish a constitutional monarchy in Spain. A constitutional monarchy involves a separation of powers by forming different heads of power and an elected monarch who serves as a figurehead. Varela published his lectures under the title *Observaciones sobre la constitución política de la monarquía española* (1821). The following year, he served as a delegate in Madrid, Spain, where he participated on various commissions and wrote a plan of provincial government that would give the Spanish colonies a high degree of local autonomy. As perhaps the first Cuban abolitionist, he also suggested a plan for the gradual abolition of slavery in Cuba.

In 1823, an absolute monarchy was established in Spain. The new leaders were traditionalists and did not approve of Varela's liberal views or his popularity among the common people. Varela fled to New York City to escape a death sentence issued by the Spanish government. He then moved to Philadelphia, Pennsylvania, where he established *El Habanero,* a literary and political paper. Varela spoke plainly about the atrocities committed by the Spanish Crown, and from 1824 to 1826, he lived under the danger of possible assassination. His paper was clandestinely circulated throughout Cuba, where it was forbidden. He translated Thomas Jefferson's *A Manual of Parliamentary Practice* and Humphrey Davy's *Elements of Agricultural Chemistry* into Spanish. In 1825, he went to New York City to minister to the Latin members of St. Peter's Church. He served as pastor there until 1835. Through his religious work, Varela established several parochial schools, one of the first total abstinence societies, and a day nursery for the children of laboring women.

In the late 1820s, Varela released *Miscelánea filosófica* (Miscellaneous philosophy), edited the

poems of the Cuban poet Manuel de Zequeira, and published in two volumes his *Cartas Elpidio sobre la impiedad, la superstición y el fanatismo* (Elpidio letters on impiety, superstition, and fantasy). He continued to write journalistic work, contributing to *Truth Teller, New York Weekly Register, Catholic Diary, El Mensagero Semanal* of New York, *Revista Bimestre Cubana* of Havana (1831), and the *Young Catholics' Magazine.* In 1837, Varela became the vicar general of New York. From 1841 to 1844, he edited and contributed articles to the *Catholic Expositor and Literary Magazine.* In 1851, he retired to Saint Augustine, where he died on February 18, 1853.

Further Reading
Guinta, Peter. "Father Varela Moves Closer To Canonization." St. Augustine. Available online. URL: http://www.staugustine.com/varela/varela18.shtml. Downloaded on July 27, 2005.

Kanellos, Nicolás, et al., eds. *Herencia: The Anthology of Hispanic Literature in the United States.* New York: Oxford University Press, 2003, pp. 522–531.

Schweiger, Tristan. "Priest with St. Augustine Ties on Road to Possible Sainthood." *Florida Times-Union.* June 10, 2003, p. 4.

Véa, Alfredo, Jr.
(1950–   ) novelist

Alfredo Véa, Jr., represents an emerging class of writers who prefer to be known as authors who are Chicano, rather than as Chicano authors. Although his characters' personae are based on his Chicano heritage, his work expands beyond nationalism to encompass an unrelenting search for truth.

The son of Lorenza Véa, a migrant farmworker of Yaqui and Spanish parentage, Alfredo Véa, Jr., was born on June 28, 1950, in Buckeye, Arizona. (Some reports say 1952.) His father abandoned him and his mother, who was only 13 at the time, shortly after Alfredo's birth. When he was six years old, Véa's mother left her son in the care of her parents, Manuel Carvajel and Josephina Castillo de Carvajel, so she could work in the fields as a day laborer. Véa's maternal grandparents greatly influenced their charge with threads of magic, mysticism, and faith woven into their stories, teachings, and mannerisms. His grandmother was proud of her Spanish heritage. His grandfather was trilingual and a Yaqui Indian who introduced Alfredo to visionary practices that enabled the child to strengthen his conviction for truth while expanding the realm of what is possible. With his grandfather's assistance, Alfredo had a vision of Aztlán, the utopian, pre-Columbian Mexico. The vision was enhanced by peyote prepared in a mind-expanding tea, in a ritual honoring the transformational process that Yaquis believe occurs at nine years old. With this multicultural basis, Alfredo developed a worldly and broadminded awareness with a loyalty to Yaqui traditions.

Alfredo's mother returned when he was 10 years old. She took him to California, where he was made to work in the fields. Véa established friendships with French Canadians, inspiring him to study French at Livermore High School in Alameda, California. He briefly attended the University of California–Berkeley but returned to the fields due to financial pressure. In 1967, the U.S. military drafted Véa to serve in the Vietnam War. He took his case to court, identifying himself as a conscientious objector. He lost his case when he would not swear allegiance to or recognize a supreme being. Véa returned to Yaqui territory, his grandfather's homeland, before his service began. Building on a childhood aptitude for and interest in electronics, Véa served as a radio telephone operator (RTO) in Vietnam. Véa summarized in an interview with John Bowdreau in 1993 his experience and perception of war: "In order to survive, you can kill an entire family, including the children; you are given the license, the uniform, and every weapon under the sun. You could get away with anything, and that's when you find out who you are. You realize

that kindness and gentility are acts of will. You have to choose a side." This stark realization of war and the many levels and variations of causalities it wreaks and demands seeped deep into the consciousness of the budding writer.

After his military service, Véa worked as a truck driver, fork lift operator, and with a carnival. He spent a year in France, absorbing the culture while working as a janitor. Upon his return to California in 1971, he again enrolled in the University of California–Berkeley, earning a B.A. in English and physics in 1975 and a J.D. in 1978. He worked one year at the Centro Legal de la Raza (Legal Center of the People) in San Francisco. Véa worked at the San Francisco Public Defender's Office from 1980 to 1986, after which he opened a private practice. During a death penalty case in 1989, the judge commented that he did not know Mexican lawyers existed. Véa rented a trailer in the small central California town where the case was argued for the duration of the trial and channeled his anger and the prejudicial comment into his first novel, *Maravilla* (1993; *The Wonder*).

In *Maravilla,* Véa's main character has a coming-of-age journey. Highly autobiographical, the book includes the peyote tea ritual. Véa said he wrote this book, which is suffused with the mysticism of his childhood, "in a way that an English reader could read it and understand what it felt like to have a childhood in Spanish." The novel gives depth and credence to love and folklore while denouncing gentrification.

Silver Cloud Café (1996) connects the lives of migrant peoples from all nationalities. Converging at the Silver Cloud Café in the Mission District of San Francisco, the novel depicts a divergent mix of wanderlust characters. Véa gives a haunting account of the Vietnam War in *Gods Go Begging* (1999). Stripped of gory battle scenes, the author goes deep into the human psyche to expose the primordial desire inherent and behind all wars. Véa's writings forge a new direction in Chicano letters. They represent characters who begin with Chicano or indigenous ingredients yet by the nature of their journeys blend experiences and introduce other cultures to create a dynamic amalgam.

Further Reading

Lomelí, Francisco A., and Carl R. Shirley, eds. *Dictionary of Literary Biography*, Vol. 209: *Chicano Writers, Third Series*. Detroit: Gale Group, 1999, pp. 269–274.

Véa, Alfredo, Jr. *Gods Go Begging*. New York: Plume, 2000.

West-Durán, Alan. *Latino and Latina Writers, Volume I*. Detroit: Thomas-Gale, 2004, pp. 511–526.

Veciana-Suarez, Ana
(Ana Sira Veciana)
(1956–   ) *journalist, novelist, young adult writer, essayist*

An award-winning *Miami Herald* columnist and author of six books, Ana Veciana-Suarez uses her varied skills to address universal social issues through family experiences. Of Catalan and Cuban decent, Ana Sira Veciana was the second of five children. She was born on November 28, 1956, in Havana, Cuba. Veciana's mother, Sira Muiño, was born in the Catalonian region of Spain and moved to Cuba when she was 10 years old. Born in Cuba, Veciana's father, Antonio Veciana, also claims Catalan heritage. In 1961, Ana, her older brother, her younger sister, and her mother moved to Barcelona, Spain, to live with her mother's family for nearly 10 months before moving to Miami, Florida. Soon afterward, Ana's paternal grandparents joined them, filling the home with Catalan food and language. Ana often returned home from school to eat comfort food made by her grandmother—a Catalan treat of squeezed tomatoes and olive oil drizzled over bread. Ana attended a Catholic school, which inspired her dream of becoming a nun. Alternatively, she aspired to build bridges as a civil engineer, as she excelled in math.

When she was in junior high school, her family moved to La Paz, Bolivia. Veciana attended an American cooperative bilingual school through her sophomore year. Then the family moved back to Miami when Veciana was in the 11th grade. Encouraged by her English teacher, Veciana joined the writing team of her high school paper. Normally an introvert and an avid reader, Veciana established good friendships while working on the paper.

From 1974 to 1976, Veciana attended Miami Dade Community College and worked full time at a savings and loan institution. She transferred to the University of South Florida and studied mass communications from 1976 to 1978. She earned a B.A. in 1978. She served as an intern at the *Miami News* for one semester while in college. Her bilingual abilities helped her secure a job after graduation at the *Miami News* as a reporter, where she worked for four years. In 1980, Veciana married Leo Suarez.

Veciana-Suarez worked at the *Miami Herald* as a reporter for seven years from 1982 to 1989 and wrote an occasional column for the paper about family life. She wrote two reference books for the Media Institute, a think tank in Washington, D.C.: *Hispanic Media, USA: A Narrative Guide to Print and Electronic Hispanic News Media in the United States* (1987) and *Hispanic Media: Impact and Influence* (1990). Her husband, a newspaper editor, took a job at the *Palm Beach Post* in 1989. Veciana-Suarez followed him and gained a position as a regular columnist at the paper, a post she held until 1992. She then returned to the *Miami Herald* to write a column that addressed the effects of social issues on the human condition. During these years, Veciana-Suarez gave birth to five children.

In 1995, Veciana-Suarez's husband died of a heart attack. Four years later, Veciana-Suarez's older sister gave birth to a child with trisomy 18, a hopeless condition in which most children die in infancy and all die before reaching adulthood. Veciana-Suarez channeled her grief into writing her first novel. The widely acclaimed *Chin Kiss King* was released in 1998. Inspired by her sister's journey, Veciana-Suarez tells the story of three generations of Cuban-American women who struggle to care and provide for Victor Eduardo, who has been born with trisomy 18. Veciana-Suarez effectively deals with this immensely sad and bleak situation by ameliorating the pain through magic realism.

In 1998, Veciana-Suarez married David Freundlich. Her honest and genuine syndicated column caught the interest of a New York editor who asked her to compile several articles into a book. The result, *Birthday Parties in Heaven* (2000), is a collection of 17 humorous and thought-provoking essays about life and love. While on tour for *Birthday Parties in Heaven,* an editor from Scholastic asked Veciana-Suarez to write a book about an adolescent immigrant for their First Person Fiction series. Veciana-Suarez drew on her experiences to tell the story of Yara Garcia, age 13, and her arrival in United States from Cuba. Written in diary form, *Flight to Freedom* (2003) portrays Garcia's loss and aching desire to begin creating a new life.

Veciana-Suarez's commentary has appeared in several magazines, including *Readers Digest; O, the Oprah Magazine; Woman's Day; Washington Post Magazine; Parenting;* and *Latina.* She is the recipient of several honors and awards, including a nomination for the prestigious International IMPAC Dublin Literary Award for *The Chin Kiss King,* a Sunshine State Award from the Society of Professional Journalists, and an Excellence in Feature Writing award from the American Association of Sunday and Feature Editors.

Further Reading

Bach, Jackie. "Flight to Freedom." *ALAN Review* 1 (Winter 2003).

Sutten, Jonathan, Tiffany Vance, Sarah Huffner, and Daniel Douglas. "Ana Veciana-Suarez. Available online. URL: http://voices.cla.umn.edu/vg/Bios/entries/vecianasuarez_ana.html. Downloaded on April 10, 2006.

Veciana-Suarez, Ana. *The Chin Kiss King.* New York: Plume Books, 1998.

Velásquez, Gloria
(Gloria Louise Velásquez, Gloria Louise Velásquez-Treviño, Gloria Velásquez-Treviño)
(1949–   ) *poet, young adult writer, short story writer, novelist, activist*

Gloria Velásquez is one of the most preeminent Chicana voices of our times. She has won awards for her poetry and books and has extended her talents to embrace the needs and concerns of the young adult market with her highly successful Roosevelt High School series.

Gloria Louise Velásquez was born in Loveland, Colorado, on December 21, 1949. When she was a young girl, Velásquez's parents, Francisca Molinar and Juan Velásquez, worked as field-workers on farms from Colorado to Texas. During these early years, Velásquez's grandfather spoke Diné (Navajo) to her, introducing her to a world and culture she loved and appreciated. She is proud of her Diné heritage and had she become fluent in Diné, it would be Velásquez's third language, as she is fluent in English and Spanish. Velásquez greatly appreciates her ability to be bilingual. As she said in a 2005 interview, "Being bilingual is having a dual identity. I feel blessed to be able to create either entirely in Spanish, entirely in English, or naturally bilingually, as I do with some poems. It is a natural part of my soul."

Velásquez attributes her creative genesis to her first guitar, a present her parents brought from Juárez, Mexico, when she was seven or eight years old. She taught herself to play and wrote her own songs. Despite or perhaps because of the hardships of poverty and discrimination, Velásquez views her parents as models of strength and inspiration. In 1963, her parents abandoned the migrant life, settling down in Johnstown, Colorado, as factory and hospital workers. While attending Roosevelt High School, Velásquez started and wrote her own underground high school paper. She included satirical poems and featured her friends, as they were not part of the high school paper.

When Velásquez graduated from Roosevelt High School, she cried, not tears of joy, but rather tears of longing and hopelessness. She desperately wanted to go to college, but the family could not afford it. Velásquez worked as a motel maid, a transformer stacker, and a field-worker. In 1978, she married Kirk Velásquez Vriend and had a daughter, Brandi Lynn Treviño, all while pining for higher education. Undaunted, she worked as a secretary at a local Hewlett Packard plant and occasionally attended classes at Aims College in Greeley, Colorado, at night. Velásquez worked as a teacher's aide at Letford Elementary School. George Keating, who always saw her reading in the teacher's lounge, asked why Velásquez was not in school. When Velásquez replied that she had no money, Keating found her a business law grant, resulting in a fellowship for Velásquez to study at the University of Northern Colorado in the late 1970s.

Velásquez's political consciousness grew out of her involvement with the Movimiento Estudiantil Chicano de Aztlán (MEChA), an organization that raises political, social, and cultural awareness about the Chicano experience, and the Crusade for Justice. Velásquez was very active in college; she often rallied with her fellow students for equality and peace. Her poetry began to reflect her activism, concentrating on issues such as Chicana history, experience, and identity; antiwar protests; male dominance; the farmworkers' plight; motherhood; and problems with alcohol, old age, and medical care. She graduated with a double major in Spanish and Chicano studies, earning a B.A. in 1978.

From 1977 to 1979, Velásquez participated in Canto al Pueblo (Song of the People) festivals, traveling through Texas, New Mexico, and Wisconsin. She became involved with the Floricantos festivals and performed her poetry alongside JOSE ANTONIO BURCIAGA and Jose Montoya. Inspired by the popularity of the events and fueled by the energy of the Chicano movement, Velásquez pursued higher education at Stanford University. She won the Department of French and Italian's Premier

and Deuxième Prix awards in poetry in her second year at Stanford. During this time, she gave birth to her second child, Bobby, and had many of the prose pieces from her unpublished novella, *Toy Soldiers and Dolls,* published in a variety of journals. Velásquez received a Ph.D. in Spanish literature in 1985 with the completion of her dissertation, "Cultural Ambivalence in Early Chicana Prose Fiction." Later that same year, Velásquez accepted a position at California Polytechnic State University in San Luis Obispo, California, where she is currently a professor in the modern languages and literatures department.

Velásquez created the Roosevelt High School series to address the specific needs and concerns of adolescents of different ethnic backgrounds. The series includes *Juanita Fights the School Board* (1994), *Maya's Divided World* (1995), *Tommy Stands Alone* (1995), *Rina's Family Secret* (1998), *In Search of Ankiza's Rainbow* (2000), *Teen Angel* (2003), and *Tyrone's Journey* (2005). The series reaches the hearts and souls of young adult readers, helping them cope with issues such as violence, sexuality, prejudice, and interracial dating in a divergent world. The *Stanford Alumni Magazine* labeled Velásquez the "Latina Judy Blume" in its May 1996 issue.

Velásquez released her first collection of poetry, *I Used to Be a Superwoman,* in 1997. This emotive bilingual collection of poetry stirs the blood to challenge complacency, rise to create a world of justice, and, in Velásquez's own words, "refuse to be silent / to be buried in obscurity." Shortly afterward, Velásquez released her *Superwoman Chicana* CD. In 2005, Velásquez released *Xicana on the Run,* a bilingual book of poetry. Velásquez has received numerous awards and honors, including the 11th Chicano Literary Prize in the Short Story from the University of California–Irvine, in 1985; becoming the first Chicana to be inducted into the University of Northern Colorado's Hall of Fame for her achievements in creative writing in 1989; and a spotlight feature during Hispanic Heritage Month on KTLA in Los Angeles in 1996.

Gloria Velásquez sings while playing her guitar at a local function. *(Courtesy of the author)*

Velásquez has been reviewed and interviewed nationally as well as internationally. Her poetry and short stories have been published in numerous journals and anthologies such as *Chicanos y chicanas en diálogo* (1989), *Best New Chicano Literature* (1989), and *Neueste Chicano Lyrik* (1994, New Chicano music, German translation). Velásquez was recently featured in *Latino Voices in Literature* (1997). Her songs have been featured in the PBS documentaries *Soldados* and *La Raza de Colorado*. Velásquez has spoken as a guest author at various universities worldwide and continues to perform her poetry and sing her songs of empowerment and reclamation of justice.

Further Reading

Heide, Rick, ed. *Under the Fifth Sun: Latino Literature from California.* Santa Clara and Berkeley, Calif.: Santa Clara University/Heyday Books, 2002.
Lomelí, Francisco A., and Carl R. Shirley, eds. *Chicano Writers: First Series.* Detroit: Gale Research, 1989, pp. 302–305.
Samaniego, Danielle. "Professor Reflects on Her Beginnings" *Mustang Daily.* Available online. URL: http://cla.calpoly.edu/~gvelasqu/mustang.html. Downloaded on April 15, 2006.

Vigil-Piñón, Evangelina
(Evangelina Vigil, Evangelina Piñón)
(1949–) *poet, journalist, editor, children's book writer*

Evangelina Vigil-Piñón, poet, broadcast journalist, singer-songwriter, editor, and children's book writer, is credited with being one of the first Hispanic writers to effectively re-create life in the barrio in her writings. Honored with numerous awards, her diverse interests and talents have brought to life the universal concerns of relationships, the passage of time, and transformational processes.

Evangelina Vigil is the second of 10 children of Juan and Maria Soto Vigil. Born on November 29, 1949, Vigil spent her entire childhood in San Antonio, Texas. A child attracted to the sensory delights of the natural world, she loved to listen to katydids, watch geese migrate, and walk among flowers. The sounds of her beloved barrio became a comforting harmony that would later inform her work. Vigil also paid close attention to the stories her grandmother and great-uncle told of life in Mexico during the tumultuous years of the Mexican Revolution of 1910, when the poor, working-class people sought to overthrow the cruel dictator Porfirio Díaz, and then the transition into life in the United States. Her grandmother taught her to observe and listen for the wisdom and guidance that arise from experience.

Her father, a shoemaker, often played the guitar and sang with neighbors and friends, instilling a love of music in Vigil. She sang in the school choir and created lyrics when she did not know the lines of popular music. Her mother gave her a love of the written work. Vigil wrote her first poem at age eight and won third prize in a writing contest. Her aptitude for the visual arts was encouraged by prizes won in arts and poster contests, as well as time spent at Inman Christian Center, a private art school, where she and only one other classmate were of grade school age; the rest were in their early 20s. In high school, Vigil focused her varied creative talents on music. Harkening back to her bucolic childhood days, she suffused the vivacity and love of life's rhythms into poems she wrote for herself and songs she created and played with her cousins in the neighborhood. Vigil describes her muse as "the rhythm of time, the ticking of clocks, hearts beating. To me poetry is music. It is that song in our heart. Life is the dance to that music." Although creativity flowed freely through her veins, she was forced in the direction of secretarial science in high school.

In 1968, Vigil enrolled in Prairie View A&M University, where she earned a scholarship for business administration. The predominantly black university gave Vigil the opportunity to explore African-American music, pride, faith, and culture. This experience helped her discover her Hispanic identity. An artist at heart, Vigil could no longer ignore her creative talents and urgings. She transferred to the University of Houston to study English. She read a variety of poets and other writers extensively, finding inspiration in the writings of Frederick Douglass, James Baldwin, Nikki Giovanni, and Ntozake Shange.

After graduating with a B.A. in English in 1974, Vigil worked in community affairs, television, and counseling. She taught English and literature at the Universidad Jacinto Treviño, served as a writer in residence for the Harlandale Independent School District and Texas Commission of the Arts, and received a National Endowment of the Arts award, which enabled her to travel to the Caribbean and Central America. Vigil released her first collection of poems, *Nade y nade* (Deeper and deeper), in 1978. These poems explore self-identification, the effects of time, and relationships. Critics called Vigil's approach to these weighty topics gentle, with a meditative spirit. From 1976 to 1979, she read Latin-American writers extensively and penned several poems.

Vigil moved to Galveston, Texas, in 1981 to serve as the poet in residence with the Galveston Cultural Arts Center. A year later, she moved to Houston to become a guest lecturer in the English department at the University of Houston. The same year, Vigil released *Thirty an' Seen a Lot.* Her most lauded work, *Thirty,* a collection of poems that celebrate life's simple pleasures shared with nature and people, received the American Book Award. From 1982 to 1989, she worked as a paralegal and in various positions at the Cultural Arts Council of Houston and Harris County. She married musician-artist Mark Anthony Piñón in 1983. That same year, she edited *Woman of Her Word: Hispanic Women Write,* a major collection

Broadcast journalist Evangelina Vigil-Piñón is also a poet and singer. *(Courtesy of the author)*

formed as a singer-songwriter in a Latin and Brazilian trio known as Houston Tranquility Base. In 1993, she coedited *Decade II: An Anniversary Anthology* (1993). Two years later, she became an editor at Arte Público Press. In 2001, Vigil-Piñón released her first bilingual children's book, *Marina's Muumuu.* This book weaves together the special bond a child shares with his or her grandparents. In a 2005 interview, the author explained how Hawaiian culture captivated her: "[A]s a kid I was fascinated with the beauty of the far-away Polynesian islands—the vast sea, graceful palms, exotic blossoms, vibrant colors, lush greenery, beautiful people. It was a world so far far away, so remote—inciting a distinct sense of beauty—and a setting which contrasted dramatically with the urban setting in which I grew up, San Antonio's inner-city Westside barrio, in a region that's semi-arid and more known for cacti, dusty weeds, sunflowers, and Mesquite trees, albeit the abundant palm trees (which I love.) I remember, as a young girl studying art, I loved drawing island scenes. And in the late 1950s and 1960s, the muumuu was a popular dress in the U.S. We all had our muumuus. I loved muumuus, so free and loose and colorful."

Further Reading

Lomelí, Francisco A., and Carl R. Shirley, eds. *Chicano Writers: Second Series.* Vol. 122. Detroit: Gale Research, 1992, pp. 306–312.

Olivares, Julián. "Seeing and Becoming: Evangelina Vigil, *Thirty an' Seen a Lot.*" In *The Chicano Struggle: Analysis of Past and Present Efforts.* Edited by Juan A. García, Theresa Córdova, and Juan R. García. Binghamton, N.Y.: Bilingual Press/Editorial Bilingüe, 1984, pp. 152–165.

Peña, Carmen. "Evangelina Vigil-Piñón." Houston Institute for Culture. Available online. URL: http://www.houstonculture.org/people/pinon.html. Downloaded on September 17, 2005.

Telgen, Diane, and Jim Kamp. *Notable Hispanic American Women.* Detroit: Thompson Gale, 1993.

of literature and criticism by Hispanic women. Three of her poems appear in this work. In 1984, Vigil-Piñón wrote and directed a videotape called *Night Vigil* and gave birth to her son, Marc Antony. Three years later, she translated TOMÁS RIVERA's *. . . no se lo tragó la ierra/. . . and the Earth Did Not Devour Him* and published *The Computer Is Down,* a collection of poems that address the challenge of modernizing without losing culture and identity.

Vigil-Piñón joined KTRK-TV, a Houston ABC affiliate, in 1989, where she served as public affairs director as well as host and producer for the show *Community Close Up: Viva Houston.* During this time the ever-evolving artist per-

Villanueva, Alma Luz
(1944–   ) *poet, short story writer, novelist*

Alma Luz Villanueva had an impact on Chicano literature with her adamant yet poignant perspective on feminine strength and women's universal contributions. She is an acclaimed writer whose varied works appear in several anthologies.

Alma Luz Villanueva was born on October 4, 1944, in Lompoc, California, a small town north of Santa Barbara. She never knew her German father, and her Mexican mother left her in the care of her grandmother, a Yaqui Indian, at an early age. Her maternal grandmother provided the psychic, emotional, and spiritual support young Alma needed. Raised in the Mission District of San Francisco, California, Villanueva's grandmother taught her Mexican traditions, about her German heritage, and the healing and visionary spells she had learned from her own mother. Alma developed a deep connection with the land, nature's cycles, and all living beings. She also learned of the essential role women play in the cosmic game of life. These early lessons created an identity that helps Villanueva recognize herself today as a "Native person of the Earth."

Her grandmother died when Villanueva was 11, and her mother returned to take care of her through her teen years. At 15 years old, Villanueva gave birth to her first son. She experimented with poetry to unravel her emotions but would not take her writing seriously for many years to come. She dropped out of high school and soon found herself in a violent marriage with three children. Her husband, a U.S. Marine, often worked overseas, leaving Villanueva alone with her children in the poorest and most brutal neighborhoods in San Francisco. Villanueva divorced her husband and moved with her children to a remote farming town in the Sierra Nevada range in central California. In this agricultural lifestyle, she reconnected with nature and its innate cycles of ebb and flow.

She married Chicano artist Wilfredo Castaño and had another child. In her late 20s, Villanueva began to use poetry as a means to explore her life's journey, the impact of female relationships, and transformational processes. Her collection of poems *Bloodroot* (1977) employs the power of women's intuition, relationships, and nature as the lens to delve into a wide variety of themes. That same year, Villanueva won the Third Chicano Literary Prize for a collection of 22 of her poems. Critics noted the visceral verses that contained explicit sexual and violent imagery. With an unapologetic conviction, Villanueva wrote *Mother, May I?* in 1978. This epic autobiographical poem recounts the journey from maiden to womanhood in a patriarchal society. Despite the fact that Villanueva begins with a highly personal epicenter, her writing is celebrated for its ability to span out and reach a diverse audience. Villanueva acknowledged to Contemporary Authors Online in 2006 the beauty of writing in "the paradox, the mystery of writing: that when we touch the most personal, the most hidden within ourselves, we touch the other, the outer, the universal. To the 'beginning writer': writing takes all your courage to stand by your work and see it through to publication—courage and luck (and discipline, discipline, discipline)."

La Chingada (1985; The violated woman), another lengthy and passionate poem, explores a universal rather than regional or personal look at the traditional role of woman, including mythical and historical feminine archetypes. As Villanueva's maturity deepens, her poetry reflects an inner, unfettered happiness. The verses in *Life Span* (1985) explode with a jubilant love of life, people, and her role in life.

Sticking to strong female energy, Villanueva successfully ventured into fiction with *Ultraviolet Sky* (1988). The novel recounts Rosa's struggles against the people closest to her to create a life of her choosing. Villanueva's debut novel received fantastic critical acclaim, including an American Book Award. Her second novel, *Naked Ladies* (1994), juxtaposes mundane everyday life with larger-than-life issues such as cancer, domestic and sexual violence, alcoholism, infidelity, and suicide. *Weeping Woman: La Llorona and Other Stories* (1994) is a collection of uninhibited short stories that examines the effects of drug abuse, murder, prostitution, rape, and incest on women's sexuality. Villanueva possesses a keen eye that bears witness to society's ills, and yet this appears as a mirage sitting upon a potential paradise bequeathed to humankind. Villanueva's passion and inclusive love spill forth in the poems of *Desire* (1998).

With her unique style of shamanlike visionary conviction and willingness to use her life as an example, she produced a poignant young adult novel in *Luna's California Poppies* (2002). This compelling coming-of-age novel employs informal epistolary writing as the protagonist uses writing as a means to develop inner strength. In homage to the poet's Yaqui lineage, the poems collected in *Vida* (2002) reflect Villanueva's reverence for life and the sacred symbolism inherent in nature and intimate relationships. *Soft Chaos,* a book of poetry, was released in 2006. During her writing career, Villanueva has served as an artist in residence in many communities and universities. She currently lives in Mexico.

Further Reading

Heide, Rick, ed. *Under the Fifth Sun: Latino Literature from California.* Santa Clara and Berkeley, Calif.: Santa Clara University/Heyday Books, 2002.

Lomelí, Francisco A., and Carl R. Shirley, eds. *Chicano Writers: Second Series.* Vol. 122. Detroit: Gale Research, 1992, pp. 313–317.

Sanchez, Marta Ester. *Contemporary Chicana Poetry: A Critical Approach to an Emerging Literature.* Berkeley: University of California Press, 1985.

Villarreal, José Antonio

(1924–   ) *novelist, essayist, short story writer, editor, journalist, educator*

José Antonio Villarreal, often called the founder of Chicano literature, wrote the groundbreaking novel *Pocho,* which is considered the predecessor to the Chicano literary movement. José Antonio Villarreal was born in Los Angeles, California, on July 20, 1924. His parents, Felícitaz Ramírez and José Heladio Villarreal, had 17 children, 12 of whom survived to adulthood. They had recently emigrated from Zacatecas, Mexico, prior to Villarreal's birth. His father had been a follower of Pancho Villa, one of the insurrectionists of the Mexican Revolution of 1910, when the common folk rose to fight the dictator Porfirio Díaz. Violence continued throughout Mexico until 1920. For the first six years of his life, José constantly moved with his family as migrant field-workers following the crops. José loved the campesino ways of his early years. He listened to the workers share stories of their Mexican regions and knew at an early age he wanted to become a storyteller. The Villarreals settled in Santa Clara, California, in 1930. He credits his first-grade teacher, Miss Uriell, for introducing him to the written word. Upon discovering the local library José fell in love with books. He began to write while in grade school.

Typical of his generation, Villarreal lived the double life of speaking only Spanish at home and only English in school. Ensconced in this space between the Mexican and Anglo cultures, Villarreal felt confusion and frustration. The label and experience of being a *pocho,* a person living between the Mexican and American cultures, served as inspiration for his writings. Eventually the term *pocho* took the negative connotation of someone out of touch with his or her Hispanic roots.

After he graduated from high school, Villarreal enlisted in the U.S. Navy to fight in World War II. He spent three years as a sailor in the Pacific theater. After the war, he enrolled in the University of California–Berkeley with the aid of the G.I. Bill. He graduated with a B.A. in English literature in 1950. He took graduate courses but did not obtain a master's degree. He married Barbara Gentles in 1953 and eventually became the father of three children. While Villarreal attempted to get his novel *Pocho* published, he worked at a variety of jobs, from public relations work to driving a delivery truck and working as a technical editor and writer.

Finally, in 1959, Villarreal found a publisher for *Pocho.* However, the author was a bit ahead of his time in explaining the trials and tribulations of a young person seeking to close the gap between Mexican and American cultures. His novel quickly went out of print but was rereleased at the height of the Chicano movement in 1970. This time, the book received the attention it deserved. Highly autobiographical, the book explains what life was like in the 1930s and led Villarreal to editorial positions, guest lectureships, and teaching positions at such institutions as the Stanford Research Institute, the University of Santa Clara, the University of Colorado, the University of Texas–El Paso, the Preparatoria Americana of the American School in Mexico, Pan American University, and California State University–Los Angeles.

Villarreal moved his family to Mexico in the early 1970s to research firsthand experiences of the Mexican Revolution. The result of this work was *The Fifth Horseman* (1974), which essentially is the chronological predecessor to *Pocho.* Villarreal's second novel found little commercial success until it was rereleased in 1984, the same time his third novel, *Clemente Chacón,* was published. This last book explores the success of immigration while maintaining one's national inheritance. The author returned to Santa Clara in 1992. In addition to his novels, Villarreal has contributed essays to various publications. Some of Villarreal's papers are held at the University of Santa Clara.

Further Reading

Bruce-Novoa, Juan. *Chicano Authors: Inquiry by Interview.* Austin: University of Texas Press, 1980, pp. 37–48.

Heide, Rick, ed. *Under the Fifth Sun: Latino Literature from California.* Santa Clara and Berkeley, Calif.: Santa Clara University/Heyday Books, 2002.

Meier, Matt S., Conchita Franco Serri, and Richard A. Garcia. *Notable Latino Americans: A Biographical Dictionary.* Westport, Conn.: Greenwood Press, 1997.

Villaseñor, Victor
(Victor Edmundo Villaseñor)
(1940–   ) *novelist, screenwriter, short story writer, young adult writer*

Known best for *Rain of Gold,* hailed as the Latin-American version of *Roots,* Victor Villaseñor has helped foster cultural pride and resolve in generations of Mexican Americans. The third of five children, Victor Edmundo Villaseñor was born on May 11, 1940, to Lupe Gomez and Juan Salvadore Villaseñor in Carlsbad, California. He grew up on the family's 166-acre ranch in Oceanside, dreaming of someday becoming a cowboy. He attended the U.S. Army and Navy Academy, where he faced an onslaught of abusive teachers and resentful classmates who constantly teased and humiliated him, crushing his tenderness, depleting his confidence, and erasing pride in his heritage. He struggled with reading and writing, which only served to fuel his growing frustration with life and school. He felt that violence seemed the only answer to his pain. He sought support in the strength of his close-knit family, especially his brother Joseph "Chavaboy." Chavaboy taught Victor to look for little miracles daily—a practice he has maintained for well more than 50 years. Victor was nine years old when his brother died of a rare, unexplained disease.

Villaseñor channeled his mounting anger into wrestling. He returned to his roots during his junior year of high school, when he quit school and moved to Mexico. While in Mexico, he found dignity and developed an appreciation for the value of his Mexican heritage. At the age of 20, Villaseñor returned home. His dormant frustration and rage bubbled to the surface like an old volcano when he witnessed the degradation of poverty-stricken Mexican Americans. Fortunately, he discovered James Joyce's *Portrait of the Artist as a Young Man,* which made him realize a writer could explore and confront his or her problems and perhaps assist the reader to gain empathy. He began writing a book about his youth but received many rejections from publishers. After receiving advice from a writer and family friend to give up writing because he lacked talent, Villaseñor joined the army but continued to write.

Later, he took courses at the University of San Diego and earned a little from construction jobs. After penning 65 short stories and nine novels, he still had not made a penny from his writing. Finally, in 1970, after 265 rejections, Villaseñor sold his first novel, *Macho!* The *Los Angeles Times* compared this raw, powerful, and heartbreaking story of a migrant farmworker to the writings of John Steinbeck.

In a fateful event in 1973, Villaseñor gave an impromptu keynote speech to 30 English teachers during which he exploded with rage and tears at the shame and disgrace he had endured from his teachers, crying so hard and with such venom-

ous anger he rocked the podium. About 30 minutes later, some teachers had left, but the majority remained and to his amazement gave him a standing ovation. This moment provided the impetus he needed to become a public speaker and motivational lecturer.

In 1975, Villaseñor married his editor's daughter, publicist Barbara Bloch. Villaseñor began investigating and studying his family's history soon after the birth of his first child, David. (Joe was born two years later.) He wrote *Jury: The People vs. Juan Corona* (1977), a documentary that reveals the shocking truth behind a murder case, and the screenplay for *The Ballad of Gregorio Cortez* (1982), starring Edward James Olmos.

When Villaseñor was 45, he and his wife took their two boys to a reading specialist. On a whim,

Victor Villaseñor brought the Mexican migration during the Mexican Revolution to the attention of the mainstream audience with *Rain of Gold*. *(Courtesy of the author)*

Villaseñor took the test, too. The results revealed a severe case of dyslexia, which handicapped him in both the visual and auditory areas. He finally had an answer to the cause for many of his learning problems in school.

In 1989, after 12 years of interviews, exploration, and writing, Villaseñor sold *Rain of Gold,* the compelling saga of his family's immigration from Mexico to California. There were just a few catches: The publisher wanted Villaseñor to slash the 540-page manuscript by 75 pages, change the title to *Rio Grande,* and call it fiction in hopes of boosting sales. Villaseñor became enraged. At lunch in Manhattan with the publisher, he bent his fork out of shape and shouted, "I want a divorce! You've been an unfaithful mother to my book!" Villaseñor desperately needed *Rain of Gold* to be marketed as nonfiction to instill the same dignity for Latin Americans that *Roots* had given to African Americans. Alex Haley supported and advised Villaseñor during this tumultuous time. "I wanted my children to see examples of real Mexican heroes," Villaseñor explained on his personal Web site and in the September 1992 issue of *People.* "I grew up thinking Mexicans could only wash dishes and work in the fields."

Villaseñor mortgaged his house, borrowed his mother's life savings, and bought back the rights to the book. He then turned to a small publisher, Arte Público Press, who published *Rain of Gold* in 1991. The book was an instant success. The following year, a New York publisher released *Rain of Gold* in paperback. The book became a best seller, has been translated into seven languages, became required reading in schools across the nation, and received glowing reviews. *USA Today* called it "One of the best books of this or any year." NBC hired Villaseñor to develop a miniseries about Mexican Americans.

Villaseñor's adage became "We are all one race, the human race." He created Snow Goose Global Thanksgiving in 1992 for devoting a day for people to focus on similarities over differences with a sense of community. Celebrated at the Villaseñor home in Oceanside, California, the only request is a dish prepared with love. One year later, Villaseñor self-published *Snow Goose: Global Thanksgiving* to celebrate life, honor Mother Earth, and promote peace from within.

Driven to bring literature to children everywhere, Villaseñor wrote *Mother Fox and Mr. Coyote* (1994), "a sly adaptation of a folk tale for children," as noted by the publisher. Villaseñor continued to explore his family's history, and in 1996, *Rain of Gold*'s prequel, *Wild Steps of Heaven,* was released. This majestic retelling of his father's family's plight in northern Mexico on the eve of the Mexican Revolution weaves together magic, danger, and perseverance. The family's welfare and heart rest solidly on the Villaseñor women, especially his paternal grandmother, an indomitable Indian matriarch, who protects and guides her family with the resolve of unconditional love and a touch of magic. That same year Arte Público Press rereleased *Macho!* and published *Walking Stars* (1996), a collection of short stories to inspire young people to find the brilliance within themselves.

Ever vigilant, Villaseñor continued to research the wealth of wisdom left to him by his ancestors and strong women in his life. The third memoir of his family's saga, *Thirteen Senses* (2001), reveals the unconditional love and fortitude of his parents and explores the limitless realm of the sensory world during Prohibition and the Great Depression.

Burro Genius (2004), the first book of his second trilogy and nominated for a Pulitzer Prize, draws on the brutality of prejudice, the strength of family, and the determination to keep alive the spirit and faith within. Villaseñor searches for the bridge between the lines that divide him against himself and from connecting to the world. He wrote in *Burro Genius* that it is "very hard for me to sometimes known where my Catholic-Christian upbringing stopped and my grandmother's Indian teachings began. For me it was like one big river running together with all these different waters." Villaseñor released two additional children's books in 2005: *Frog and His Friends Save Humanity/La*

Rana y sus amigos salvan a la humanidad and *Little Crow to the Rescue/El Cuervito al rescate.*

October of 2005 saw the opening of the world premiere of the play *Rain of Gold* in the Monterey Bay area of California. Villaseñor has earned many awards and endorsements, including the founding John Steinbeck Chair appointment. In his impassioned lectures, he asks the audience who believes that people have had peace for 5,000 years and promises that at the end of his talk, everyone will agree that, yes, people have had peace for 5,000 years. Women of Substance, as he calls them, or the nurturers, he insists, have ensured this peace by feeding the human spirit, encouraging laughter, and portraying examples of true strength—grace under fire. The women tell stories, mend broken bones, cook, and tend to the heart and soul of their families. This has been the peace that humans have known for 5,000 years, claims Villaseñor. Villaseñor writes and speaks to the fact that peace prevails and that personal suffering is also human suffering; through understanding, family, love, adventure, and laughter, he believes that people can all come together.

Further Reading

Heide, Rick, ed. *Under the Fifth Sun: Latino Literature from California.* Santa Clara and Berkeley, Calif.: Santa Clara University/Heyday Books, 2002.

Villaseñor, Victor: *Burro Genius.* New York: HarperCollins, 2004.

West-Durán, Alan. *Latino and Latina Writers, Volume I.* Detroit: Thomas-Gale, 2004, pp. 537–548.

Villegas de Magnón, Leonor
(Leonor Villegas)
(1876–1955) *memoirist, essayist*

Leonor Villegas de Magnón chronicled the role women played in the Mexican Revolution, a turbulent, violent period from 1910 to 1920, when the common people attempted to wrest themselves free of corrupt politicians. Leonor Villegas was born into wealth and prestige on June 12, 1876, in Nuevo Laredo, Tamaulipas, Mexico. Her father, Joaquín Villegas, originally from Spain, had made his money through ranching, mining, and his import-export business. Her mother, Valeriana Rubio, came from a well-established family as well. Villegas was born just a few days after Porfirio Díaz took control of Mexico City, beginning a dictatorship that would last 34 years. When the military came searching for hidden revolutionaries, they heard the newborn Leonor crying and assumed she was a hidden rebel fighter. From that day, her father affectionately called her "la Rebelde," a name she would grow into and assume as the title for her autobiography.

Villegas enjoyed an idyllic, pastoral life on her family ranch with her three siblings, Leopoldo, Lorenzo, and Lina, until their mother died prematurely. Her father remarried Heloise Monsalvatge, who insisted the family move to Laredo, Texas, and then she promptly sent the children off to boarding schools. Villegas attended the Ursuline Convent in San Antonio, Texas, from 1882 to 1885. She then transferred to the Academy of the Holy Cross in Austin, Texas, where she stayed until she graduated in 1889. She moved to New York in 1889. After receiving a bachelor's degree and teaching credentials from the Academy of Mount St. Ursula in New York in 1895, she returned to Laredo.

On January 10, 1901, Villegas married Adolfo Magnón, a U.S. citizen, with whom she would have three children, Leonor, Joaquin, and Adolfo. The couple moved to Mexico City, where Magnón worked as an agent for several steamship companies. In Mexico, Villegas de Magnón enjoyed a life of luxury but became increasingly aware of the poverty surrounding her. She became involved with revolutionaries, such as Ricardo Flores Magón, who supported Francisco Madero, a leader opposed to Mexican president Díaz. Without her husband's knowledge, she began writing insurgent articles against the Díaz government, which she signed with her maiden name. In 1910, Villegas de Magnón took her children to visit her dying father in Texas, who told his daughter that much of his Mexican land holdings had been confiscated by the government as punishment for Villegas de Magnón's writings.

Villegas de Magnón remained in Laredo and became an active member of the Junta Revolucionaria (Revolutionary Council). She provided housing for political exiles and wrote articles covering the latest events of the revolution to *La Crónica* (The Chronicle), a paper owned by JOVITA IDAR's family, and to her brother's *El Progreso* (The Progress). She opened one of the first bilingual schools in Laredo for young children in 1911. She founded the organization Unión, Progreso y Caridad (Union, Progress, and Charity), calling for women to become more involved in the public sphere through such work as the education of children, charity work, city beautification, and cultural and social events.

In January 1914, Villegas de Magnón founded and financed the Cruz Blanca (White Cross), a medical relief group of women, including Idar, from the border area who traveled with the Constitutionalist forces into war-torn Mexico in support of military insurgent leader Venustiano Carranza. Her efforts were so important that NICOLÁS KANELLOS wrote in *Herencia* that Villegas de Magnón served "practically as a general of women, [who] took charge of the hospital in Nuevo Laredo, [Mexico.]" After the revolution, Villegas de Magnón resumed her role as a teacher and worked for the Women's Division of the State Democratic Executive Committee of Texas. By 1940, Villegas de Magnón had begun to run out of money. She returned to Mexico City and joined the Club Internacional de Mujeres (Women's International Club). After years of lobbying, she and other women finally received official recognition as veterans of the revolution. In 1946, she left her job at the National Department of Statistics in Mexico City to work her own *parcela* (agricultural plot) in Rancherías Camargo, Tamaulipas, as part of the land redistribution program. The program failed, and she returned to Laredo having spent her inheritance.

In the late 1940s, Villegas de Magnón began a memoir to recount the heroic deeds of the Cruz Blanca and "those worthy nurses and brave women who so patriotically defended their country." After several unsuccessful attempts, Villegas de Magnón could not secure a publisher for either the Spanish original or English translation of her book, entitled *La Rebelde* and *The Lady Rebel,* respectively. She died on April 17, 1955. Many years later, however, her granddaughter Leonor Smith placed the collection of drafts of both the English and Spanish versions of the memoir, as well as scrapbooks, letters, and albums, into the hands of editor Clara Lomas, who edited the collection and released *The Rebel* in 1994.

Further Reading

Kanellos, Nicolás, et al., eds. *Herencia: The Anthology of Hispanic Literature in the United States.* New York: Oxford University Press, 2003, pp. 425–428.

Lomas, Clara. "Leonor Villegas de Magnon." In *Longman Anthology of World Literature by Women.* Edited by Marian Arkin and Barbara Shollar. New York and London: Longman, 1989, pp. 181–184.

Lomelí, Francisco A., and Carl R. Shirley, eds. *Chicano Writers: Second Series.* Vol. 122. Detroit: Gale Research, 1992, pp. 318–322.

Villegas de Magnón, Leonor. *The Rebel.* Edited by Clara Lomas. Houston: Arte Público Press, 1994.

Viramontes, Helena Maria

(1954–   ) *short story writer, anthologist, poet, essayist, novelist, educator*

Helena Maria Viramontes is an essential voice of wisdom and clarity in Chicano literature. She hones her anger at the injustices suffered by impoverished Mexicans and Latinas who are oppressed by their dominant culture into finely structured imagery and prose. She thereby transforms the

Helena Maria Viramontes is celebrated for invoking humanity despite the serious themes she tackles. *(Photo of Helena María Viramontes is reprinted with permission from the publisher [APP Archive Files] [Houston: Arte Público Press—University of Houston, © 2006])*

stark, untouchable realities of society's invisible members into a connection among and deepening of humanity.

Born on February 26, 1954, Helena Maria Viramontes is one of nine children. Her father worked at construction while her mother stayed at home to care for the children. Their house was often filled with people who had just crossed the U.S.-Mexico border. Late night stories revealed the desire they all had of obtaining a life on "the other side." These sojourns of dreams, laughter, and crying stayed with Helena for years and formed the foundation for her later writings. To supplement

their income, the entire family, including Helena and her siblings, would work in the fields, picking the crops. Viramontes recalled with the vivid imagination of a skilled writer picking grapes under a sweltering sun and the horrible conditions, such as working all day without the convenience of water or access to a toilet.

The Viramontes household rules were typical of most Latino families of the 1960s: The boys got the privileges, and the girls got the chores. There was not a book in the house until Helena's father brought home an encyclopedia. Helena would steal it away into the bathroom and devour the words, which she came to revere as sacred. She attended Marianna Elementary School, Belvedere Middle School, and Garfield High School in East Los Angeles. Her experience as a nurses' aide during her teen years increased her desire to study and solidified her identity as a bookworm and a scholar. Much to the chagrin of her family, particularly her father, she attended Immaculate Heart College on a scholarship and received a B.A. in English in 1975. Viramontes transferred to the University of California–Los Angeles (UCLA) to study English. She was told by a college professor that she did not belong at UCLA because she wrote about Latin subjects and people. While in college, she began to write seriously. Her first works were published in anthologies, literary journals, and magazines such as *Maize* and *XhismArte Magazine,* the latter of which Viramontes coproduced.

In 1979, Viramontes enrolled in the creative writing program at the University of California–Irvine (UCI). Although she graduated from the program two years later, she unfortunately encountered resistance to her writing when a professor claimed she should not write about Hispanics or Chicanos but people. Outraged, Viramontes commented in a 1995 interview with the *Arizona Republic,* "I knew in my heart that I was writing about people I loved very dearly. I was giving honor to them. Maybe I wasn't the greatest writer—you can criticize me on my craft. But please, please don't say that Chicanos are not people." This piercing ability to see to the root of the issue, the humanity that must be restored, is what gives Viramontes's work its long-standing place within Chicano literature. Her stories, featured in several anthologies and the recipients of several awards and recognitions, speak to the trials and tribulations of Chicanos with such delicate yet powerful prose and verses that one does not focus primarily on the sadness but instead on the redemption and hope inherent in all life. Her writing seeks to break deeply rooted oppressive roles for women held in conventional Latino homes and to inspire her readers to give some thought to the people who launder their clothes or pick the food that appears on their tables day after day.

While at UCI, the author was quite active in promoting Latino and Latina cultural events and creative endeavors and organized two national conferences. She collaborated with MARÍA HERRERA-SOBEK, and together they coedited two volumes that study the contributions of Chicana authors: *Beyond Stereotypes: The Critical Analysis of Chicana Literature* (1985) and *Chicana Creativity and Criticism: New Frontiers in American Literature* (1988).

Viramontes's first book, *The Moths and Other Stories* (1985), focuses on the struggles and spirits of Chicana daughters, mothers, and grandmothers. The short stories in this collection document the political and social personae of Latina women and their efforts to find peace within themselves and a place within society. In the mid-1980s, Viramontes met Eloy Rodriguez while presenting an essay at a reading, which had won the UCI Chicano Literary Contest. Within two years, the couple was married and eventually had two children. In 1989, Viramontes received a National Endowment for the Arts fellowship grant and was able to attend a workshop given by Colombian Nobel Prize–winner Gabriel García Márquez at the Sundance Institute.

In 1993, Viramontes wrote *Paris Rats in E.L.A.,* a collection of stories based in the barrios of the 1960s. She later adapted this work into a screenplay, which the American Film Institute produced. That same year, she accepted a post to teach creative writing at Cornell University, where she is currently an assistant professor of English. Her best known work, *Under the Feet of Jesus* (1994), is a powerful novel that takes readers into the heart of a family of Mexican farmworkers in California. With poignancy and poetic prose, Viramontes tells the story of Estrella, a young woman who comes of age against the backdrop of the brutalities and yet magical strength of farmworkers' lives.

Their Dogs Came with Them (1996) draws a parallel to the brutality of the Spanish conquest of Mexico with the harshness of life for Chicanos in East Los Angeles in the period of the Vietnam War. Congruent to her style, Viramontes tackles cruelties of life and history that most find too appalling to witness with an unflinching yet sensitive pen that enables readers to piece together the fragments of what was lost and create a more soulful worldview.

Further Reading

Davidson, Cathy N., and Linda Wagner-Martin, eds. *The Oxford Companion to Women's Writing in the United States.* New York: Oxford University Press, 1995.

Fernandez, Roberta. "The Cariboo Cafe: Helena Maria Viramontes Discourses with Her Social and Cultural Contexts." *Women's Studies* 17, no. 2 (1989): 71–85.

Fox, L. C. "Chicana Creativity and Criticism: Charting New Frontiers in America." *College Literature* 18, no. 1 (1991): 103–106.

West-Durán, Alan. *Latino and Latina Writers, Volume I.* Detroit: Gale-Thomas, 2004, pp. 549–568.

W

Williams, William Carlos
(1883–1963) *poet, essayist, novelist, playwright, short story writer*

Pulitzer Prize–winner William Carlos Williams was a prolific writer who is best remembered for his poetry and helping to develop imagism—the clear, precise delineation of imagery in poetry—in the early part of the 20th century. William Carlos Williams was born on September 17, 1883, in Rutherford, New Jersey, a town in which he would spend most of his life. His father, William George Williams, was a socialist, a businessman, and cofounder of the Unitarian Society of Rutherford, who never gave up his British citizenship or the austere expectations of a Victorian gentleman. Williams's mother, Raquel Hélène (Elena) Rose Hoheb Williams, was a cultivated, aloof woman whose ancestry included Puerto Rican, Dutch, French, Jewish, and Spanish roots. She pined to return to Paris, spoke mainly Spanish at home, and entertained cosmopolitan guests from Paris and the Caribbean. Young Williams longed to be close to his mother but never seemed to penetrate her Puritan, gentile front. His paternal grandmother, Emily Dickinson Wellcome, provided the earthy stability Williams needed. This woman of immense stubbornness and fierce independence took the boy under her care. Williams attended public schools in Rutherford throughout his primary education.

In 1897, when Williams was 14 years old, his father spent a year abroad in Venezuela. His mother seized the opportunity to travel to Europe, where Williams and his young brother, Edgar, attended schools in Geneva and Paris. They returned to Rutherford in 1899. Williams and his brother commuted from New Jersey to Manhattan's Upper West Side to attend Horace Mann High School. There, English teacher William Abbott introduced Williams to the systematic study of poetry and the works of John Keats and Walt Whitman. Both poets would prove to have a profound impact on Williams's writings. Williams's parents demanded their son's education be directed toward a more suitable profession, forcing the dutiful son to hide his passion for writing. He studied medicine at the University of Pennsylvania, in Philadelphia, from 1902 to 1906. During his medical studies, he maintained his interest in poetry. While at the university he met Ezra Pound, who was a couple of years younger than Williams. Pound was a visceral writer and freed Williams from the idealistic, rather boxed writing he had developed. He helped his friend to be more creative, authentic, and spontaneous in his work.

Williams completed medical studies in Philadelphia in 1906. He served as an intern at the French hospital in New York City for two years. He spent six months at Child's Hospital before becoming dissatisfied with the administration. He went to Germany in 1909 to study pediatrics for a few months before returning to Rutherford to open a private practice. Williams practiced medicine for approximately 40 years.

About 1911, the imagism movement dawned in London and America. Pound was at its epicenter, and while Williams never officially became a member, his works were often included in imagist anthologies. Williams felt his work lay in describing, through poetry, the love and landscape of his country and his hometown. His poems are marked by a distinct voice, a palpable place. Williams met Charles Demuth, a painter who would affect the writer's work by creating, as he put it, "an atmosphere of release, color release, release from stereotyped forms, trite subjects." In 1912, he married Florence (Flossie) Herman, with whom he would have two children, Eric and Paul. In 1913, Williams released his second book of poems, *The Tempers,* and by that time had formulated the style of poetry he would maintain for the rest of his life. Williams wrote only one collection in Spanish, *¡Al que quiere!* (1917); all other works appear in English. Other books of poetry by Williams include *Spring and All* (1923); *Collected Poems, 1921–1931* (1934); *An Early Martyr and Other Poems* (1935); *The Complete Collected Poems* (1938); *Selected Poems* (1949); *The Pink Church* (1949); *The Collected Earlier Poems* (1951); *The Collected Later Poems* (1950); *The Desert Music and Other Poems* (1954); *Journey to Love* (1955); *I Wanted to Write a Poem,* reported and edited by Edith Heal (1958); and *Pictures from Brueghel and Other Poems* (1962). Many of these works have been revised and enlarged over the years and have enjoyed publication into the 21st century.

Williams proved himself a prose writer with *Kora in Hell: Improvisations* (1920), a collection of prose "improvisation;" *The Great American Novel* (1923), a short novel; *In the American Grain* (1925), a collection of historical essays; and his first full-length novel, *A Voyage to Pagany* (1928). Williams penned a plethora of essays, novels, and short stories, including *A Novellette and Other Prose (1921–1931)*

(1932), *The Knife of the Times and Other Stories* (1932), *White Mule* (1937), *Life along the Passaic River* (1938), *In the Money: White Mule—Part II* (1940), *Paterson (Book One)* (1948), *Paterson (Book Two)* (1948), *Paterson (Book Three)* (1949), *Make Light of It: Collected Stories* (1950), *A Beginning on the Short Story [Notes]* (1950), *Paterson (Book Four)* (1951), *The Autobiography* (1951), *The Build-Up: A Novel* (1952), *Selected Essays* (1954), *Paterson (Book Five)* (1958), *Yes, Mrs. Williams: A Personal Record of My Mother* (1959), *The Farmers' Daughters: The Collected Stories* (1961), and *Paterson (Books 1–5 and Notes for Book 6)* (1963). Of these works Williams is best known for *Life along the Passaic River* and his collection of *Paterson* works.

Williams was also a playwright. His plays include *A Dream of Love: A Play in Three Acts and Eight Scenes* (1948), *Tituba's Children* (1950), and *Many Loves and Other Plays: The Collected Plays* (1961).

Williams died on March 4, 1963. In October of that same year, he was posthumously awarded the Pulitzer Prize for his book *Pictures from Brueghel and Other Poems.* Other prestigious honors include the Dial Award, National Institute and American Academy of Arts and Letters Gold Medals, Bollingen Prize, and an appointment as consultant in poetry to the Library of Congress. After his death, several authors and editors compiled Williams's works and critical analysis of its importance in American literature into more than 70 books, including *A Recognizable Image: William Carlos Williams on Art and Artists* (1978); *The Doctor Stories,* compiled by Robert Coles (1984); and *The Collected Poems of William Carlos Williams,* two volumes (1986).

The majority of Williams's manuscripts and letters are housed in three libraries: the Lockwood Memorial Library at the State University of New York–Buffalo, the Beinecke Rare Book and Manuscript Library at Yale University, and the Humanities Research Center at the University of Texas–Austin. There are also small but important collections of papers at the Alderman Library at the University of Virginia, the University of Delaware library, and the Lilly Library at Indiana University. Williams's success hinges on the fact that his writings speak to the human condition and create images of everyday life. He infused the magic and mystery of poetry into the mundane world with tenderness and conviction.

Further Reading

Breslin, James E. B. *William Carlos Williams, an American Artist*. New York: Oxford University Press, 1970.

Laughlin, James. *Remembering William Carlos Williams*. New York: New Directions, 1995.

Rosenthal, M. L. *The William Carlos Williams Reader*. New York: New Directions, 1966.

Williams, William Carlos. *The Autobiography of William Carlos Williams*. New York: New Directions, 1967.

———. *William Carlos Williams: Selected Poems*. New York: Library of America, 2004.

Y

Yglesias, Jose
(1919–1995) *novelist, short story writer, journalist*

Jose Yglesias wrote a series of books exploring bicultural living for the working-class Latino. His best-known book is *The Goodbye Land,* a tribute to his father and his father's hometown in Spain.

The son of immigrant cigar makers, Jose and Georgia (Milian) Yglesias, Jose Yglesias was born on November 29, 1919, in Tampa, Florida. His father was originally from Spain, and his mother was Cuban. His father died at an early age, which profoundly affected the budding writer, as did experiences of the riotous "Cigar City" during the 1920s and living through the depression as a young man. In 1886, cigar makers Vicente Martinez-Ybor and Ignacio Haya had moved their cigar factories from Key West, Florida, to Tampa, thereby creating Ybor City, a haven for Cuban, Spanish, and Italian immigrants. As a youth, Yglesias was well aware of the trials and tribulations of immigrants, which he committed to his memory and heart. The experiences of those around him were not relegated to some sociological assemblage of events but rather were individual life events and relationships. He was a humanitarian who appreciated the unique experience of the individual.

Throughout the late 1930s and early 1940s, Yglesias held several jobs, from dishwasher and stock clerk to assembly line worker and typist-correspondent. He served in the U.S. Navy from 1942 to 1945. After World War II, Yglesias attended Black Mountain College in North Carolina for a year. From 1948 to 1950, he was the film critic at *Daily Worker* in New York City. Yglesias married Helen Bassine, a novelist, on August 19, 1950. The couple had one son, Rafael. Yglesias served as the assistant to the vice president of the pharmaceutical company Sharp Dohme International from 1953 to 1963. He translated several works, including *Island of Women* (1962), *Sands of Torremolinos* (1962), *Villa Milo* (1962) and *The Party's Over* (1966). Yglesias released his first book, *A Wake in Ybor City,* in 1963. The book was one of the first to depict the experiences of Cuban immigrants. It follows a Cuban-American family in 1958 as they are confronted by a series of crises.

Yglesias traveled with his wife and son to Spain to better understand his father and their shared ancestry. *The Goodbye Land* (1967) was a result of interviews with his father's relatives and friends, as well as his observations of the quaint, mountainside village. He followed with *In the Fist of the Revolution: Life in a Cuban Country Town* (1968), a book based on the opinions of the Cuban Revolution held by the people he met during his three-month stay in Mayari, Cuba. *An Orderly Life* (1968) contains sociopolitical themes. Yglesias then met with young revolutionaries of Brazil, Cuba, Chile, and Peru to form the basis of *Down There* (1970). He received a Guggenheim fellowship in 1970 and again in 1976. He was also the recipient of a National Endowment for the Arts grant in 1974.

Yglesias continued his study of individual awareness, behavior, and reaction through his writing. Additional books by Yglesias include *The Truth About Them* (1971), *Double, Double* (1974), *The Kill Price* (1976), *The Franco Years* (1977), *Home Again* (1987), *Tristan and the Hispanics* (1989), *The Old Gents* (1996), *Break-In* (1996), and *The Guns in the Closet* (short stories, 1996). The latter three books were published posthumously by Arte Público Press. Yglesias died of cancer on November 7, 1995, in Manhattan. His short stories were published in collections after his death. When Arte Público Press rereleased his earlier works, Ygelsias received the recognition as a predecessor in chronicling the immigrant experience that he deserved.

Further Reading

Brown, Susan Windisch, ed. *Contemporary Novelists.* 6th ed. Detroit: St. James Press, 1996.

Kanellos, Nicolás, et al., eds. *Herencia: The Anthology of Hispanic Literature in the United States.* New York: Oxford University Press, 2003, pp. 231–233.

Yglesias, Jose. *The Goodbye Land.* New York: Pantheon Books, 1967.

Z

Zamora, Bernice
(Bernice Ortiz)
(1938–   ) *poet, short story writer, essayist, educator*

Bernice Zamora is considered one of the leading voices of the Chicano movement. Zamora's poetry has been widely anthologized and recognized for its imagery, rage, and originality.

The eldest of five children, Bernice Ortiz was born on January 20, 1938, in Aguilar, Colorado, a farming and coal mining community. Both of her parents, Marcela Valdez and Victor Ortiz, a coal miner and farmer, claimed long-standing heritage to the region along the Apishapa River in south-central Colorado. When she was three years old, Bernice attended catechism classes, where the nuns discovered she had taught herself to read English from household items such as cereal boxes. They encouraged her to use English whenever possible. Bernice's linguistic development focused on English; she spoke Spanish only with her grandparents and older relatives. An excellent student, Bernice attended Catholic schools in Pueblo and Denver, Colorado, until the eighth grade. Then, her father sustained a work accident that disabled him. Ortiz worked long hours after school throughout junior high and high school to supplement the family's income.

In 1957, Ortiz married and assumed her husband's surname, Zamora. The couple had two daughters, Rhonda and Katherine. At 28, Zamora decided to further her education. She graduated from the University of Southern Colorado with a B.A. in French and English in 1969, later earning an M.A. in English literature from Colorado State University in 1972. She studied in the doctoral program at Marquette University before her marriage ended in divorce in 1974. She then drove with her daughters to northern California, where she enrolled in the doctoral program at Stanford University.

During the 1970s, Zamora contributed her poetry and essays to a number of journals and magazines. She met ALURISTA, RON ARIAS, and JOSE ANTONIO BURCIAGA while at Stanford. These influential writers would often gather to read their works and lend support and energy to one another. Zamora and Burciaga combined their poetry in *Restless Serpents* (1976), which explores Chicano culture, language, and gender relations. Zamora's title poem, "Restless Serpents," has been widely anthologized. JUAN BRUCE-NOVOA praised Zamora's writing saying, "Like those serpents, Zamora's poetry fascinates: inscrutable signs of life and death in beautiful poems, capable of demonic possession; gods of mysterious, lost worlds, only accessible to us in the surface of the images they themselves are."

In 1979, Zamora moved to Alburquerque, New Mexico, to become the editor of the Chicano journal *De Colores*. She wrote short stories and made other contributions to the magazine yet always found her lifeline in poetry. Zamora participated in the Chicano literary festival Floricanto and coedited an anthology based on the works from the festival entitled *Flor y Canto IV and V: An Anthology of Chicano Literature* (1980). Zamora became quite ill in 1982 and returned to California. She recovered and continued her education, receiving a Ph.D. in English and American literature from Stanford University in 1986. She accepted a teaching position in the English department of Santa Clara University in 1990, where she taught world, Chicano, Native American, contemporary, and American literature. She published *Releasing Serpents* in 1994. That same year, *The Nation* commented on Zamora's poetry, "What makes her short, imagistic poems so magnificent is the way she captures decades-old history, then thrusts it forward into the present without hesitation."

During the late 1990s, Zamora's short stories appeared in anthologies. Although many of her writings speak to the injustices done to women and evoke a need for empowerment, Zamora does not consider herself a feminist writer, claiming "to be a purely feminist writer is to ignore the issue of race—racial discrimination, division, and deprivation." Zamora's seminal poetry deals head-on with cultural oppression with a ferocious anger.

Further Reading

Heide, Rick, ed. *Under the Fifth Sun: Latino Literature from California.* Santa Clara and Berkeley, Calif.: Santa Clara University/Heyday Books, 2002.

Magill, Frank N. *Masterpieces of Latino Literature.* New York: HarperCollins, 1994.

Meier, Matt S., Conchita Franco Serri, and Richard A. Garcia. *Notable Latino Americans: A Biographical Dictionary.* Westport, Conn.: Greenwood Press, 1997, pp. 406–409.

Tardiff, Joseph C., and L. Mpho Mabunda, eds. *Dictionary of Hispanic Biography.* Detroit: Gale Research, 1996, pp. 965–966.

Zavala, Val
(Valerie Zavala)
(1955–   ) *journalist*

The success and track record of award-winning broadcast journalist and executive Val Zavala exemplifies what strength of character, dedication to community, and receptivity to divergent cultures can accomplish. Throughout her career, Zavala has earned nine Emmy Awards, four Golden Mike Awards, the Best of the West Award, the Imagen Award for Excellence, and the Greater Los Angles Press Club Award. Even as a young child, Zavala felt a deep concern for people around her. She thought she would work in politics intending to change the world for the better. Today, as one of the highest-ranking Latinas in local television news, she carries out her dream but through a different medium than she originally imagined.

Born to Salvador Zavala and Dorothy Kraus in Chicago, Illinois, on July 5, 1955, Valerie Zavala is of Mexican, French, and German descent. While she was still quite young, Valerie, her four siblings, and their parents moved to the Mexican-American border towns of Calexico and Chula Vista of southern California. Valerie attended Catholic schools and enjoyed many comforts in life. However, in a bilingual and bicultural environment, she could not help but notice the socio-economic disparities.

As a child and still today, Zavala draws inspiration from her father, whose family emigrated from Mexico City when he was eight and whose widowed mother raised six children on the south side of Chicago during the Great Depression and World War II. Despite the hardships, he became fluent in English, earned a college degree, and went into banking. It was precisely his success that influenced Zavala's ambitious nature.

After graduating from high school in Chula Vista, Zavala won admission to Yale University. Living on the East Coast gave Zavala exposure to a subculture immersed in politics, with an orientation completely different from a southern California border town. This eye-opening experience would prove important in developing Zavala's journalism skills. In 1978, she graduated with a B.A. in Latin-American studies and applied to the Peace Corps. While she eagerly awaited an assignment in Latin America, the corps underwent reorganization. The delay caused Zavala to obtain work as a secretary at the National Public Radio station in San Francisco (KQED), where she discovered an interest in broadcasting. The following year, she received a fellowship from NBC and attended American University in Washington, D.C., to study in the master's program in journalism. Upon graduation in 1980, Zavala worked for three years as a production assistant in Baltimore, Maryland. She spent the next three years working as a general assignments reporter in San Luis Obispo, Fresno, and San Diego, California.

Zavala became disillusioned with commercialism in broadcast journalism and its obsession with ratings. She remembered in a 2005 interview that she "learned a tremendous amount about how to put a story together quickly. But it was clear that news directors paid more attention to the choice of clothes and hairstyles than the choice of words. There is an eternal quest for high ratings. Newscasts have become news 'shows.' Broadcasters have become news 'personalities.' The average story is forty-five seconds long. And cameras can't resist flashing orange flames or a hot pursuit."

In 1987, Zavala found refuge at KCET as a senior producer at the West Coast's flagship public television station. "I was lucky to have found my calling," said Zavala. "Instead of covering shootings or the world's longest banana split, we were reporting on serious issues, ideas, local history, culture, and arts." Clearly in her niche, Zavala began to win awards, such as the Los Angeles Area Emmy Award for Best Public Affairs Special for "Hispanics and AIDS."

In 1992, Zavala took a mid-career break as a John S. Knight Fellow at Stanford University, one of only 12 journalists selected nationwide. She returned a year later to KCET as executive producer of *Life & Times*. In November 1996, Zavala was promoted to vice president of news and public affairs to oversee the transition of *Life & Times* to a nightly broadcast, which premiered in January 1998.

In her work, Zavala seeks to offer southern Californians a different perspective on community than they perhaps currently have. She takes the time to delve deeper into subjects such as policy and education and truly represents the community and its diverse needs. "With Latinos fast becoming the majority in southern California . . . it's important that Latinos are really in the decision-making end of things—especially in this market," said Zavala in a March 15, 2005, press release. "It's great to see brown reporters out there, but what's important is that there be people behind the scenes who are making the decisions of who and what ought to be in front of the camera." She is dedicated to offering stories that dig beneath the surface to find the universal quality that connects us all. Zavala commented in a 2005 interview that she believes that "beyond race or background, it is the individual skills, people skills; the essence of character that gets you where you want to go." In seeking out the human element and responding to the public interest, she personifies integrity in the newsroom, bringing the community together one show at a time.

Further Reading

Baldwin Hills Conservatory. "The Baldwin Hills Conservancy Honors Val Zavala." Available online. URL: http://bhc.ca.gov/Val_Zavala.html. Downloaded on June 2, 2005.

Lambert, Laurel. *"Life & Times,* KCET's Signature Newsmagazine, Covers Station's Communities with Val Zavala as Sole Anchor Reporting from the Field." URL: http://kcet.org/lifeandtimes. Downloaded on May 25, 2005.

BIBLIOGRAPHY AND RECOMMENDED SOURCES

Anthologies

Christie, John, and Jose Gonzales. *Latino Boom: An Anthology of U.S. Latino Literature.* Englewood Cliffs, N.J.: Longman, 2006.

Cortina, Rodolfo, ed. *Hispanic American Literature: An Anthology.* Lincolnwood, Ill.: NTC, 1997.

Flores, Lauro. *Floating Borderlands: Twenty-five years of United States Hispanic Literature.* Seattle: University of Washington Press, 1998.

González, Ray, ed. *Currents from the Dancing River: Contemporary Latino Fiction, Nonfiction, and Poetry.* New York: Harcourt Brace, 1994.

Heide, Rick, ed. *Under the Fifth Sun: Latino Literature from California.* Santa Clara and Berkeley, Calif.: Santa Clara University/Heyday Books, 2002.

Hernández-Gutiérrez, Manuel de Jesús, and David William Foster. *Literatura chicana, 1965–1995: An Anthology in Spanish, English, and Caló.* New York: Garland, 1997.

Heyck, Deni Lynn Daly. *Barrios and Borderland: Cultures of Latinos and Latinas in the United States.* New York: Routledge, 1994.

Kanellos, Nicolás, et al., eds. *Herencia: The Anthology of Hispanic Literature in the United States.* New York: Oxford University Press, 2003.

———. *Hispanic American Literature: A Brief Introduction and Anthology.* New York: HarperCollins, 1995.

López, Tiffany Ann, ed. *Growing Up Chicana/o: An Anthology.* New York: William Morrow, 1993.

Milligan, Bryce, Mary Guerrero Milligan, and Angela de Hoyos, eds. *Daughters of the Fifth Sun: A Collection of Latina Fiction and Poetry.* New York: Riverhead Trade, 1996.

———. *Floricanto Sí: A Collection of Latina Poetry.* New York: Penguin Books, 1998.

Olivares, Julián, and Evangelina Vigil-Piñon, eds. *Decade II: A Twentieth Anniversary Anthology.* Houston, Tex.: Arte Público Press, 1993.

Poey, Delia, and Virgil Suárez, eds. *Iguana Dreams: New Latino Fiction.* New York: Perennial, 1992.

Rebolledo, Tey Diana, and Eliana S. Rivero. *Infinite Divisions: An Anthology of Chicana Literature.* Tucson: University of Arizona Press, 1993.

Rio, Eduardo del. *Prentice Hall Anthology of Latino Literature.* Englewood Cliffs, N.J.: Prentice Hall, 2001.

Santiago, Robert. *Boricuas: Influential Puerto Rican Writings—An Anthology.* New York: One World/ Ballantine, 1995.

Stavans, Ilan, ed. *New World: Young Latino Writers.* New York: Delta/Dell, 1997.

Tashlik, Phyllis, ed. *Hispanic, Female and Young: An Anthology.* Houston, Tex.: Arte Público Press, 1994.

Tatum, Charles M., ed. *New Chicana/Chicano Writing.* 3 vols. Tucson: University of Arizona Press, 1992–1993.

Biographical Sources

Bruce-Novoa, Juan David. *Chicano Authors: Inquiry by Interview.* Austin: University of Texas Press, 1980.

Hospital, Carolina, ed. *Cuban American Writers: Los atrevidos.* Princeton, N.J.: Ediciones Ellas/Linden Lane Press, 1988.

Kanellos, Nicolás, ed. *Biographical Dictionary of Hispanic Literature in the United States: The Literature of Puerto Ricans, Cuban Americans, and Other Hispanic Writers.* Westport, Conn.: Greenwood Press, 1989.

Lomelí, Francisco A., and Carl R. Shirley, eds. *Dictionary of Literary Biography*, Vol. 82: *Chicano Writers, First Series.* Detroit: Gale Group, 1989.

———. *Dictionary of Literary Biography*, Vol. 122: *Chicano Writers, Second Series,* Detroit: Gale Group, 1992.

———. *Dictionary of Literary Biography,* Vol. 209: *Chicano Writers, Third Series.* Detroit: Gale Group, 1999.

Martínez, Al. *Rising Voices: Profiles of Hispano-American Lives.* New York: New American Library, 1974.

Meier, Matt S., Conchita Franco Serri, and Richard A. Garcia. *Notable Latino Americans: A Biographical Dictionary.* Westport, Conn.: Greenwood Press, 1997.

Meyer, Nicolas E. *Biographical Dictionary of Hispanic Americans.* New York: Facts On File, 1997.

Palmisano, Joseph M. *Notable Hispanic American Women.* Book 2. Detroit: Gale Research, 1998.

Ryan, Bryan, ed. *Hispanic Literature: A Selection of Sketches from Contemporary Authors.* Detroit: Gale Research, 1991.

———. *Hispanic Writers.* Detroit: Gale Research, 1991.

Tardiff, Joseph C., and L. Mpho Mabunda, eds. *Dictionary of Hispanic Biography.* Detroit: Gale Research, 1996.

Telgen, Diane, and Jim Kamp. *Notable Hispanic American Women.* Detroit: Thomson Gale, 1993.

West-Durán, Alan. *Latino and Latina Writers.* 2 vols. Detroit: Gale Thomas, 2004.

Critical Studies

Augdenbraum, Harold, and Margarite Fernandez Olmos. *U.S. Latino Literature: A Critical Guide of Students and Teachers.* Westport, Conn.: Greenwood, 2000.

Bruce-Novoa, Juan David. *Chicano Authors: Inquiry by Interview.* Austin: University of Texas Press, 1980.

Candelaria, Cordelia. *Chicano Poetry: A Critical Introduction.* Westport, Conn.: Greenwood Press, 1986.

Herrera-Sobek, María. *Beyond Stereotypes: The Critical Analysis of Chicana Literature.* Birmingham, N.Y.: Bilingual Press, 1995.

Herrera-Sobek, María, and Helena Maria Viramontes. *Chicana Creativity and Criticism: New Frontiers in American Literature.* Albuquerque: University of New Mexico Press, 1996.

Kanellos, Nicolás. *Hispanic Literary Companion.* Detroit: Visible Ink, 1997.

Kevane, Bridget. *Latino Literature in America.* Westport, Conn.: Greenwood Press, 2003.

Leal, Luis. *Decade of Chicano Literature, 1970–1979: Critical Essays and Bibliography.* New York: Presidio Press, 1982.

Lomelí, Francisco A., and Donald W. Urioste. *Chicano Perspectives in Literature: A Critical and Annotated Bibliography.* Albuquerque, N.Mex.: Pajarito, 1976.

Madsen, Deborah L. *Understanding Contemporary Chicana Literature.* Columbia: University of South Carolina Press, 2000.

Magill, Frank N. *Masterpieces of Latino Literature.* New York: HarperCollins, 1994.

Martinez, Julio A., and Francisco A. Lomelí, eds. *Chicano Literature.* Westport, Conn.: Greenwood Press, 1985.

Robelledo, Tey Diana. *Women Signing in the Snow: Cultural Analysis of Chicana Literature.* Tucson: University of Arizona Press, 1995.

Tatum, Charles. *Chicano Literature: A Critical History.* Boston: Twayne, 1982.

Ventura, Gabriela Baeza. *U.S. Latino Literature Today.* Englewood Cliffs, N.J.: Longman Publishing, 2004.

Genres and Literary Movements

Algarín, Miguel, ed. *Aloud: Voices from the Nuyorican Poets Cafe.* New York: Henry Holt, 1994.

Augenbaum, Harold, and Ilan Stavans, eds. *Growing Up Latino: Memoirs and Stories.* Boston: Houghton Mifflin, 1993.

Carlson, Lori M., ed. *Cool Salsa: Bilingual Poems on Growing Up Latino in the United States.* New York: Henry Holt, 1994.

Castillo-Speed, Lillian, ed. *Latina: Women's Voices from the Borderlands.* New York: Touchstone/Simon & Schuster, 1995.

Cortés, Eladio, and Mirta Barrea-Maryls, eds. *Encyclopedia of Latin American Theatre.* Westport, Conn.: Greenwood Press, 2003.

González, María C. *Contemporary Mexican-American Women Novelists: Toward a Feminist Identity.* New York: Peter Lang, 1996.

González, Ray, ed. *After Aztlán: Latino Poets of the Nineties.* Boston: David R. Godine, 1992.

———. *Mirrors Beneath the Earth: Short Fiction by Chicano Writers.* Willimantic, Conn.: Curbstone Press, 1992.

Herrera-Sobek, María, et al. *Chicano Renaissance: Contemporary Trends in Chicano Culture.* Tucson: University of Arizona Press, 2000.

Hospital, Carolina, and Jorge Cantera, eds. *A Century of Cuban Writers in Florida: Selected Prose & Poetry.* Sarasota, Fla.: Pineapple Press, 1996.

Kanellos, Nicolás. *The Hispanic American Almanac: A Reference Work on Hispanics in the United States.* Detroit: Gale, 1993.

Madsen, Deborah L. *Understanding Contemporary Chicana Literature.* Columbia: University of South Carolina Press, 2000.

Poey, Delia, and Virgil Suárez, eds. *Little Havana Blues: A Cuban-American Literature Anthology.* Houston, Tex.: Arte Público Press, 1996.

Romero, Rolando, and Amanda Nolacea Harris, eds. *Feminism, Nation and Myth: La Malinche.* Houston, Tex.: Arte Público Press, 2005.

Sommers, Joseph. *Modern Chicano Writers: A Collection of Critical Essays.* Englewood Cliffs, N.J.: Prentice Hall, 1979.

Stavans, Ilan. *Wáchale! Poetry and Prose about Growing Up Latino in America.* Peru, Ill.: Cricket Books, 2001.

Steiner, Stan. *La Raza: The Mexican Americans.* New York: Harper and Row, 1970.

ENTRIES BY SUBJECT MATTER/STYLE

Barrio Experience

Baca, Jimmy Santiago
Cisneros, Sandra
de Hoyos, Angela
Galarza, Ernesto
Hernandez Cruz, Victor
Mohr, Nicholasa
Morales, Alejandro
Piñero, Miguel
Rodríguez, Luis J.
Salas, Floyd
Sánchez, Ricardo
Soto, Gary
Thomas, Piri

Border Culture

Cantú, Norma Elia
Chávez, Denise
Cisneros, Sandra
de Uriarte, Mercedes Lynn
Gaspar de Alba, Alicia
González, Jovita
Hinojosa-Smith, Rolando
Idar, Jovita
Islas, Arturo
Martínez, Demetria
Martínez, Rubén
Méndez, Miguel
Mora, Pat
Paredes, Américo

Villarreal, José Antonio
Viramontes, Helena Maria

Chicano Movement

Acosta, Oscar Zeta
Alarcón, Francisco X.
Alurista
Anaya, Rudolfo A.
Anzaldúa, Gloria
Arteaga, Alfred
Bruce-Novoa, Juan
Burciaga, Jose Antonio
Castillo, Ana
Cervantes, Lorna Dee
Corpi, Lucha
de Hoyos, Angela
Delgado, Abelardo
Gonzales, Rodolfo
Herrera, Juan Felipe
Hinojosa-Smith, Rolando
Islas, Arturo
Kanellos, Nicolás
Méndez, Miguel
Morales, Alejandro
Paredes, Américo
Ríos, Alberto
Rivera, Tomás
Rodríguez, Luis J.
Rodríguez, Richard
Salas, Floyd

Salazar, Rubén
Salinas, Luis Omar
Sánchez, Ricardo
Soto, Gary
Tafolla, Carmen
Ulibarrí, Sabine R.
Valdez, Luis
Velásquez, Gloria
Villanueva, Alma Luz
Villarreal, José Antonio
Viramontes, Helena Maria
Zamora, Bernice

Cuban-American Literature

Cabrera, Lydia
Engle, Margarita
Fornes, Maria Irene
García, Cristina
García-Aguilera, Carolina
Hijuelos, Oscar
Martí, José
Muñoz, Elías Miguel
Prida, Dolores
Suárez, Virgil
Yglesias, Jose

Expatriate Experience

Alegría, Fernando
Allende, Isabel

Carrillo, Adolfo
de Burgos, Julia
García, Cristina
Martí, José
Varela, Félix

Feminist Issues

Agosín, Marjorie
Anzaldúa, Gloria
Castillo, Ana
Chávez, Denise
Cisneros, Sandra
Cofer, Judith Ortiz
Corpi, Lucha
Cortina, Betty
Davidds, Yasmin
de Acosta, Mercedes
Estés, Clarissa Pinkola
Gaspar de Alba, Alicia
González, Jovita
Idar, Jovita
Jaramillo, Cleofas Martínez
Lopez, Josefina
Martínez, Demetria
Moraga, Cherríe
Nogales, Ana
Ponce, Mary Helen
Ruiz de Burton, María Amparo
Ruiz, Vicki L.
Santiago, Esmeralda
Tafolla, Carmen
Villanueva, Alma Luz
Villegas de Magnón, Leonor
Viramontes, Helena Maria

Folklore and Oral Storytelling

Alcalá, Kathleen
Anaya, Rudolfo A.
Cabrera, Lydia
Carrillo, Adolfo
Chávez, Fray Angélico
De Zavala, Adina

Fornes, Maria Irene
Gilbert, Fábíolá Cabeza de Baca
González, Jovita
Haslam, Gerald
Hernández-Ávila, Inés
Herrera, Juan Felipe
Herrera-Sobek, María
Huerta, Jorge
Jaramillo, Cleofas Martínez
Lopez, Josefina
Mares, E. A.
Mohr, Nicholasa
Morales, Ed
Morton, Carlos
Nava, Yolanda
Niggli, Josephina
Otero, Nina
Paredes, Américo
Pineda, Cecile
Piñero, Miguel
Portillo Trambley, Estela
Prida, Dolores
Rojas, Arnold
Serrano, Nina
Tafolla, Carmen
Valdez, Luis
Véa, Alfredo, Jr.
Velásquez, Gloria
Vigil-Piñón, Evangelina
Villarreal, José Antonio
Williams, William Carlos

Gay and Lesbian Issues

Alarcón, Francisco X.
Anzaldúa, Gloria
Castillo, Ana
de Acosta, Mercedes
Gaspar de Alba, Alicia
Moraga, Cherríe
Rechy, John

Immigrant Experience

Adame, Leonard
Agosín, Marjorie
Alarcón, Francisco X.
Alvarez, Julia
Cofer, Judith Ortiz
Colón, Jesús
Delgado, Abelardo
Diaz, Junot
Fornes, Maria Irene
Galarza, Ernesto
Gonzales, Rodolfo
Hernandez Cruz, Victor
Hijuelos, Oscar
Limón, Graciela
Martínez, Rubén
Muñoz, Elías Miguel
Prida, Dolores
Rivera, Tomás
Santiago, Esmeralda
Suárez, Virgil
Yglesias, Jose

Latin-American Writers

Agosín, Marjorie
Alegría, Fernando
Allende, Isabel
Benítez, Sandra
Goldemberg, Isaac

Magic Realism

Alcalá, Kathleen
Allende, Isabel
Anaya, Rudolfo A.
Arias, Ron
Corpi, Lucha
Escandón, María Amparo
Urrea, Luis Alberto
Véa, Alfredo Jr.
Veciana-Suarez, Ana
Villaseñor, Victor

Native Literature
Candelaria, Nash
Chacón, Eusebio
Chávez, Fray Angélico
De Zavala, Adina
Hernández-Ávila, Inés
Jaramillo, Cleofas Martínez
Otero, Miguel A.

New Mexican Writers
Anaya, Rudolfo A.
Candelaria, Cordelia Chávez
Candelaria, Nash
Chacón, Eusebio
Chávez, Denise
Chávez, Fray Angélico
Gilbert, Fabiola Cabeza de Baca
Jaramillo, Cleofas Martínez
Mares, E. A.
Martínez, Demetria
Otero, Miguel A.
Ulibarrí, Sabine R.

Nuyorican/Puerto Rican–American Literature
Algarín, Miguel
Cofer, Judith Ortiz
Colón, Jesús
Hernandez Cruz, Victor
Laviera, Tato
Morales, Ed
Pietri, Pedro
Piñero, Miguel
Ryan, Pam Muñoz
Salinos, Maria Elena
Santiago, Esmeralda
Thomas, Piri

Postmodern/Contemporary Literature and Journalism
Allende, Isabel
Cabrera, Yvette
Cortina, Betty
Cruz, Frank
Davidds, Yasmin
del Olmo, Frank
de Uriarte, Mercedes Lynn
Diaz, Junot
Duron, Ysabel
Escandón, María Amparo
Espinosa, Maria
Estés, Clarissa Pinkola
Hatch, Sheila Sánchez
Hinojosa, María
Landres, Marcela
Martinez, Nina Marie
Martínez, Rubén
Milligan, Mary Guerrero
Moran, Julio
Moreno, Sylvia
Nava, Yolanda
Navarro, Mireya
Nogales, Ana
Paredez, Deborah
Pimentel, O. Ricardo
Ramos, Jorge
Ramos, Manuel
Rivera, Geraldo
Ryan, Pan Muñoz
Salinas, Maria Elena
Sanchez, Marcela
Serros, Michele
Sotomayor, Frank O.
Urrea, Luis Alberto
Valdes-Rodriguez, Alisa
Veciana-Suarez, Ana

Villaseñor, Victor
Zavala, Val

Social Protest Literature and Journalism
Acosta, Oscar Zeta
Alurista
Anzaldúa, Gloria
Burciaga, Jose Antonio
Carrillo, Adolfo
Cervantes, Lorna Dee
Colón, Jesús
de Hoyos, Angela
Delgado, Abelardo
del Olmo, Frank
Galarza, Ernesto
Gonzales, Rodolfo
Idar, Jovita
Laviera, Tato
Lopez, Josefina
Martí, José
Martínez, Rubén
Moran, Julio
Pietri, Pedro
Ramos, Jorge
Rivera, Tomás
Rodríguez, Luis J.
Ruiz, Vicki L.
Salazar, Rubén
Sotomayor, Frank O.
Thomas, Piri
Valdez, Luis
Varela, Félix
Velásquez, Gloria
Villanueva, Alma Luz
Villegas de Magnón, Leonor
Yglesias, Jose

ENTRIES BY YEAR OF BIRTH

1778–1850
Carrillo, Adolfo
Jaramillo, Cleofas Martínez
Otero, Miguel A.
Ruiz de Burton, María Amparo
Varela, Félix

1851–1900
Chacón, Eusebio
de Acosta, Mercedes
De Zavala, Adina
Gilbert, Fabiola Cabeza de Baca
Idar, Jovita
Martí, José
Otero, Nina
Rojas, Arnold
Villegas de Magnón, Leonor
Williams, William Carlos

1901–1920
Alegría, Fernando
Cabrera, Lydia
Chávez, Fray Angélico
Colón, Jesús
de Burgos, Julia
Galarza, Ernesto
González, Jovita
Niggli, Josephina
Paredes, Américo
Ulibarrí, Sabine R.
Yglesias, Jose

1921–1930
Candelaria, Nash
de Uriarte, Mercedes Lynn
Fornes, Maria Irene
Gonzales, Rodolfo
Hinojosa-Smith, Rolando
Méndez, Miguel
Portillo Trambley, Estela
Salazar, Rubén
Thomas, Piri
Villarreal, José Antonio

1931–1940
Acosta, Oscar Zeta
Alvarez, Julia
Anaya, Rudolfo A.
Burciaga, Jose Antonio
Cruz, Frank
de Hoyos, Angela
Delgado, Abelardo
Espinosa, Maria
Haslam, Gerald
Islas, Arturo
Limón, Graciela
Mares, E. A.
Mohr, Nicholasa
Pineda, Cecile
Ponce, Mary Helen
Rechy, John
Rivera, Tomás
Salas, Floyd
Salinas, Luis Omar

Santiago, Esmeralda
Serrano, Nina
Valdez, Luis
Villaseñor, Victor
Zamora, Bernice

1941–1945
Algarín, Miguel
Allende, Isabel
Anzaldúa, Gloria
Arias, Ron
Benítez, Sandra
Bruce-Novoa, Juan
Candelaria, Cordelia Chávez
Corpi, Lucha
Estés, Clarissa Pinkola
Goldemberg, Isaac
Herrera-Sobek, María
Huerta, Jorge
Kanellos, Nicolás
Mora, Pat
Morales, Alejandro
Nava, Yolanda
Pietri, Pedro
Prida, Dolores
Rivera, Geraldo
Rodríguez, Richard
Sánchez, Ricardo
Sotomayor, Frank O.
Villanueva, Alma Luz

1946–1950

Adame, Leonard
Arteaga, Alfred
Cantú, Norma Elia
Chávez, Denise
del Olmo, Frank
Duron, Ysabel
García-Aguilera, Carolina
Hernandez Cruz, Victor
Hernández-Ávila, Inés
Herrera, Juan Felipe
Laviera, Tato
Morton, Carlos
Piñero, Miguel
Ramos, Manuel
Ryan, Pam Muñoz
Velásquez, Gloria
Vigil-Piñón, Evangelina

1951–1955

Agosín, Marjorie
Alarcón, Francisco X.
Alcalá, Kathleen
Alurista
Baca, Jimmy Santiago
Castillo, Ana

Cervantes, Lorna Dee
Cisneros, Sandra
Cofer, Judith Ortiz
Engle, Margarita
Hijuelos, Oscar
Milligan, Mary Guerrero
Moraga, Cherríe
Moreno, Sylvia
Muñoz, Elías Miguel
Nogales, Ana
Pimentel, O. Ricardo
Rodríguez, Luis J.
Ríos, Alberto
Ruiz, Vicki L.
Salinas, Maria Elena
Soto, Gary
Tafolla, Carmen
Urrea, Luis Alberto
Véa, Alfredo, Jr.
Viramontes, Helena Maria
Zavala, Val

1956–1965

Escandón, María Amparo
García, Cristina
Gaspar de Alba, Alicia

Hatch, Sheila Sánchez
Hinojosa, María
Martínez, Demetria
Martínez, Rubén
Morales, Ed
Moran, Julio
Navarro, Mireya
Ramos, Jorge
Suárez, Virgil
Veciana-Suarez, Ana

1966–1975

Cabrera, Yvette
Cortina, Betty
Davidds, Yasmin
Diaz, Junot
Landres, Marcela
Lopez, Josefina
Martinez, Nina Marie
Paredez, Deborah
Sanchez, Marcela
Serros, Michele
Valdes-Rodriguez, Alisa

Entries by Ethnicity or Country of Orgin

Argentina
Nogales, Ana

Chile
Agosín, Marjorie
Alegría, Fernando
Allende, Isabel

Colombia
Sanchez, Marcela
Serrano, Nina

Cuba
Cabrera, Lydia
Cortina, Betty
de Acosta, Mercedes
Engle, Margarita
Fornes, Maria Irene
García, Cristina
García-Aguilera, Carolina
Hijuelos, Oscar
Martí, José
Morton, Carlos
Muñoz, Elías Miguel
Prida, Dolores
Suárez, Virgil
Valdes-Rodriguez, Alisa
Varela, Félix
Veciana-Suarez, Ana
Yglesias, Jose

Dominican Republic
Alvarez, Julia
Diaz, Junot

Ecuador
Landres, Marcela
Davidds, Yasmin

El Salvador
Martínez, Rubén

Mexico
Acosta, Oscar Zeta
Adame, Leonard
Alarcón, Francisco X.
Alcalá, Kathleen
Alurista
Anaya, Rudolfo A.
Anzaldúa, Gloria
Arias, Ron
Arteaga, Alfred
Baca, Jimmy Santiago
Bruce-Novoa, Juan
Burciaga, Jose Antonio
Cabrera, Yvette
Candelaria, Cordelia Chávez
Cantú, Norma Elia
Carrillo, Adolfo
Castillo, Ana
Cervantes, Lorna Dee
Chávez, Denise

Chávez, Fray Angélico
Cisneros, Sandra
Corpi, Lucha
Cruz, Frank
Davidds, Yasmin
de Hoyos, Angela
del Olmo, Frank
Delgado, Abelardo
de Uriarte, Mercedes Lynn
De Zavala, Adina
Duron, Ysabel
Escandón, María Amparo
Estés, Clarissa Pinkola
Galarza, Ernesto
Gaspar de Alba, Alicia
Gonzales, Rodolfo
González, Jovita
Haslam, Gerald
Hatch, Sheila Sánchez
Hernández-Ávila, Inés
Herrera, Juan Felipe
Herrera-Sobek, María
Hinojosa, María
Hinojosa-Smith, Rolando
Huerta, Jorge
Idar, Jovita
Islas, Arturo
Jaramillo, Cleofas Martínez
Limón, Graciela
Lopez, Josefina
Mares, E. A.

277

Martínez, Demetria
Martinez, Nina Marie
Martínez, Rubén
Méndez, Miguel
Milligan, Mary Guerrero
Mora, Pat
Moraga, Cherríe
Morales, Alejandro
Moran, Julio
Moreno, Sylvia
Morton, Carlos
Nava, Yolanda
Niggli, Josephina
Paredes, Américo
Paredez, Deborah
Pimentel, O. Ricardo
Pineda, Cecile
Ponce, Mary Helen
Portillo Trambley, Estela
Ramos, Jorge
Ramos, Manuel
Rechy, John
Ríos, Alberto
Rivera, Tomás
Rodríguez, Luis J.
Rodríguez, Richard
Rojas, Arnold
Ruiz de Burton, María Amparo
Ruiz, Vicki L.
Salazar, Rubén

Salinas, Luis Omar
Salinas, Maria Elena
Sánchez, Ricardo
Serros, Michele
Soto, Gary
Sotomayor, Frank O.
Ryan, Pam Muñoz
Tafolla, Carmen
Urrea, Luis Alberto
Valdez, Luis
Velásquez, Gloria
Vigil-Piñón, Evangelina
Villanueva, Alma Luz
Villarreal, José Antonio
Villaseñor, Victor
Villegas de Magnón, Leonor
Viramontes, Helena Maria
Zamora, Bernice
Zavala, Val

Peru
Goldemberg, Issac

Puerto Rico
Algarín, Miguel
Benítez, Sandra
Cofer, Judith Ortiz
Colón, Jesús
de Burgos, Julia
Hernandez Cruz, Victor

Kanellos, Nicolás
Laviera, Tato
Mohr, Nicholasa
Morales, Ed
Navarro, Mireya
Pietri, Pedro
Piñero, Miguel
Rivera, Geraldo
Santiago, Esmeralda
Thomas, Piri
Williams, William Carlos

Spain
Baca, Jimmy Santiago
Candelaria, Nash
Espinosa, Maria
Gilbert, Fabiola Cabeza de Baca
Jaramillo, Cleofas Martínez
Otero, Miguel A.
Otero, Nina
Paredes, Américo
Ryan, Pam Muñoz
Salas, Floyd
Ulibarrí, Sabine R.
Valdes-Rodriguez, Alisa
Véa, Alfredo, Jr.
Veciana-Suarez, Ana
Villegas de Magnón, Leonor
Yglesias, Jose

INDEX

Boldface locators indicate main entries. *Italic* locators indicate photographs.